RICKY
A LIFE WORTH SHARING

Volume 1

Ricardo J. Bordallo
with
C. Sablan Gault

Published by University of Guam Press
Richard F. Taitano Micronesian Area Research Center (MARC)
303 University Drive, UOG Station
Mangilao, Guam 96923
(671) 735-2153/4

www.uogpress.com

ISBN-13 Hardcover: 978-1-935198-87-1
ISBN-13 Paperback: 978-1-935198-88-8
ISBN-13 Institutional E-Book: 978-1-935198-89-5
ISBN-13 Trade E-Book: 978-1-935198-90-1
Library of Congress Control Number: 2024948359

Editor: Victoria-Lola Leon Guerrero
Copy Editors: Verna Zafra-Kasala
              Rindraty Limtiaco
CHamoru Language Orthography Editors: Anna Marie Arceo
                                       Robert A. Underwood
Photo Editor: Jess Merrill
Cover and Interior Layout Designer: Ralph Eurich Patacsil
Cover Artist: Jerrold Dwayne Castro

Ricky

A LIFE WORTH SHARING

VOLUME 1

Ricardo J. Bordallo
with
C. Sablan Gault

Praise for
RICKY: A LIFE WORTH SHARING

"Ricky Bordallo's early life before his ascendency into business and political success is marked with extraordinary experiences and hardships. But it is also a tale of hope in which a young CHamoru man finds his footing in spite of challenges with colonial authority, broken hearts, and strained relationships. His journey gives us incredible insights into the lives of young CHamorus on the cusp of World War II. In Ricky's story, we see the struggles of that special generation in full, vivid color and in bold relief, as well as some of our own."

— **Robert A. Underwood**, Ed.D., former Guam congressional delegate, U.S. House of Representatives and President Emeritus, 10th president, University of Guam

"For those of us who have no memory of when Guam and CHamoru identity were synonymous, this book eloquently fills that gap. *Ricky: A Life Worth Sharing* is a must-read for students of Guam history. The resilience and character of the CHamoru people are in full display in the twists and turns of this narrative."

— **Laura M. Torres Souder**, Ph.D., educator and author of *Daughters of the Island: CHamoru Women Organizers of Guåhan and Other Writings*

"Ricky's recollection of life in Guam and the once densely populated urban center of Hagåtña prior to the Japanese invasion is starkly vivid and extremely riveting. There may not be another literary work that effectively captivates the imagination while sewing together fragments of the forgotten history of a city and people that are forever changed. We are front-row witnesses to the loss of dignity and life and the widespread bombing and destruction of a beautiful island home. So, too, are we witnesses to acts of humanity and love, the emergence of heroes, and the remarkable recovery of a people."

— **Joshua F. Tenorio**, 10th lieutenant governor of Guam

"Tormented by concerns about his legacy, Bordallo urged author Catherine Sablan Gault to complete a 'romantic, poetic, and historical' account of his life. Here she has succeeded admirably, assembling a richly detailed narrative that leaves no doubt of Bordallo's love for Guam and its Indigenous CHamoru people. Bordallo's presentation is valuable for reasons other than the purely autobiographical. Readers interested in the Pacific theatre during World War II will appreciate his eyewitness accounts of the growing tensions between the U.S. and Japan and the very real impact that the Japanese presence had."

— **Marie Marmo Mullaney**, Ph.D., historian, author of
*Biographical Directory of the Governors of the United States
1988-1994*, and professor at Caldwell University

"This book provides readers with insights into the early life and experiences of one of Guåhan's most prominent politicians. This is essential reading for anyone who wants to learn more about the history of Guåhan from the pre-World War II era to the U.S. reoccupation of the island in the early 1950s."

— **Alfred Peredo Flores**, Ph.D., author of *Tip of the Spear: Land, Labor, and US Settler Militarism in Guåhan, 1944-1962*
and associate professor of Asian American Studies
at Harvey Mudd College

"In telling his life story, Gov. Bordallo simultaneously tells Guam's story. Reading this book is a way for us to witness the CHamoru world before the war. Through his life, the reader rides the waves of Guam's history from life in Hagåtña in the 1930s to the controversial militarization of Guam after the war. He is insightful and unapologetically honest. We simply need more books like this."

— **Kenneth Gofigan Kuper**, Ph.D., associate professor
of Political Science, CHamoru Studies, and Micronesian
Studies at the University of Guam and director of the
Pacific Center for Island Security

Contents

Contents

Foreword

When I think of a life worth reading about, I think of my uncle Ricky's life. As the son of his younger sister Norma, I have learned from Uncle Ricky, and from the whole family, that your work and your life must be bigger than you — whatever you do, make sure you are doing it to help someone other than yourself. For Uncle Ricky and our family, their obligation has always been to serve our island and our people. This is what I have proudly inherited. They showed me that no matter how hard things get, no matter what people think, when you are doing something for the right reason, you keep at it. There is no excuse to stop. At the end of the day, whether your work is known or appreciated, your work must matter, to be of import.

Our family's experience during World War II was horrific. As you will read in this book, Uncle Ricky suffered immense physical and emotional pain, but what broke his heart and stayed in his memory was an incident that occurred near the end of the war. The occupying forces had sent him to retrieve supplies from a warehouse owned by a family of collaborators in Hagåtña, which American forces were bombing relentlessly. To Uncle Ricky's shock, the warehouse was filled with canned foods and milk and other supplies. He had just lost his baby brother to poor nutrition and was heartbroken. The family, whom he would not name, had a stockpile of food. Hagåtña was in flames, and bombs were falling around him, but seeing that stockpile devastated him the most. People were starving, yet this family hoarded food. He couldn't understand how they could think only of themselves.

I remember Uncle Ricky telling me, "Things were bad, Mike. People would go from house to house asking for food. When they came to us, we would always give a little bit, even when we didn't have enough for ourselves."

He grew up understanding that he was part of one village, one island, and that they were all one big family.

Family was important to Uncle Ricky. And he had a way of making people feel like they were close family, no matter how distantly they were related to him. My first recollection of Uncle Ricky is embodied in a picture taken at the beach. The photo was fortuitous because it could have been any one of my cousins, but I was the one standing next to him that day. I was about 4 years old, and I was watching as he and my uncles cut up fish. Our family did things like this often. I didn't know he was a wealthy man back then. He never carried himself as one.

I also remember the night of Guam's first gubernatorial election in 1970. Uncle Ricky had run for governor and lost. I was about 8 years old, and my parents decided to stop by his campaign headquarters on our way home to Santa Rita. It was very late, and Uncle Ricky and his running mate Dick Taitano were standing outside, talking. I didn't know what they were talking about, but I could see that it was intense, and I remember the look on his face. That stuck in my mind.

By the time I was in high school, I was an active campaigner, not just for my uncle, but also for the issues. Back then, we were issue prone. Everyone passionately followed their party and their candidates — I wouldn't take away from that — but we also talked about the issues.

Until then, I had not met anyone who I thought spoke better CHamoru than Uncle Ricky. It was not just his command of the language but his eloquence. My mom said he learned to speak like that from the flatbed of a truck. In the early days of Uncle Ricky's political career, candidates for public office rode from village to village on big-rig trucks with 40-foot flatbeds. They would stand on the bed and speak to the voters, sharing their ideas entirely in CHamoru. Uncle Ricky was younger than other candidates when he first started running and had to be able to compete with the likes of some of Guam's most seasoned and respected politicians. He had to speak at their level. And boy, were they rough back then. He did this almost every other night during campaigns and perfected his CHamoru. It wasn't just what he said, but how he said it that made him stand out. There was a poetry to the way he would make a point that really distinguished him from a lot of his contemporaries.

Uncle Ricky and I had serious talks about politics after he lost the 1978 election. During the campaign he handed out flyers — we called them Xerox tickets — listing the details for meetings. He gave me one and told me to come if I was interested. From that day on, I don't think I ever missed a meeting. I worked with him all the way to the next gubernatorial election in 1982 and co-chaired the Young Adults for Bordallo/Reyes. While it took a while, I was able to convince my parents to allow me to defer my acceptance to the University of Hawai'i a semester so I could stay for the campaign. I was very fortunate that I had that time with Uncle Ricky.

I got the good and the bad, because boy, when I didn't deliver, I would hear it. I remember one night it was very late, and I was hanging around with three or four other people at the campaign headquarters when Uncle Ricky came down and saw me. He asked about a survey project I had been assigned to help Bob Rogers with just the day before. Dr. Rogers had given us two weeks to go from house to house and conduct surveys. When I told Uncle Ricky this, he said, "Oh yeah. You know, by now I would have had it done." I reminded him that we had just been given the assignment the day before, and he said, "That's my point." I replied, "I got it," finished in 48 hours, asked for a second set of surveys, and did them all by myself.

Uncle Ricky taught me what it meant to be a hard worker. When his wife, Madeleine, opened her shoe store, Zapatos, she wanted some tropical trees planted in front of the store. He asked me to help him plant on the weekends. He used a fusiños to dig holes, but the ground was hard coral. Each time he jammed the fusiños down, the coral "clinked." But he kept at it. After a while, his hands started to bleed. He didn't make a big thing out of it and just went to the hardware store, bought some gloves, and continued the work. He was determined to finish the task, despite the blood. Seeing that humbles you.

After Uncle Ricky died, I became chairperson of the Democratic Party of Guam. I worked hard and managed to bring to Guam the former U.S. presidential candidate and famous civil rights movement activist, Reverend Jesse Jackson. At a welcoming reception, many among the local party stalwarts struggled to converse intelligently with him. Dan Tydingco, the party's executive director, leaned over to me and said, "If there was ever a time I miss your uncle, it's now." He was right. Uncle Ricky would have held his own with Reverend Jackson. That would have been something to see.

I have not met anyone who could tell a story the way Uncle Ricky did. He had so much to tell and so many thoughts to share that his book needed to be divided into two volumes. From these volumes, you will learn about what it is like to be a CHamoru, to be from the generation that survived the war. You will learn from someone who reached the pinnacle of local politics as a senator, founder of the Democratic Party of Guam, and two-term governor; who met the Kennedys, the Queen of England, and many other luminaries; and who, as a businessman, brought Toyota and more to Guam in a short lifetime.

Uncle Ricky once asked me if I knew why his father (my grandfather) B.J. Bordallo went to Washington, D.C. in 1936. I had recalled reading a speech my grandfather wrote and replied, "In order to obtain full, civil, human, and political rights, we needed U.S. citizenship."

"Exactly," Uncle Ricky said. "That's what Dad told me." I felt validated because I had understood my grandfather's speech. I understood the magnitude of what he had hoped to achieve. He made the decision to endure leaving his family for many months and traveling thousands of miles because our people were being denied basic rights. That is the power of history that is passed on orally.

When a story is good, it will last. My grandfather passed his story to Uncle Ricky and to me when I read it decades later. We came from two different eras, three different generations, but we understood my grandfather's purpose. Reading Uncle Ricky's book was reaffirmation for me. Much of what he shares in this book are stories I heard him tell throughout my life. They still hit me the same way when I read them now.

The adage "walk a mile in my shoes" fits this experience. This book is only a mile in the life of a man whose purpose was much bigger than politics or business. His purpose was the CHamoru cause. He once explained to me that the CHamoru word irensia meant more than heritage (its English translation). He said irensia is not passive; it is also a verb. Yes, it is something that is given to you, but an obligation comes with it. You have to recognize your responsibility to the obligation that comes with your inheritance and act on it.

Uncle Ricky's life was a call to action. He wanted to be remembered as a farmer of people, especially young people. He would remind us that we stand on the shoulders of those who came before us, and we lift those who come after us. He has been gone for almost 35 years, but I know, without a doubt, that the work I and others do today is attributed in part to the spirit he cultivated in us.

Michael F. Bordallo Phillips
Hagåtña, Guam
2024

Introduction

Ricardo J. Bordallo, or Ricky, as many people called him, began working on his autobiography with freelance writer Judy Alderton in 1979, after his first term as the governor of Guam. They completed a few chapters about his childhood, but Ricky's personal and political motivations overtook his focus and attention, and they never finished the book. In February 1987, after his second gubernatorial term, and while his trial on federal corruption charges was still ongoing, Ricky asked me to help him restart his autobiography. I was his second term press secretary; beyond that, we were second cousins — my mother and both his parents were first cousins, members of the Kotla Pangelinan clan. More than our being related, I think he felt most secure expressing himself both in English and CHamoru, which he could do with me.

Ricky invited me for an initial meeting to discuss the project at his home in Tamuning. I thought his autobiography was to be the narrative of his life, business, and political accomplishments. But he liked Judy's romanticized description of Guam in the first iteration — the land, the sea, and the clouds — and said he wanted that sort of "romantic, poetic, historical" account of his life. He laughed at the dubious look on my face and asked, "You think you can do it?" Knowing Ricky better now, after having spent four years as his press secretary and three years collaborating on his autobiography, I think I accurately put into words what he wanted to say.

I brought a pocket tape recorder with me and recorded our initial conversation. Because he was in the midst of his humiliating public trial, his anger and disillusionment are clear in that recording and in later ones, and feature prominently in his preface. Once past his catharsis, Ricky gave in to nostalgia as he talked about his childhood and his family in prewar Guam, and what enemy occupation was like during World War II. Even then, whether he recalled fond memories or frightful ones, his despondency and resentment over the trial never went away.

We met at his home almost every workweek afternoon. Our work sessions consisted of long conversations and back-and-forth questions. We tape-recorded almost all our sessions in his home office, but since we were not sound engineers, the quality of our recordings varied from good to poor, and sometimes to no recording at all. Still, we filled more than a hundred 60-minute and 90-minute audio tapes. I catalogued the tape numbers, dates, and my notes in a thick notebook, and collected daily newspaper clippings (there was no internet back then). Ricky chose what to talk about. He often jumped from one incident and timeframe to another, only loosely speaking in chronological order. He sometimes invited guests to sit with us and share their recollections on tape. These included Richard "Dick" Taitano, Paul Souder, Joe Dizon, B.J. Cruz, and others. He often recorded his thoughts when he was alone. When I listen to those recordings now, I can hear the sadness and bitterness in his voice.

At home, I would listen to the day's tape, add to my notes, and write — sometimes blocks of text, sometimes several pages. As I completed the piece about Ricky's Army service (which he never talked about publicly and for which his detractors invented outlandish stories), a sudden power glitch erased everything I wrote. My primitive little Radio Shack computer did not automatically store data. Ricky called me at that moment. I burst into tears and explained what happened. He calmly, almost fatherly, said, "Maybe it's God's way of saying it needs to be better." I cried even harder. Since that day, his first words to me on phone calls were, "Did you punch 'save'?" reminding me to save my work before taking his call.

Ricky was fun to be with when you had his attention. He talked enthusiastically about his childhood, and since we share many of the same relatives, we could laugh over stories about them. He also was impossible to interrupt when he was on a roll, usually digressing to ramble about the injustice done to him. The first time I dared to interject, to get him back on topic, my impudence shocked him. He froze midsentence; his eyes flared, then he softened and said, "What's your point?" Ricky did not just talk at me; I dug, probed, and pressed for explanations and details. He never got tired of my questions, and I never got tired of listening. Whenever he remembered some detail, or a recollection came to his mind, he would call me at home and say in his commanding governor's tone, "Cathy?! I just had a thought flash! Write this down so we can talk about it tomorrow." He had many "thought flashes."

We often sat at his kitchen dining table and ate candy bars as we talked. His candy stash was like a Halloween haul. He had a terrible sweet tooth. Once, before going into his office and setting up the tape recorder, we left empty candy wrappers and greasy fingerprints on the glass tabletop. Madeleine had a fit. She showed us (me, actually) where she kept the Windex so that we could clean up after our candy binges. I once came upon him having lunch at the kitchen sink. He was eating with his hands — digging handfuls of rice from a pot in the sink and chunks of steak on a plate nearby. He always offered me whatever he was eating.

Ricky did not just talk about events in his life, he insisted on showing me the places he described, pointing out specific locations, even if they had changed or no longer existed. We rode his little red Suzuki jeep around the island along Marine Drive and the village backroads to places I had never seen. We went to what had been the vast Bordallo landholding in Agat, to what had been Mayanghulo', his family's summer estate. He pointed out where our Uncle Carlos's and Uncle Tomas's houses were, and where all the machines and pens and fields were. We drove toward Umatac and to the place where he hosted a farewell picnic for Madeleine's family. He took me on a tour through the jungle from Pado, behind Mongmong, down to the Cha'ot River and up the utility road onto Route 4, between Ordot and Sinajana. He said the prewar road from Sinajana down into Hagåtña was narrow and steep, and terrifying in the dark on the night he drove into the burning city during the World War II American bombardment. On a walk around Hagåtña, Ricky pointed out where prewar landmarks and his family's home had been, and he wondered whether some buried bottles of whiskey might have survived. We stood atop the old Spanish bridge, and he described where the river used to course, where the old power plant and tall black smokestack stood, and where the prewar Japanese soda bottling plant once was.

Ricky's early life, as chronicled in this volume, was the most enjoyable for me — to hear him talk about times and places I knew about only from elders, who spoke freely about life "before the war" but not about "during-the-war". The second half of Ricky's life, which will be captured in the second volume of this autobiography, is when he established himself in business and politics. It was full of highs and lows, as he succeeded as well as failed in business and both lost and won elections. These years were contemporary for me, and I remember much of them. Then came his come-back triumph in the 1983 gubernatorial election, his defeat in 1986, his trial, the jury verdicts, his appeal in 1987, the Ninth Circuit Court's decision in 1988, and Ricky's suicide in 1990.

I stopped working on Ricky's book after his death. He stored the audio tapes and copies of the original 5.25-inch floppy diskettes in his home office. I kept my own copies of the diskettes, transferring them to newer storage devices over the years, and losing many parts of the unfinished manuscript along the way. In 1997, Super Typhoon Paka ripped the roof off my house and destroyed much of my family's belongings as well as my notebook catalogue, news clippings, and all the drafts of the manuscript.

Ricky's brother Paul offered to pay for the autobiography to be published, but it was in scattered bits and pieces and not ready for print. The project was at a standstill until 2020, when Madeleine gave Victoria-Lola Leon Guerrero, the director of the University of Guam Press, permission to help me complete and finally publish Ricky's book. He would have approved and been delighted to have UOG Press and the University of Guam, our island's highest educational institution, as his publisher. I could almost hear him react and say, "No kidding?" and watch a smile come to his face.

Madeleine, Debbie, Nicole, and I hope you will enjoy this volume and discover, as we did, the times and tides that made Ricky Bordallo.

C. Sablan Gault
Agaña Heights, Guam
2024

Preface

THE REQUIEM OF A PEOPLE

As I write this, I stand convicted of corruption and discredited before my people. I am not certain what the history of my island will say about me. I fear it will be with condemnation rather than praise. On reporting the outcome of my trial, Guam's news media opined that their portrayal of my life would influence my place in history. That prospect alarms me. I have never been a media darling; hence, I offer my own account of my life.

As a seven-term legislator and two-term governor of the U.S. Territory of Guam, I shall share the same historical reference as other elected American officials:

Bordallo, Ricardo Jerome; born December 11, 1927; Democrat; Senator, Fourth through Tenth Guam Legislatures, 1956-70; Governor of Guam, 1975-79 and 1983-87.

The chronological order of governors will list me as the second and fourth man to have won the mandate of my people. Their right to elect their governor is a mere 20 years old. Other rights remain ungranted. After 88 years, the United States of America continues to deny that it is a colonial power in Guam and has not allowed the people of Guam to exercise their right of political self-determination.

Special interest groups in the U.S. government continue to erect obstacles to the Guamanian desire for equality. They do so by keeping the American public ignorant about Guam and her indigenous people, the CHamorus, and their long history. Americans are often surprised to learn that Hagåtña,

Guam's capital, is older than St. Augustine, Florida, touted as America's oldest city. These forces are the same as the perpetrators of the Iran-Contra arms scandal[1] who prove themselves capable and willing to lie to the American people. They use the might of the United States government and the guise of protecting national security to treat Guam like a back-alley mistress. Instead of a legitimate proposal of political marriage and mutual commitment, the United States plies Guam with debilitating federal handouts and saddles her with ambiguous, contradictory, and often stifling policies. Rather than stroll proudly arm-in-arm down Main Street, the United States keeps Guam secreted away, out of sight, out of mind. Rather than show us the best side of America, the United States sends us an inordinate number of those who use their positions, Guam's distance, and Washington's apathy to plunder and pillage. We call them "federalis." It is a derogatory term.

Because I dared to buck this system in the ways truest to the American principles of justice and fair play, a federalis agent with the blessing and might of the federal government accused me of the very same crimes that so many of his kind have perpetrated in Guam for years. My prosecutor, the new U.S. attorney, arrived proclaiming his intention to root out government corruption. He touted his reputation as a Reagan administration henchman in association with those who defied Congress, interpreted the law to their advantage, and lied to the nation.

Guam, the largest and southernmost of a 15-island chain in the western Pacific, lies about 6,000 miles west of California. It was not deserted when Ferdinand Magellan stumbled upon it in 1521. It was home to an established society of brown-skinned people, my ancestors, the CHamorus. They were a peaceful, hospitable people who called their home "Guåhan," which means "the bounty we have." They welcomed Magellan and his men, but the bearded white strangers overstepped their welcome. They helped themselves to Guam's bounty. Upon seeing this, and with as much gusto, the CHamorus boarded Magellan's ships and helped themselves to what they prized most: iron. They gathered every iron tool and ship fitting they could find, not realizing that the white man's ideas about entitlement only worked one way.

The incident prompted Magellan to call the archipelago "Islas de los

---

1 The secret U.S. arms deal in the mid-1980s to trade missiles and arms to free Americans held by terrorists in Lebanon and to use the sale of such to support armed conflict in Nicaragua.

Ladrones," the Islands of Thieves. He and his men retaliated with guns, which were unknown to the CHamorus. Not satisfied with the bloodshed, Magellan and his men sacked a village. Records do not say how our ancestors perceived Magellan, but they do praise the Filipinos who fought back and killed the explorer for "discovering" the Philippines after leaving Guam.

Magellan paved the way for Spanish missionaries and soldiers. The Jesuit, Diego Luis de San Vitores, renamed the islands the Marianas, after Queen Mariana of Austria, who funded San Vitores' request to Christianize the CHamorus in 1668. San Vitores died in Guam at the hands of a CHamoru chieftain on April 2, 1672.

Two hundred and thirty years after San Vitores arrived in the Marianas, on June 20, 1898, Henry Glass, the American Navy captain of the USS Charleston, sailed into Apra Harbor to engage the Spanish colony in battle. By then, Guam was typical of other European colonial communities: it had a palace and grand plaza, a large cathedral and "college" for young men, an administrative center and bustling commercial sector, a system of roads, and a network of armed forts. Unaware that Spain and the United States were at war, the Spanish governor mistook the Charleston's warning shot as an arrival salute. He hurried to greet the Americans who demanded his immediate surrender. Thus, the Spanish rule of the Marianas came to an end, and the political separation of the CHamoru people began.

The 1898 Treaty of Paris, which ended the Spanish-American War, required Spain to relinquish its colonies in the Atlantic and Pacific. Of the Marianas, the United States wanted Guam only; Spain ceded the rest of the islands to Germany. Guam became an American possession, and we became "wards" of the United States.

"The civil rights and political status of the native inhabitants of the territories hereby ceded to the United States shall be determined by the Congress," reads part of Article IX of the Paris Treaty. We were subject to the whims of a Spanish viceroy and his advisers, then we became subordinate to the foibles of an American Navy captain, his superiors, and the U.S. Congress. As wards of the United States, we faced a new language and new customs and ideas but the same regimentation, condescension, and supremacist arrogance. Only our colonial administrators changed. The new ones, too, had absolute control.

Under U.S. Navy rule, transient captains or lieutenants served both as commanding officer of the naval base and as governor over island residents.

The Navy sealed the port of Guam and restricted access. In World War II, the clamp tightened even further, to include the air space above Guam. The Navy required anyone seeking to enter or exit the island to obtain a security clearance from the State Department.

Guam remained under Navy rule for 52 years until 1950, when Congress enacted the Organic Act of Guam. The Act transferred jurisdiction over Guam to the U.S. Department of the Interior but kept the Department of State's security clearance requirement intact. The requirement shrouded Guam in mystery and kept her frozen in time. It prevented the normal growth and development of the community and the economy. President John F. Kennedy abolished the requirement by executive order[2] in 1962.

The Organic Act decreed Guam's status as an unincorporated territory. It established a three-branch civilian government and granted island residents limited U.S. citizenship. A similar decree in 1681 made Guam's people subjects of the Spanish Crown. Both actions were arbitrary and made without consultation or the advice and consent of the CHamorus.

The new office of a civilian governor of Guam became the impressive but unglamorous payola for political friends and presidential "hangers-on." All came from the United States. Perhaps as compensation for the hardship of a far-flung overseas assignment, the appointed governors wielded more power and authority over CHamorus than state governors and even the president himself over Americans.

In 1968, 18 years after the Organic Act and 70 years after the Treaty of Paris, Congress, in uncustomary generosity, granted the people of Guam the right to elect their own governors, but it failed to amend the provisions of the governor's powers and authority. Written expressly for appointed governors, the gubernatorial provisions of the Organic Act continue to haunt Congress and Guam's five elected governors. Congress has had to amend the Act numerous times over the past 36 years to address its flaws and shortcomings. Its greatest flaw is that it is not a constitution written and ratified by the people it was meant to govern. It is only a cheap imitation of the scope and grandeur of the Constitution.

Before permitting my constituency the fundamental right of American

---

2 Executive Order 11045—Discontinuing the Guam Island Naval Defensive Sea Area and Guam Island Naval Airspace Reservation, August 21, 1962.

democracy — for the governed to sanction their government — the United States distorted it. The government of Guam is a creation of federal law and remains subject to the caprice of Congress. We, the people of Guam, have been, and may always be, treated as mere features of the landscape. Congress controls — and can abrogate — our fundamental right to self-government.

If I sound disillusioned and bitter, I confess I am. The threat of unwarranted imprisonment, the methods used to disgrace me before my people, and the continuing failure of the United States to live up to its own principles where my island and my people are concerned give rise to my bitterness. I am disillusioned because this government chooses to practice cultural genocide, waiting for the last CHamoru to fall in line and meld into the apathetic American society. Americans may never accept that we, as a distinct people, as CHamorus, can be true Americans — the courageous, freedom-loving, justice-seeking kind espoused by the founding fathers who forged this great Nation. In time, we may also say, "Oh, what the hell..." and give up.

I am not anti-American. On the contrary, I am a very loyal American, but I feel betrayed by a national government that would rather destroy me and the CHamoru people than adhere to the letter and spirit of the democracy it espouses and that I respect, admire, and fervently wish to have applied to my island homeland.

During my trial, while deliberating on a defense motion to dismiss on the grounds that the federal government had no legal jurisdiction in Guam, the judge, whose position was pending in Washington, asked why I did not just move to another country if I did not "like" the American system. The question was asinine and typical of the federal colonialist mentality. I am CHamoru; Guam is my home. It will always be my home. I want no other. If Guam is American, then I should be also.

It is clear to me now that CHamorus are not in the warm embrace of an appreciative and understanding American family because we are unwanted, illegitimate beings. Our ancestors are not among those who founded the United States. We are not among the immigrants who fled oppression in their homelands to seek freedom and equality in the greatest nation on earth. We do not believe that the only legitimate way to become part of this nation is to sever all ties to a mother country. That is a price only a people so oppressed, so affected by tragedy, can willingly pay. CHamorus did not flee an oppressed motherland. We are not shipwrecked castaways encroaching on American soil. We came with this island. Above all else, CHamorus are citizens of Guam. We would never renounce that. But we are also unwanted stepchildren whose only possession is an island homeland too strategically valuable for us to keep.

To become Americans, immigrants must renounce their previous national allegiance. We were Spanish subjects not by choice but by Spanish domination. It was easy to renounce what we neither asked for nor wanted. Immigrants must also pass written tests of American history knowledge and pledge allegiance to the American flag. We took no such tests, save those in grammar school. Our pledges were no more formal, albeit official, than the perfunctory routine at school every morning. The occupying Japanese of World War II also required a pledge of us. By force, we had to bow and swear allegiance to the emperor or die.

After the war, reciting the Pledge of Allegiance became a more meaningful and profound privilege for us, but our loyalty and unabashed patriotism have gone unappreciated and unrewarded. My fellow CHamoru "Americans" are hybrid citizens not recognized as a people belonging to themselves first. Without regard for our ethnicity as a distinct Pacific people with a 4,000-year-old tradition that guides our relationship to one another and our environment, the federal government demands our immediate and complete assimilation into its individualistic and materialistic society. These are alien concepts to isolated island peoples whose values are opposite.

Guam is an American jurisdiction in which so many injustices and inequuities remain unsettled. The very nation that espouses equality and justice as legal guarantees denies them to us. Ours is a benevolent subjugation, but it is subjugation, nonetheless.

The proclamation of Guam's first naval governor, Richard P. Leary, reads, "Now, therefore, by virtue of the authority vested in me by his Excellency, the President of the United States, I, Richard P. Leary, Captain, United States Navy, and Governor of the Island of Guam, do hereby announce and publicly proclaim my actual occupation and administration of this Island, in fulfillment of the Rights of Sovereignty thus acquired and the responsible obligations of government thus assumed . . ."

Where are CHamoru Rights of Sovereignty? How can a nation of people and their sovereignty be "thus acquired"? Leary should have proclaimed outright, "CHamorus, you are a conquered people and have no rights." Then we would have known what to expect, but to preach and promise equality and justice, then deny them is more than dishonest. It is immoral. Subjugation, whether brutal or benevolent, is the issue. It is difficult to accept from an administering government that "holds such truths to be self-evident — that man was endowed by his Creator with certain unalienable rights." Guam is so far from the American consciousness that few Americans know how CHamoru sovereignty was taken from them, and that they resent it. Ours is a three-and-a-half-century struggle for human rights, first under the Spanish and then under the Americans.

The United States has become an apathetic and neglectful giant blind to its own failures. It no longer lives up to the great ideals, the principles of justice, and the spirit that made it great. The flawed CHamoru-American relationship has been an uncomfortable shotgun marriage of convenience — the dowry of geographic location. Guam was stolen property when the United States acquired it. It is still stolen property. The supremacists who have been our conquerors do not acknowledge that we are not chattel for sale, trade, or their denial of our dignity and human rights.

This great nation denies CHamoru human rights and political self-determination in the name of strategic importance and national security. The importance of U.S. Nuclear Fortress Guam on the doorstep of Communist Asia is the barrier to our complete protection under the Constitution. No American state would tolerate such an excuse for the arbitrary denial of constitutional protection of its citizenry. Its power to say "No" lies in its state constitution, in the U.S. Constitution, in its voting powers, and in its elected officials. Americans would not deny that it is they who grant governing power and authority to their state governor and legislators. For Guamanians — the CHamorus and others who now make Guam their home — the ability to grant those powers and authorities is superficial, a facade to hoodwink the nation and the world into believing justice prevailed. Saddest of all is that the U.S. treatment of CHamorus is unnecessary. Loyal CHamorus would still give up their lives and properties to protect the national interests of the United States. CHamorus only want to be real Americans.

As a youngster, I tried to fuse my mind and soul as the complete equivalent of a white American, but over the years, I learned I was wrong to try. Despite my efforts to learn correct, well-educated American English; despite my successes as a businessman, legislator, and governor; and despite my apparent triumph in achieving the American Dream, I have discovered I cannot be part of this great nation because I am "different." Yet I remain convinced that the greatness of the United States is inspirational, admirable, and worthy of appreciation, emulation, and respect. But elitist and possessive forces who fear differences are the ones in control. They do not appreciate differences; they are suspicious of them, threatened by them, even hateful of them. I have encountered such forces many times in my life, and they have cemented this notion for me. Yet despite all my encounters with un-American Americans, I have believed since childhood that the bad Americans were the ones sent to Guam, the ones who took advantage of their authorities. The good ones, the noble, inspirational ones who did not tarnish true Americanism, lived somewhere in the heart of America. The noble Americans I have met keep my faith in Americanism alive, even now.

I have never allowed myself to feel inferior. Quite the contrary, I have always felt a sense of superiority as a true American, true to the soul of the Constitution, to its principles and ideals, its concept and spirit. The U.S. Constitution adapts to the changing and varying needs of a diverse citizenry. It is the greatest political document ever written, but it is not infallible.

The Constitution's bicentennial anniversary, the sordid Iran-Contra arms deal, and the television mini-series Amerika were causing a national stir while I stood trial in Guam. How was I to celebrate the Constitution's 200th birthday? I had taken oaths more than a dozen times to uphold and defend it, yet I did not receive a reciprocal promise: My right to a fair trial by an impartial jury was a farce. The federal chicanery that put the president in hot water over the arms scandal did not surprise me. It is typical of the federal conduct in Guam. I felt a kinship with the Amerika's character, Devin Milford, who single-handedly tried to rekindle the conscience and spirit of the American people to save the country from Soviet occupation. I, too, feel alone in trying to rekindle the dampened spirit of my fellow CHamorus and the conscience of my fellow Americans.

When I was reelected governor of Guam in November 1982, I set Guam's quest for political self-determination as a top priority of my second administration. The political status issue had languished during the four years of my predecessor's tenure before coming to a vote in January 1982. The people of Guam opted for closer ties with the United States and selected a commonwealth status. Had it been possible or practical, Guamanians would have voted for full statehood which, for many, remains a lofty goal. In January 1983, I chaired the commission that drafted the Guam Commonwealth Act. By 1986, the draft act was ready for presentation to the people of Guam and eventual submission to Congress.

In pushing the political status issue, I discovered that as a lawfully elected American governor, sworn to uphold the U.S. Constitution, I may not champion my people's rights to full and equal protection under that great law. I found out how far vested partisan authorities would go to keep national defense interests first, the CHamoru people second, and Ricky Bordallo last.

I also placed equal priority on government integrity and launched an offensive against white collar crime within the government of Guam, which was steeped in the corrupt traditions of its Navy forerunner and role model.

On September 3, 1986, three days before Guam's primary election, a federal grand jury served a 12-count indictment charging me with bribery, extortion, and conspiracy — the very criminal acts I had vowed to fight. The indictment came as no surprise. Rumors about the grand jury's not-so-secret deliberations circulated for more than a month. The timing of the indictment was suspicious, as was the U.S. attorney's public assertion that I was guilty of wrongdoing. The defamation tainted the free election process in Guam. Despite the indictments, I won a resounding victory in the four-way gubernatorial primary on September 6. I garnered more votes than any other party nominee in Guam's brief election history.

The victory was a powerful reaffirmation of my leadership and a clear indication that the people of Guam would hand me a third term, which meant that as an outspoken and implacable advocate for commonwealth, I could shepherd the Guam Commonwealth Act's passage into law and put an end to the federal government's stranglehold on Guam. To prevent it, partisan federal officials launched a second, insidious assault to chip away at my strong position in the polls. Guam's U.S. attorney appeared in the media, condemning me as a common thief and a "Judas" to my people.

On October 4, a month before the general election, my trial date was set for January 12, 1987. The date was bandied repeatedly. I stood little chance against all the damaging news. The whispered aspersions unnerved the electorate and caused my defeat to a fawning Republican on November 4, 1986. As if I needed more humiliation, on November 20, a superseding indictment charged me with an additional six counts of witness tampering, wire fraud, obstruction of justice, and accepting an illegal gratuity.

My trial ended on Friday, February 13, 1987. The jury acquitted me on seven counts that required proof of criminal intent. They convicted me on 10 counts — all on technicalities of the law. When news reporters pestered me for a reaction, I said the verdicts were as I expected. By clever manipulation, application, and unyielding interpretation of the colonial power's law, I was adjudged guilty. But to my accusers' chagrin, I showed no remorse. I am innocent of wrongdoing, and my conscience is clear. I am guilty only of adhering to my CHamoru values.

The complicated legal definitions given to the jury included the declaration that circumstantial evidence was sufficient for conviction. In his closing arguments, my prosecutor argued for the validity of such evidence. He said it was like footprints in the sand. "If you see the footprints of a bird, that's circumstantial evidence. You do not see the bird. You only see footprints, but that's equally persuasive — tells you he was there," he said.

I, too, see footprints. Tracks appear many times throughout my life. I offer them now, throughout this book. There is plenty of circumstantial evidence — footprints — to suggest that I threw a wrench into the federal works. My political successes and my promotion of CHamoru political self-determination may have been the catalyst for persecution. Though I did nothing treasonous or subversive, worried forces in Washington sent a band of FBI agents here to dredge up anything to destroy me. Some among my supporters likened the federal effort against me to rabbit hunting with elephant guns. At my sentencing on April 3, 1987, an assistant U.S. attorney called for my immediate incarceration, as if I posed a danger to the community. Indeed, footprints abound; I do not have to see the bird.

Much is at stake in the Pacific. The Trust Territories are negotiating with the United States to end the trusteeship. The United States seeks to continue as their protectorate in some sort of political status arrangement. Meanwhile, the Libyans and the Soviets are increasing their incursions into the region. It is naive to think the Iran-Contra deal was the National Security Council's only concern. The United States' direct intervention in the Philippines' "People Power" revolt proves it was more than inclined to interfere in Guam's political process to secure its ends. Guam is too strategically important to let a nationalistic, pro-autonomy leader like me gum up federal objectives.

I was ousted as governor in 1978 by political underhandedness. A whisper campaign portrayed me as a budding dictator with delusions of grandeur. The electorate, the highest court of the democratic system — the jury that renders a verdict of satisfaction or dissatisfaction — voted me out. Yet four years later, having realized the deception, the people returned me to office. The subterfuges used in 1986 were more heinous. To ensure I did not win a third term, partisan federalis made me out to be a money-hungry power broker and betrayer of the public trust. My name, my reputation, my record had to be discredited and my political career destroyed by legal means so that I can never again hold public office in Guam.

But if I made a comeback, at whose pleasure do I serve — the federal government or the people of Guam? If I won election again, would the mandate of the people supersede the Organic Act? No, it would not, because the government of Guam is the creation of the federal law imposed on the people of Guam. They did not write, ratify, or consent to it. I took oaths to uphold the Constitution. I am not above the law, but neither am I equal before it. Guam is a schizophrenic dichotomy.

After my trial, lawmakers amended the Organic Act of Guam to prohibit convicted felons from holding the office of governor. On August 8, 1987, the draft Commonwealth Act went before the people of Guam. As a convicted felon, I wondered whether I could cast my vote in the referendum for the instrument I had nurtured into existence. I do not know at this point whether history will repeat itself and vindicate me in the appeals process or whether my future holds only years of federal imprisonment. Other factors are not yet manifest.

Some say one's life flashes before his eyes when he faces death. I have had that experience but not in a single flash. For the four weeks of my trial, while watching others determine my fate, I would recall incidents in my life. Some were poignant and pleasing, others painful and regrettable. In trying to come to grips with everything that has transpired this past year, I took a hard look at my life, trying to relate my past, present, and future, to contemplate the footprints and find the bird. This book contains the thoughts that came to me during this trying, painful time.

In this process of self-examination, I find the story of a life worth sharing. This is a collection of someone who, just by circumstance, was very much exposed to Life. I hope the family I had, my education and everyday experiences, the exceptional elements and encounters in my life, and the footprints will add more than my name to the record. I am not a special person, but I wish to share the interesting stories — all the joys, sorrows, and hazards —

that shaped my character and influenced my actions. Somewhere in the telling, the people of my island and my nation may come to recognize that this is more than the life story of one man. It may be the requiem of a people.

Ricardo J. Bordallo
Hagåtña, Guam
1987

L-R: *Catherine Sablan Gault, Ricardo J. Bordallo, and Michael F. Phillips leaving the District Court of Guam, then located in the Pacific News Building in Hagåtña, after Bordallo's resentencing in 1989.*

PART ONE

The Land of the CHamoru

GUAM BEFORE WORLD WAR II

BORDALLO
Family Tree

**1. Baltazar Jeronimo "B.J."
Pangelinan Bordallo**

1900-1984

**3. Irene
Delfina**

1923-1990

**5. Roy
Jerome**

1926-1926
(not pictured)

**7. Barbara
Louise**

1929-2015

**9. Norma
Ann**

1931-1988

**4. Sylvia
Lorraine**

1924-1980

**6. Ricardo
Jerome**

1927-1990

**8. Paul
Joseph**

1930-2007

**10. Fred
Eugene**

1933-2008

**2. Josefina
Torres Pangelinan**

1906-1945

**12. Donald
Lewis**

1936-1998

**14. Jospehine
Marie**

1938-2020

**16. Franklin
Delano**

1942-1942
(not pictured)

**18. Anita
Rita**

1945-1995
(not pictured)

**11. Rodney
Baltazar**

1934-2007

**13. Beverly
June**

1937-2011

**15. Michael
Malcolm**

1940-1997

**17. Rosamunde
Clare**

1943-2009

"We were visiting Nåna in Sumai when I got the moniker that would stick with me for life — Ricky."

11-16-32

Ricky

Chapter 1

"You've always been the one to cause a stir"

When the news broke of my federal indictment, my family was natural-ly upset. My community held my father, the late Baltazar J. Bordallo, a pioneering statesman, in high esteem. As his eldest son, I tried to em-ulate him and serve my people as best I could. Dad's honor, my fami-ly's honor, and mine were at stake. As a family, we had always shared our triumphs and disappointments. This time, despite the gravity, was no different.

My auntie, Rose looked at me and sighed. "You know, Ricky," she said, "you've always been the one to cause a stir. Even on the day you were born."

Auntie Rose was my mother's older sister. She took care of the 14 of us after Mama died in December 1945 and later married Dad after the war. I was 18 years old then, a grown man, but my siblings were still young. Anita, the youngest, was only 7 months old. Mama's death was hard on us, especially on Daddy. We had just emerged from the Japanese occupation and were looking forward to rebuilding our lives when we suffered the crushing blow. Mama left a heartbroken husband, an infant, and 13 children who needed her. I needed her as much as they did.

The nightmare of the Japanese occupation lasted nearly three years. Ma-ma's strength and courage kept us together through it all. She was very gentle and loving, the much sheltered and protective product of our serene prewar society. The obscenity of war, the brutality and hardship, the constant fear, the helpless anger, and the deep, deep heartache destroyed my mother. She was only 39 years old. I see her in my memories, in all her beauty, playing the uku-lele and singing with my sisters. I hear her voice as she spoke about Dad, the family, and life in general. I remember a home filled with love and discipline;

work and music; brothers and sisters and Mama caring for us all; as well as a circle of aunts, uncles, cousins, grandparents, and friends.

World War II arrived in all its menace on December 8, 1941, three days before my 14th birthday. I was 17 when it ended. For my generation, the occupation of Guam disrupted our youth and triggered irreparable change in our island society. Childhood was short-lived; adulthood was a matter of survival. It is not easy to become a prisoner of war at 14. Fear, terror, and the constant threat of torture and death change the way one looks at life. I grew up quickly.

I expected to grow up as Dad did, first as a boy playing and going to school, then as a young man working and building my life, and in the end, as a wise, old grandfather imparting wisdom on others. I would go off to school in the United States, as Mama and Dad had, and come home to start my own business. I would marry, raise a family, and repeat the cycle for another generation. World War II changed those expectations. I did not live my teen years in the peaceful and regimented traditional way my parents lived theirs.

The occupation and its aftermath altered life for all of us. Nothing had been as it was before. Every aspect of our prewar society changed. Even the landscape changed. American forces destroyed our world then rebuilt it, not to our specifications, but to theirs. For us, the new and alien environment became a constant challenge, which kept us trying to survive. During the occupation, we toiled to stay alive, to keep body and soul together. Afterwards, our challenge was to stay CHamoru, to keep identity and spirit intact. Under increasing pressure, our ancient culture was slowly yielding to the American efforts to erase it.

A November 1935 editorial written by Jack Flynn in the Navy's weekly publication, the *Guam Recorder*, reads: It is a fact that inasmuch as the United States governs here, the [CHamoru] people should make a determined effort to throw off the last remnants of customs, languages and ideas [...] to which they cannot be sentimentally attached as a relic of their former Government by another Nation. To assist in this process is the duty of every American on the Island.

The war and its aftermath provided for the successful execution of the "American duty."

Three centuries of Spanish rule could not make us abandon our unique culture and identity. We were not "sentimentally attached" to our former government. Our society survived despite that former government. The Americans never seemed to understand that. In their clumsy arrogance, they tried hard to deprogram us as "Spaniards" and reprogram us as "Americans," while we stubbornly refused to give up being CHamoru.

In 1986, 51 years after the editorial's publication, I realized its directive was still in force. Because of my proud adherence to CHamoru customs and ideas, the federalis twisted my actions to accuse me of bribery, extortion, and conspiracy. The deliberate distortion and denigration of CHamoru culture hurt me more than the assault against my character and integrity. Robbed of a gubernatorial election and awaiting trial on federal corruption charges, I was aware of the gravity of my situation, which weighed heavily on my mind, but I was certain of my innocence and was not afraid.

I was no stranger to controversy, but no one except the U.S. attorney had ever publicly called me a crook and a Judas to my people. Auntie Rose's reference to the clamor surrounding my birth offered pleasant relief from the weighty thoughts in my head. She smiled at the recollection and retold the story for the umpteenth time.

Church bells rang out for me on the day I was born. Påle'[3] Miguel Olano, the parish priest of Sumai, my parents' home village, rang the bells in fulfillment of a promise he made to my mother. The fourth born of 16 children, I was the first of my parents' sons to survive. An older brother, Roy, died at birth a year before me. My parents' grief at losing Roy was so deep that Påle' Olano comforted my parents by promising to ring the bells if Mama gave birth to a live son. Påle' Olano's full name was Miguel Angel de Olano y Urtega; he was a Spanish Capuchin missionary who came to Guam in 1918 and was the last to leave.

After taking possession of Guam, the American Navy government deported the Spanish Jesuits who followed two centuries after San Vitores. The Navy government viewed the Jesuits, the intellectuals of the Roman Catholic Church, as political activists who wielded too much influence over CHamorus. Most of the priests spoke CHamoru fluently and were close to the people. To undermine the priests' influence, the Navy government sent agents to circulate petitions seeking increases in rice imports. They gathered hundreds of signatures, then attached them to petitions calling for the Jesuits' ouster. The

3 "Påle'" (pronounced "pah-lee") is the CHamoru form of the Spanish "padre" used to address Roman Catholic priests.

Navy government characterized the effort as guaranteeing freedom of religion and achieved its ends. Tricked, the people grieved the deportation.

Despite the deportations, the Vatican elevated Påle' Olano to bishop and made him the Apostolic Vicar of Guam just before the war. Bishop Olano and 10 American priests spent the war years in a prison camp in Japan. Nine months after he returned to Guam, an American, Bishop Apolinaris Baumgartner replaced him. Bishop Olano retired to the Philippines but returned occasionally to visit. In June 1953, he officiated at my wedding. During a visit in 1970, Bishop Olano suffered a heart attack while swimming at San Vitores Beach, near the site where the Spanish missionary was martyred. Bishop Olano never wanted to leave the CHamorus and got his wish to remain forever. His tomb lies before the altar in the Dulce Nombre de Maria Cathedral.

After Roy's death in 1926, Påle' Olano told Mama he would pray for her next child to be a son, and if God answered his prayers, he would ring the church bells for all the world to know. Påle' Olano kept his word. I was born in Hagåtña on December 11, 1927, and Santa Guadalupe Church's bells pealed in Sumai. My parents had moved to Hagåtña, the capital of Guam, but my grandparents, many of my relatives, and several of my father's business enterprises were in Sumai and Hågat, a few miles further south. Growing up, I spent as much time in Sumai and Hågat as I did in Hagåtña. My parents celebrated my birth and christening in grand style in Sumai, with Påle' Olano officiating. Relatives tell me my christening celebration was a massive affair.

Baltazar Jeronimo Bordallo and Josephina Torres Pangelinan

My father and mother were first cousins who had to wait for papal dispensation, an official approval from the pope allowing a marriage, before they could wed. Baltazar Jeronimo "B.J." Pangelinan Bordallo was a progressive and well-educated young businessman from a prominent CHamoru-Spanish family. My mother, Josephina Torres Pangelinan, was a member of the same family. My father fell in love with my mother when he first set eyes on her.

To while away the quiet hours of uncertainty and apprehension during the occupation, Mama told us stories about her youth. How she and Daddy met, courted, and married was one of our favorites. She repeated the story many times, never growing tired of telling it. We never tired of listening, even though we knew every detail by heart.

B.J. Pangelinan Bordallo with his parents, Baltazar and Rita Pangelinan Bordallo,
and his siblings at their home in Agat circa 1910.

Front row, L-R: *Alfredo Tomas, Rita, Baltazar, and Carlos*
Back row, L-R: *Delfina, Ignacia, and B.J.*

Not many youngsters in prewar Guam went off to school in the United States. Few families could afford the expense. Mine could. My father was 15 years old when he left Guam in 1915 to attend St. Mary's College in Oakland, California. Before he returned in 1920, my mother also left Guam to attend Immaculate Concepcion Academy in San Francisco. Because going to the States meant traveling a great distance and being gone a long time, crowds of tearful relatives and friends attended every departure and homecoming. Mama returned in 1922.

Dad received the task of driving her home from the ship. As far as he was concerned, chauffeuring a returning younger cousin was not as exciting as riding the motor launches. In the days before commercial air travel, transportation to and from Guam was by ship only. Ships steamed into Apra Harbor and dropped anchor a distance from the pier in Piti. Small motor launches shuttled back and forth, ferrying welcomers out and eager returnees in. People on shore would jostle each other to get into the first launch. When Mama arrived, Pangelinans loaded themselves onto the first outbound launches. Dad managed to get a prime spot on one of the first.

Mama leaned over the ship's rail and waved as her relatives approached. She soon caught sight of a handsome young man standing on the bow of the launch. She could not take her eyes away from him. At the same moment, Dad spotted the most beautiful girl he had ever seen, and she mesmerized him. Her dark, curly hair framed a radiant, smiling face. She looked sophisticated in her neat and fashionable clothes. And she was looking at him. Dad watched in amazement as his aunts and uncles beckoned to her. To his delight, the beautiful young girl was the cousin he was to drive home. In that instant, his chore as duty driver became a coveted honor.

One of my aunts, scrambling up the gangplank to be the first to embrace my mother, ignored the gust of wind that lifted her skirt and exposed her homemade underwear. Everyone knew it was homemade because it said "Sperry Flour"[4] across the seat. This little detail was an important part of the story, especially during the occupation. It always made us laugh.

Dad could not take his eyes off Mama on the ride home. He was smitten, and Mama knew it. When I was old enough to understand the relationships between men and women, Mama shared her feelings for Dad with me. I had asked her about it one day while she ironed the clean laundry of her army of children. She looked up at me and smiled. She fell in love with him as immediately as he did, she said. Love sparkled in her eyes as she told me a love story that, for me, rivals any in great literature. I have heard it so often, and I know it so well.

At Mama's homecoming party, friends and relatives giggled and teased my red-faced aunt about her "Sperry Flour" underpants, while Mama concentrated on charming Dad. She wanted to make sure Cupid's second arrow was fatal. With skill and confidence, she played a ukulele and sang for her audience, proving that her parents' investment in her education was wise. Listening to her sing was the clincher for Dad. He decided then and there that Mama was the woman for him.

In sharing her side of the story, Mama allowed me an intimate peek into the female psyche and those wonderful ways women use to capture a man's heart. She was in love too but hid her feelings until she was certain. Mama was

---

4 Sperry Flour Co. was founded in Stockton, California around 1850 and later merged with General Mills of Minneapolis in 1929. Their flour sacks were made of strong and durable cotton and were reused as towels, bed linens, etc., and made into clothing and underwear.

eager to settle down and start a family. In those days, parents arranged marriages, but under increasing American influence, the practice began to fade, and young couples decided for themselves. American college life influenced both Mama and Daddy with modern ideas that they tempered with CHamoru customs.

Mama was more than just a beautiful young maiden recently returned from the States. She was Guam's first Island Fair Queen in 1919[5]. She was bright, outgoing, and musically gifted. She was very much a proper CHamoru lady, but she also had the spice of American boldness and independence and could converse on a multitude of subjects. She brought home a camera and took hundreds of snapshots. At a time when picture taking meant dressing up and going to a photographer's studio, Mama and her camera were curious novelties. Mama also smoked cigarettes, which only men did then. CHamoru women smoked pipes or hand-rolled cigars but only after they were old and gray, after they attained the age and wisdom to be exempt from the strict CHamoru code of behavior for women. Mama knew her cigarette smoking was too freewheeling for our conservative society, so she only smoked at home.

Mama never lacked for suitors. She was a real prize, the kind of girl young bachelors wanted to court. She had hopeful callers almost every day. Against such competition, Dad chose a different approach: he made a show of his work ethic and better-spent time.

Dad was a prize in his own right. He was a college graduate with a degree in American History and a keen sense for business. He, too, had a dash of American boldness and independence. Not long after returning from college, Dad refused to serve a mandatory stint in the Insular Guard[6]. When the Guard's American commander tried to take him into custody, Dad punched him in the face. The commander had him arrested and brought before the judge advocate who offered him a choice between a fine of $10 or two days in jail. Since he had no money, he spent two days in jail. He later argued that the Navy government could not press non-citizens into military service. He won the argument.

---

5 Popularly known as the Island Fair, the Guam Agricultural and Industrial Fair was an annual event. As reported in the July 1919 edition of the *Guam Newsletter*, Josefina Pangelinan was crowned the first queen on July 3, 1919.
6 In 1901, President William McKinley authorized the Secretary of the Navy to create an Insular Force of up to 500 natives of Guam and another native force in the Philippines to protect U.S. Naval installations in those places.

"Mama was more than just a beautiful young maiden recently returned from the States. She was Guam's first Island Fair Queen in 1919. She was bright, outgoing, and musically gifted."

After his release, Dad started building a retail store. To impress Mama, he drove his lumber and supply-laden truck slowly by her house every day. Motor vehicles were rare in those days. Only American military personnel and a few affluent CHamorus owned any. Dad and his truck rumbling through the streets of Sumai always attracted curious onlookers, but he only cared about one spectator. He made sure Mama saw him at his grimy, sweaty, workaholic best. Polished up, he came courting on weekends.

Mama told me Dad's strategy worked. He proved he could set the right priorities. While her other suitors frittered away the work week sitting in her parlor, Dad was hard at work building a source of income. He was the hard-working man who could provide for the large family she wanted. Mama was not so Americanized that she frowned on the idea of numerous children. In this, she was very CHamoru. She wanted many children to guarantee a happy home and the continuity of the family line. Dad, Mama decided, was the man for her.

Mama accepted Dad's marriage proposal, but because of their close, first-cousin relationship, the Pangelinan clan could not begin wedding preparations until their requested special dispensation[7] arrived from Rome. Mama and Daddy were married in 1923, eight months after their first meeting. They would have 16 children. Fourteen of us survived.

Complications plagued Mama's first pregnancy. She had to travel back and forth between Sumai and the hospital in Hagåtña throughout. She was so ill that the family feared for her life. After a difficult delivery, Irene was born in December 1923. Mama's difficulties, and the well-known fact that she and Dad were first cousins, sparked rumors that Irene was born without fingers. Mama was so insulted that she ordered a maid to hold Irene aloft through Sumai's streets so everyone could see she was a normal, healthy baby with five fingers on each hand.

Richard Jeronimo Bordello

Mama named her 16 children according to the color of their skin. With Spanish and CHamoru genes, her offspring varied from pale white to deep brown. She gave Anglo names to the white ones, Hispanic names to the dark ones.

---

7 The Catholic Church permits first cousins to validly marry only by canonical dispensation.

Centuries of suppression made CHamorus consider white skin beautiful and a blessing to have, while dark skin was unfortunate. Roll calls in our house were very cosmopolitan. Fair-skinned, blue-eyed Irene was born in 1923. Sylvia Lorraine, whose skin was a warm golden brown, arrived the following year. Mama gave her the middle name Lorraine because she had heard the people of Alsace-Lorraine in France had brown skin, so we called her by that name.

I was born darker than Lorraine, so Mama named me Ricardo. I think as a consolation prize, Mama gave me the English version of Dad's middle name. I am Ricardo Jerome. It is not a difficult name, but I have had to fight for my identity many times. In the lackadaisical way the prewar Navy government kept records, my birth certificate identifies me as Richard Jeronimo. In 1950, the State Department rejected my first application for a U.S. passport because I was two different people: Ricardo Jerome and Richard Jeronimo. I took the issue to court. Later, as I traveled, I began having trouble with my last name.

Bordallo is a Spanish name, pronounced with a rolling "r" and "y" for the "ll." The CHamoru pronunciation is "Boot-da-ju;" the English rendition is "Bor-dal-lio." People have mangled it into "Bordago," "Bardollo," and worse. After my election as governor in 1974, *San Francisco Chronicle* columnist Herb Caen wrote, "Something funny in the Island of Guam. They just elected a new governor whose name is Bordello."

It is not "Bordello," but I did live in two houses that served as such. After the war, our summer home in Mayanghulo' became a camp for Red Cross nurses. The Americans called it "Rocky Point." Its reputation as a fancified bordello was legendary. With our house in Hagåtña gone, destroyed in the war's bombing, we moved into a house the Japanese used as a brothel for high-ranking officers and civilian administrators. The bordello for those of lesser rank was at Adelup Point, where I relocated the governor's offices during my second administration.

Twelve brothers and sisters were born after me. They are Barbara, Paul, Norma, Fred, Rodney, Donald, Beverly June, Josephine, Michael, Rosamunde, and Anita. Franklin, who was born during the occupation, lived only nine months.

For as long as I can remember, we spent summers at Mayanghulo' and weekends at my grandmother's house in Sumai. We lived only a few miles apart, but Mama would not let more than a few days pass between visits. Although there are only about six miles between Hagåtña and Sumai, the narrow road stretched some 20 miles, meandering along the coast and through farmlands and villages, with sharp bends around steep hills and deep gullies. Our trips were always major undertakings because of the road and because there were so many of us.

Hagåtña was Guam's religious and government center. Sumai was its commercial and communications hub. Sumai was a pretty village of tree-lined streets and thatched-roofed houses nestled on the edge of Orote Peninsula, which jutted westward from the island's narrow middle. To the north of Orote, the great arc of Luminao Reef, which stretched from Cabras Island near Piti in the east toward Adotgan Point on Orote's tip in the west, formed a natural breakwater around Apra Harbor. The large, deep-water harbor's mouth lay in the west between the steep, sheer cliffs of Adotgan Point and the western end of Luminao Reef. Sumai faced northward into the harbor. The small port town of Piti lay at the eastern end.

For centuries, ships of every size, shape, and nationality called on Apra, Sumai, and Piti. In 1935, Pan American World Airways landed the first trans-pacific clipper flight in Apra Harbor and made Sumai its base of operations in Guam. Pan Am also built a seaplane ramp, a hangar, a pier, and a hotel for its travelers. Sumai was also the home of the Pacific Commercial Cable Company, which linked East with West via underwater cables. On the Orote plateau, above and behind Sumai, the U.S. Marine Corps established its first headquarters outside the continental United States. Marine Barracks Guam was an imposing facility of wood and concrete buildings, covered sidewalks, manicured lawns and parade grounds, and a golf course. After the war, the Navy seized Sumai and Orote and turned the area into Naval Station Guam.

Most of Guam's small population lived in Sumai and Hagåtña. People commuted back and forth between the two centers. Except for military vehicles, a few civilian vehicles, and some commercial trucks, buses, and taxis, motorized traffic was light. Most people traveled on foot, on bicycles, or on carabao (water buffalo) or oxcarts. My family was one of the few who owned a car.

Everyone knew when the Bordallos were on the road. We sang at the tops of our lungs as we drove along, entertaining drivers, pedestrians, and villagers from Hagåtña to Sumai and back again. Years later, when I saw The Sound of Music, it reminded me of our song fests in the car — the Bordallo Family Singers — all of us, including Mama and Daddy. Mama and I would lead as songs were decided. We always had to include Dad's favorite, "When I Grow Too Old to Dream." One of Mama's was "Someday, Sweetheart." In the days following her death, the outdoor, military movie theater next door to us played "Someday, Sweetheart." Hearing Mama's song intensified our grief.

Mama taught us to love music. We still sing together at family gatherings, even now. My family used to call me the Bobby Breen of Guam because I had a good singing voice. Bobby Breen was a young American singer popular in the 1930s. Long after his popularity faded, mine remained with my family. They would call upon me to sing, even as governor of Guam. Dad would proudly announce, "And now, we will hear from the governor of Guam. Come on, Ricky, sing us a song." And I would oblige, singing his favorites: "It's A Sin to Tell a Lie," "Bells of St. Mary," "There's No Tomorrow," "Some Enchanted Evening," "The Sound of Music," "Somewhere My Love," and of course, "When I Grow Too Old to Dream." The old songs made Dad melancholy; he would smile and sing along until tears filled his eyes. He would then disappear into his room and rejoin us a few minutes later. Dad never stopped missing Mama.

Music was an important part of life before the war. It filled Hagåtña's neighborhoods throughout the day and early evening. It seemed someone in every house owned a musical instrument of some kind. One could enjoy a range of performances from the homes of singers and musicians along the streets. One might hear a vocalist exercising scales or violinists, guitarists, and harmonica players making music. Passersby often whistled or hummed along. Auntie Rose gave voice lessons and taught piano at her house, as did another woman down the street. From the homes of Tun Jose Torres, an accomplished pianist and composer, and Dr. Ramon Sablan, the first CHamoru medical doctor, came piano concertos, classics, and original compositions. Tun Jose composed band marches on the piano, using his imagination to write parts for brass and percussion instruments. The Guam Legislature adopted and made Tun Jose's "The Guam March" the official territorial march of the island and Dr. Sablan's "The Guam Hymn" our national anthem.

Hagåtña was a city of happy people who always made music, so much so that Navy Governor William W. Gilmer issued an order prohibiting whistling in the streets and dancing after 10 p.m. According to the popular story, the whistling irritated Mrs. Gilmer, and she urged her husband to forbid it around the Governor's Palace.

"Such a long name for a little guy like you"

We were visiting Nåna in Sumai when I got the moniker that would stick with me for life — Ricky. I was about 3 years old and had fallen and injured myself. Mama rushed me to the dispensary at the Marine Barracks, which stood on the hilltop near the Pacific Commercial Cable Company station. The small dispensary took care of routine services and minor injuries while the Susana Hospital in Hagåtña was the main medical facility.

I do not remember how I hurt myself or how badly, but I remember the incident. The corpsman who took care of me was kind-hearted. I was crying hard, but he distracted me by rummaging through a cabinet and gathering medicine bottles, gauze, adhesive tape, and a pair of snub-nosed, bent scissors.

"What's your name, little boy?" the corpsman asked.

"Ricardo Jerome Bordallo," I said, relieved that he used the scissors on the gauze and tape and not on me.

"My, that's such a long name for a little guy like you," he said. "I think I'll call you Ricky. That's more your size."

And "Ricky" I have been ever since, mispronounced last name, notwithstanding.

Chapter 2

God's footprint

Guam is a speck on the map, but for those of us who call it home, it is the grandest castle in the universe. It is just an island, but it is my island. Guam is as much a part of me as I am a part of it. Guam belongs to me and to those who understand the words, *"tano'-ta,"* our land. This special sense of belonging is not unique to me. All CHamorus understand it, share it, and believe it profoundly. We are *"taotao-tåno',"* people of the land.

My ancestors, the ancient CHamorus, came here four millennia ago. They were a tall, robust, brown-skinned people who mastered astonishing navigational skills and braved the great Pacific to settle in Guam. Theirs was a society entwined with the land and the sea, a bond strong enough to withstand time and foreign conquest. The courage that steeled their ocean exploits, the determination that strengthened their perseverance and endurance, and the spirit that gave them their identity survive in their descendants. This is my legacy. Guam is my heritage. I can never give it up.

Guam is the largest and southernmost of the Mariana Islands in the Western Pacific. The island chain, the exposed summits of a submerged mountain range, arcs northward toward Japan and sits on the lip of the Mariana Trench, part of the deepest gashes in the Earth's surface. The popular local claim is that Mount Lamlam, Guam's highest point, is the world's tallest mountain if measured from the bottom of the Mariana Trench 7 miles below the surface. Mighty forces in this cauldron fuel volcanoes north of Guam and jolt the entire chain with earthquakes regularly. Guam lies almost vertically north to south. Some say it is shaped like a peanut, wide at both ends and narrow in the middle. I have always thought it looked more like a footprint, perhaps it is God's footprint.

From the sheer, 400-foot face of Litekyan Point at its northern tip to Asgådao Bay at its rounded southern end, the island measures about 30 miles long. It is 10 miles at its widest, only 4 miles at its narrowest. Mount Lamlam, which means "lightning," rises 1,334 feet on the southwestern coast. From its summit, one can look around and view the whole island stretching from north to south. To the west is the Philippine Sea and to the east, the great Pacific. Thirteen degrees to the south is the equator.

The depth of the surrounding ocean determines its color. The shallows of the fringing reef shimmer aquamarine and pale green. Crashing waves frost the reef with white foam. The open sea beyond darkens to a deep cobalt blue all the way to the horizon. The sky above is a canopy of blue from which towering white clouds preside. The air is pure, its clarity dimensional, as though one need only reach for a cloud to climb heavenward.

Guam is a tropical island of cool breezes and starlit, balmy nights. The sun shines daily, even through thick clouds, to warm the land and the seas around it. Dawn paints the clouds and sky with bright pastels of pink, yellow, orange, and peach. The colors at dusk are more intense — the sky blazes in crimson, amber, gold, and purple. Guam complements the display with the dark green of its jungles, the grayish black of its basalt formations, the red-orange and brown of its clay soils, the gray-green of fields of sword grass, and the white and ivory of bare limestone cliffs.

Guam is a peaceful island that cloaks the scars of its violent birth in beauty. It is the remnant flank of two giant volcanoes extinguished millions of years ago. On this volcanic base, billions of coral polyps lived, died, and left their calcareous skeletons to form a high island of basalt and limestone. In the north, beneath thick jungle growth, layers of limestone soak up and filter fresh water into huge subterranean pockets. Steep hills, deep valleys, and marshlands form the central interior. In the south, the red clay of decaying volcanic rock nurtures the sword grass that carpet rolling hills and savannahs.

From Guam's northern tip on a clear day, one can see the island of Rota, about 40 miles away. Only a narrow strait separates the two islands, but politically, they are oceans apart. The gulf between the CHamorus of Guam and the Northern Marianas is much wider than the few miles that physically separate us. With the stroke of a pen, the United States and Spain ignored CHamoru sovereignty and divided the Marianas. Yet in ethnicity, language, and culture, we are one people cleaved by different conquerors.

Spain offered to sell the Northern Marianas in 1898, after the Spanish-American War, but the United States declined. Instead, Germany purchased the islands. By a League of Nations mandate after World War I, the Germans relinquished the northern islands to the Japanese. In contrast, the United States demanded all 7,000 islands of the Philippine archipelago. The Filipinos revolted against the Spaniards and hailed the incoming Americans as liberators. But as in Guam, the Americans in the Philippines replaced one tyrannical regime with another. The Filipinos felt betrayed and revolted against the Americans, too. Some say the .45 caliber pistol was invented to slay the Filipino freedom fighters whose ferocity could not be stopped otherwise. The Americans then banished nonconforming Filipino political activists to Guam.

"This came from your people"

As the largest island in Micronesia, Guam has had a long and most extensive exposure to Western influences. It was the last replenishment port for the westbound Manila Galleons and last chance for disgruntled Mexican conscripts to jump ship before the galleons reached the Philippines. Guam was also a replenishment stopover for English, Dutch, French, Russian, and German explorers. Even New England whalers made port calls as they followed the whales westward from Hawai'i. Guam has one of the longest histories of human settlement and was the hub of a far-ranging trading network in the Pacific long before the Europeans arrived. The CHamorus and their Pacific cousins regularly crisscrossed the ocean in their sailing canoes.

I came to know evidence of this network in 1976 when I hosted the state visit of His Excellency Tāufa'āhau Tupou IV, the king of Tonga[8]. King Tupou is a mountain of a man, physically and politically. Standing 6 feet, 5 inches and weighing more than 400 pounds, he broke the springs of the governor's limousine on the drive from the airport. A Tongan monarch, he explained, had to be larger than his subjects. To me, his bearing and demeanor reflected the sovereignty and dignity of his people.

Over lunch at his hotel, as we spoke of the histories of our islands, King Tupou told of the ancient ties between his people and mine. I knew my ancestors had sailed the surrounding ocean but was unaware of the distance they traveled. The king then turned and said something to his wife. She left the table and returned a few minutes later with a large, finely woven, natural fiber cloth. It was brown, undecorated, and unremarkable, but the queen treated it with reverence, as if it were something valuable. Its significance to the royal couple was evident.

"This is the sacred symbol of the throne of Tonga. It is the symbol of my authority as king," Tupou said as he laid the cloth in my hands.

He said the Tongan monarchy was over 2,000 years old and that his royal family line ran unbroken from the distant past to his reign. I was deeply impressed and moved that he allowed me to touch such an important symbol. He saw the awe in my face and smiled.

"This came from your people," he said. It was the coronation gift of my CHamoru ancestors to his ancestors more than a millennium ago. He said the early CHamorus were among the oldest societies in the region and com-

---

8 The Kingdom of Tonga, the South Pacific's last Polynesian kingdom, is a constitutional hereditary monarchy. It is an archipelago consisting of 170 islands under the protection of the United Kingdom until 1970.

manded high esteem among other Pacific peoples. "That was long before the Spaniards came to your island," he said.

I looked at the cloth with renewed interest and respect. I was holding a direct link to the ancient past of my people, to ancestors who were part of a free and sovereign nation among other Pacific nations.

Our region of the Pacific, known to the world as Micronesia, is equivalent in size to the continental United States. If Micronesia was superimposed on the United States, then the Marshall Islands, on Micronesia's eastern edge, would run from Vermont to Florida. On the western edge, the Palau Islands would be well offshore from the California and Mexican coasts. The Western and Eastern Caroline Island groups — Yap, Chuuk, Pohnpei, and Kosrae — now the Federated States of Micronesia in free association with the United States, would lie scattered from Los Angeles to the Carolinas and from the Dakotas to Texas. The Northern Marianas would reach into Canada, and Guam would be in the southeast corner of Idaho. Despite Micronesia's great spread, its combined land area is smaller than the state of Rhode Island.

Micronesia is home to many distinct cultural groups that share similar societal traits. Foremost among these is the importance of interdependency and extended family systems. To survive on small, isolated islands, Pacific peoples elevated the significance of hospitality, tolerance, understanding, and humility. This impresses Western newcomers to the area.

Some Pacific people were warlike, but the CHamorus were not. We have no indigenous words for "drum" or "war." Our ancestors were competitive intellectually; they preferred sharpening tongues instead of spears and verbal eloquence instead of physical prowess. They battled with words and wits, with stories and taunts as weapons, and measured victories in deflated egos and shamed faces, not lifeless bodies. The ancient CHamorus and their descendants also did not fight against their environment; they aligned themselves to it. Their society and way of life relied on their relationship to the land and sea and to each other. It emphasized mutual dependency and defined happiness in terms of freedom of the human spirit. It scorned the accumulation of material goods as greed and celebrated contentment as true wealth.

The Spanish molded their religious concepts to fit these CHamoru values, thus making the new ones more palatable and acceptable. The Americans misunderstood this adaptation and tried to erase what they viewed as CHamoru loyalty to Spain and the Church. Despite the initial 40 years of

Americanization, basic CHamoru values helped them survive Japanese occupation. Only now, after 100 years, are CHamorus succumbing to the process of American homogenization. The process, which makes no room for CHamoru culture, is succeeding. As Jack Flynn states in his 1935 *Guam Recorder* editorial, "To assist in this process is the duty of every American on the Island."

The glories of American Democracy

Guam was a free port until the U.S. Navy took command of the island. Guam's CHamorus thought themselves more sophisticated and progressive than their neighbors in Rota, Tinian, and Saipan. But when those islands came under Japanese rule early in the 20th century, they forged ahead while the American Navy in Guam stifled progress. Garapan, Saipan's capital city, surpassed Hagåtña in just a few years. The Japanese developed an economy based on sugar production and built roads, factories, schools, hospitals, and even a steam locomotive system, the only one in the Western Pacific. They developed an economy for their own benefit, but the CHamorus there benefited as well. In Guam, the Americans concentrated on establishing a military outpost. They paid little attention to the economic development of their CHamoru wards but instead tightened their grip by issuing regulations such as prohibiting whistling, outlawing trains on women's skirts, and forbidding the sale of private property without authorization. The Navy's desire to control real estate was apparent early on.

While the Americans exploited their new authority, the Japanese exploited their proximity to the American Navy. The situation proved detrimental to CHamorus in World War II. Guam was the only organized American community given up to the enemy. Along with their fortified bases in Saipan, the Japanese were able to launch their offensive in the Pacific. Had the United States similarly fortified Guam, the Japanese might have reconsidered striking the blow that propelled the United States into World War II and the CHamoru people into slavery.

Although much touted in the halls of Washington, the Navy Department did little to prepare CHamorus for economic self-sufficiency and eventual political self-determination. Instead, the Navy in Guam expressed its resentment of this obligation by denigrating CHamorus and taking advantage of the distance from watchful eyes to exploit their authority over "docile" people.

But CHamorus were not as docile as they pretended to be. When Dad went to Washington, D.C., to lobby for citizenship in 1936, Governor Benjamin V. McCandlish retaliated by increasing the Bordallo family's property taxes over 1,000 percent, demanding full payment, and threatening immediate foreclosure. Uncle Tom, Dad's brother, fired off a cablegram to Dad, who, in turn, went to see Adm. Ernest J. King, the chief of Naval Operations. Shocked by McCandlish's vindictiveness, the CNO issued an immediate cease and desist order.

By citing poor CHamoru economic and social conditions — deliberately maintained by the naval government — the Navy Department thwarted every CHamoru attempt to secure U.S. citizenship. CHamorus tried in 1902, 1904, 1907, and regularly until 1936. Citizenship promised American equality and official recognition of CHamoru human rights. Even after CHamorus proved their loyalty to the United States during World War II, the Navy Department testified before Congress that the people of Guam still were not qualified to become citizens. The Navy government led the American people to think that Guam's native inhabitants were uncivilized, uneducated, unsophisticated ruffians in desperate need of paternal naval control. It never rendered a true portrayal of CHamoru intelligence and sophistication.

Contrary to the naval governors' annual reports to Washington, CHamorus were not wretched primitives in desperate need of paternalistic guidance. Although CHamorus were long familiar with and influenced by the West, the Navy hoax allowed for the continued violation of CHamoru human rights. In the quest to make us "throw off the last remnants of customs, languages, and ideas [...] as a relic of their former Government by another Nation,"[9] Navy administrators failed to recognize that the "relic" existed before the former government of another nation. CHamorus did not give it up for the Spanish, nor would they for the Americans. CHamorus were selective about what they would accept from new cultures. It is this discernment that preserves CHamoru sovereignty.

In another effort to impose their culture, customs, and values, patronizing Americans insist that pureblooded CHamorus are extinct, that what remains is a mixed breed of human, a hodgepodge of ethnicities. As CHamorus, we do not measure our ethnicity in terms of blood origins but in the way we look at life and relate to one another. We are CHamoru in heart and mind and

---

9 From Jack Flynn's November 1935 *Guam Recorder* editorial.

spirit. We have heard the propaganda so often and grown numb to the insult. Although we reject the argument, we have allowed it to persist.

There was a time when "CHamoru" and "Guamanian" were synonymous. After the war, it became more fashionable, more "American," to call ourselves Guamanian. The Americans, too, seemed to prefer the more Anglo-sounding term. It was not as alien or native as "CHamoru." In our zeal to become Americans, we assumed the new label, but among ourselves we still are CHamoru. Now, a Guamanian is a Guamanian like a Californian is a Californian. But only a CHamoru is a CHamoru. There are CHamorus who are not Guamanian and Guamanians who are not CHamoru. Biology and genetics are not the determinants. No matter what mingles in his blood, a CHamoru answers "Yes" to the question, *"Kao CHamoru hao?"*

While learning about the great glories of American democracy, we soon discovered a distinct difference between theory and practice. CHamorus were at the mercy of the character and integrity of every new naval governor. Some were despots; others were humane; many just did not care. They all commanded their Navy base as if it encompassed the entire island, tolerating its indigenous people as annoyances. Many among mainland Americans think Guam is only a military base, even now.

No matter their caliber, the naval governors and their deputies, as practitioners of the prevailing racial attitudes of the times, subjected the CHamorus to varying degrees of degradation and discrimination. The "Ugly Americans" detailed to Guam outnumbered those who tried with sincerity to understand CHamoru culture and perspectives. Though few, those Americans exemplified America's greatness for us. They gave us the steadfast belief that the United States of America was the greatest nation on earth.

The city of Hagåtña, heart of the CHamorus

Saipan's railroad system, a marvel at the time, could not compare with the beauty and majesty of Hagåtña's Plaza de España, the Palascio de Gobiernador or Governor's Palace, and the Dulce Nombre de Maria Cathedral. The lawns, the avenue lined with palms, and the kiosko where the Navy band performed every Sunday presented a striking view from anywhere in town. The Spanish built the complex in traditional style and design in the 17th century. Thick manposteria columns and walls enclosed the Almacen, the private gardens, the stables, and the storehouses. The Governor's Palace was the seat of the Spanish colonial government; it was a two-story building with administrative offices on the first floor and the governor's living quarters on the second. The Americans continued the arrangement throughout the prewar administrative period, keeping themselves and their children behind the protective walls.

The Governor's Palace faced north, toward Hagåtña Bay and the Philippine Sea. The plaza laid in front of it, bound on the west by Dorn Hall and on the east by the Dulce Nombre de Maria Cathedral. The Navy's Bank of Guam, the courthouse, the jail, the library, the commissary, the public market, Leary School, the Susana Hospital, the lieutenant governor's official residence, and several red tile-roofed haciendas surrounded the Plaza and government complex. American bombs destroyed the palace and most of the complex in 1944, but the plaza remains Hagåtña's centerpiece.

Hagåtña before the war was a lot like the small towns I have visited in Spain, Mexico, Puerto Rico, and the Philippines. I feel an instant familiarity in such places. Hagåtña's plaza was only about a hectare, with the kiosko at its center. The Spanish complex was small also, but it contained the same features as the larger ones in the New World — armories, stables, barracks, commissary and galley, storage buildings, and smithies.

The cathedral was not as large or as ornate as some I have seen, but even St. Peter's Basilica in Rome reminds me of the old Dulce Nombre de Maria. The cathedral, and each succeeding structure, was built on the site of San Vitores' original mission, on land given to him by Kepuha, the high chief of Hagåtña, in 1668. Over the centuries, typhoons, earthquakes, fires, and the war destroyed several successive structures on the same site. The new cathedral, built after World War II, is stark and austere. It lacks embellishment and is not as ornate and beautiful as its predecessors. Nor does it reflect the Roman Catholic Church's long and rich history in Guam.

Hagåtña lays on a narrow shelf between the bay and the cliffs of Tutuhan. A vast swamp east of the city was the breeding ground of mosquitoes, tropical diseases, and floods, which frustrated both the Spanish and American colonial governments. From the swamp, the Hagåtña River meandered through the eastern part of the city into a large pond called the Minondo. From there, it forked: One tributary snaked to the sea through the San Antonio District, the other coursed through the city, parallel to the sea for about a mile, before emptying into the bay in Aniguak, near the city's western limits. Several foot and traffic bridges spanned the river throughout the city.

The Spanish divided the city into districts, or barrios. San Ignacio, the oldest and largest, was the center of town. San Antonio and Santa Cruz lay between San Ignacio and the bay. Toggai and San Ramon lay at the base of San Ramon Hill and Tutuhan. Hulåli and Aniguak marked the city's western edge. The barrios of Padre Palomo and Bilibek, where military families rented many of the homes, were on the northern edge of the bay. Bilibek was also known as "Lågon Såddok," which means "north of the river."

A grid of parallel streets and perpendicular alleys divided Hagåtña into long narrow blocks. Few people owned motor cars, so wider streets were unnecessary. Homes and buildings of Spanish, Chinese, Japanese, and European architectural styles competed for space with CHamoru thatched-roof homes. The Americans introduced corrugated roofing sheets and concrete, which replaced manposteria as the common masonry. Manposteria was a thick sandwich of coral rubble and gravel between facings of cement. Such walls were massive and as much as 3 to 4 feet thick. Manposteria identified the older Spanish era buildings.

Despite the availability of modern construction materials, CHamorus did not give up their thatched-roof homes. For all the permanence of tin or tile, thatch remained the preferred choice for roofs. Tin and tile could not match it for cost or coolness or for the gentle music of rain on packed palm fronds. Thatched roofs needed replacement about every five years. The materials were cheap and plentiful, and thatching time was a social event. Family, friends, and neighbors came together to strip away the old roof and prepare and weave hundreds of palm fronds for the new one. These were pleasant times for gossiping, joking, and laughing.

Expert cutters would gather young palm branches and split them in two for the weavers. The weavers would sit cross-legged on mats and weave thousands of fronds until there was enough for a roof. Then as many as 20 men would balance themselves on the roof's frame, and from the edge, begin tying down the fronds, one atop another, to ensure a waterproof seal. The work would last all day amid camaraderie and celebration. Like other youngsters, I learned to weave fronds, to throw them spear-like up to the thatchers, and to thatch like an expert. It took a long time to master that aspect of the craft.

I lived on Hernan Cortez Street in San Ignacio until the war. The cathedral, the plaza, and the Governor's Palace were on the same street. It was Hagåtña's main thoroughfare where much of the city's activity occurred.

Stores, shops, restaurants, taverns, and residences lined both sides of the street. It bustled with life on weekends when folks turned out to shop, see a movie, stroll, and visit. Neighbors called out to each other and chatted from doorsteps and front porches.

We lived on the north side of Hernan Cortez. The Mayhew house and store was next to us to the west. Across a side street and several houses beyond were the Johnston home, Tun Pedro Martinez's house with Elliott's Drug Store on the ground floor, the Shinohara home, and Dad's garage and repair shop. His taxi stand was on the next street over beside our first home, a house Dad rented from his uncle, Tun Ignacio "Kotla" Pangelinan. Further west were Suzuki's store and bar; Tun Jose Flores' retail store; Tun Tebutsio, the shoemaker's shop; Tun Francisco Torres' store; the Navy enlisted men's club and bowling alley; and Limtiaco's taxi stand and repair shop. Beyond these, Hernan Cortez continued into a residential area. To the east of us, on our side of the street, were the Atkins Kroll company store, Tan Chai Perez's house across a side street, and Tan Beck Guzman's store and home.

On the opposite side of Hernan Cortez, across from Tun Tebutsio's shoe shop, was our Santa Cruz meat and vegetable market. Dad's hardware and auto parts store and his retail bicycle outlet were there also. His office was in the building next door. The auto parts store, with its one-time dance hall on the top floor, was originally located further east, but Dad vacated the building, and Uncle Butler moved in to expand his Coca-Cola bottling plant. Dad leased another building just before the Japanese invasion and opened a cold storage market. Uncle Butler's home, with a soda fountain and department store on the ground floor, was on the next street over. Eastward from Butler's were the Shinohara Restaurant; the Gaiety Theater; Tun Tabus, the other shoemaker; and Dejima's store. Other landmarks I recall were Murphy's Tavern, the Palting property, and Seaton Schroeder School, where the Navy's director of education had his office. Hernan Cortez ended a block from the San Nicolas bridge.

Sounds that seem like music in my memories

Dad owned and operated a cockpit in Bilibek, on the ocean side of Hagåtña, and kept at least 100 of his warrior roosters in our backyard. I woke up every morning to their ear-splitting voices. Their crowing and many other sounds now seem like music in my memories.

Women shuffling off to the first Mass of the day filled the streets with the soft rustle of their long skirts and the whispered flapping of their leather church slippers. Until outlawed by the naval government as health hazards, mature women wore skirts with trains trailing behind them. Whenever she encountered dusty floors or ventured outdoors, a lady would lift her train and tuck an end into her waistband. The cinched-up skirt allowed a peek of the white cotton slip underneath. For me, the skirts with the trains were hallmarks of feminine grace and charm. I mourn their passing and resent the notion that they were hazardous to health. I have always felt that because trains on ladies' skirts connote royalty, the naval government banned them to reserve the connotation only for themselves.

After returning from church, the matriarchs of the homes would prepare breakfast as the city came to life. The naval captain-governor would take his morning exercise, resplendent on horseback. His horses were healthy and handsome, his leather saddle shiny and impressive. His saddle blanket was royal blue with gold braids and trim that flashed in the morning sun. Dressed in his dazzling white uniform, the captain-governor would ride through the city, eyes straight ahead, chin high, ignoring the bows and curtsies of people in the streets. Although as Americans, they were supposed to be averse to the symbolisms of royalty, none of the naval governors ever ordered a halt to the public bowing and scraping. I would watch people bow low as the governor passed and felt humiliated. With head held high, I would look the governor in the face. Sometimes he would ignore me, sometimes he would glare at me. But I refused to bow down. I would watch him ride off toward Apotguan before tending to my chores.

The sound of men chopping preceded the smell of cooking fires that signaled breakfast in the making. Burly woodsmen, with their bull carts stacked high with cords of firewood, would unload cords at the designated woodpiles of their customers in the neighborhood. Icemen and their wagons delivered heavy blocks all day long. Peddlers with fresh, hot bread and pastries roamed the streets. Most were children carrying baskets or boxes or large pans on their heads. They sold *potu*, which were steamed, fluffy, sweet rice cakes made with tuba, the fermented sap of the coconut blossom; *bibingka*, a tarter, baked version of *potu*; *fensil*, the edible nuts of the pandanus fruit; and *apigige'*, the sweet, gelatinous meat of green, unripe coconuts mixed with arrowroot starch and griddle-baked in banana leaf jackets. After selling their wares, vendors trudged home with their profits and then went to school.

Street traffic picked up after breakfast as farmers in their bull carts rumbled out of town to their farms in the vicinity. I could identify individual drivers outside my bedroom window by the distinctive sound their solid wooden wheels made against the pavement, the creak and squeal of wood-against-wood axles, and the slow, plodding *clop-clop* of carabao hooves.

Smoke rising from cook fires carried the scents of fresh ground coffee brewing, of eggs and the many other traditional selections of a generous breakfast, the major meal of the CHamoru day. Hardworking people who had few labor-saving devices needed heavy meals to start their day. Breakfast tables always had large selections — bacon, eggs, venison, chicken, pigeons, fish, fresh and dried beef, and fried pork strips. There were soups and stews, and always *titiyas*. Ours were larger and thicker than Mexican tortillas and made with one of four kinds of flour: corn, wheat, *mendioka* (tapioca), or *fadang*, a much-processed flour made from poisonous federico nuts.

Scientists now suspect *fadang* is a factor in the high incidence of dystrophic diseases in Guam. At one time, Guam had the world's highest per capita incidence of Parkinson's disease and ALS, or amyotrophic lateral sclerosis, also known as Lou Gehrig's disease. Although still higher than the U.S. average, the rates in Guam have declined since the end of the war. It may be because few people have the time, patience, or knowledge to prepare *titiyas fadang* anymore.

Like the sound of distant, gentle applause emanating from every household, the *pat-pat-patting* of hands making *titiyas* meant that breakfast would soon be ready.

When I was old enough, Dad put me in charge of opening the grocery store in San Nicolas. It was my first chore of the day. Dad's chief butcher, Tun Encho Sablan, as well as John Taitano, a good-humored employee and friend who taught me much about life and women, and the other employees would be waiting for me. I would turn on the lights, open the day's cashbox, and unlock the reefers. My next task was to take Dad's Cuban fighting roosters through their paces, exercising their leg and wing muscles to keep them in top fighting form. I would sometimes help Dad cut off a rooster's comb with a razor blade. Cocks cannot fight if they cannot see, and the combs hampered their vision.

Cockfights at Dad's cockpit took place a few nights a week and on weekends. Joaquin "Kin Inda" Cepeda, Dad's cockpit manager and long-time business foreman, collected admission at the door: 50 cents for spectators and bettors. Cockfighters got in free. The men who kept tabs of the bets were amazing. Without computers or calculators, they could — and still can — remember who made what bet on which rooster. They had incredible memories. Losers who thought they could get away without paying up rarely escaped the bet keepers.

With 3-to-4-inch razor sharp blades strapped to a spur, fighting cocks battled to the death while owners, spectators, and gamblers cheered them on. Equally matched birds fought long, bloody battles that ended only when the victor made one final peck at his dead opponent before dying himself. Oftentimes the winning peck was just the bird's final convulsion. Since Dad's roosters did not often lose, their dead opponents, sometimes in the dozens, came home to our kitchen. Because their muscles were rock hard, Mama had to stew them for as long as two days to make a chicken *kådu* (soup) we could eat. We ate lots of fighting cock soup.

Chapter 3

Going to the Guam Institute

Once done with the rooster exercises, I would head to school. Irene, Lorraine, and I attended the Guam Institute, a small, private grammar school run by Mr. Nieves Flores. It went from grades one through nine and was in a two-story building on San Ignacio Street. Tun Jose "Atdot" Lujan, a prominent carpenter, built and owned the building.

The old Guam Institute building was one of few to survive American bombardment in 1944. It also escaped the Seabee bulldozers that pushed Hagåtña's ruins into the sea. Abandoned, it deteriorated. In 1976, Super Typhoon Pamela made a direct hit and caused destruction islandwide. I was governor then, trying to come to grips with the disaster. Eager to clear public properties of debris, my parks director, Bob Cruz, ordered the derelict Lujan building razed. Bulldozers were ready to start when I dashed to the site and countermanded Bob's demolition order.

I did not want the building destroyed at my administration's hands. It had nurtured the early education of so many, including mine, and was too valuable and historic to destroy. I chided Bob's insensitivity. He and many of his postwar generation were apt students of the old Navy government's ingrained "no room for sentimentality" attitude. If something is old, replace it; if it serves no purpose, get rid of it. Bob knew little about Guam history — or that our personal histories intertwined.

"You see that window there?" I asked him, pointing to one on the second floor. Bob nodded. "That was your mother's classroom. That is where your mother taught many of us how to read and write. And you want to tear it down?"

Like other schoolboys, I had a crush on my pretty, young teacher, Miss

Rosita Perez. My schoolmates and I were heartbroken when she married Alan Cruz, Bob's father.

I sought federal historic preservation grant money and restored the building. The Lujan House is now on both the federal and local Register of Historic Places. As an adult, I appreciated the Lujan building's significance, but as a child, I wished I did not have to go there.

I wanted to attend public school, which offered many fun extracurricular activities. My younger sisters and brothers were fortunate. As they grew to school age, they went to public school. I had to wait until I finished eighth grade to be transferred to George Washington High School. That was in 1940. George Washington opened in 1936 and was the only high school then.

The Guam Institute was Hagåtña's only private school, but there were many public grade schools, among them Dorn Hall School, Richard P. Leary School, Seaton Schroeder School, Bilibek School, Padre Palomo School, Roy C. Smith School, and others. There was also an industrial arts school at the foot of San Ramon Hill and George Washington. Now only two schools remain in Hagåtña — the Cathedral Grade School and the Academy of Our Lady of Guam, the all-girls high school. Both are private Catholic schools. There are no more public schools, nor are there many residents. Hagåtña remains Guam's capital, but it is a strange one.

Our classes at the Guam Institute broke for recess at midmorning. Most of us would head to the nearest place to buy snacks. We could buy rock candy at Tun Vicente Martinez's store or *dos-put-uno* (two for a penny) candy at Tun Jose Flores' general store. Many families around the school also catered to the students by selling soup, pastries, or breads. My favorite treats were cream-and-bread pudding with cinnamon and a large hard candy we called *chåda' ngånga'*, duck eggs.

The public schools did not often include the Guam Institute in their extracurricular activities. They held annual baseball games, foot races, drill marching competitions, and oratorical contests for students, islandwide. The oratorical contest was the most popular and highly esteemed event. I was 10 years old when the Guam Institute accepted the invitation to participate for the first time. Although the competition was stiff, I was determined to win a slot to represent my school. I worked hard on my speech and practiced as often as I could, hoping I could make an excellent showing for the Guam Institute. I won first place overall.

The only other programs that involved all schools were the Red Cross' Christmas gifts and the Navy government's annual de-worming treatment. The Red Cross packages came without fail before every Christmas. They contained school supplies, a book bag, and some small toys. Every student in every school received one, even us at the Guam Institute. We all anticipated receiving the Red Cross packages but not the de-worming treatment.

Both colonial governments tried with limited success to control the diseases, infections, and infestations our tropical climate produced. Navy government workers regularly sprayed gallons of diesel oil to kill mosquitoes. Still, everyone, at least one time or another, suffered from dysentery, head lice, and parasites. All school students had to report as a group to the Susana Hospital for one treatment or another several times a year. The annual de-worming treatment was the most awful and most dreaded. The announcement of a scheduled treatment would send children into a panic. I would even have nightmares about it.

The de-worming medicine, Chenopodium, was a thick, black liquid served in little paper cups. It smelled horrible and tasted even worse. It left an aftertaste so bitter nothing could wash it away. Taking it was worse than getting a spanking or a shot. Many of us cried, but no pleading, struggling, gagging, or vomiting spared us. Nurses, corpsmen, and teachers made sure each of us swallowed a dose. With my spine tingling, I would wait in line for my turn. My stomach would revolt even before I could bring the paper cup to my mouth. I think we would have preferred living with worms. The cure was worse than the disease.

The children of Hagåtña knew every nook and cranny of the city. The entire city was our playground, with friends and relatives at every turn. The adults knew every child, or at least what family the child belonged to. In so tight-knit a community, family problems often became community gossip. People hid their disagreements to keep the peace, but the gossips always found out. Word of any incident spread until all details were known, discussed, and often, distorted for greater effect. No child could get into trouble without everyone finding out.

The Navy's newsletter, the *Guam Eagle*, and its monthly magazine, the *Guam Recorder*, catered mainly to the military community and upper levels of Guam society. The publications were of little interest to ordinary people unless their names appeared. My name appeared in the *Guam Recorder's* January

1928 edition under December births. Neither publication could compete with the rapid local grapevine, the *tilifon alaihai*. *Alaihai* is the beach morning glory which grows along the shore in long, tangled webs. The *tilifon alaihai* worked faster and better than official news sources or the regular telephone system. Its "lines" extended further than its mechanical counterpart.

Dad had telephones at the market and the taxi stand, but we did not have one at home until 1938, after we moved into the house Dad bought from Tun Pedro Martinez. My sisters were delighted. The phone was a large, wooden box mounted to the wall in the dining room. It had a crank handle on one side and a bell-shaped listening piece tethered by a long, black cord on the other. A horn-like mouthpiece stuck out in front. Even though the Mayhew girls lived next door, just yards away, my sisters would call them on the telephone. They could have chatted face-to-face from window to window. Houses in Hagåtña were so close together that one could hear a neighbor's telephone ring, and the footsteps running to answer. And, sometimes, even the conversation.

At home on Hernan Cortez Street

For the first few years of my life, home was the tin-roofed, two-story concrete house Dad rented from Tun Ignacio. It was on the corner of Hernan Cortez Street's commercial district. After Bobbie's birth in January 1929 and Paul's in May 1930, our household numbered eight, so Dad moved us into a house his brother, Uncle Carlos, owned. Their sister, Auntie Butler, lived across the street. Dad's taxi garage and a side street separated our first house from the second. Uncle Carlos' house had a tin roof and whitewashed walls, one of many in the city. The carbide for whitewashing came from the cable station in Sumai. Carbide was available in abundance and cheaper than paint but became discolored easily. Older houses, with multiple whitewashings, were dazzling white. Newer walls needed many washings before they achieved the same whiteness.

A short flight of stairs led to a small, screened porch of our new house. A foyer, with a hat rack and an umbrella stand, opened into a large parlor, four bedrooms, a bathroom that I always thought was dingy, and a spacious double kitchen. Part of it was inside the house, part was outside. The outside kitchen was a traditional one with a raised hearth for open-fire cooking. The indoor kitchen was modern with a huge iron stove and an icebox, which Dad later replaced with an electric refrigerator. We kept vigil beside the new refrigerator, waiting to see if the water in the ice trays would really freeze. After it did, we made hundreds of popsicles until the novelty wore off.

Dad's taxi stand was next door. The garage and auto repair shop were behind us. I spent hours in the repair shop tinkering with the tools and machinery. I built things like scooters out of kerosene tins and packing crates. Watching Dad's mechanics work on the taxis allowed me to see the latest technological advances coming out of Detroit, the home of the Ford Motor Company. Dad held the franchise for Ford vehicles. I used my status as the owner's son to get drivers to teach me. At 8, I cajoled them into letting me steer during runs about town. By the time I was 9, I had mastered the Ford Model T. At 11, I could drive the Model A.

As part of my secret driving lessons, I also learned to crank up a Model T like an expert, an accomplishment I am proud of even now. If not done properly, and if the engine backfired, it could mean injury for the operator. I knew just when to pull the choke lever at the lower left corner at the front of the vehicle, to give the crank a good turn, pull the choke lever, and crank again. An incomplete cycle would cause the pistons to burn prematurely, and the crank would flip back. I have seen arms broken by such flipping. In time, I also learned to manage a stubborn engine. I figured out how to position the crank, stand on the lever, and when to give a quick downward thrust. I also learned how far to jump away.

Just before the war, Dad bought a large house from Tun Pedro Martinez, a prominent Hagåtña merchant. It was our first real home. Tun Pedro was not selling it, but Mama asked. He had a soft spot for Mama and agreed to Dad's offer. The purchase was necessary because by then, there were 11 of us: Irene, Lorraine, me, Barbara, Paul, Norma, Fred, Rodney, Donald, Junie, and Josephine. Michael's birth in 1940 brought our total to 12.

There were so many of us that we ate at separate tables. As firstborns, Irene, Lorraine, and I had the privilege of sitting at Mama and Dad's table, where they imparted their wisdom and where conversations and discussions were grown-up. Bobbie, the eldest child at the children's table, made sure our younger siblings behaved and ate properly. The eldest at each table always served, which meant they also got the best selection. For my brothers and sisters, promotion to the grown-ups' table was a rite of passage that occurred only after they had mastered fork, knife, and spoon, as well as pouring and drinking without spilling or knocking over the glassware.

Mama was a stickler for proper etiquette. We had to be gentlemen and ladies not only at the supper table but also in our behavior and manner of speech. If any of us failed to be polite or courteous, especially in the presence of elders, Mama would punish us. She never raised her voice or lost her patience, no matter how angry she became, but a scolding or a stern look was all she needed to make us behave. She never spanked us; she left that kind of discipline to Dad, who was not stingy with the strap. Mama would not tolerate cussing and rough or vulgar speech of any kind. I could never bring myself to say "goddamn it" or "shit" until well after the war, when we all seemed comfortable with the American right to self-expression. By then most of us, me included, were numb to even the vilest expletives.

My politeness and practiced good manners sometimes hindered, sometimes helped, my efforts to impress girls. Some thought I was a real gentleman, others thought I was an oddball. Unfortunately, many of the girls I liked found me too odd for their tastes. With others, I was luckier. I took my cues from Mama, learning from her how to relate to women, how to conduct myself, and what to expect from my efforts. She taught me what to do and not do. She also taught me what women looked for in a suitor. Her advice led me to a girl who shares many of Mama's traits. My wife Madeleine is a lot like Mama. She, too, is a refined and gentle person who loves music.

Slingshot, marbles, and champion tops

My parents' families, the Bordallos and the Pangelinans, owned large tracts of land, and many considered them prosperous. Most of my aunts and uncles were in business on their own as well. I was a member of Hagåtña's circle of prominent families, but I did not often play with my cousins and the other affluent children. The entrepreneurial legacy my father inherited he bequeathed in turn to my brothers and me. I went to work at many of his enterprises at an early age, as did my brothers until the war disrupted the process. Working left me little time for boyhood games and frolic, but I managed to find time. When I did, it would be with neighborhood children whose families were not as well-off as mine.

Before school started in the morning, and after it ended at noon, I would report to Dad for my assignments. He always had a lengthy and unpredictable list. I never knew what he would have in store for me. I swept floors and restocked shelves in the auto parts store or the cold storage room at the San Nicolas Market. Sometimes he had me run errands on a bicycle or help prepare the cockpit for a fight. He had me operate the gas pump at the taxi stand, unpack and assemble new bicycles, or assist the auto mechanics. I also helped slaughter hogs and cattle at the abattoir, helped make sausage and *chachalon* (deep-fried pork rinds) and helped make salted fish.

Between assignments, I could often sandwich in some target practice with a slingshot, a quick game of marbles, or rise to the challenge of a tops fight. I was always ready to steal time for play. I carried a slingshot in my hip pocket, a bag of marbles in my left pocket, and my champion, handmade top in my right. These were every boy's standard equipment, as universal as the machetes dangling from the belts of farmers and workmen.

No boy would be without his slingshot, at least. Made from *lemmon di china* branches and inner tube rubber, our slingshots were no mere toys. We used them for hunting and defense, as well as for sport. We shot birds for food; giant toads, rats, and other small vermin for target practice; and vicious dogs and wasp nests in defense. I could bring down game birds at 50 yards even though my eyesight was poor. I was not aware of it until years later, but I must have developed a kind of sensing system — a sixth sense — that has served me well. I suspect we inherited some prowess from our CHamoru ancestors who astonished European explorers with their skill and accuracy. With his sling, a CHamoru marksman was as deadly as any rifleman.

Playing marbles also required good hand-eye coordination, skill, and a good supply of unchipped glass marbles. Marbles was a friendly, entertaining game, not as competitive or violent as tops fighting. Tops fighting was a test of manhood — or boyhood. To start, two guys would fling their tops at a bullseye scratched into the ground. The top closest to the bullseye became the first striker; the other top became the victim. It was like an execution. The victim had to remain in place while its owner prayed for it to survive or for the first striker to miss. With as much force as he could muster, the first striker would hurl his top down upon the victim, aiming for a direct hit. If he missed, the roles reversed. The strikes continued until one of the tops was "dead" — either fractured or shattered to pieces.

The owners of "dead" tops walked away humiliated by their loss and their inferior workmanship. Store-bought tops were fragile; they split too easily. The best tops were hand-carved from *åbas* (guava) or *lemmon di china* wood and fitted with a spike or sharpened nail. Champion tops, the victors of many battles, were only nicked and dented. Luckily, championships changed often enough for each of us to taste victory.

On weekends, we took our competition to the open field at Bilibek and challenged one another with *saranggolas*, which are special kites armed with sharp blades. They were not for show but for airborne dogfights. They had no tails and were difficult to control. We tethered them to strong cords, heavier than ordinary kite string. Crowds would gather to watch whenever we mobilized for kite battles; they would cheer for their favorites, especially if those managed to get airborne. Once aloft, *saranggolas* filled the air with zinging, whooshing sounds as they dipped and twirled in the sky, chasing and attacking other kites. Kite flyers had to struggle to keep their cords taut and away from the blades of other kites. Only the best flyers could stay in control. The spectators' gasps and shrieks added to the tension and excitement. After a while, few kites would still be flying, and splintered kite frames and shredded paper would litter the ground.

In 1944, as I raced into the burning city of Hagåtña, the whistling whine of bombs and mortar shells reminded me of battling *saranggolas*. I was scared to death but found myself remembering the peaceful, carefree days when we flew kites. Survival had a different meaning then.

I was one of the few boys who owned a Daisy BB air rifle. It cost a steep $2.50 in the 1930s, but I shared the rifle with boys who were not as fortunate to own one. We spent hours shooting giant toads along the Hagåtña River. Toads were not as challenging as birds and fruit bats. If we were lucky, we could even bring down a wild pig or deer. I was an excellent marksman by the time I was old enough for shotguns and .22 or .30 caliber rifles. As an adult, I often entertained myself with a high-powered 30-30 rifle, shooting targets in the surf below the cliffs at Nasgan on my Yoña estate. I also kept a rifle on board my yacht, in case sharks attacked my catches of fish.

As a boy, I had many playmates my own age but never developed close friendships. My most loyal companion was a mongrel named Ranger. Among neighborhood playmates, we let our dogs fight to settle our disputes. It was hard on our pets but better than having to explain lacerations and black eyes to our parents. I look back now and realize how cruel we were. Once, during a fight, Ranger lunged at Greg Perez, who was watching. Greg was 12 at the time. Ranger slashed Greg's top lip. The injury healed but left his face scarred.

Although I got a good licking for it, I never stopped feeling guilty. Greg and I remained friends. Years later, Greg did not return from a fishing trip. Searchers never found his body.

If chores permitted, I spent some time building model airplanes with Richard Arriola. We hung our finished models from the ceiling in our homes. Richard never outgrew his interest in tiny, intricate things and became a watchmaker. The two friends I hold dear were older than me: Jesus "Gådi" Laguaña and Arthur Anderson. We liked and respected each other, and during the occupation, we depended on each other. Gådi remains a friend. The Japanese executed Arthur.

I spent most of my time alone or with adults. Perhaps because I was Dad's eldest son, his contemporaries allowed me into their conversations. They let me pick their brains and answered my questions.

"Son, we are different ... we are not their equals"

Of all the children in my family circle, I was closest to Dolly Butler, my first cousin who lived across the street. We were the same age and regular companions and playmates at family gatherings. Dolly's mother, Ignacia Butler, is Dad's older sister who married Chester Butler, an American civilian. Dolly was fair-skinned and looked Caucasian, but no one considered her "white." Her father tainted his status when he married her mother.

Dolly and I were in the same class in *eskuelan påle'*, which translates to "priests' school" and refers to Catholic catechism classes. All children in Hagåtña had to attend an hour of *eskuelan påle'* every weekday afternoon at the St. Vincent de Paul Hall adjacent to the cathedral. I sometimes skipped *eskuelan påle'* to go swimming at the Minondo, a deep part of the Hagåtña River, but that ended when Påle' Dueñas tattled on me. *Eskuelan påle'* ended before *mirienda*, a late afternoon teatime the Spanish introduced. *Mirienda* helped stave off hunger until supper at 8 o'clock. *Eskuelan påle'* gave us a last chance to see friends and playmates before *orasión*, or evening prayers, which ended outdoor activities and signaled the coming of suppertime and bedtime.

One day, when we were about 7, Dolly and I walked to *eskuelan påle'* through the plaza and the Governor's Palace. As we passed the high wall of the palace complex, we heard the American children laughing and playing in what we assumed was their play area. Their school was inside the complex.

They rarely ventured outside it, and if they did, they acted superior and were snobbish. Their Navy fathers, no matter what their rank, had power and authority over us, and they knew it. We had no way to fight back. Even Dolly, who was half American, had no rebuttal.

I had just finished my chores and was heading to another sort of school. I wondered whether the American children had chores to do and how their lives behind their stone wall differed from ours. That afternoon, I scaled the wall to find out.

"What are you doing?" Dolly asked in alarm.

"I'm going to see what they're doing," I said.

"Ricky, get down," she insisted. "You'll get caught and get us in trouble."

"You go on ahead. I'm going to look," I whispered and continued up the wall.

Either out of loyalty or because we both would get in trouble, Dolly stayed. "Be careful," she whispered. She was curious too.

I reached the top and peered over the edge. The sight took my breath away. There was a small, well-kept courtyard. The lawn was smooth and green and bordered by clipped hedges and flowering shrubs. The children were playing on the most incredible play equipment I had ever seen — swings with wide, wooden seats hanging from chains on sturdy A-frame pipes, teeter-totters, monkey bars, and a tall, shiny slide. There was also a little merry-go-round. Some boys were spinning it and making the girls on it giggle and scream. It was a children's paradise.

"What do you see?" Dolly whispered up at me. "Ricky, what do you see?"

Before I could answer, a Navy man stepped into the play yard and spotted me. "Hey, you!" he shouted. "What are you doing up there?"

The American children froze and looked in my direction. The man yelled again. Without answering, I shimmied back down. Dolly had heard the man yelling and followed me running toward the cathedral.

"Ricky, what was there?" she asked as we reached the church. I looked at her but did not answer. I did not have the heart to tell her.

The scene in the courtyard bothered me. The difference between the American children's playground and ours was astounding. Our playground in San Antonio had four squeaky see-saws, a few broken swings, and a chain-and-handlebar merry-go-round. Instead of manicured green lawns, our playground was a dusty, rock-studded field with patches of tall weeds.

I went home dejected that afternoon and told Dad what I had done and seen. I expected him to scold me, but I needed an explanation. Dad could see my hurt and confusion. He listened and sighed before he answered.

"Ricky," he said, "those children have those things because the Navy provides for them. The Navy brings them far from their homes and feels it has an obligation to make their lives as comfortable here as where they come from. The Navy can do that. You cannot compare their resources with ours."

Dad's answer did not satisfy me. The Navy was supposed to take care of us, too. Why then was there such a difference in what the Navy provided for its children and what it provided for us? Why couldn't we have a playground like theirs? I pressed for answers.

"Son, we are different from them," Dad said. "We are not their equals. We are not American citizens. You are just beginning to see what that means. As you get older, you will understand better. It may change someday. I am going to try to make that change for all our people. For now, just remember that we are different. Not better, not worse, just different."

Dad was right; I did understand as I grew older. But the more I understood, the more I resented. I took solace in Dad's words about changing the unequal situation, even though justice seemed slow coming. I had great faith in Dad and knew he would indeed take on the task someday.

The picture of that playground has remained vivid in my mind. From that day on, each time I passed that wall and heard the American children in their playground, my resentment grew. Fifty years later, with a twinge of satisfaction, I talked about the American children's playground. I included it in my remarks at the dedication of the Playground for All Children in Dededo. I launched the playground project during my first term as governor. It was unfinished when I left office in 1978. My successor did not continue the work. After returning to office in 1983, I completed the project and dedicated it to all of Guam's children. It is a fully equipped, state-of-the-art playground surpassing the little one I saw behind the palace walls.

Like their children, adult military dependents did not often venture past the palace walls to socialize with the locals. I recall one exception, Mrs. Waskey, who would call on Mama now and then. She would bring her piano accordion and spend the afternoon making music and singing with my mother and sisters. I never met Mr. Waskey. He never came to our house. Navy men did not fraternize with native men. In my deepening understanding of the differences between the Americans and us, I realized racial prejudice was most obvious among men.

Even Hagåtña's American civilians had their prejudices. Many, like Uncle Butler, were married to CHamoru women but did not consider CHamoru men as equals. The prewar Elks Club of Hagåtña was exclusive to American civilian men. No CHamoru man could even approach the clubhouse steps. The Elks often hosted parties to which only CHamoru girls received invitations. The insulting selectivity prompted CHamoru men to form their own club. They called it the Young Men's League of Guam and opened their headquarters across from the Elks Club. Dad was a charter member. He served as president from 1936 until the invasion and afterward from 1945 until 1947. He continued active membership for many years thereafter.

Uncle Butler's amazing Coca-Cola plant

Dad was always getting involved, always doing things, particularly in business. He tried just about everything. He and his brothers, Tomas and Carlos, and sister, Ignacia, got a head start by inheriting my grandfather's properties and business. Dad and his brothers got an expansive agribusiness and the cattle ranches. Their sister inherited Pappa's two-story house and general merchandise store fronting Hernan Cortez Street. She and Uncle Butler developed it further to include a soda fountain, a movie theater, and a soda bottling plant. In 1923, they were the first ever to secure a Coca-Cola franchise outside Coca-Cola's home in Atlanta, Georgia.

Coca-Cola arrived at the Butler plant in syrup form, then was mixed with carbonated water, and bottled. The formula and mixing technique were trade secrets so private that few were privileged to know them. Tun Lino Sablan, the Butlers' head chemist, was one of the privileged. According to local lore, he took the secret to his grave. Tun Lino also supervised the brewing and bottling of sarsaparilla, root beer, and several kinds of carbonated fruit drinks.

After securing the Coca-Cola franchise, Uncle Butler expanded the bottling plant and installed new, modern machinery. He brought specialists from the States to install and inspect it. Uncle Butler also installed a plate glass window on the street side of the bottling plant so that passersby could watch the amazing machinery at work. It offered a peek into the future and the magic of automation. It also meant the plant workers who washed, filled, and capped bottles by hand lost their jobs.

Uncle Butler's machinery drew little, brown faces to the big window daily. The conveyer belts and the assembly line, working independent of human control, mesmerized everyone who watched. Like clinking toy soldiers, the soda bottles rattled along in single file. They would pause beneath a machine that filled them then moved on to another that stamped on the caps. We loved to watch and listen to the rhythmic *whoosh* and *hiss* of the machines and the clinking of the bottles tapping against each other on the conveyers. But I did not have to watch through the window from outside. As the plant owner's nephew, I could go into the plant and watch up close.

I could roam anywhere except the top-secret upstairs room where Tun Lino and a few others worked. Pipes from that room led down to the Coca-Cola blending tank. The mixture then went into the machine that filled each bottle with the correct amount. Sometimes Uncle Butler would pull a filled, but not yet capped, bottle from the line and hand it to me. It always made me feel guilty. It was hard to drink the soda in front of all the faces pressed against the window. I often wished I could open the doors and let them join me.

When it came to drinking Coca-Cola before an audience, no one could beat Mr. Mayhew, a big, heavyset American who was married to a CHamoru lady. Mr. Mayhew did not just sip his Coca-Colas — he guzzled them down in one swallow.

Mr. Mayhew and his family lived in a two-story house next to us. The family lived upstairs. Downstairs was their store, which carried photography supplies and featured photo displays. Mama bought her film and got her pictures developed there.

More than photo displays in his shop, Mr. Mayhew himself provided the most interesting entertainment. He would sit in front of the store almost every afternoon, relaxing with several bottles of Coca-Cola. Since he owned the store, he could drink as many bottles as he wished. And he drank many. People often gathered to watch him pour one cola after another straight down his throat. Adult spectators made bets on how fast he could down an entire bottle or on how many bottles he would drink. We would just watch in awe. All of us would applaud and cheer when Mr. Mayhew held up each empty bottle.

Mr. Mayhew's Coca-Cola ritual continued for several years. As time passed, he grew fatter and fatter. Before he and his family moved away from Guam in 1939, Mr. Mayhew was gigantic. His addiction to Coca-Cola, no doubt, contributed to Uncle Butler's prosperity. Uncle Butler was one of the wealthiest men in Guam at the time.

Chapter 4

Affluence born out of hard work

I never understood why Dolly's parents went by their last name. We had always called them Auntie Butler and Uncle Butler, and it never seemed strange until someone pointed it out. Their contemporaries called them by their first names, Ignacia and Chester, but not their nieces and nephews. Everyone else in the family was conventional. Auntie Rose was Auntie Rose, Uncle Tom was Uncle Tom, and Uncle Carlos was Uncle Carlos. Dad's friends called him either B.J. or "Batasalito," the CHamoru pronunciation of Little Baltazar, after his father, his namesake. Mama's name, Josefina, was shortened to Sufina. Auntie Rose's name is Rosalia. Their sister Gloria, who we called Auntie Lolang, died of tuberculosis when I was 9 years old. Her funeral was my introduction to death. I wept throughout her funeral, as did everyone else in the family.

Nearly everyone had at least one nickname. A nickname could stem from a cumbersome first name, one's clan name, a teasing name, or for some state or condition one is known for. Or all three. Since several people could share the same first, middle, and last name, nicknames identified one from another. One Jose P. Cruz might be "Pepen Kotla" while another might be "Ping Happy." Pepe and Ping are common nicknames for Jose, Joseph, or Joe. Obituaries that read "also known as..." often puzzle newcomers to Guam.

My parents' Pangelinan clan is a large one. Mama and Dad were "Kotla" Pangelinans, distinguishing their family from other Pangelinan families. Nicknames helped everyone keep track of who was who. Thus, CHamorus did not have identity problems. Children knew who they were and who their relatives were just by the family nicknames. Children also had to address all elders, whether blood relatives or not, with respect, prefacing their first names with "tun" or "tan," the CHamoru derivatives of the Spanish "tío" and "tía" for

uncle and aunt. The CHamoru usage acknowledged seniority. Tun and tan
were more common than the Spanish "don" and "doña." Dad's father was a
Spaniard; people addressed him as Don Baltazar.

My paternal grandfather left his general merchandise store in Hagåtña
to Auntie Butler. He left his vast land holdings to my father and two uncles.
These included cattle ranches at Mount Lamlam, Hågat, and at Kotot in the
Talo'fo'fo Valley, as well as rice fields, fruit orchards, and farmlands in Sumai
and Mayanghulo', just outside Hågat. We had a liquor distillery and more than
1,000 head of cattle and hogs, a slaughterhouse, and a meat market. These
were labor-intensive operations that turned me into a cattleman and butcher
even before I reached my teen years. I enjoyed working the ranches and the
cattle. With so much work, so many responsibilities, and so little time for play,
I learned how to turn work into play. It became a way of life for me. I grew
up in affluence born out of hard work, mine as well as Dad's. Dad was always
trying something new in business and always tasked me with some duty for it.

In addition to his share of the family agribusiness, Dad independently
owned the general merchandise store and taxi company in Sumai. In Hagåtña,
he operated the grocery with cold storage facilities, a general merchandise
store, an auto parts store, a boxing stadium, a dancing school, a bus line, an
auto dealership, and a rental service for bicycles and pickup trucks. The trucks
also served as hearses. In time, he would also run a cockpit, a coffee shop, a
restaurant, and a nightclub. Not all his ventures succeeded. His dance studio,
which was above the auto parts store, was supposed to be a serious school
of dance, but it was really a taxi dance hall. It was known around town as a
place of drunken carousing. When the priests began condemning the dance
hall from their pulpits, Mama forced Dad to shut it down. Dad then moved
the auto parts store a few doors down the street and returned the building to
Uncle Butler for the new Coca-Cola bottling plant.

After Dad expanded to Hagåtña, his chief accountant, Antonio B. Won
Pat, managed the businesses in Sumai. Like Dad, Mr. Won Pat was a member of the Guam Congress, a pseudo-legislative body that served only as an
advisory council to the Navy governor. Mr. Won Pat was among the Guam
congressmen who stormed out of the legislature in protest in 1949. The following year, in 1950, he became speaker of the First Guam Legislature and, in
1965, Guam's first delegate to U.S. Congress. I chaired his campaign for the
congressional seat.

As a boxing promoter, Dad arranged for boxers to come from the Philippines. He housed them at my grandmother's sister's home in Hågat, where they could set up a makeshift training camp and prepare for their bouts. I learned how to box and skip rope from them. Dad's boxing stadium had the distinction of once having Jack Dempsey referee a fight. Dempsey, who was the world heavyweight boxing champion from 1919 to 1926, came to Guam on the Pan American China Clipper in 1939.

"You must always respect a man's dignity"

Dad was a stern, no-nonsense person. He took life seriously and demanded absolute obedience from his children. He was a shrewd and careful businessman, but he was careless with money — not his investment capital but the cash in his pockets. Mama took care of this shortcoming and parlayed it into a secret and sizeable household fund. Sometimes Dad left loose change in his pockets, sometimes a few dollars. Mama once found $300 wadded up in a trouser pocket. Dad never missed it, never asked about it, or told Mama he had lost it. Mama opened an account at the Navy's Bank of Guam for the windfall from Dad's pockets. Since I made the deposits for her, I shared her secret. I opened a savings account of my own and deposited my hard-earned nickels and dimes. By the time the war came, I had saved $12.

Dad's friend and political colleague, Eduardo "Jake" T. Calvo, worked at the bank. As young as I was, Jake would take time to manage my bank business himself. Jake always dealt with me man to man. I enjoyed talking with him whenever I came into the bank. Dad's contemporaries accorded me and Jake's eldest son Paul as eventual successors of our prominent and respected fathers, a measure of adult standing, even though we were mere boys.

Despite my youth, Dad charged me with supervisory duties over the people in his employ. That meant I had authority over men twice and thrice my age. A firm disciplinarian, Dad would not tolerate foolishness on my part and would set me straight whenever I got too big for my britches. It did not take long for me to learn about the burdens of responsibility that come with authority.

"You must always respect a man's dignity," Dad told me, warning me against becoming arrogant and insensitive. "You must be forceful and firm, but always be fair and honest. Never forget that the authority you have over someone is yours only if you can earn his respect, only if you remain mindful of his dignity as a person." I have tried to live my life according to Dad's words.

To temper my sense of balance as a leader, Dad gave me as many menial tasks as managerial ones. I could manage the stores, but I also had to sweep floors. I could head cattle roundups, but I also had to learn how to butcher beef. I could sit in the company of important men, but I also had to serve as an errand and delivery boy. I hated making deliveries, trudging around town with my wagon, but now I appreciate the insights I gained from it and how deeply I became steeped in the CHamoru way of life. I ran many errands and interacted with all sorts of people. I never felt out of place anywhere. Now, I am as comfortable with kings as I am with paupers. They are my equals as surely as I am theirs.

Sharing was a significant part of CHamoru community life. Fishermen gave away whatever their families did not need, as did farmers with their produce; hunters with their catches of venison, game birds, or fruit bats; and ranchers with their beef or pork. No one kept more than they needed. Surpluses were always either traded or given away. Everyone took turns being givers or receivers of good fortune. There was no shame in asking either. If someone down the street made something special, like *fritada*, a rich blood stew made with beef or pork organs, the aroma would waft throughout the neighborhood. The makers of such delicacies always knew to make enough for the neighbors who wanted some.

"Ricky, Tan Maria is making *fritada* today," Mama would say. "Give her that fish in the icebox and tell her I want some *fritada*." Sometimes, as I made my rounds, I would get similar instructions from neighbors. "Ricky, tell your mother I want some of her cooking bananas," a neighbor might say. "Tell her my brother is making salt, and I'll give her some. Be sure to come tomorrow to get it. And bring me those bananas as soon as you can."

I would moan and groan — even cry sometimes — whenever my parents received anything in large quantities. The windfalls meant I would spend my entire day delivering shares to friends, neighbors, and relatives scattered throughout town. I would pull my wagon back and forth and up and down the streets of Hagåtña to deliver beef or fresh vegetables to Nanan Chong, my grandmother's sister, and to Tun Pedro Martinez, or to pick up baskets and bundles of this and that for Mama. Every Saturday morning, I had to follow her with my wagon to the public market behind the Navy commissary.

Mama insisted on doing her own shopping rather than send a *muchacha*, or maid, to do it for her. While most of the status-conscious women in Mama's circle would never dream of going to the public market themselves, Mama rather enjoyed it and did not think it beneath her. My counterparts in that same circle also kept themselves separate, living sheltered lives. I never saw any of them at the public market.

The public market was an important forum for socializing and a colorful place to buy all kinds of goods. Although most families were self-sufficient, they always needed something from the market. City folk and government office workers depended on the market. With children in tow, buyers and sellers would come in from the outskirts of Hagåtña and beyond, to do business and catch up on the latest news and gossip. While they did, their children would frolic around the stalls. I would join in while Mama browsed. The squeals and laughter of children and the voices of haggling grown-ups blended with the cackling of live chickens, goats, and livestock and made the market a noisy, wonderful place. It was always busy, always crowded.

The market also featured handicrafts as well as fresh fruit, produce, and other foodstuffs. One lady sold elegant, handmade christening gowns. Another, Mrs. Tomas Mesa, sold bags and purses made with pastel-colored *akaleha'* shells. *Akaleha'* were tiny snails once abundant in Guam. Mrs. Mesa cultivated the snails and developed a lucrative market for her wares. She expanded her shell craft business and employed several other women. Few Navy wives ever returned to the States without some of Mrs. Mesa's handiwork. Mrs. Mesa did not survive the occupation. The Japanese executed her and 29 other Malesso' villagers in 1944. The dainty little snails are gone too, displaced by ugly, giant African snails that infested the island after the war.

For being her obedient delivery boy and loyal shopping companion, Mama catered to my likes. Depending on the time of year and what was in season, she would buy things, especially for me. In the summer and fall, it would be sacks of *hutu*, the seeds of the *dokdok* (*Artocarpus mariannensis*), a relative of the breadfruit. They are delicious boiled, and I loved them. I still do.

Until I was about 8, I also made milk deliveries every morning. Dad entered the dairy business to accommodate the tastes of American military families who had to depend on local suppliers. My delivery route was not long, and the task did not take a lot of time, so I did not mind it, especially since it was interesting work. It gave me a peek at the private lives of military families and, I thought, a glimpse of American life.

One of their strangest but nicest practices was kissing on the doorstep. Fascinated but embarrassed, I would try not to ogle as American husbands kissed their wives before going to work. I never saw my father kiss my mother and was unaccustomed to open displays of affection. Although it made me uncomfortable, the American goodbye kiss seemed like a caring way to begin the workday. I liked the practice.

I could not leave milk bottles in the heat on my customers' doorsteps. Nor did customers leave the empty bottles outside. I had to go into their homes to make deliveries and retrieve empties. This allowed me to see how they lived — their parlors and kitchens and other interesting things. Because of the heat, Americans stripped off their clothes in their homes. We often snickered at how they ran around undressed in their homes. As a milkboy, I knew it firsthand. A Navy wife wearing only a robe once met me at the door. I delivered the milk then ran off to tell the other boys what I had seen. Many offered to make deliveries for me just to see for themselves.

Of all my milk customers, a couple named Lyons stands out in my memories. They gave me a gift one Christmas, the first I ever received from strangers. I could not believe they would be so kind and generous to the CHamoru boy who delivered milk. Their thoughtfulness was unlike the haughtiness of many military personnel. The couple gave me a present every Christmas during their tour and seemed tickled by my shy "thank yous." They also gave me a going away gift when they left Guam. I do not remember what any of the gifts were, but they left me with the belief that not all Americans were stingy and mean.

Milk was not an important part of the CHamoru diet then, but through her exposure to American life, Mama insisted we drink it with our meals. I did not like it and told her once that "milk is a wonderful thing, Mama, but I just don't care for the taste." The ploy did not work; I still had to drink it.

Milk deliveries fell to my younger brothers when I graduated to bigger responsibilities. For a while, I supervised Dad's bicycle sales and rentals, a division of his Hagåtña taxi service. I was responsible for the care and maintenance of more than 50 bicycles, but at first, I could not own one myself. Through Mama's intercession, Dad allowed me to purchase one. He increased my salary to 10 cents a week so I could pay him 40 cents a month until the new bicycle was mine. The transaction was my first experience with credit buying. It seemed like years before I was free of the $15 debt. Not long after I got the bicycle, I crashed into a moving jitney on San Ignacio Street, between the Notley residence and the rear of Gaiety Theater. I was unconscious for a day and a half.

Most of my bicycle customers were sailors from the transport ships that pulled into Apra Harbor every three months. The ships ferried Navy men and dependents from the States to new duty stations in Guam or the Philippines. When the ships arrived, I would do brisk business renting bicycles to the hordes of sailors who flooded into Hagåtña for the two or three days the ship was in port.

Everyone prospered when the transports arrived. Anyone with anything to sell would set up roadside stalls from Piti to Hagåtña. Vendors offered everything from fresh fruits and vegetables, homemade candy, pastries, and cooked delicacies to handicrafts and souvenirs. In a carnival atmosphere, peddlers would bellow the praises of their wares in the hopes the sailors and transport passengers would stop and buy. The biggest spenders were the transports themselves. Since their holds did not have electric refrigeration, the transports would take on ice from Tun Pedro Martinez's ice plant, and fresh fruits and vegetables from farmers who earned the bulk of their income from transport orders.

Tun Pedro would stockpile tons of ice between transport arrivals, and crowds would gather to watch the loading. The ice handlers, like my friend Jesus "Gådi" Laguaña, were entertaining professionals who could sling huge blocks of ice with amazing skill. We would watch in wide-eyed fascination and scramble for any ice chips that broke off. Chunks of ice were highly prized on warm afternoons.

While the ship was in port, Hagåtña would sparkle with white crackerjack sailor uniforms. Curious sailors filled every tavern, pool hall, restaurant, and merchandise store. They crammed into every one of Dad's taxis and rented my entire fleet of bicycles. And they did not just ride around town; they explored Hagåtña and beyond. They also performed interesting bicycle tricks, but as the sailors got drunk, their tricks were less successful and funnier to watch.

Drunken sailors were entertaining. They would weave and stagger through the streets, whooping, whistling, hollering, and making all kinds of racket until Shore Patrols hauled them off. It was like watching an end-of-the-trail shindig in a cowboy movie. The sailors were like wild cowboys, although they did not fire six-shooters in the air. Raucous behavior was common among off-duty, drunken Americans but was most uncommon among CHamorus.

The bars were always the busiest places. When the Navy's enlisted men's club got too crowded, sailors would fill the local bars. My playmates and I could watch their brazen antics at the Suzuki Bar, which was in the cellar beneath the Suzuki store on Hernan Cortez Street. A narrow window at street level allowed us a view of the goings-on inside. We watched drunk sailors try to do more than steal kisses from the bar girls. Their crude advances, their hands groping under the girls' skirts were scandalous to 7-and-8-year-olds but also arousing.

Hagåtña would bustle with extraordinary activity while the transports were in port. Everyone would profit as best they could until the next ship arrived. Except for the salaries of Navy government workers, revenue from the transports was the extent of the Navy's contribution to CHamoru economic development. At the time, the money spent by the visitors was the island's only source of new revenue. The Navy made much ado about the thousands spent on infrastructure improvements, but those were for its own benefit. The Navy made no improvements to the CHamorus' social, political, or economic conditions.

In the years before World War II, many of Guam's able-bodied male workforce were without salaried jobs. In desperate need of cash, for taxes and the like, men would wait outside the gates of the Navy Public Works yard, hoping for a day's work and wages. Many would carry live chickens in baskets to give to the hiring boss if he offered them a job.

Guam's economic condition was not always so grim. Early in the 20th century, while the world demand for copra still existed, Guam prospered. Export companies like Atkins Kroll and Rothschild would pay $3.25 for a *piku* (200 pounds) of *sine'so'* (coconut meat stripped from the shell and dried). Anyone with the wherewithal to gather coconuts and make copra could reap a hefty income. But advancements in technology and the depression of the 1920s killed the copra market. The Japanese were among the world's last large customers for copra. By the 1930s, as relations between the United States and Japan chilled, the Navy revoked Japanese access to copra from Guam. The Japanese controlled millions of coconut trees in Micronesia but did not have as effective or as centralized a collection point as U.S.-held Guam.

Until the Americans ceased trade with Japan, Japanese merchandise was abundantly available in Guam. Japanese goods poured in from Saipan[10]. When the flow of goods slowed, CHamorus in Guam had access only to expensive U.S. goods. Shipping costs for the great distance to Guam made prices out of reach for average, cash-poor people. To make the cash, many families worked doubly hard at farming, fishing, and hunting so they could sell their surpluses. Others specialized in some exclusive endeavor, like shoemaking, or starting a small business. To support his large family, Dad started several.

"Get the hell outta here, gook"

Dad's garage serviced both his taxi and bicycle sales businesses. It was a full-service garage complete with its own gas pump outside. The gas pump was a tall, cylindrical column topped with a large, glass-measuring container. It drew gasoline from an underground storage tank. To work it, one pumped a lever on the side of the column. The wizardry that made gasoline rise from the underground tank and gurgle and slosh in the glass container fascinated me.

Until Standard Oil established an office in Guam, which was before the war, Dad ordered gasoline from the States in 55-gallon drums and stored them in a warehouse in Pigo'. I liked to help unload the drums at the Piti docks, as well as to roll and stack them in the warehouse. We would then drive them to Hagåtña to fill the underground tank at the garage.

Dad never discarded the empty drums. He and Mama did not throw anything away. No one did. People saved and recycled everything. Nothing ever went to waste. Dad had the empty drums cleaned, painted, and stored under the stadium. When space ran out, he had them stacked inside. While empty gasoline drums filled the stadium, empty bottles, jars, and cans of all sizes filled Mama's kitchens. I did not understand until a few years later why Dad insisted on saving the drums. When Standard Oil made importing gasoline unnecessary, 55-gallon drums became scarce. Only Dad could meet the demand for them.

Standard Oil also brought the first gasoline tanker truck to Guam. It was a technological marvel. I made sure I was on hand whenever it came to refill the underground tank. I loved to watch the gasmen manipulate the hose and

---

10   From 1914 until 1944,, Saipan and the other islands in the Northern Marianas were ruled and colonized by Japan.

valves and levers on the panel of dials and gauges on the back of the tanker. I would go anywhere that had interesting machines and processes to watch. Whenever I was free, I would be at Tun Ben Herrero's sawmill in Aniguak, at Ada's soap factory, or at Tun Pedro Martinez's yards, watching his foreman Tun Jose Guzman, or Tun Jesus Crisostomo at the ice plant, or Tun Felix "Felis" Dungca at the machine shop. Tun Felis was the only mechanic I knew who could take apart an engine, put it back together in working order, and still have parts leftover.

I liked working at Dad's garage because the gas pump was fun. When business was busy, there was plenty to do. When it was slow, I was free to do as I pleased so long as I stayed put. To kill time, I would practice my aim with my slingshot, marbles, or top.

One day, when I was about 9, Dad ordered me to watch the garage until his return. There was little to do, so I started playing marbles. I squatted in the dust beside the gas pump and concentrated on a game of "fish." I lost track of the time and did not notice that it was almost sunset. Nor did I notice that someone had come up behind me. I sensed a presence and turned to see the big, black boots of a Marine policeman watching me. I twisted around and looked up at him.

"Hey, you," the policeman barked. "It's getting dark. You should be inside. Go home!"

I stared at him but said nothing. I had a legitimate reason to be outside and no one, not even a policeman, could countermand Dad's orders.

"You better be gone by the time I come back or else," he said and strutted away.

I did not know where Dad went or what was keeping him, but I could not leave until he returned, so I continued my game. The policeman returned about half an hour later, but Dad still was not back. The policeman glared at me because I had not obeyed him. I would see the same disgusted look on a government prosecutor's face 50 years later.

Without a word, and before I could protect myself, the policeman grabbed the back of my collar and yanked me up. He dangled me in midair. Bunched at my throat, the front of my shirt was choking me, but the policeman did not ease up. He shook me like a dust rag. To this day, I do not know what I did to provoke such anger or merit such treatment.

Still clutching me by the nape of my neck, the Marine policeman dragged

me down the alley connecting Hernan Cortez and San Ignacio. He turned onto
San Ignacio, passed behind Auntie Butler's house and the Gaiety Theater, then
turned right at the Notley house corner. He crossed a side street, Santa Cruz
Street, another side street, and passed the Bronton house on the next block.
He turned onto Dr. Hessler Street and passed Butler's Emporium. I struggled
all the way. He passed the Elks Club, turned right at the Leary School toward
the Governor's Palace, then left onto San Juan de Letran Street, and headed
to the jailhouse on the corner. We had come quite a distance from the garage,
but my feet scarcely touched the ground. In a show of force, the policeman
dragged me into the jailhouse and slammed me against its heavy door. As I
picked myself up, he kicked me in the seat of the pants.

"Get the hell outta here, gook," he growled.

The Americans called us "gooks" the same way they used ugly slurs for
Blacks, Mexicans, Italians, Germans, the Chinese, and the Japanese. "Gook"
was as hurtful and insulting as all other bigoted labels. It sounded like a kind
of despicable insect. I was only a boy, but I fiercely resented the insult, especially from a policeman who was supposed to uphold the law, protect the
innocent, and defend freedom and justice. My shirt rumpled, my neck and
butt sore, I filled my eyes with hatred, scowled at him, and left with my pride
intact. I swore never to let any man call me a gook again.

The incident made me realize that the American principles of liberty and
justice for all were exclusive, and that Americans would ignore them whenever they wished. We studied those principles in school, but they did not apply
to us because we were not Americans. Nor were we white, which made denying them acceptable. I could not reconcile the contradiction and vowed to become an American of Abraham Lincoln's caliber someday. I did not want to be
like the ones in Guam who had not studied their own history. I kept my vow,
but in 1986, another Marine lawman decided to drag me through the streets
of Hagåtña again, to try me as a crook. He did not call me a gook; he called me
something worse — a Judas to my people.

The version of Americanism displayed for us differed from what we were
learning in school. We studied the 13 colonies and the tyranny that led to the
Declaration of Independence, the pioneers and the wagon trains, the Civil
War and the Indian wars, and the taming of the West. We took pride in the
works of the presidents and the heroes who epitomized American freedom,
justice, and fair play. We believed in the principles of equality and justice for

all, in the sanctity of individual rights and freedoms. We learned to accept them as fundamental truths. But the "self-evident truths" did not apply to us, and that was the comfortable justification.

The Americans in Guam were unlike us. Their attitudes and behavior differed. Few seemed unselfish or caring and generous; most were self-centered and condescending. Many reveled in our differences, never tolerating the idea that we were equals in any way. We were simply wards in their custody, a responsibility they did not relish.

Yet their conduct and sense of superiority made them fascinating and entertaining to watch, especially the women. American women were audacious and gregarious, more outgoing than CHamoru women, who abided by a code of modesty and refinement. CHamoru men viewed American women as unapproachable and unattainable. Few dared to court one, even if she showed interest, which sometimes happened. It became regular sport among young men and boys to spy on the immodesty of American women, especially if they were at the beach with a lover. Most of the Americans were unaware that their antics, scanty bathing suits, and love trysts on the secluded beaches reserved exclusively for their recreation provided entertainment for the many eyes watching them from the jungle. In their curiosity about the female anatomy, especially white ones, many adolescents became shameless Peeping Toms. I might have joined the peeping circuit, but the Japanese occupation engulfed my teen years.

The shocking behavior of drunken American women at the Navy officers' club also was a popular attraction. Except for a rare glass of wine, CHamoru women of good breeding never got drunk. And they never hiked up their skirts, exposed their legs and underwear, cackled loudly, or behaved so "unladylike." The club was in the middle of town, near Nanan Chong's house, where Mama often sent me on errands. Men would gawk at the women inside from the curbsides, and until the Navy moved the club, I did my share of gawking, too.

Aware of the attention the officers' club was drawing, the Navy government built a new club in Tutuhan, overlooking the city. In the new location, officers' club patrons could indulge in their activities without a lot of prying eyes. After the war and the establishment of the civilian government of Guam, a new governor's residence was built on the site of the old officers' club. I lived there for eight years.

I never dreamed I would grow up to become governor of Guam — twice.

I never aspired to the office. My only ambition was to become a rich and successful businessman like Dad. I wanted to follow in his footsteps. But Dad also succeeded in politics. He exposed me to both fields since my childhood. Yet, as the boy who refused to bow to the Navy governor, I never dreamed I would earn his title in a free election or that the burdens of so high an office would be mine.

In a strange way, becoming governor may have been the fulfillment of a recurring dream that haunted me until I was about 8 years old. It was not a nightmare and did not frighten me. Instead, it puzzled me. I never understood what it meant. The dream was always the same: I was gazing up into a vast, black void. A small sphere high above began to descend toward me, growing larger and larger. By the time it reached me, it was the size of a planet. I would feel its great weight pressing down on my head and shoulders. I would wake up before it crushed me. In the 1960s, when the first photos from space appeared on television, chills ran down my spine. The blackness of outer space looked like the void in my dream. The great weight of a small world did not press upon me until I became governor in 1975.

The magic of the movies

Long an observer of human activity, I loved watching movies. I could never resist an opportunity to see a film, even if I did not have the money or the permission to do so. I loved movies so much that I was willing to risk punishment, time and time again. I spent many nights sleeping in the car in the garage after coming home late from a movie. I was of the innocent and erroneous belief that I could hide from Mama and Daddy, but they figured it out. Paul, who they sent most often to fetch me, would go to the garage to wait for me or jostle me awake. Of the hundreds of lickings I brought upon myself, most were for sneaking off to the movies without permission.

Since Uncle Butler owned the Hagåtña Theater, I could often get in for free, depending on who was taking tickets at the door. If I did not have the 10-cent admission, I would often join others who also did not have the money. With our rumps in the air, we would crouch on the floor and watch from the space under the theater doors. Outside the Gaiety Theater building, which the Johnston family owned and operated, there was a narrow ledge below the open windows. We would perch there like roosting chickens until a theater employee came out to shoo us away. We would scatter like chickens but return when the employee went back inside. On rainy days, watching from the ledge was miserable, but no one chased us away.

To my good fortune, I was also able to watch movies from behind the theater screen and through the tiny window of the projection room. Like others in the audience, I would jump at sudden gunshots or recoil when a larger-than-life posse, a runaway stagecoach, or a speeding locomotive thundered toward us from the screen. The production of such magic lured me to sneak onto the stage to examine the movie screen from behind. More than the plots and actors, the mechanics of the movies fascinated me. To me, the real movie heroes were the men who ran the projectors. I thought they were brilliant technical engineers. When allowed, I would go into the projection room and watch the projectionists manage the huge reels of movie film. I was more fascinated by the film winding around the projector's cogs and spools than in watching the movie screen. The big, black movie projectors looked like whirring, clicking, one-eyed robot monsters eating miles of film.

The movie serials of every Saturday matinee would spawn costume crazes among us young fans. We copied whatever Hollywood offered. When it was Zorro, dozens of make-believe Zorros in homemade black masks and capes swaggered through the streets of Hagåtña, brandishing swords of scrap lumber. When it was Buck Rogers, kettle-helmeted spacemen aimed scrap metal ray guns and littered the streets with "dead" alien invaders. Cowboys, like Hopalong Cassidy, or swashbucklers, like Errol Flynn, were easy to imitate. Buck Rogers was harder, but improvising costumes was a challenge that never daunted us.

Hopalong, Errol, Buck, Zorro, Shirley Temple, and Tom Mix came to us the same way they came to other kids: in black and white on a theater screen. They were our heroes, too. It was easy then to distinguish the good guys from the bad. I was too naive, too trusting, and too unsuspecting to realize my re-programming. It never occurred to me that I could never be the swashbuckling pirate hero or that I was more akin to the Indians fighting for their homelands and way of life than invading white settlers. I cringe now at all the times I rooted for the cavalry and cheered when Indians bit the dust.

Because the Butlers owned the theater, I had access to the films themselves. Auntie Butler stored them in her attic where they would await return shipment to the States. I could watch a movie again by stretching out the film against the light and examining it frame by frame.

Auntie Butler's attic was a treasure room full of wonderful things to play with and wonder about. There were stacks of movie posters — Hopalong, larger than life, and Shirley Temple, blonde ringlets and all — just waiting for me to examine up close. There were boxes of books and photographs and all kinds of bundles to investigate. I was always careful to put things back as I found them, lest the Butlers prohibited me from returning. The attic was my special place, the only place I could keep all to myself. I had permission to go up there whenever I wanted, but I would sneak up when no one was around. I did not want to have to share it with my cousins Mae, James, Benny, Dolly, and Bea or with my brothers and sisters.

Of all the treasures, the most valuable and wonderful was a stamp collection. The stamps were like miniature postcards of all the faraway places I longed to see. I spent hours adding to the collection, cataloguing, and studying the stamps with a pair of tweezers and a magnifying glass. Some rare specimens were valuable even in those days, priceless today. I would examine each one with awe, knowing they came from exotic places around the world. Whenever I could, I would escape to the attic to be alone with my beloved stamps, but the collection did not survive the war.

The attic was a quiet retreat for a boy with many responsibilities and a burning curiosity about the world beyond Guam's shores. I would get ideas about what that world was like at the Piti docks, just north of Apra Harbor. It was a busy, exhilarating place, a worldly thoroughfare when a ship came in. Freighters arrived every four to six months with the new supplies and merchandise. Off-loading them drew a crowd that would watch and wonder about the contents of the wooden crates. I would be there too, looking for crates addressed to Dad. I liked watching the tugs, barges, and steamboats shuttling back and forth and the stevedores, who, like the ice handlers, made their work look easy.

The arrival of Uncle Butler's new Coca-Cola sign created a real stir; no one had ever seen a sign so big or so fancy. Uncle Butler ordered it special from the States after he expanded the bottling plant. It came in a massive crate. It was the red script letters of Coca-Cola's logo measuring 15 feet high and 30 feet long. Uncle Butler put Uncle Tom in charge of installing it on the rooftop of Auntie Butler's two-story house. I could not imagine how he was going to do it, so I watched every phase of the project. It was an incredible feat of engineering. An army of workmen constructed scaffolds in front of the Butler house then used a block and tackle to hoist the sign up to the roof. The giant Coca-Cola sign was the biggest, tallest, and most handsome commercial billboard in Guam at the time. It was visible from everywhere in Hagåtña. Thirty years later, when I went into business, I wanted a sign as impressive and commanding as Uncle Butler's. Mine said "Ricky's Auto Company" in fancy script.

Dad's shipments of new automobiles also attracted a crowd. Dad was the Guam distributor for Nash, Willis Overland, and Lafayette Motors, as well as International Harvester, Willard batteries, Goodyear tires, and other products. There was always cargo addressed to him. It always impressed me that someone somewhere in the United States of America packed automobile tires, batteries, and car parts in the wooden crates then stenciled Dad's name and address on them. New automobiles also came in crates. They were uncrated at the port and then driven to Hagåtña. Because most people could not afford motor vehicles, many would gather and inspect the new ones. They would test the cigarette lighter and the radio knobs, which was useless since there was no commercial radio station in the island.

There was one once. The Butler Broadcasting System only lasted two or three years because there were few radio sets to receive its broadcasts. My cousin Benny was the announcer, commentator, and host. It went on the air for two hours on Wednesday evenings. Whenever Benny could coax her, Auntie Rose would sing — mostly to a family audience. I suspect Benny's monologues and limited programming led to the station's end. Guam did not have a commercial radio station again until 1954, when Harry Engles started KUAM. Engles hired a crew of local people, including my then-new bride, Madeleine.

Forty years after Benny's stint as a radio personality, his nephew Denny Butler, James' son, would be the only voice heard over the airwaves throughout the long and terrible night in May 1976 when Super Typhoon Pamela struck Guam. Denny was a disc jockey at KATB, which belonged to Uncle Tom at the time. KATB was the only radio station that could continue broadcasting; others lost their antennae and electricity. Rather than abandon the safety of KATB's transmitter site in the Mañenggon Valley and the thousands of listeners anxious for storm news, Denny entertained his unseen audience nonstop for more than 24 hours. For many, Denny's exhausted voice was their only link to the world outside their shelters.

For 72 hours after the storm, the island's entire commercial communications system was down. Typhoon Pamela left Guam battered, broken, and cut off from the outside world. And I was governor.

Chapter 5

The arrival of the Pan American Clippers

In 1935, Guam's connection to the outside world was by ship, cable, and wireless radio. On October 13 of that year, a Pan American "flying boat," on a trial run from San Francisco to Manila, touched down at Apra Harbor and made aviation history. The feat linked East with West by air and brought Guam into the mainstream of air transportation. Pan American established its operations base in Sumai. A year later, on October 14, 1936, another Pan Am flight brought the world's first trans-Pacific passengers to Guam.

CHamorus treated the Clipper's arrival like a major holiday. Nearly 85 percent of the population turned out in Sumai to see history in the making. They wanted to be part of it, to see and welcome the first passengers, who consisted of airline officials, national media representatives, and some celebrities. Islanders had high hopes Pan American World Airways and the regular Clipper flights would bring Guam out of isolation and obscurity. In the days when only the wealthy and powerful could afford the luxury of Pacific air travel, CHamorus hoped that such influential people would take back the message that Guam was more than a military outpost. The luminaries who have transited Guam over the years are impressive, but Guam and her people remain relatively unknown among America's public. To our deep disappointment, most references to Guam are derogatory.

Dad and Uncle Butler were among the local dignitaries and Navy officials who welcomed the inaugural flight in 1935. Dad was chairman of the Guam Congress' House of Council, and Uncle Butler held the franchise for *Collier's* magazine. Mr. Tom Beck, chairman of the board of Collier-Crowell Publishing Company, was among the passengers. Dressed in their best white suits, Dad and Uncle Butler looked as dignified and important as the Navy officials. I looked on with pride as photographers took pictures of a gathering that included my father. I was only 8 years old, but I knew I was witnessing something important.

B.J. Bordallo (*second from left*) with local and Navy officials welcoming Pan American World Airways' inaugural transpacific flight in 1935.

Photo courtesy of Guampedia and R.O.D. Sullivan/Pan American Historical Foundation.

After meeting Mr. Beck, Dad invited him to be a guest at our house. He accepted and spent hours talking with Dad. Beck was curious about Guam and expressed sincere concern for CHamorus. Dad told him about the quest for American citizenship and how he and Mr. "F.B." Leon Guerrero, a member of the House of Assembly, planned to travel to Washington, D.C., to lobby for it. Dad and F.B. were to leave as soon as fundraising efforts raised enough for the trip. Before continuing his journey the following day, Mr. Beck invited Dad to visit him in New York. Several months later, Dad did call on Mr. Beck, who used his influence to arrange a meeting for Dad and F.B. with President Franklin D. Roosevelt.

The weekly Clipper flights always carried a celebrity or two. It became almost commonplace to hear that someone famous was stopping over. Each flight stayed overnight then continued to Manila the following day. Pan American later built a hotel in Sumai for its passengers. Watching hotel guests lounge on the veranda became popular among the townspeople. Our weekly trips to Nåna's house gave my sisters a chance to see the latest fashions Pan Am's female passengers wore. I looked forward to watching the Clippers land and take off. The seaplanes would descend from the clouds, glide toward the harbor, then touch down. Their boat-like underbellies skimmed the water and kicked up arcs of spray. The passengers then disembarked into launches that shuttled them ashore. Watching Pan Am's planes fueled my curiosity about the outside world and my wanderlust.

Except during the war years, Pan Am's flights to Guam continued for half a century. The airline was an integral part of our community until it decided to pull out on April 1, 1984. In October 1985, Pan American commemorated the 50th anniversary of the first Clipper flight by recreating the original route — from San Francisco to Honolulu, Midway, Wake, Guam, and Manila — and filling a Boeing 747 with airline officials, media representatives, and special guests. As governor, I hosted a welcoming reception at the Guam International Airport and attended a ceremony at the U.S. Naval Station in a barren field where the Pan Am hotel and the village of Sumai once stood. The Navy razed Sumai, relocated villagers to a hillside in Santa Rita, and took control of the Orote Peninsula after the war. A tiny cemetery, a few crumbling foundations, Santa Guadalupe's cement cross, and a small plaque marking the site of the Pan Am Hotel are all that remain of Sumai.

The ceremony was sentimental for me. The beautiful village of Sumai, where I spent much of my youth, exists now only in fading photographs and old memories. My audience probably expected to hear a long-winded, self-serving political speech from me. Instead, I explained why we were in an empty field inside a Navy base. I wanted them to know about the bustling community that once existed there. I told them about how, as a young boy, I watched passengers on the hotel veranda and how I longed to join them in great adventures on a seaplane. I received praises for my speech, but the recollections filled me with melancholy. I found myself looking back to a time in my youth when all I could do was look forward with great hopes and expectations.

Madeleine and I joined the commemorative flight to Manila and returned to Guam two days later. By then, I was a seasoned traveler, and the flight, while luxurious and comfortable, was just another plane ride, an inescapable entry on my busy schedule.

The Island Fair

We used to drive to Sumai in an old, black Hudson sedan Mama won in a raffle. It belonged to a Navy officer who offered it as a prize at the annual Fourth of July Agricultural and Industrial Fair. The first fair, which took place in 1917, was such a success that it became an annual islandwide event and was simply called the Island Fair. In 1919, the fair included a contest for a queen to reign over the week-long festivities. A bevy of pretty teenagers vied for the title, but Mama won it. She was the first Island Fair queen. Mama presided with a court of princesses, pageboys, and trumpeters dressed in colorful medieval costumes. She wore an elaborate, white gown with a long train. Two costumed pageboys held up the end of it. Pictures of her coronation often appear to illustrate aspects of life in prewar Guam. Except during the war years, there have been Island Fair queens from Mama's reign to the present. Now they are known as Liberation Day queens. Candidates do not compete based on their looks but on who raises the most money.

The Island Fair was a genuine "state" fair. It was set up in the Plaza de España and was always full of color, excitement, music, and pageantry. The fair's main attractions were the displays of produce, livestock, and new farm machinery and equipment. Farmers from all around the island would bring bushels and baskets of their best crops and their showiest livestock — cattle, hogs, goats, chickens, ducks, pigeons, and others. The women competed in cooking, canning, and sewing contests. Prizes and ribbons went to the best, the biggest, and the tastiest. And there were fireworks, rides, games of skill and chance, and food concessions of all kinds.

My favorite booth was "Knock the Cannibal," a throw-and-dunk booth. A costumed and painted "cannibal" would sit over a tank of water and heckle the ball throwers. The aim was to hit a target, release a spring, and drop the cannibal into the water. A cannibal had to be a good heckler; only the best got the job. They were always entertaining and funny. Nowadays, pretty girls in skimpy swimsuits have replaced the obnoxious cannibals of yesteryear.

Dad sometimes ran a gambling booth, and I helped operate it. I would watch serious gamblers lose all their money but not give up; they would come back later with more money to lose. Fortunately, the fairs only lasted a few days; otherwise, addicts would have risked much more. Those who could not afford to lose were the most pathetic, but once hooked on hopes for instant wealth, they returned again and again. And lost again and again. The addictive power of gambling frightened me. I have seen firsthand what it can do to the weak-willed and desperate. My boyhood exposure to addiction made me a life-long and implacable opponent of legalized gambling.

The fireworks were launched from our dusty playground behind Tun Kiko Cruz's "Fixin" shop alongside the *guinaddok laida*, the channel dredged for the Navy's coal barges. The playground was the tamped-down sand and silt dredged from the channel.

The American-style contests were popular but not as exciting as tradi-tional sporting events like coconut tree climbing, coconut husking, coconut grating, or tuba drinking. These were everyday tasks to which we could all re-late. The Americans were often impressed even by the slowest coconut husk-er, flabbergasted by the fastest. A good husker could peel a coconut in less than three seconds. The real crowd pleasers were the carabao races around the plaza. Although usually placid and lumbering, carabao can pour on the steam. Frisky, eager racers were crowd favorites. The grand finale of the con-tests was the canoe races from Sagua' Mañagu, a beach area near Alupang Cove, to the *guinaddok laida*. Canoes called *galaide'* were the descendants of ancient CHamoru flying proa, the lightning-swift craft that astounded the first Europeans who came to Guam.

I have watched traditional island sporting events in America and West-ern Samoa and in other Pacific islands and have seen the pride with which my Pacific brethren hold fast to their cultures and traditions. To prove they are not "backward natives," modern CHamorus ignore contests of tradition-al skills in favor of new ones, and they have lost much in the process. Now, instead of coconuts, carabao, and canoes, they compete in drag racing, disco dancing, and "battles of the (rock'n'roll) bands."

During the week of the Island Fair, we children enjoyed greater liber-ties. We could stay up later in the evenings and spend time at the fairgrounds as soon as we finished our chores. As someone with many responsibilities, I reveled in the extra freedom and took every opportunity to instigate or par-ticipate in pranks that often resulted in a good ear twisting or a spanking. One of our standard tricks was to lie in wait and frighten homeward-bound girls. Since there were no streetlights to brighten the way home, we would take advantage of the darkness and hide in alleyways, snickering while we waited for unsuspecting girls to step into our traps. We would position sheaves of dry grass tethered on long strings in the middle of the path. As girls passed by, we would yank the string, entangle their legs, and howl with laughter at their terrified screams and wild jigs. The girls, of course, chased after us. Faster on our feet, we would disappear into the darkness, still laughing.

In addition to the fair's contests, games, and races, drill teams from the different public schools competed. Dressed like toy soldiers in military uniforms of varying colors and designs, the marching teams attracted large, enthusiastic audiences. While spectators were generous with their applause, the teams took the competitions seriously, doing their best to impress the judges and win top honors for their schools. Those from outside Hagåtña often made grand entrances into the plaza, while the Hagåtña teams stood at rigid attention. Because the Guam Institute did not have a marching team, I could only watch and envy the competitors, especially my cousin Alfred Bordallo, Uncle Tom's son, who was a platoon captain of his school's team.

Alfred's team wore uniforms patterned after those of West Point cadets. In addition to his smart, gray uniform with black piping and shiny, brass buttons, he also wore a tall, black helmet with a leather chin strap and carried an ornate baton. He would stand out in front and command the crowd's attention as well as his men's.

Precision marching remains popular in Guam, but in recent times, it is no longer a part of public school activities. Enthusiasts have formed drill teams or drum-and-bugle teams to represent their villages and march in parades, but without leadership, sponsorship, and a venue for competition, such teams lose heart and quit. I reinstituted drill competitions in Guam's public schools during my second term as governor. Before then, precision marching was only available to high school ROTC students whose enthusiasm and fervor continue to win them high honors in national competitions.

Armed with ball peen hammers and thumbtacks

Lent, the days between Ash Wednesday and Easter Sunday, was a solemn and quiet time for us. For almost a month, the bustling city of Hagåtña would grow quiet. People stayed indoors, street traffic decreased, and unnecessary noise-making ceased. Even whistling and music-making came to a halt. Children, especially, had to stay still and silent, lest they rouse the *babuin Kuaresma* — the Lenten pig which ate naughty, noisy children. Even at home, the usual clatter of meal preparations quieted in observance of this much-revered holy time. Despite the enforced solemnity, pranksters chafing under such restrictions found ways to rebel. Good Friday services at the cathedral was a favorite time and place.

Our Lenten services were ritual reenactments of Jesus' last hours. They began on Holy Thursday with the Last Supper, the washing of the Twelve Apostles' feet, the Agony in the Garden, and Jesus' arrest and imprisonment. If his disciples could not stay awake one hour with him, Guam's Catholics would stay up even longer in atonement. They would keep vigil throughout the night in the church before the tabernacle serving as Jesus' jail.

The vigil ended on Good Friday afternoon with rituals commemorating Jesus' trial, his carrying of the cross, and his crucifixion, death, and burial. At 2:30 p.m., the cathedral's doors and window shutters would close, and all the candles were extinguished. The darkened church represented the darkened skies as Jesus hung on the cross. At 3 o'clock, the hour of Christ's death, parishioners would begin stamping their feet on the floor and banging sticks against the pews, simulating the thunder heralding Jesus' death. The deafening noise would fill the darkened church for several minutes.

For mischievous little boys, the noise and darkness hid the perpetration of a favorite annual prank. During the ruckus, while no one paid attention, several of us would sneak from our seats, meet in the aisles, and crawl under the pews where the old ladies knelt. Armed with ball peen hammers and thumbtacks, we would nail their long skirts to the floor then sneak back to our seats. When the noise stopped, the windows and doors opened, and the service ended, the ladies would try to stand up. We would watch their astonishment and alarm and then their fury. Our laughing and chuckling always gave us away. The cuff on the ear after church was almost an annual thing as well.

After a few successful years of the prank, the priests, altar boys, and parishioners began scrutinizing all suspicious-looking boys between the ages of 6 and 13. To get around the searches, we would stick tacks to the undersides of pews with chewing gum a week before Good Friday. In place of tell-tale hammers, we used sewing thimbles, which were less suspicious but equally effective. In a good year, we would manage to tack down at least two dozen skirts; in a bad year, maybe only 12 or 14. The unbroken record was more than 50.

Games, toys, the Emporium, and the smell of America

Our pranks stemmed from the audacious ingenuity of children eager to test the many layers of authority above them. In a community governed by the military, wherein the lowest-ranking military man commanded more authority than the highest-ranking civilian, children were at the bottom of the heap.

We did not have the fancy playground equipment the American children had, nor could many of us afford expensive, American-made toys like those pictured in the Montgomery Ward catalogues or displayed at Butler's Emporium. We made our toys out of ordinary things or discarded scraps. Our balloons came from the slaughterhouses, where butchers saved the *bihiga*, or cow bladders, for us. Cleaned, dried, and inflated, *bihiga* balloons were tougher than rubber balloons but not as colorful or pretty.

Chongka, an ancient game for two players, was also popular among children and adults. Almost every household had a chongka board and the small cowrie shells, or *cheggai*, to go with it. The rules were simple, and the object of the game was to collect more shells than the opponent. Each player goes around the board, dropping a shell into each pit and in a large "home" pit.

Chongka is a game of mathematical strategy. The real champions could keep track of each round, of the number of shells in each pit at any time during the game. They knew which pit to start from at each turn. They also knew when and how to "kill" an opponent by forcing him to land at an empty pit. Children and adults spent hours playing chongka and mastering its mathematical complexities. The *click, click, click* of dropping shells and cries of *"måtai!"* (dead!) would resonate from porches and parlors.

Every child had access to chongka but not to store-bought toys, especially American-made ones. We could only gaze at those at Butler's Emporium on Hessler Street. The toy department was on the second floor and was a wonderland. Like the rest of Hagåtña's children, I would roam the toy department, transfixed by the wonders on display. I would await my turn to climb into and "drive" a bright red, miniature automobile with pedals under the hood. The child-sized car was the most popular toy at the Emporium and the most expensive. I do not think anyone ever bought it. Unlike cheap but affordable Japanese toys, the Emporium's American toys were priceless treasures few could afford. Because there were so many of us, Mama never considered buying such expensive playthings.

The Emporium on Hessler Street replaced an older, smaller one on Hernan Cortez. Uncle Butler bought the larger building a few years before the war and turned the new Emporium into the largest, most modern department store in Guam. He and Auntie Butler spent a small fortune making it just like the department stores pictured in American magazines. It had shiny linoleum floors and sparkling glass showcases and merchandise that emitted a distinctive scent.

To me, the scent, combined with that of new pinewood, was clean and fresh. It was American — what I thought America smelled like. The same smell came from the boxes and crates of Dad's shipments from the States. Whenever I walked into the Emporium, the scent allowed me to imagine myself entering the United States of America. It was a wonderful smell, and I took deep breaths of it to keep my imagination sparked.

I always associated the smell of new merchandise with the places of their origin and with the local stores that carried them, but never in negative ways. The Navy commissary, which carried a wide selection of fruits and vegetables from the United States, smelled fresh, clean, and sweet. The nearby public market smelled of fish and livestock, of coconut oil and basketry, and of fresh produce; it smelled very CHamoru, musky, earthy, and reassuring. Dejima's and Sayama's stores, which carried Japanese-made goods and foodstuffs, smelled like dried fish, seaweed, soy sauce, and *daikon*, a white radish which we called *daigo'*. Tun Josen Anga's store carried goods from the Philippines and smelled like mahogany, pickled fish, and wicker.

Although Mama had local stores to choose from, she shopped for our Christmas presents in the Montgomery Ward catalogues, which featured many of the same toys available at the Emporium. But to my disappointment, Mama never ordered toys. She ordered practical things instead, like shoes, clothing, and underwear for us. About six months before Christmas, she would peruse the latest catalogue, make her selections, and send off her order. My siblings and I would scramble for the book and search for any marking or clue as to what she ordered.

It was always my job to post the all-important order. I would carry it as if it was a valuable and important document. For us, it was. The postal clerk would weigh it and tell me how much for postage. Mama gave me enough, but I would always add a few cents of my own and ask the clerk to add an extra stamp, just to make sure. As soon as I left the post office, I would begin an imaginary journey, following Mama's order halfway around the world, not knowing how long it would take. I would allow a few days for the letter to leave the post office, weeks to cross the ocean by ship, then overland by truck or rail to Montgomery Ward's headquarters in Chicago.

I imagined a kindly mail-order clerk receiving Mama's order and reacting with surprise: "Oh, this comes all the way from Guam!" He would fill our order quickly, knowing the goods were Christmas gifts for deserving children — at least that was how I hoped he would react. Sometimes I worried the order would reach an uncaring clerk who could delay or deny us our Christmas presents. I would lie awake, unable to sleep, worrying about all the terrible things that could happen to our order on its long journey. I would even wake up breathless and sweaty from a nightmare that the ship with our order sank. As the months passed, my obsession would grow.

"Mama, what if it doesn't get put on the ship?" I would ask again and again.

"Don't worry, Ricky, it will come." Mama's unwavering confidence was reassuring.

In November, when the last freighter before Christmas docked at Piti, I would be in a panic. Mama's order had to be on that ship or else we would have no presents. The next ship would not arrive until February. I would chase after the postal trucks from Piti and watch them unload, worried that our order missed the boat. Not even my chores could keep me from dropping into the post office several times a day to check. I would peer through the bars, searching for newly arrived parcels. Finally, the clerks who watched my anxiety grow would announce, "Ricky, it's here!"

The good news would lead to a new worry. Although the package was safe at the post office, Mama could not pick it up until she had the cash to pay for it. Her orders came COD — cash on delivery — and averaged $200 or more, a hefty sum in the 1930s. I could not be happy until I was trundling home with the Christmas order in my wagon. I often hoped damage would occur in transit so I could peek inside. Would we get what we wanted? Would everything look as grand as they did in the catalogue? The answers would be as we hoped. One Christmas, I wanted a pair of black, steel-toed work boots. I never mentioned it, but somehow, Mama knew. I got the boots.

My family practiced the American tradition of opening our gifts on Christmas day. Other families kept the Spanish tradition of gift giving on January 6, the Feast of the Three Kings. Christmastime in our community was a prolonged and happy time steeped in the importance of peace and friendship and joy. Gift giving was secondary. In this special atmosphere, I learned the joy and greater pleasure of giving rather than receiving.

We welcomed the New Year with *"Burego'* Night," which was a children's time much like Halloween. *"Burego'"* means dirty or ugly face. Dressed in homemade costumes, our faces garishly painted, we roamed the streets, asking for sweet treats. We played harmless tricks on anyone who did not give us treats. Halloween replaced *Burego'* Night but not until years after the war.

When the winds howl and the sea revolts

It was great sport among my brothers and sisters and me to guess where we would go on weekends. We would fidget in anticipation until Mama made the announcement at week's end. No matter what she decided, we were eager to be off.

Mama sometimes chose Apotguan, which was acceptable to us. Apotguan, on the outskirts of Hagåtña, was "out in the sticks." It was where certain families made salt. Their little shacks dotted the beach. We would park by Dungca' Beach and swim to Sagua' Mañagu or play in the shallows in the icy cold *bo'bo'*, the bubbling freshwater springs escaping into the sea. There were dozens near the shore. One could drink the freshwater if he put his face close to the bubbling sand. Too close and he would get a mouthful of sand, too far and he would get a mix of warm seawater and cold freshwater.

We were thrilled if Mama said we were going to Tomhom, which was further north, below the cliffs of the Tamuning peninsula. Tomhom was a wild, untouched area of breathtaking beauty. To get there, we drove a narrow dirt road deep through thick stands of *ifit, da'ok, dokdok,* and *lemmai* trees [11]. The road then descended the steep cliffs and coursed through huge coconut groves from the base of the cliffs to a wide stretch of white, sandy beach. Some of the coconut trees curved out over the water and served as jumping platforms. We would spend hours swimming, exploring, building up our appetites, and getting deep-brown tans.

---

11 Ifil (*Intsia bijuga*), palomaria (*Calphyllum inophyllum*), seeded breadfruit (*Artocarpus mariannensis*) and breadfruit (*A. altilis*), respectively.

In addition to cook fires, the air in Tomhom smelled of wildflowers and jungle vegetation, of clean sea breezes and drying seaweed. To some, the smell was *pao mata* — fishy, smelly, and unpleasant; to others, it was nature's beach perfume, made rich and full-bodied by life, death, sea, and sunshine. Islanders and coast dwellers long for that smell when they are far from the sea.

Mama was never without her camera. She took hundreds of pictures of our weekend outings and all our activities, creating a pictorial record of our increasing numbers and physical growth. How I wish some of those photographs survived. They would mean more to me than any of the thousands Madeleine and I have collected over the years.

Tomhom, now pronounced Tumon, is no longer the pristine paradise of my childhood. In 1984, during my second term as governor, I officiated at the dedication of a small park built by the Chinese Community of Guam. The park overlooks Tomhom Bay and features a statue of Buddha. As I waited for the ceremony to begin, I looked down on the bay, saddened by how much it had changed. Development replaced the jungle and coconut groves with high-rise luxury hotels, commercial buildings, and parking lots. A four-lane highway replaced the old, narrow dirt road. Japanese tourists were splashing in the water or sunning on the sand, overpowering the beach perfume with the odor of suntan oil. I shared my recollections of old Tumon with my audience, but they just stared at me blankly. The contrast was beyond their imagination.

As people of a small island community, all of us, both children and adults, were close to the land and sea. Our environment was our larder and our playground. We knew how to survive in it, how to enjoy it, how to take only what we needed. We respected nature's power as well as its bounty. We were no strangers to typhoons, earthquakes, and floods. We knew how to shelter ourselves from nature's wrath, when the winds howl and the sea revolts. After a storm, while the seas were still rough and choppy, we would have fun swimming at Tomhom, pitting ourselves against 30- and 40-foot breakers. Almost every child knew how to swim; learning how was a sink-or-swim proposition. Watchful adults tossed children into deep water and waited. The lessons did not always work; some children refused to go into the water ever again. For those of us initiated, the ocean became part of our playground. We could play in the waves and dive to great depths. Some could hold their breaths for as long as five minutes.

Those of us willing to risk the adventure would also tackle the ocean another way. We would collect empty, wooden Kirin beer crates from Dad's grocery store and modify them into tiny boats. We would caulk the seams, add a bow, and scrounge for something to use as a paddle. The resulting "boats" were just large enough to seat a single captain-navigator. In our little Kirin beer crate boats, we would sail off to glory in the reef flats of Hagåtña Bay, careful not to go too near the reefs or the *guinaddok laida* at the Hagåtña Boat Basin.

Just as I had a boat, so did Dad. But his was a ship as far as I was concerned. I was more excited than Dad about his "new" boat. It was an old, 24-footer in poor condition. He bought it in Sumai and managed to sail it north to Hagåtña. To tow the boat through the channel, he called in more than 50 men from his enterprises — the stores, the taxi and bus stand in Hagåtña, and the cattle ranches in Hågat. The men secured ropes to the boat from the shore then pulled it over the reef at high tide. They hauled it through the channel to the water's edge behind Dad's stadium. They made the job look easy.

I was determined to be a part of the massive project and "supervised" from my beer box boat, paddling alongside the ship, shouting unnecessary orders ignored by the workmen who did not need them. I docked long enough to eat lunch with the hauling crew then returned to my boat to watch the next step. After lunch, the men lifted the ship out of the water and onto a cradle. I reveled in our having a real boat, but Dad knew how much work it needed. It took months for repairs and needed extensive rebuilding.

Dad hired Tun Juan Yamaguchi, a wise, old Japanese builder from Asan, to transform the broken-down boat into my father's dream yacht. Tun Juan, who spoke fluent CHamoru, did not mind my inquisitiveness or enthusiastic assistance. I spent many days helping him pound white caulking strips between the new planking and putting putty over the caulk. After he rebuilt the cabin, Tun Juan carved two beautiful name plates out of hardwood for both sides of the bow. Dad named his boat the *Josephine*, after Mama.

Despite Tun Juan's expert workmanship, the *Josephine* was crude compared to the launches the Navy used to ferry dignitaries from ship to shore. Their launches had shiny brass rails and fittings, a metal canopy, and upholstered lounge chairs. They were the most luxurious craft in Guam at the time and were like real yachts. The Navy kept the launches moored in garages at the Piti harbor. I often snuck inside to admire them. I promised myself I would own one someday — a bigger, finer, more luxurious yacht. As a wealthy businessman, I fulfilled that promise in 1973.

Unlike the Navy launches, Dad did not reserve his boat only for important visiting officials and special guests. Our boat was for our family and friends to enjoy. And it was more practical — we could go fishing in it. Dad was a flamboyant person and an avid fisherman. I am sure this motivated his purchase of the *Josephine* and his renovation of it. He killed two birds with a single stone: He had both a pleasure craft and a fishing vessel. We used it that way for several years, sailing back and forth between Hagåtña and Sumai. We took it out into the open sea but always stayed close to shore.

If I were deserving, Dad would take me along on his five- or six-hour fishing trips. If it got too late, Dad would leave the *Josephine* in Sumai and have a car pick us up. The short trips were fun but not as adventurous as those that lasted two or three days and took us north to Tangison and Litekyan. To me, those trips were brave and courageous encounters with the open sea. Sometimes we would go ashore on a secluded beach along the rugged northern coast, and I would pretend to be an explorer setting foot on a virgin shore.

Often, as we headed out, Dad would tow out the 60-foot outrigger canoes of net fishermen. They were an impressive lot with their hair bleached blond and their skins burned dark by the sun. They were jovial and carefree and could swim like fish in the open ocean. Their large canoes, loaded with their fishing gear and provisions, would be their home for days while they fished. We would tow them to a spot about a mile offshore from Såtpon Point, also called Two Lovers Point after the CHamoru legend, and pick them up again when we returned a few days later. After leaving the fishermen at their fishing grounds, we would head north to ours.

My main job on board was as shark killer. We trolled for red snapper, dolphin, tuna, and other large fish. Sharks often gathered to claim our catches. We would watch for them in the clear water and haul in our fish before the sharks attacked. We were not always quick enough; there were many times when we hauled in only fish heads. Sometimes we would catch sharks in the act and haul them in, still clinging to our fish. Once landed, the sharks flapped about and gnashed at anything. Dad kept a baseball bat as standard fishing equipment. My job was to beat a landed shark with the bat until it was no longer a danger. Most of the sharks averaged 6-to-8-feet long. The largest we ever caught measured over 14 feet and weighed more than 1,000 pounds. We kept the dead sharks and gave them away to friends and acquaintances who liked the taste. Parts of the 14-footer went for pig feed.

We had many adventures on the *Josephine*. Most were pleasant, a few were dangerous and frightening. Dad once took the *Josephine* out alone for a short trip, but when he failed to return, we thought we had lost him forever. Mama was worried. When he did not return the following day, she grew frantic. Searchers kept vigil at high points and scanned the ocean, watching for the *Josephine*. I joined a search party on the third day. By then, my entire family feared the worst. There was no moon that night and the weather was foul with thunder and lightning. As we drove to Litekyan, lightning struck a tree beside the road ahead of us. I watched with wide-eyed terror as the tree split down the middle and the halves curled back like banana peels. With the road blocked, we had to give up and return to town. Dad showed up safe and sound the following day.

The most frightening adventure involved my brother Paul and me. I was 8 years old, and Paul was only 6. Dad had taken us with him on a day-long outing to Litekyan with his regular fishing partners, Tun Jesus Paulino and Tun Enrique "Po." As we headed for home that night, the *Josephine* ran aground at the mouth of the *guinaddok laida*, the barge channel. Without lighted buoys to mark the channel entrance, the men tried to guess their way through the narrow opening in the shallow reef. While Dad and the men debated which direction to take, the *Josephine* hit the reef with a loud, grinding crunch.

Dad feared the heavy boat would flounder and sink, so Tun Enrique swam ashore for help. Dad and Tun Jesus put Paul and me on an outcropping on the reef.

"Stay here, and hold on," Dad said. "We'll come back to get you as soon as we can."

The moonless sky was pitch-black that night, and the sea was choppy. Waves crashed unto the reef and washed over us, but Paul and I held on tight. We were not afraid until we realized the *Josephine* was drifting away. Each time Dad called to us, his voice grew fainter. Before long, we were alone in the dark. We could not see anything, not even the lights of Hagåtña several hundred yards from where we were. We got cold and scared when the waves grew larger and stronger. I was afraid the next wave would knock us off the rocks. I thought about wading ashore, but I could not tell where we were. If we were to the left of the channel, we could wade most of the way and paddle through the deep spots. But if we were to the right, we would walk straight into the deep channel. That was too dangerous. I rejected the idea.

Cold and shivering, Paul and I hugged each other and began reciting the Our Father prayer through chattering teeth. We clung to the rocks for what seemed like hours. We later learned it was about two. Finally, we spotted a light on shore. There was only one at first, then two, then more and more until the whole shoreline was aglow. Hundreds of torches began moving toward us like a rescuing cavalry. Paul and I shouted to indicate our position. Minutes later, volunteer rescuers scooped us off the rocks and carried us ashore.

The same volunteers lashed the *Josephine* with ropes to shore that night. The following day, Dad's men hauled her over the reef and through the channel the same way they did before. They hoisted her onto the cradle again for hull repairs. Forty years later, as a typhoon swept over Guam, my yacht, the *Madeleine*, would run aground at the same place. Her pilot, a new man who was unfamiliar with the Hagåtña channel, misjudged the entrance. I had men lash the Madeleine to trees and moorings on shore, but she did not survive the night. Rough seas battered her to bits on the reef.

The *Josephine* was luckier in her bout with a typhoon. Not knowing of an impending storm, Dad took her out to sea. Despite the darkening skies, he let me come along with Tun Enrique and Uncle Felix Pangelinan, Mama's brother. Uncle Felix was another one of Dad's frequent fishing companions. We made our way along the Pan Am channel in Sumai, out of Apra Harbor and the breakwater, into the open sea. With only a small, four-cylinder inboard engine, the *Josephine* bobbed about like a toy. We motored around Orote Point and Adotgan rock, a huge limestone boulder that must have fallen from Orote's face eons ago. A narrow channel separates the boulder from a beach pretty enough to impress a Hollywood set designer. To enjoy its pristine beauty, the Spanish built steps from the top of Orote to the beach, 100 feet below. I have always loved the grandeur of Orote Point from the vantage at sea.

The water outside the harbor was choppy, and the wind was stiffer than usual, but no one seemed concerned. We dropped our trolling lines and headed south toward Hågat. Fish began striking right away. My job was to haul in the catches. We were so busy catching fish that we did not notice the wind picking up and the sky growing ominous. We were off Hågat, bouncing like a cork, when Uncle Felix pointed out the worsening weather. By then, no one could ignore it. The wind was blowing hard, and the sea was alive. A dark curtain of hard rain was heading toward us.

"I don't think it's wise to stay out here; it doesn't look good. I think we better head back!" Uncle Felix shouted.

But Dad, having been in a storm at sea once already and survived, was unconcerned. Uncle Felix turned to him and said, "Don't forget we have Ricky with us. I don't know how safe he'll be if we run into trouble."

I pretended not to hear. I was already scared, but I did not want Dad to know. He looked down at me, then up at the sky. Night was coming.

"You're right. This isn't good," he said. Uncle Felix and Tun Enrique agreed.

Dad turned the *Josephine* into the wind to head back to Orote. Huge, white-capped waves crashed against the boat, jolting us hard and washing over the decks. The howling wind forced the men to shout out their orders. At full throttle, the *Josephine* seemed stationary. Its only movement seemed wildly upward, well out of the water, then down again, slamming hard against the surface. Rain and spray blurred the coastline. Dad finally realized we were in trouble.

"Ricky!" Dad shouted. "Get below and start pumping!"

I scrambled below, my heart pounding with fear, and grabbed the handle of the bilge pump. I began pumping as hard as I could, but with each wave, seawater cascaded down the open hatch, soaking me and sloshing in the confined space. Almost in tears, I pumped harder and harder, trying to keep ahead of the gallons of water pouring down on me. I could hear Dad, Uncle Felix, and Tun Enrique shouting above me: "Grab the line! Watch out, watch out! Man the wheel! Hold it!" There was panic in their voices. In the blackness below, I fought back my own.

"Ricky, are you still pumping?" Dad yelled down at me.

"Yes, Daddy," I hollered back, trying not to cry.

"Good! Keep pumping, son, keep pumping."

Despite our engine at full throttle and my pumping, we did not seem to make headway.

"Maybe we should abandon ship and try to swim for shore. We're never going to make it like this," Uncle Felix shouted.

"No, we'll get there," Dad shouted back.

It took four hours to make the few miles to Orote and the mouth of the harbor. It was pitch-dark when we got there. With only a red-lighted marker buoy to guide us, we inched our way toward Apra's mouth. Uncle Felix took command, negotiating our reentry from memory and guesswork while Dad and Tun Enrique kept watch for the reef and the channel with flashlights. As we entered the mouth, a huge wave washed us in and suddenly we were in the calmer water inside the harbor. But the wind was still stiff, making visibility difficult. The *Josephine* inched forward little by little until we reached the Pan Am channel and safety.

As we pulled alongside the pier, Tun Enrique jumped off to secure the lines. Before he could finish, the *Josephine's* engine sputtered and died.

"How did that happen?" he asked, puzzled.

"I don't know, it just quit," Dad answered.

Until that moment, the men had forgotten about me in the hold. I was shin-deep in water and still pumping. Someone flashed a light down on me while Dad shined another into the engine compartment. Water filled the compartment but did not reach the spark plugs and kill the engine until we were safe.

Chapter 6

Nåna's nickels and Auntie Butler's soda fountain

If we did not go to Sumai for the weekend, Nåna would come to Hagåtña instead. We loved her visits and would wait in line for the nickels she gave each of us. Unlike our hard-earned and budgeted pennies, Nåna's nickel was *chenchule'*, a windfall given without restriction.

Chenchule' is based on generosity. It may take different forms — spending money for a traveler; food offerings for a wedding, christening, or fiesta; or helping hands for a roof-raising or when illness or death strikes a family. The money given for a funeral is *ika*, a specialized *chenchule'*. No matter what its vehicle, *chenchule'* is motivated by compassion. It implies reciprocal generosity, sometimes stated, but more often left to the conscience and ability of the recipient. In a cash-poor society that relied on bartering and trading, *chenchule'* was the way to share resources in times of need.

In 1986, a federalis agent stripped *chenchule'* from its CHamoru context and applied the Western definition of "gratuity" to accuse and convict me of illegally accepting money. The defamation and devaluation of my culture pains me more than the personal insults hurled at me.

Nåna did not expect anything in return when she gave us her nickels; she was teaching us the value of caring, generosity, and sharing. We belonged to an affluent family, but we were not pampered children. Dad and Mama had too many mouths to feed to be generous with extra pennies. My brothers and sisters and I worked for our pocket money and could not afford to spend foolishly. Sometimes we would spend our nickels, and other times we would save them. Sometimes I added my nickel to my savings account at the Navy Bank of Guam. Other times my brothers and sisters and I would head to a favorite store. Like other kids in the neighborhood, we too would drool over the wonderous candy assortment at Butler's, Dejima's, Elliott's, Suzuki's, Flores', and Torres' stores. We always drew a bunch of neighborhood kids, each recommending what to buy. In those days, a nickel could buy five different penny candies. Nåna knew we would spread the wealth.

We sold hard candy at the Santa Cruz market, but our selection was nothing like the offering at Butler's Soda Fountain or Dejima's Store. Butler's had an entire showcase filled with candies of all sorts and colors. The variety was mind-boggling. There were huge jars of multicolored bubble gum, sourballs, hard candies, and all kinds of candy bars and chocolates. My favorite was Planter's chocolate-covered peanuts in small packets.

I could have eaten candy by the ton if I had the money. I had such a sweet tooth that by the time the war ended, my teeth were in terrible shape. I never saw a dentist until after the war. Since then, I have spent a fortune on my teeth, but I still have a sweet tooth. As governor, I reserved one desk drawer for my cache of candy. There were candy jars in my chambers as well. I could help myself to the candy jars at our Santa Cruz market, but to buy Planter's chocolate-covered peanuts, I would shortchange the cashbox at the garage.

Occasionally, I would indulge in a chocolate milkshake at Auntie Butler's soda fountain and enjoy two treats in one. The soda fountain looked just like the ones in magazines, with a long marble counter, tall wrought-iron stools, and a real soda jerk in a starched white jacket and cap. I would climb onto a stool, rest my elbows on the counter, and order a chocolate ice cream milkshake as if it were an ordinary thing to do. And then I would watch in awe. For me, the making of my milkshake was as much a treat as drinking it. The soda jerk would put two scoops of ice cream into a metal tumbler, add chocolate syrup and cold milk, then place it under the paddle of the mixing machine and flip the switch. As he poured my milkshake into a glass, I would worry he would not give me my entire money's worth. Thanks to Nåna, I enjoyed enough milkshakes to have them among my fondest memories.

Nåna had a funny way of smoking cigars. First, she peeled away the veins of locally grown tobacco then stacked enough leaves to roll into a thick cigar. She tied the cigar in three or four places then cut it into short chunks to fit the bowl of her pipe. She smoked it by the chunk in her pipe.

Nåna outlived three husbands. Her third husband, Tun Antonio Torres, was the grandfather we knew best. Tun Antonio was a wealthy man who had been in love with her for many years. Despite their marriages to other people,

Tun Antonio vowed to marry Nåna before he died. He made good on the vow after his first wife died. By then, he and Nåna were quite old.

Nåna's first husband, Jose "Tuan" Cruz, was the high commissioner of Tinian at the turn of the century. She was 16 when she married him and left Guam for Tinian about 100 miles north. The sight of a man hanging by his thumbs greeted her arrival. Shocked, Nåna demanded an explanation and learned the man was a thief undergoing punishment. Nåna ordered the man released or else she would not stay, so her husband complied. The thief was so grateful that he offered himself as her servant and remained loyal to her during her stay in Tinian. When Tun Jose fell ill, Nåna's servant battled savage currents to ferry the couple to Saipan where they took the *guleta*, a kind of schooner, to Guam. Tun Jose died in the hospital in Guam. Nåna did not return to Tinian.

Nåna's second husband, Felix Pangelinan, was Mama's father and my grandfather. His sister, Rita Pangelinan Bordallo, was Dad's mother. Since my parents were first cousins, we nieces and nephews addressed our elders as figurehead parents, calling them "Nanan," or "mother," and "Tatan," or "father" along with their CHamoru nicknames.

Mama was especially close to Nanan Chong, the youngest of her aunts. Nanan Chong's name was Asuncion Borja Pangelinan Cruz. Like all my other grandaunts and uncles, I was related to her on both sides.

Nanan Chong's eldest daughter, Serafina, and her eldest son, Augusto, were my baptismal godparents. I addressed them as Nino and Nina, short for *patlino* and *matlina*, the CHamoru derivatives of the Spanish words for "godparents."

Nanan Chong and her husband, Francisco "Tun Kiko" Martinez Cruz, lived in Hagåtña. Tun Kiko ran the "Fixin," a machine shop where he fixed bicycles and small motors. They owned a large *låncho*, or farm, with a small chapel in Tutuhan. Every year, Nanan Chong offered a novena in honor of Santa Cruz in the chapel, and we looked forward to the celebration when it ended. Nanan Chong grew and roasted coffee beans and made delicious coffee. She served it in small, deep bowls that concentrated its aroma. One did not just drink Nanan Chong's coffee — one savored it. Nanan Chong's Santa Cruz fiesta also meant carefree leisure time for playing sandlot baseball. We only played with two bases, and I always pitched. I was not as good a hitter as I was a pitcher.

Nanan Lia and Nanan Acha lived in Hågat. Throughout the year, we would travel from village to village, visiting one grandaunt or another. Or we would go on big family picnics at Apotguan or Tomhom. At least twice a year, the Pangelinan clan would gather at Mayanghulo', where the Bordallo agribusiness was located. We had a large house on a promontory overlooking the beach. Uncle Tom and Uncle Carlos had summer homes there also. We all moved to Mayanghulo' after school got out, and a large family gathering would take place then.

Our clan gathered and socialized with other clans and participated in many other community activities. Nearly everyone did; it was our nature as CHamorus and very much an important part of our lifestyle. Everyone, even children, would be eager and excited to *fangade'*. *Gade'* is an ancient way of fishing as a large group. It was as important a social event as it was a food-gathering method. And it was great fun. As many as 40 to 50 people would turn out at night. The biggest and strongest men would wade waist-high into the water and position themselves in a large semicircle with a long fish net stretched among them. Everyone else would form a line in the water several yards away from the net. At a given signal, the people would move toward the net, making a great commotion, beating, and splashing the water, herding the fish into the net. The men holding the nets would then close the ends, and everyone would help pull it ashore. The adults would then sort the catch and divide it so that everyone received a share. They would even cook some fish on the beach to eat on the spot. The merriment would last long into the night around the cook fires. And the tuba would flow as freely as the singing and storytelling.

Caravans and fiestas: adventures to the South

Every year on March 6, families from Hagåtña traveled to Umatac to celebrate Magellan Day, the day in 1521 when Ferdinand Magellan landed in Guam. The Spanish regime made it an annual observance. It remains a public holiday but is no longer called Magellan Day. The old explorer has fallen out of favor with modern-day CHamorus who resent his getting the credit for discovering Guam. It is now Discovery Day, commemorating our ancestors who preceded Magellan by thousands of years.

Umatac lies on Guam's rugged southwestern coast. Prior to the war, getting there was not easy unless one sailed. For Magellan Day, the Navy made the USS *Penguin* available to the public for free passage to Umatac. Much to my disappointment, we never went by ship, but our trips to Umatac were exciting, nonetheless. We always drove in a caravan with several other Hagåtña families and would spend more time traveling than celebrating. The overland trek, which would begin at dawn, took almost all day.

There were two roads to the south, but only one reached all the southern villages. The Camino Real, the road southwestward from Hagåtña, ended in Hågat, a few miles south of Sumai. Beyond Hågat there were only meandering footpaths and bull cart trails that led down and around the southwestern coast or along the old Spanish routes around Seya and Sette bays. The bays remain unspoiled and beautiful even now. There is an old Spanish stone bridge at Seya, and CHamoru archaeological sites abound in both places.

In the early 1970s, the Navy announced plans to condemn both bays and the surrounding government of Guam land to build a new ammunition wharf and storage facility. Without considering the CHamorus' regard for the area, the Navy planned to tunnel into the hillsides and seal off a large swath of land as an "explosive arc zone." The arbitrary decision became controversial immediately. No longer tolerant of the Navy's imperiousness, many people voiced vehement opposition. The Navy's plan, they said, was as profane as building a dam at Niagara Falls. I had just lost my first bid for the governorship and was out of office at the time, but my brother Paul, a senator in the Eleventh and Twelfth Legislatures, led the legislature's protest. Having witnessed the accidental explosion of an ammunition dump after the war, I supported Paul's arguments.

After the public outcry, the Navy withdrew the Seya/Sette plan and decided instead to build the new ammo wharf at Adotgan, the pristine cove on the Orote Peninsula, which the Navy condemned in the name of national defense after the war. Although they have little say in the matter, the Naval Station's resident dependent families did not relish the idea of bomb trucks rumbling through their neighborhoods, something Guam's civilian community endured during the Vietnam War.

The road from Hågat to Umatac, Malesso', and Inalåhan did not exist until after 1950. To establish Naval Station Guam, the Navy seized Orote Peninsula, razed the ruins of Sumai village, relocated the villagers to a hillside inland from Hågat, and sealed off the Camino Real between Sumai and Hågat. A new route skirts the base and courses through what used to be Bordallo property. People now reach Hågat by going through what was once our farm and cattle ranch.

Before the war, the only road to the south ran eastward from Hagåtña and across the island's narrow waist to Yoña. From Yoña, the narrow country road followed the eastern coastline to Inalåhan and around the island's southern tip and northward again to Malesso' and Umatac. The eastern route was no easier than the shorter western one, but it was the only one that could accommodate motorized traffic. This was our route to Umatac for Magellan Day, and I loved it. It was like a long roller coaster ride, full of dips and curves and hair-raising ascents and descents.

With other neighborhood family groups — the Torreses and Martinezes, in particular — we would set out in a caravan of about 30 or 40 cars, trucks, and jitneys. The roller coaster ride would begin immediately as the heavily laden vehicles labored up San Ramon Hill one at a time. The caravan would string out across the 4 miles through Guam's hilly, narrow waist, through the villages of Sinajana, Ordot, and Chalan Pago. A rickety, wooden bridge spanned the Pågu River, then the road rose the steep incline to Pågu Point and Yoña.

The road then led downhill and over the Ilek River to Ipan where some of Guam's most beautiful beaches stretched along the coast. These were long strands of white sand peppered with craggy limestone outcroppings, some in the water, some in the sand and capped with furry, gray-green-leafed *hunek* (*Messerschmidia argentea*), shiny-leafed *nanåsu* (*Scaevola taccada*), and the dense, low-growing *Pluchea indica*. Carpets of *alaihai*, beach morning glory, reached across the sand, their pink trumpet blossoms facing the sun. Coconut palms swayed in breezes that whispered through strands of *gågu* (*Casuarina equisetifolia*). Muffled in the distance, breakers crashed against the fringing reef. Navy submariners would claim part of this area as their exclusive rest and recuperation retreat after the war. They dubbed it Camp Dealy. I could never begrudge the submariners their claim. Anyone who would risk his life to fight wars in such potential tombs as submarines deserved to enjoy nature at its loveliest.

The drive along the beach provided the break we needed before tackling the *Atkiya*, the most perilous part of the journey. *Atkiya*, which means "hairpin," described the road. Once over the Talo'fo'fo bridge, the road rose sharply and zigzagged on a narrow lip chiseled out of the vertical flanks of a high bluff. In many places the road was barely the width of a vehicle. Above and below the narrow stretches, there were only sheer rock faces. Each vehicle had to negotiate the Atkiya ascent one at a time. Drivers had to depend on spotters to keep them on track and pilot them through tight curves. Many of the women would choose to walk rather than risk the heart-pounding, white-knuckled ride. I loved every minute of it.

At Malohloh, the caravan would turn inland and onto a plateau, the backsides of the mountains that jutted upward from the Hågat side of the island. We would follow a dusty dirt road to Tun Pedro Martinez's cattle ranch in Dåndan. The same road leads to NASA's former satellite tracking station. Tun Pedro's men would have watermelon, cold drinks, and other midmorning refreshments waiting for us. After a brief rest, the caravan would head out again to reach Umatac by lunchtime.

The last leg of the journey was through rolling hills and an easy descent into Inalåhan, a little village clinging to a narrow strip of flatland between a small bay and more rolling hills. The caravan would clear Inalåhan and the village of Malesso' in a little less than an hour and arrive at last in Umatac, but not before one final thrill. For a third time, the caravan would go one at a time to descend steep Mount Toguan and enter the village. Riding into Umatac was so much fun. To ensure a safe descent and prevent runaways from careening headlong into the village, villagers carrying large rocks would meet the caravan at the top of the hill. They would sprint alongside a descending vehicle and use the rocks as chocks if brakes did not hold.

Because they lived in such a remote area and did not often receive guests, the people of Umatac welcomed visitors like returning heroes, whooping, waving, laughing, and running alongside the caravan not just as rock carriers. We would greet them back with cheers, enthusiastic waving, and horns blaring.

Before the feasting, there would be a program of speeches by village officials and presentations by Umatac's schoolchildren, the students of Tun Francisco Q. Sanchez, a respected village leader and teacher who devoted his life to education. He composed songs to help his students learn arithmetic and wrote funny poems to entertain them. Tun Francisco was deeply committed to the quest for CHamoru political rights. He wrote the theme song for the fundraising effort to send Dad and F.B. Leon Guerrero to Washington. Umatac's people named their postwar elementary school in his honor.

No one can beat the hospitality and generosity of southern CHamorus. Their distance from Hagåtña and Sumai, from Spanish and American administrators, and from sustained outside influences allowed them to hold truer to CHamoru culture and traditions. As hosts, they excelled in CHamoru virtues and rekindled ours as "city folks." For an occasion as important as Magellan Day, they would prepare long tables with their best offerings of fresh fish, lobsters, crabs, shrimp, octopus, and clams, as well as land crabs, coconut crabs, beef, pork, venison, chicken, game birds, pigeons, and fruit bat cooked in every conceivable way. Yams, sweet potatoes, taro, and fresh vegetables and fruits from their farms and gardens served as side dishes, centerpieces, and desserts. Baked goods and sweets in a mouth-watering variety of shapes, colors, and sizes would fill separate tables alongside huge pots of *åhu* (sweet coconut soup), *apigige'*, and other coconut desserts.

CHamoru fiesta meals have always been gastronomic orgies limited only by the capacity of one's stomach. But offering of bounty is not meant to encourage gluttony; it is the way CHamorus express pride in themselves and their joy in living. We believe food, like air and water, is a life necessity to share freely. To be generous with these life necessities is to earn honor. Above honor, pride and dignity rank highest in the way CHamorus look at life and death. Denied these, a CHamoru views life and death as one and the same.

As guests of the village, we would stand in awe of Umatac's *na'taotaotumano'*, the fiesta meal prepared by the entire village for all visitors. We children would fidget nervously, waiting for the program to end and for the parish priest to bless the table before we could eat. It was wonderful when that time finally came.

By late afternoon, after everyone heard all the latest news and gossip, and the children got their fill of swimming, fishing, romping on the beach, and exploring the abandoned Spanish forts, it was time to regroup and head for home. For those of us in the caravans, departing at the right time was crucial. The circuitous route home was dangerous at night. Any delay meant camping out or trying to negotiate the Atkiya in the dark, which was out of the question.

A stowaway on the USS *Penguin*

We had always gone to Umatac overland in the caravans, but I so wanted to be among those who came in on the USS *Penguin*. Like our caravan, it also had to leave by late afternoon to get back to Apra Harbor. The *Penguin* was an old Navy minesweeper commissioned in 1918. The Navy converted it into a gunboat. It patrolled the Yangtze River in China after World War I. The Navy decommissioned it in 1921 and assigned it to Guam. It was 187 feet long, 35 feet wide, and had a crew of 75. It was a small vessel, but to me, it was huge.

On Magellan Day in 1935, as my caravan gathered for the return trip, I dallied by the Umatac pier and watched with envy as boats shuttled people back to the *Penguin*. I knew a grand adventure would await me if I went home on the *Penguin*, but Dad would not have allowed it, so I dared not ask. I toyed with the idea of getting on one of the boats and going anyway, knowing I would get in trouble. I argued back and forth with myself, trying to decide. When the last group of passengers got on the launch, I jumped onboard just as the launch pulled away.

Regret began to gnaw at me as the launch motored ahead; I knew I was going to pay a high price for what I had done. But as we neared the *Penguin*, my remorse evaporated. I looked up the ship's ladder and felt only excitement and anticipation. The *Penguin* was nothing like the *Josephine*. It was a ship — a real ship. I forgot all about the caravan and Dad as I climbed aboard. I could not contain my amazement and curiosity, and I dashed about, soaking up the novelty of being on the deck of a real ship. It was a whole new experience for me. I began exploring, examining every fitting, every piece of machinery, every stretch of deck from bow to stern.

When the *Penguin*'s huge engines rumbled to life and the ship began to move, my heart leaped into my throat. I felt as if I was sailing away to the United States of America. I joined some people leaning over the rails and watched in awe as the *Penguin*'s bow sliced through the deep blue ocean. It was mesmerizing. From the wind-blown bow, I marveled at the flight of hundreds of flying fish skittering through the waves. I even spotted pods of dolphins, undulating in the sea ahead of us.

From my vantage high above the water, I had a spectacular view of Guam's southwestern coastline; of Fuha Bay, Sette Bay, Seya Bay, Fåkpe Point; of Anae Island and Bangi and Alutom islands; of Hågat Bay and the little point of Mayanghulo' where our summer house was; of Tipalao and Neyi Island, and of the high cliffs of Orote Peninsula. Everything was much more beautiful from the deck of the *Penguin* than from the *Josephine*. In my best authoritative stance, I puffed out my chest and, for a brief imaginary moment, I was captain of the vessel. But it ended too soon. In no time at all, the *Penguin* made the four-hour trip to Apra Harbor and was making for the docks at Piti. My great sea adventure was over. The next one lay ahead of me — at home with Dad.

I hitched a ride from Piti to the Santa Cruz District at the western edge of Hagåtña. It was almost 9 p.m. The caravan from Umatac had not yet arrived. It would be another two hours before it did. I decided to kill time by walking home the long way; I was in no hurry. The streets were dark and quiet as I walked to Bilibek School, contemplating my fate. I knew what I did was wrong, but the enormity of it did not register until the fun ended. My family would have looked for me and that would have delayed their departure from Umatac. I wondered how long they searched, what time they left, and when they would get home. I thought about how angry Dad would be and how Mama would worry. Upsetting Mama would have doubled Dad's anger. He was not one to spare the rod, so I knew I was in for more than a twisted ear, and I shivered. I was in serious trouble and wondered if I would live to see my children and grandchildren.

"Ricky!" Cristobal Hines, one of Dad's taxi drivers, called out to me. "Where have you been? They're looking for you in Umatac." Part of the caravan left on schedule. The rest stayed behind with Dad and Mama to look for me. "Your dad was really upset, and your mother was worried. I think you're in trouble," he added.

What an understatement. I slowed my pace even further. There was no sense rushing into the lion's den. The *tilifon alaihai* spread the news that I was missing in Umatac, and the return word that I was seen in Hagåtña spread just as rapidly. The first report would have worried people. Had something terrible befallen little Ricky? Poor Batasalito. Poor Sufina. But wait a minute … isn't that Ricky out there? He is not missing; that's him right outside. *Toka.*

Sure enough. *"Toka hao,"* someone taunted from an open window. *Toka* is the CHamoru equivalent of "danger is impending." *Hao* is the CHamoru second person pronoun. *Toka hao* means "Boy, are you going to get it!"

My neighbors had pieced together obvious clues and unraveled the mystery. I must not have had permission to leave the caravan and had done so without my parents' knowledge. The only way I could have reached Hagåtña so quickly was to have come on board the *Penguin*. Ah-ha! So that is what happened. All along my route home, neighbors passed the word.

"Toka hao, Ricky!" The message came at me from every direction, from windows and doorways, from porches and yards. Even Dad's taxi drivers at the garage, sitting on their fenders, snickered, *"Toka hao*, boy!" as I walked by.

"So, there you are! Don't you know they're looking for you in Umatac? *Toka hao!*" I must have heard it 50 times before I got home. Some spat the warning like a sentence of doom. Others were more sympathetic. They all knew that such a serious offense would reap an equally serious punishment. Everyone knew my transgression was going to unleash a great tragedy in the Bordallo house. And I had no hope of reprieve. Word would reach Dad that I was in Hagåtña even before he parked the car.

I turned onto Hernan Cortez and slowed my pace for the short distance home. I tried to gather up courage as I neared the house. My brothers and sisters had already unloaded the car, and everyone was inside. Just as I was about to mount the front steps, my brother Fred came bounding out the door. He stopped short and stared at me, wide eyed. Without a word, he whirled around and dashed back into the house, shouting, "Mama! Daddy! It's Ricky! He's alive! He's home!"

My sisters Irene and Lorraine came running to the door. Seconds later, Bobbie, Paul, and Norma gathered also, crowding the doorway. They all spoke at once, repeating what I was already sick of hearing. My heart pounded as I walked into the house. Mama ran to me. She scooped me up and began kissing me, mumbling, crying, and thanking God I was not dead. But her relief quickly gave way to anger. She withdrew her affections. With an icy look, she nudged me into the living room where Dad was waiting. *"My life is over,"* I thought to myself.

Dad's face was like gray stone. He had his belt looped in his right hand, ready. It was a thick leather belt made by local leather smiths. It was strong and durable. At that moment I hated the pride and effort CHamoru craftsmen put into their work. That well-made belt was going to taste my flesh.

In a voice surprisingly calm, Dad said, "I can't understand why you would do a thing like that." It was all he said. He did not raise his voice, but I could hear his deep disappointment. He raised the belt over his shoulder, and I braced myself for the blow. *Whap!* I tried to be brave but could only manage for a few minutes.

From the security of their homes, my relatives and neighbors heard B.J. Bordallo mete out justice. Up and down the street, the households around ours listened without sympathy to my howls and the whacks of Dad's belt. After several minutes, those who kept count gave up. Legend has it that no child in Hagåtña got as many lashings as Ricky Bordallo did on that Magellan

Day. It was the worst licking in anyone's recollection.

That night I went to bed without supper and with stinging welts on my body. I rubbed some of the sorest spots and relived my ocean adventure. I stood once more at the railing and watched the white foam of the *Penguin's* wake. I recalled the wind blowing in my hair and the cold salt spray on my face. I remembered flying fish at my feet and the sailors scurrying about. I had no regrets. My adventure was worth the spanking and the pain.

And I deserved every lash. I found out later that my failure to make roll call in Umatac sparked one of the biggest manhunts ever seen in the village. CHamorus never take life lightly, particularly that of a child. When I did not turn up after a quick search, the entire village turned out. People organized search parties, believing I had fallen and injured myself and was helpless somewhere in a deep ravine or the surrounding hillsides. Another group set out in boats to search the bay. Village fishermen and divers even searched under the water. Women gathered at the San Dionisio church to offer a rosary for my safe return. My mother and sisters were in tears, and Dad scurried from one search group to another for news. My disappearance left the village in an uproar of worry and fear. The search continued until an old man approached Mama and suggested I might have gone onboard the *Penguin*.

"I could be wrong, Sufina, but I thought I saw a boy that looked like Ricky on the last launch," he told Mama.

When the searches yielded nothing, and the hour grew late, Mama and Dad decided to leave Umatac while it was still safe to travel. They left hoping the old man was right. The episode was the talk of Hagåtña for months. The following Magellan Day, parents warned their children not to "pull a Ricky on us." And at every Magellan Day after that, no unescorted children could board the launches. The *Penguin's* crew checked for stowaways and lone children, and caravan roll calls were mandatory. No one wanted to share the Bordallo family's experience.

My hunger for adventure has always been insatiable. As governor, I have unintentionally given my staff a few scares. After a while, even my security guards gave up trying to keep up with me. On several of my off-island trips, I would go off to do some exploring and forget to inform the staff traveling with me.

I gave Dave Santos, my tax director, quite a scare in 1984 while we were in Washington, D.C. I was going to attend a National Governors Association meeting and then with Dave to testify before the House Committee on Insular Affairs. Since we had accomplished our mission and had a free weekend before our return to Guam, I rented a car and drove to Atlantic City without telling Dave. I figured he, a bright, conscientious man half my age, would prefer his own diversions rather than taking in Atlantic City's nightlife with his boss. But Dave spent the weekend frantically searching for me. Fearing the worst, Dave considered calling home long distance as a last resort but hesitated because he did not know how to explain that he had "lost" the governor. When I returned late Sunday evening, an angry Dave Santos was waiting outside my hotel. He gave me a piece of his mind as diplomatically as he could.

"Hell must look like this"

Since childhood, I have always needed to discover things for myself, to experience new things, and to experiment, even if I got into trouble for my antics later. I never outgrew it. I made it my business to keep up with the goings-on in town so that no opportunity for adventure could pass me by. I knew every nook of the Martinez warehouse and lot, as well as every footbridge that spanned the Hagåtña River between the warehouse yard and the Martinez store and ice plant. I watched the ice men at work and marveled at their skill. I knew how freezing hundreds of gallons of water made huge blocks of ice. I watched the processing of copra at the Torres copra warehouse and the cutting of lumber at Tun Ben Hererro's sawmill in Aniguak. I was also an eager and faithful spectator of the coal barges that came up from Piti.

The barges chugged up along the *guinaddok laida* loaded with coal that came from Kobe, Japan. I had learned that fact, and many other technicalities of commerce and trade, from listening to the conversations of Hagåtña's businessmen. Learning such things made me feel knowledgeable and mature. I could speak with some authority to playmates who also gathered to watch the coal barges.

Large cranes on the dock at the end of the channel would lift coal-filled boxcars from the barges and lower them onto a set of inclined tracks that led to the top of a 40-foot-tall storage bin beside the power plant. Cables pulled the boxcars from dockside along the track and up the ramp to the storage bin. The boxcars reminded me of huge, hungry cockroaches climbing the track, lifting the massive bin cover, and peering inside for something to eat. But unlike cockroaches, the coal cars disgorged their contents into the bin and rolled away for the next car.

The boxcars were black. So was the coal. Everything at the power plant was black. The plant and its 200-foot-tall smokestack were black. The smoke that belched from it was always thick and black. Even the ground around the power plant was black with a thick carpet of sparkling cinders.

The power plant sat on the north bank of the Hagåtña River, adjacent to the old, Spanish-era San Antonio stone bridge not far from the Navy's cold storage plant and our house. The Jota Bottling Company, owned and operated by a Japanese family, also was on the riverbank near the bridge. They were soft drink makers and Uncle Butler's main competitor until he landed the Co-ca-Cola franchise and put them out of business. Near the bridge also, the river bubbled and boiled beneath a blanket of steamy, white foam where the power plant discharged hot water. The water a few feet away was always crystal clear. We could watch minnows, shrimp, and *ito'* (catfish) darting along the bottom.

Inside the power plant, winches moved loads of coal to piles near massive furnaces that stokers manned around the clock. I often peeked inside to watch them — their muscles bulging, their skin shiny with sweat, shoveling coal into the roaring furnaces. I imagined they were stoking sinful souls in the fiery furnace of Hell and thinking, *"Hell must look like this."*

Chapter 7

"To act with the wishes of the people"

In May 1931, Captain Edmund S. Root relieved Commander Willis J. Bradley, Jr. as Navy governor of Guam, just two months after Bradley called for the first free general election in Guam. Captain Root condemned Bradley's extension of democracy and abolished Bradley's policies. Bradley had earlier proclaimed a "bill of rights" for CHamorus and embarked on a program of islandwide infrastructure improvements, including the construction of buildings to house the Guam Congress in Aniguak just outside Hagåtña. Bradley's sensitivity to CHamoru needs and desires made him popular in Guam but not in Washington.

Bradley reorganized the Guam Congress, which Governor Roy C. Smith[12] established in 1916, as an appointed advisory council to the governor. Bradley called for the popular election of members to the bicameral Second Guam Congress — a 13-member House of Council (the upper house) and a 33-member House of Assembly (the lower house). Like its predecessor, the second congress remained an advisory body, but for the first time, the people of Guam could exercise the right to choose their own representatives. High hopes for more exercises of self-government crumbled when Root assumed command.

The 1931 election also included races for village commissioners' seats. Like the congress members, village commissioners served as appointed advisers to the governor. Bradley's policies sparked enthusiasm for direct political involvement but fizzled when the Navy government's indifference resumed under Root's administration. In his 1933 annual report to the Navy Depart-

---

12 Roy Campbell Smith (1858-1940) was an American naval officer and the governor of Guam from 1916 to 1918.

ment, Root decried the free election of commissioners as an "unsuccessful scheme."

"The commissioners are basically employees of the Government and are the agencies through which the Governor is able to demand certain things of the people of the districts," he wrote. "Sometimes these things are not in accordance with the personal desires of those concerned and as long as the commissioners were elected, they were inclined to act with the wishes of the people rather than the desires of the Governor." Root halted the election of commissioners and returned them to appointed positions.

I was only 5 years old when Root filed his report. I was not old enough to understand what it meant, but Dad did. He had won a seat in the Second Guam Congress and the confidence of his colleagues who elected him chairman of the House of Council. Jake Calvo won a seat in the House of Assembly and chairmanship of the lower house.

Although the congress convened only once a month, Dad and his colleagues spent countless evenings in discussions. They had no power or authority as lawmakers, but they took their responsibility seriously. They made earnest efforts to offer the governor well-reasoned policy recommendations. But Larry Ramirez, who was a clerk in the governor's office, reported to the disheartened congressmen that most of their resolutions ended up in the governor's wastebasket. Larry would embark on a distinguished political career himself years later. He became a colleague of Dad's and mine also.

Despite the futility of their efforts, the congressmen persisted. Their appointed predecessors in the First Congress sought to be more than advisers and asked Governor Smith for some lawmaking authority. Smith's response became legend. He told the congressmen, "The only lawmaking authority here is this." He opened his mouth and pointed to his tongue.

Apathy among succeeding congressmen grew until Bradley's administration. Between Smith's administration and Bradley's, the Guam Congress was nothing more than a forum for debating local issues. Frustrated by the fruitlessness of their efforts, many congressmen ceased attending sessions or resigned. Although the Second Guam Congress was to continue as an advisory body, Bradley's call for free congressional elections rekindled CHamoru hopes for political autonomy and administrative sensitivity to public desires. Root's abolishment of Bradley's policies led to widespread disenchantment. Congressional elections continued under Root, but with lawmaking authority still denied the congress, the exercise was merely a pantomime of democracy. CHamorus lost heart and interest in the election process. Fewer and fewer bothered to go to the polls. Nonetheless, Dad retained his congressional seat in the elections of 1933 and 1936 and continued to serve as chairman of the upper house.

In July 1936, the Guam Congress unanimously passed a resolution petitioning the United States to grant American citizenship to CHamorus. A similar petition was sent to President Franklin Roosevelt in 1933, but he ignored it, as had been done with several other petitions before it. This time, two representatives — Dad, as chairman of the House of Council, and F.B. Leon Guerrero of the House of Assembly — would take the petition to Washington, D.C., and deliver it directly to the U.S. Congress in person. The planning, scheduling, and preparation for the journey took eight months and began long before the funds were available. The 1936 resolution also sought $5,000 from naval government funds for the delegates' trip.

Dad went to see Governor Benjamin V. McCandlish about the funding request. McCandlish expressed sympathy for what he called the CHamorus' "ambition" toward citizenship but denied the funding. In jest, he offered to chip in $20 toward the trip. Dad took offense to McCandlish's callousness but remained undaunted. Dad and his colleagues sought other means to raise money.

In October, Senator William Gibbs McAddo of California and his wife Eleanor, the daughter of President Woodrow Wilson, arrived in Guam. The visit gave the Guam congressmen what they hoped was a unique opportunity to win powerful political support for the citizenship cause. They welcomed the McAddos with an extravagant public reception in the Plaza de España in front of the Governor's Palace. During the ceremony, Dad and Jake Calvo spoke passionately about the citizenship quest and tried to gain McAddo's support.

I sat with Mama and the rest of the family listening to Dad's speech. Jake's family was there also. At the time, neither Jake's son, Paul, nor I dreamed we would grow up to become governors of Guam. Forty-two years later, in 1978, Paul, a Republican, would win the governorship from me and become the third elected governor of Guam. After his term, I retook the governorship. In 1936, Paul and I were just boys listening as our fathers earned their places in our history.

Despite Dad and Jake's fine words, Senator McAddo was unmoved. He told the congress to "conduct your efforts through proper channels." McAddo's rebuff prompted an immediate response from the people of Guam. In less than a month, our cash-poor community raised more than $6,000 for the Washington trip. Singing a song composed by Tun Francisco Sanchez, volunteers, including Tun Francisco himself, wandered village streets with outstretched blankets collecting donations. People pitched pennies, nickels, and dimes into the blankets. Mr. Leon Guerrero even sold some of his family's land, and Tun Jose Estaquio and Jake Calvo made sizeable contributions to total $10,000. Dad even pressed Governor McCandlish to make good on his $20 pledge.

"Remember the words I'm saying to you now"

After I had climbed the palace compound wall and seen the American children's playground, Dad told me I would begin to understand the CHamoru political condition. He told me he would try to secure political rights for the people of Guam. I never doubted him and knew the time would come. His trip to Washington was to be his major effort. I had always assumed that his insistence on my early training was to ensure my future success in business. I did not realize it was also to prepare me to take on, at age 9, an even bigger responsibility.

On the eve of his departure, Dad summoned me to his bedroom. His bags, packed and stacked by the door, made me realize he was going to be away for a long time.

"Come in, son, and close the door," he said. Dad was sitting on the bed. With sadness in his eyes, he motioned for me to sit beside him. We were to have a private, man-to-man exchange, not simply a list of chores for me to do while he was away. Mama would have witnessed his instructions, but it was just the two of us.

"Yes, Daddy," I said, conscious of his grave manner.

"Ricky, you're very young, but you're much older than your age," he said. "I know you understand because I brought you up to understand what is happening. I must leave your mother to go on this long journey. I do not know what might happen, and there is a chance that I might not return. While I am gone, you must fulfill my responsibilities. You must look after your mother and your sisters and brothers. Always. Do not fail me on this."

I nodded but knew that such a heavy burden would not be mine alone. In Dad's absence, I knew Tun Kin "Inda" Cepeda, Dad's trusted and loyal right-hand man, would be helping me. The elders in our family would be looking after us also. Dad knew that. At first, I thought Dad was reminding me of my responsibilities and that I was not free to shirk them, but I sensed he had deeper reasons for our talk.

"Remember the words I'm saying to you now, Ricky. I must go on this mission because I am fighting for the rights of our people. Our people under-stand what I am trying to do. They are depending on me to follow through," he said. "I will ask one more thing of you. If anything should happen to me, and if, at any time in the future, the people come to you and ask you to lead them and help them, I want you to leave your personal ambitions behind and do as they ask."

"Yes, Daddy, I will," I answered with only a vague understanding of the commitment I was making — to him and to anyone who might someday call upon me. I wanted to be like Dad, honorable and true to his word, to be like him, a *kabayeru*, a man of integrity. From then on, I waited for the call and heeded it each time. I have yet to fail my father or my people.

Dad and Mr. Leon Guerrero were prepared to face Washington, to bring Guam's petition for American citizenship to Congress and the president him-self, if possible. The Navy Department successfully blocked many previous efforts contending that the CHamoru people were not "politically mature" enough to understand or fulfill the obligations and responsibilities of Ameri-can citizenship.

Mr. Leon Guerrero, who worked for the Navy government's agriculture and fisheries department, was aware of Navy arrogance. Like Dad, he went to jail for insubordination. A few years before winning his congressional seat, Mr. Leon Guerrero was at work in Piti when the Navy governor arrived on horseback to inspect the agriculture facility. After dismounting, he ordered Mr. Leon Guerrero to tie up his horse. "Tie it up yourself. I'm not your slave," Mr. Leon Guerrero told the governor. He received 15 days in jail. On the last day of his confinement, as a final humiliation, the governor ordered Mr. Leon Guerrero to collect garbage at the Navy Yard during an awards ceremony for yard employees.

Another future political leader, Mr. Jesus "Okie" Okiyama, earned 30 days of hard labor at the coral pits at Adelup for bouncing a check for $1. Okie, an astute analytical thinker, became a respected statesman. He was a delegate to the 1968 National Democratic Convention in Chicago and heard a booming voice over the loudspeaker in the huge convention center. The convention's presiding officer announced, "Mr. 'Hay-soos Okinawa,' you have a phone call." Mr. Okiyama always chuckles at the recollection.

Dad and Mr. Leon Guerrero left Guam on November 17, 1936, on board the USS *Gold Star*, which first sailed to Manila. They waited there for three weeks before they could secure passage on another ship to Yokahama. They waited another three weeks in Japan for a liner to San Francisco. Then they traveled across country by train and arrived in Washington, D.C., in time for the convening of the 75th Congress.

L-R: B.J. Bordallo and F.B. Leon Guerrero

Dad addressed that Congress, explaining his mission and appealing for action. The congressional record for that day included his remarks. After the war, my cousin Clara Mae Butler Champion gave me several original pages of Dad's typewritten testimony.

Without a prearranged appointment with the president, Dad and Mr. Leon Guerrero waited for weeks while sympathetic senators and Washington staffers tried to secure one for them. They were heartbroken and ready to give up. They had carried the hopes of the people of Guam and faced having to return in defeat. After exhausting every channel available to them, Dad remembered Tom Beck's invitation. In desperation, he called Mr. Beck and asked for help. Mr. Beck invited Dad to *Collier's* New York offices and to his home in Connecticut. Dad took the next train.

The offices of Crowell, Collier, and McMillan Co. were in a skyscraper. Several staffers met Dad at the door and treated him like an expected important person. They ushered him into Mr. Beck's office right away. After renewing acquaintances, Dad explained the difficulty he and Mr. Leon Guerrero were having in Washington. Mr. Beck listened then asked if there was something he could do. That was when Dad discovered how important and influential Mr. Beck was.

Mr. Beck lifted his phone and dialed. "Franklin," he said into the receiver. "I have a friend here you must meet."

Dad listened in amazement as Mr. Beck spoke directly with President Franklin Roosevelt, saying how Dad had come thousands of miles to meet with him and what an embarrassment it would be if he could not spare the time to meet. Mr. Beck grinned and nodded at Dad. He got an appointment. Elated and impressed, Dad rushed back to Washington.

On the day of their appointment, Dad and Mr. Leon Guerrero went to the White House with symbolic gifts for the president from the people of Guam: a handmade ifit wood coffee table, a silver-handled ifit wood walking stick, and a pair of shell lamps. Ifit is a dense and heavy hardwood. The coffee table was small but heavy. Carrying the table and lamps into the White House, Dad and Mr. Leon Guerrero must have looked like furniture movers in business suits. Secret Service agents did not search them or their gifts and escorted them into the Oval Office, courtesies Dad boasted about to us.

Dad and F.B. explained their mission, but the discussion about American citizenship was brief. President Roosevelt sympathized and expressed hopes for their success then turned the conversation to fishing in Guam. As a fisheries expert, F.B. told Roosevelt about the abundance in Guam's waters. While F.B. talked of fish species and habits, Dad told of lures, techniques, and memorable catches. Roosevelt's secretary interrupted three times, advising him of the time and that an ambassador he expected had arrived and was waiting. The president brushed aside the reminders. Despite his full appointment schedule and a waiting ambassador, President Roosevelt kept Dad and F.B. 15 minutes longer than their allotted time. As governor, I know what it is to entertain appointments one after another. My appointment secretary often had to remind me that "We're behind schedule, people are waiting, and the waiting room is full."

After Dad and Mr. Leon Guerrero's visit, Senators Ernest W. Gibson of Vermont and Millard Tydings of Maryland introduced S.1450, "A Bill to Confer United States Citizenship upon Certain Inhabitants of the Island of Guam and Extend the Naturalization Laws Thereto," on February 10, 1937, the first session of the 75th Congress. The bill passed in the Senate but failed in the House.

The Navy Department again undermined the effort and opposed the bill. In written testimony dated March 20, 1937, Navy Secretary Claude A. Swanson wrote:

"At the present time, as citizens of Guam, the people of that possession enjoy the privileges of United States citizenship and have few, if any, of the obligations connected therewith. They are accorded passport privileges, have no Federal taxes or tariffs to pay, receive free medical and educational services, and are, in general, a particularly privileged people."

After stating that the Navy's policy was to protect CHamorus and guard them from exploitation, Swanson said CHamorus not only needed federal economic help, but "careful training and supervision from the paternal island government."

Swanson continued, "There is every indication that these people have not yet reached a state of development commensurate with the personal independence, obligations, and responsibilities of United States citizenship. It is believed that such a change of status at this time would be most harmful to the native people..."

While the Navy considered us "a particularly privileged people," we thought of ourselves as kept in abeyance. The Navy's "careful training and supervision" was little different from dictatorship. A velvet cage is still a prison. A pampered mistress has no honor. If the cage is not velvet-lined and the mistress has no say in her condition, she is oppressed.

We would not become U.S. citizens for another 14 years after Dad and Mr. Leon Guerrero's visit to Washington. By then, it came from Washington's worried reaction to growing CHamoru dissatisfaction and unrest in response to the questionable military land-taking. The pursuit for self-government began again immediately after the war. With it came the quest to define CHamoru political status.

The Guam Congress of 1941 reconvened in 1945 amid postwar optimism and enthusiasm for a promised election in 1946. Adm. Charles A. Pownall, the last Naval governor of Guam, pledged to extend limited lawmaking authority to the new congress, thus renewing the CHamoru appetite for the political process. The 1946 election resulted in victory for Dad, F.B. Leon Guerrero, Jake Calvo, Antonio Won Pat, Jesus Okiyama, and Rosa T. Aguigui, Guam's first congresswoman.

Despite Pownall's assurances, the new congress remained powerless. It was so helpless it earned the sarcastic nickname *"kongresson dammot"* — the flaccid penis congress. In March 1949, Governor Pownall denied the Guam Congress the authority to summon and question naval government employees suspected of profiteering. A bitter clash ensued, and the members of the House of Assembly walked out in protest. Pownall dismissed the assemblymen and threatened to replace them with his appointees. The standoff made national news, which led to action in Guam's behalf in Congress.

In 1950, President Harry S. Truman signed the Organic Act of Guam and transferred jurisdiction over the island from the Navy to the Department of Interior, where it remains. In Congress, jurisdiction over Guam rests with the Committee of Energy and Natural Resources. Throughout my terms as governor, I opposed our relegation to the category of natural resources. Washington has scoffed at my efforts to lobby for a cabinet-level Department of Native American Affairs. The United States continues to devalue her native peoples — the hundreds of different native peoples of North America, Alaska, and the Pacific islands. I also lobbied for the creation of an Organization of Micronesian States, but that too fell on deaf ears.

"With my love and tears, Father"

At the end of 1935, a series of earthquakes rocked Guam. Aftershocks continued almost daily for more than two months. In December of the following year, while Dad was away, another earthquake shook the island. It was the worst one in 30 years and occurred in the dead of night. I was asleep but woke up to a strange, high-pitched whistling whine. I sensed it more than heard it. A low, distant rumble followed. It grew closer and stronger, then the house began to shake. Everything started rattling — the floorboards and ceiling creaked, the windows clattered, the cupboards in the kitchen flew open. Dishes, glassware, pots, pans, and canned goods tumbled from the shelves. In the living room, knickknacks, vases, and picture frames crashed to the floor. We all jumped from bed in a panic and struggled to stay upright. The floor undulated. Terrified, we fled into the street.

In the dark night, people staggered and stumbled out of their homes. Many started crying and praying. Some fell to their knees or flat on the ground. The quake lasted a few minutes and subsided slowly. The ground trembled to a stop, then a strange silence enveloped the city. We climbed to our feet, our hearts pounding, and looked to make sure everyone was present. Like our neighbors, we were barefoot and dressed in nightclothes. For a long time, no one wanted to go back inside their houses. They sensed aftershocks would follow the main quake. All of us — Mama and her nine children — gathered on Auntie Butler's porch, all babbling at once.

In the rush to get out of the house, Mama grabbed Donald from his crib and ran. When her panic eased, she realized she did not have a blanket or dry diaper for him. She worried about his exposure to the early morning chill and dampness because he was sick and had been feverish. Donald, who was 11 months old, had gone into convulsions several times since his birth. The only time I ever saw my mother frightened and unnerved was when Donald convulsed. His bout with high fever made matters worse. He was so ill she feared he would die. On top of the pressures of Dad's absence and Donald's convulsions, Mama was also pregnant for the 11th time.

Mama sent me back into the house for Donald's things. I was scared to be indoors, but Mama scolded me to hurry. I entered our dark and quiet house and tripped over toppled furniture. The house was eerie and tomb-like. The floor seemed solid and steady, but I did not trust it to stay that way. I dashed to the bedroom, grabbed whatever baby things I could find, and ran out, panting.

Nearly everyone stayed outside until around 5 a.m. There were a few aftershocks but only minor ones. When all seemed safe, people went back inside. We straightened our house then went to school as usual. The earthquake was everyone's only topic of discussion that day. As school let out that afternoon, another strong tremor shook the island. Panic began again as the ground moved, and frightened people stumbled and fell. In the daylight, we could see the ground undulating like the ocean.

My cousin Dolly and I had just rounded the corner near Tun Vicente Martinez's store and were in front of Alan Cruz's house when the quake knocked us down. Spread-eagled on the ground, we watched in horror as a fissure opened up a few feet in front of us. It ripped raggedly along the street for several yards. It left a gash about 2 feet wide. I do not know how deep it went; we could not see the bottom. Two other fissures opened in other parts of the city, and for the rest of the day, people went from one to the other, crowding around all three. The fissures seemed bottomless and sparked rumors they reached all the way to Hell. Navy trucks loaded with coral gravel filled the cracks a day or two later. Infrastructure damage was minor and repaired quickly.

The quakes of 1936 occurred just weeks after Dad left for Washington. He had to have heard about them while waiting in Manila and was likely worried. He was away from us for eight months and missed us as much as we missed him. He had a photograph portrait made of himself in Washington and sent it to us with a telling inscription. It read, "To my dearest ones, my wife and children. I present this living memory of myself with my love and tears, Father. May 10th, 1937." The portrait remains in my possession. It hung in my chambers during both terms and hangs now in my office at home. I keep it in sight to remind me of the promise I made to him and for the comfort of knowing he still watches over me.

Not long after we received Dad's portrait, Mama gave birth to my sister Beverly June on June 8, 1937. Junie, as we call her, brought our number to 10. Donald recovered from his fever and convulsions, but his growth and development suffered. An adult now, Donald lives in humble self-sufficiency, gathering and selling coconuts to support himself. He knows he can rely on the family but prides himself on his independence. I often envy him the freedom and simplicity of his lifestyle.

"To my dearest ones, my wife and children. I present
this living memory of myself with my love and tears,
Father. May 10th, 1937."

— B. J. Bordallo

Dad came home in July 1937 to a huge welcoming celebration at the stadium. Mr. Leon Guerrero remained in the United States another year. Governor McCandlish, who had been ordered by Adm. Ernest J. King, the chief of Naval Operations, to rescind his exorbitant property tax hike and immediate payment demand, was also ordered to apologize to the Bordallo family. Everyone believed McCandlish's action was in retaliation for Dad's going over his head and straight to Washington. Uncle Tom cabled Dad about the hike and payment demand, and he went to the Navy Department to protest. McCandlish complied with King's order but was standoffish for the remainder of his tour. Commander James T. Alexander relieved McCandlish in February 1938. The harassment of the Bordallo family continued.

"Now I know you are a white man"

When I was about 8 or 9 years old, I listened to Uncle Tom relate a story that has troubled me ever since.

The Navy's public works director, a commander, ordered the removal of topsoil from Bordallo property. The Navy government arbitrarily took topsoil from other private properties, but the landowners were too intimidated to protest. Angered by what he considered theft of property, and suspicious of the commander's authority to order the removals, Uncle Tom went directly to Governor George Alexander to lodge a formal complaint. As Uncle Tom headed home from his meeting, the public works commander confronted him at the corner of Dorn Hall and Leary School. The officer berated Uncle Tom, talking down to him as though he were an errant underling. The commander demanded to know what Uncle Tom told the governor. Uncle Tom refused to be intimidated; it was none of the commander's business. The commander called Uncle Tom a son-of-a-bitch to his face and said, "Who the hell do you think you are?"

It was not the name-calling that enraged Uncle Tom; it was the question of his identity. Already embarrassed by the public dressing-down, Uncle Tom exploded in anger.

"Why you son-of-a-bitch," he snarled. "You come here and think because you're a Navy officer you can walk all over us. You come into our properties and do whatever the hell you want. Who the hell do *you* think you are?"

The commander realized he had aroused Uncle Tom's indignation and backed down. Uncle Tom was the bigger and heavier of the two. The officer's demeanor changed; he smiled, offered his hand, and apologized, even addressing Uncle Tom as "Mister Bordallo."

"Now I know you are a white man, Mr. Bordallo," the commander said.

I listened to Uncle Tom relate the episode to the rest of the family. The handshake did not placate Uncle Tom. In those days, the Americans were blatantly racist, supremacist, and colonialist. They looked down on us as lesser beings. We all knew it and felt it. The commander's statement to Uncle Tom has puzzled me since. Did being a white man mean one had to be forceful, foul-mouthed, and belligerent?

The Navy guarded its power and authority over Guam and went to great lengths to exhibit its control, no matter how trivial. The Navy government levied taxes on tuba production and required tuba producers to paint the bases of their coconut tree trunks white to show that they paid the tax. Painted tree trunks became a much-disliked symbol of Navy government regimentation. After I renovated Government House in 1975, Madeleine drew criticism for having the base of tree trunks on the grounds painted white. She thought it gave the grounds a neat and finished look, but to CHamorus it symbolized Navy oppression.

The great Jack Dempsey and the mysterious Professor Polansky

In December 1939, two years after Dad's Washington, D.C., trip, news came from Sumai that the China Clipper was bringing the great Jack Dempsey to Guam. Dempsey was on his way to Manila. Throngs gathered at the Pan Am pier in Sumai to greet the former world heavyweight boxing champion. At a Rotary Club luncheon in his honor at the Elks Club, Dempsey announced he would referee a fight in Guam to help raise funds for the local chapter of the American Red Cross.

Hundreds of us crowded outside the Elks Club to catch a glimpse of him. As shy children, none of us dared to accost him, but I decided the risk was worth it. I mounted the steps of the Elks Club and positioned myself where I knew Jack Dempsey would pass. When he emerged with a large group of other men, I reached out and grabbed his hand. Dempsey's hand was so big I could only grasp his thumb. He smiled down at me and let me, grinning from ear to ear, shake his thumb.

Word that he would referee a fight spread around the island. There was no need to advertise. On Christmas evening 1939, spectators packed Dad's stadium to watch Dempsey referee the main event.

The first fight on the card featured Tony Palolo against Slugger Quitugua. The fight ended in a draw. The second fight pitted Piston Sakai against Kid Mafnas. The fight had to be stopped, and Piston was credited with a technical knockout. In the third fight, Nick de Mike defeated the Umatac Caveman, Gorilla Topasna.

During the intermission, local talent entertained the restless, eager crowd. Mama's friend, Mrs. Waskey, played her piano accordion; the Elks Club Minstrel Show performed some skits; then Professor Veth, a Navy crewman on the USS *Gold Star* and amateur aerial acrobatics performer, stunned the crowd. The Umatac Minstrels, a group of school children under the direction of Tun Francisco Q. Sanchez, sang for the audience. Jack Dempsey and the main event were next.

Bill Lujan, Dad's stadium manager and announcer, was a colorful and imaginative character who loved the drama and action of the boxing ring. With a packed house and the former world champion waiting in the wings, Bill was in his glory. He stepped into the ring and milked the crowd's excitement.

"Laaadies and gentlemen," he bellowed, drawing out his words for better effect. "And now, for the main event of the evening..." He introduced the boxers at each corner. K.O. Salas and Dynamite King bounced forward, gloved hands raised, prancing before the audience. They knew their fight was not really the main attraction.

"And our special referee for this bout is none other than the Heavyweight Boxing Champion of the Wooorld," Lujan said. The crowd's roar nearly drowned him out. "Ladies and gentlemen, it gives me great pride and pleasure to introduce the one, the only Champion of the World, Jack Dempsey!" The cheers, the applause, the stamping and whistling, and the yelling were deafening.

I watched the entire fight from the ring skirt and felt every jolt and vibration of the action. My eyes darted from the fighters to Dempsey. I do not remember who won the fight, but after it ended, I got a chance to meet Jack Dempsey at ringside. Bill introduced me as the stadium owner's son. Towering above me, Dempsey said, "How do you do, Ricky?" Then he offered his huge hand for a real handshake. Awed, I could only answer, "Fine." When he asked me if I liked boxing, I overcame my shyness and answered with enthusiasm. I tried to impress him with my knowledge of the sport and of famous bouts.

Dempsey was supposed to leave Guam the next day, but Pan Am canceled the Clipper flight for some reason. Dempsey stayed an extra day in Guam, and we children followed him everywhere he went until he left the island.

To draw audiences to the stadium, Dad and Bill dreamed up attractions. A promoter himself, Bill came up with catchy, American-style names for local boxers so spectators would come out of curiosity. They would want to know what the Umatac Caveman looked like or how good a slugger Slugger Quitugua was. What CHamoru boxers lacked in height and mass, they made up for in strength, endurance, and speed. Hard physical labor, training, and a diet of natural foods every day made them formidable athletes. They could hold their own against American servicemen who boxed in the regular smokers. They did not often lose to the American boxers in their own weight class. The bouts between CHamoru and American boxers were popular and well-attended, but Dad and Bill never left attendance to chance. They were masters at CHamoru-style promotion.

To advertise fights, they would decorate a jitney with balloons, streamers, and posters of the boxers. Bill would drive it around town, often with me riding along. One year, we entered the decorated jitney in the Island Fair parade. Public exposure for the stadium was too good to pass up. The annual parade began in front of the library, made its way to the Santa Cruz intersection near the Torres house, turned onto Hernan Cortez Street and passed in front of our house, then went past Seaton Schroeder School, turned at the Elks Club, and ended at the Plaza de España. There the floats could undergo public inspection. Our float featured a makeshift boxing ring on a flatbed truck. Dressed in boxer shorts and our own, child-size boxing gloves, Paul and I would prance about, sparring in the ring throughout the parade.

In addition to the roaming jitney and boxing float, Dad also promoted the stadium as an all-purpose public hall. Indoor basketball games and track meets, cockfights, and the annual governor's ball took place there. It had ample room for an orchestra, a dance floor, and the governor's guests. Once a year, decorators transformed the stadium from a smoky, sweaty sports arena into a glittery, colorful wonderland, peopled by Navy officers in fancy uniforms, men in tuxedos, and ladies in beautiful gowns.

Dad and Bill also looked for interesting local talent to enlist for intermission entertainment. The more offbeat and unusual the acts were, the better the chances of packing the house. The act that sticks in my memory was Professor Polansky's. I knew Professor Veth was a sailor who often performed his acrobatics routine during his tour in Guam, but Professor Polansky was a mystery. I tried to find out about him and his trick, but no one would tell me anything. Even Mama, who always spoke the truth, was evasive. Dad and Bill were secretive about Polansky but promoted the act to the hilt. The Polansky posters took top billing over fights on the card.

It was Dad's idea to mount a black coffin on an open jitney and drive it around town, touting that Polansky would escape the coffin before everyone's eyes without breaking the seals. The gimmick worked better than expected. Because coffins were associated with death, people flocked around the jitney, curious, skeptical, and suspicious. Sealing someone alive in a casket was dangerous and almost sacrilegious. It seemed too incredible to believe. If Polansky could do as the posters claimed, he was a true magician.

I was not the only one trying to figure out who Professor Polansky was and where he came from. It seemed everyone was curious. There were no unfamiliar faces in town, not even among the military people. Accustomed to being in the know, I was frustrated by the lack of inside information. I heard a rumor that Polansky almost died during rehearsals and ended up in the hospital. On the big night, I positioned myself at ringside and examined underneath the ring for a trap door or some other device that explained the trick. As spectators filed into the stadium, I examined every part of the ring but found nothing unusual. I looked for Dad, but he was nowhere in sight.

The audience filled every seat in the stadium. The act was so incredible the whole community turned out. There were more servicemen than usual, as well as several progressive but conservative CHamoru ladies. Most women considered boxing an uncouth male pastime, improper for them to witness. The Polansky act prompted a bending of the rules.

The main event had little appeal; the crowd came for Polansky. When the preliminary fights ended, Bill stepped into the ring.

"Ladies and gentlemen, tonight you will witness an incredible feat of magic," Bill said as stagehands carried the coffin into the ring. They placed a small table, a candle, and a box of matches beside it. Bill then invited anyone in the audience to examine the coffin. Several eager fellows jumped into the ring and inspected the coffin, evaluating the sides and lid. Satisfied, they nodded to the crowd and exited the ring. Then the house lights dimmed.

"Ladies and gentlemen," Bill said, his voice low and dramatic, "Professor Polansky!"

The stadium lights switched off, leaving only the spotlight above the ring. It cast a swirling, smoky cone of light around the coffin. A figure in a black robe, his face hidden by a hood, emerged from the dressing rooms and made his way to the ring. Without unveiling himself or speaking, he climbed into the coffin and laid down. The stagehands replaced the coffin lid and screwed it down. Afterwards, a boisterous group of sailors climbed into the ring and announced they were not satisfied with the sealing. They produced a long rope, looped it around the coffin, and knotted it tightly.

"Let's see him get out of that," one of them said. They climbed out of the ring, laughing and certain the trickster would fail.

The stagehands placed four black screens around the coffin. Then the spotlight flicked off, plunging the stadium into darkness. The crowd gasped, then fell silent, listening for any sound, any movement, but there was nothing. I struggled to adjust my eyes but could only stare blankly toward the center of the ring. After about five minutes, a faint glow appeared behind the screens. As it grew brighter, we realized it was the candle on the table. Someone lit it.

The stadium lights flicked back on, and stagehands rushed to remove the screens. The candle was burning, but the rope was still tied around the coffin. The sailors climbed back into the ring and untied the rope. The stadium hands removed the coffin lid. It was empty. The audience applauded wildly, whistling and hooting with delight. But Professor Polansky did not reappear, nor did he return to the ring to receive the applause. He vanished and never appeared again.

I never stopped wondering about Polansky, how he did his trick, and what happened to him afterward. I pestered Bill, but he refused to tell me. I also asked Dad countless times over the years, but he ignored my questions. Before Dad died in 1984, I asked him again. I was a grown man, the governor of Guam, but Dad became irritated and shushed me like an impudent child. He took the secret to his grave. Now Polansky will always remain a mystery.

Chapter 8

I could be a cowboy but not a Boy Scout

Josephine's birth in July 1938 brought our number to 11 and prompted Dad's search for a larger, permanent home. Mama had always longed for one, but Dad delayed the search until we outgrew rented housing. He offered to buy Tun Pedro Martinez's house on Hernan Cortez, two blocks further east from our old house across Auntie Butler's. Tun Pedro rejected Dad's offer until Mama added her request. Tun Pedro was fond of Mama. He respected her talent and education and admired her integrity and propriety. He would not refuse her.

Tun Pedro was arguably the most prominent and wealthiest business-man in Hagåtña. He owned the island's only ice plant, which the Navy built and assigned to Tun Pedro by special arrangement. His holdings included several other buildings and city lots, and his warehouses and supply yards occupied most of the block behind our old house. Tun Pedro also owned a beautiful summer home on a hilltop in Sasa', between Piti and Sumai.

Tun Pedro's cattle ranch in Dåndan, west of Yoña, was the largest one at the time. His biannual cattle roundups were wonderful. We would join several other Hagåtña families in a caravan to the ranch to help round up his cattle, as many as 1,000 head at a time. Chasing cattle in Dåndan's dusty hills and valleys fueled my imagination. Working under the hot sun, I would pretend we were in the desert badlands of the American West, just like in the cowboy movies.

Tun Pedro showed his appreciation by spreading a huge feast. His cooks and ranch hands always made special effort to include all kinds of wild fruits — *månha* (young, green coconuts) and thick stalks of *tupu* (sugarcane) arranged in piles already cleaned, peeled, and ready to eat. These treats were made especially for the children. There would also be fresh and dried beef, pork, ham, chicken, game birds, fish, and huge pots of rice. I remember gazing into two gigantic basins of hard-boiled eggs. There were thousands of them. The feast was lavish because there were so many families to feed. In addition to Tun Pedro's extended family, there were the Johnstons, Torreses, Villardes, Uncle Tom's family, and mine. The families of Tun Pedro's ranch hands and household help would be there also.

Tun Pedro and his wife, Tan Maria, had 12 children whose ages corresponded with ours. His fourth son, Luis, was a few years older than me, but we shared many of the same duties as working sons. Luis' nickname was To', and he was Tun Pedro's *kiridu* — his favorite. I sometimes envied how close To' was to Tun Pedro. Mama and Dad showed no favoritism toward any of their children. The Martinez child closest to my age was Josephina, nicknamed "Peng." Antonia, whose nickname was "Noning," was a strikingly beautiful girl. I had a crush on her, but she was Paul's age, and I had no chance of winning her affections. She thought of me only as a big brother.

My interest in women, especially beautiful ones, developed early. I was 11 years old and thought of myself as a mature young man. Mama and Dad treated me like an adult, and I conducted myself as one. But outside our home, my cousins, friends, and playmates did not credit me with much maturity. I had crushes on many girls, some older, some younger than myself, but most of them thought of me only as dependable, little "Ricky Boy." I did not always gain their favors.

There were many pretty girls to admire in Hagåtña. Beauty surrounded me. Everywhere in town, girls of all ages sat on their doorsteps or porches, combing each other's hair for hours until their locks shone like satin. Long, shiny hair was a hallmark of CHamoru femininity esteemed by CHamoru men. As young as I was, the romance of the ritual enamored me, and I would watch admiringly. I never had to go far to appreciate beauty. There was an abundance in my immediate vicinity: my own sisters and cousins and their friends, Patsy Notley, the Martinez girls, the Johnston girls, the Torres girls, the Villarde sisters, the Underwood sisters, and the Mayhew sisters next door.

Our new house and the Mayhew house were back-to-back. The Navy's cold storage plant was a few yards up the street on the Mayhews' side of the block. Not far from it was Auntie Rose's house on Soledad Street in front of the San Antonio Bridge (now landlocked within the Old Spanish Bridge Park).

The south side of our house faced Hernan Cortez. This area of Hagåtña was the center of commercial activity. It was where I grew up.

In addition to the house, Dad also bought a race car from a Navy officer who, for some unknown reason, brought it to Guam. No one could figure out why the man would go to the trouble and expense of bringing such a vehicle to a small island. We had no raceways, and our narrow, winding roads were not for racing machines. The speed limit was only 25 mph in the country and 10 in the city. Why Dad would buy the car was also something no one could figure out, but I was glad he did.

The car was a real racer, sleek and futuristic, like the ones in the newsreels about the Indy 500. It was bright red and shiny with broad, cupped fenders like the "Maria Clara" bell sleeves of a lady's gown. The body was cylindrical and narrow. It looked like an airplane fuselage with a bullet-shaped tail. The driver's seat was in a small, cramped compartment. Its angled glass windshield curved low in front of the driver. Dad put the car up on blocks in the garage. I often climbed into it and imagined myself a begoggled race driver speeding around a raceway in a cloud of dust. Until the occupying Japanese confiscated it, the car never left the garage.

I could only imagine myself a race car driver, but I could be a cowboy and, better still, a real-life cattle baron. Someone once said there was a difference between a cowboy and a cattleman. Real cowboys led rough, hard lives on the range while cattlemen lorded over their cattle on a ranch. At our ranches, I got a taste of both work styles. The Bordallo family owned three large cattle ranches: one in Kotot in the hills near Talo'fo'fo, another in Hågat, and a third behind Mount Lamlam, a few miles south of Hågat. We owned about 7,000 acres and over 1,000 head of cattle, including several that belonged to me.

Dad's livestock agent, Francisco "Galabook" Delgado, was a spry womanizer with a wonderful talent for relating his exploits, but he did not look like a Don Juan. He was less than 5 feet tall and very skinny. His trademark was a weather-beaten Stetson worn sideways with the upturned brim on his forehead. I called him Sir Gallahad because it sounded like his nickname and matched his reputation. I enjoyed accompanying him on livestock-buying trips because he would tell me about his bedroom adventures, and we would laugh. He taught me as much about charming ladies as he did about judging livestock and bargaining prices.

In time, I started buying cattle with my own money. I felt like a cattle baron the day I registered my personal brand with the Navy government's Department of Records and Accounts. By the outbreak of the war, I owned about 20 cows and bulls. They were in with the rest of the family herd but bore the brand "RJB."

Our Hågat estate was a huge working farm and ranch. There was always plenty of work to do, but it was fun work. For two weeks a year, I would live with our vaqueros to round up cattle for de-ticking. Cattle ranching gave me a chance to be a real cowboy, a real-life Hopalong Cassidy without the bad guys. On horseback, I would yip and whoop just like in a cowboy movie. De-ticking time was especially cowboy-ish. After corralling the herds, we would drive them down a narrow chute, one at a time, into the dipping vats.

We would switch from horses to carabao to round up steers in the high country. Carabao were slower but stronger and more efficient on rough, steep terrain. These placid, lumbering beasts are more sure-footed than horses and more intelligent than cattle. They also have excellent homing instincts, and with careful training, could even harness themselves to the plow. Their exceptional intelligence and homing instinct were the stuff of jokes and stories, some real, some fanciful. Farmers and ranchers enjoying "agi," *aguayente*, (CHamoru moonshine) could rely on the carabao of their unconscious comrades to get them home. One popular story was of a Yoña farmer who boasted that not only could his carabao harness itself, but it could also plow his fields while he took a siesta under a tree. But the punch line to prove he was not that clever was, "Yeah, but if you were truly smarter than your carabao, you would have trained it to plant and harvest as well, no?"

In comparing the intelligence of carabao and men, people laughed at attempts to mix CHamoru, Spanish, and American English into a single situation. One joke told of an "Americanized" CHamoru who ordered, "Eleven the carabao and let's go to Fly." Those who appreciated wry CHamoru humor thought the joke was hilarious. *"Onse,"* the Spanish word for "eleven" also means "to harness." *"Lålo',"* an area in Barrigada, is also the CHamoru word for "fly," the insect pest. The humor stemmed from the forced mixture of cultural dissimilarities and the innocence that tried to blend them.

I think CHamorus seek humor in all situations, no matter how tragic. During the smallpox epidemic of the early 20th century, people died by the hundreds, but the tragedy spawned an anecdote that survived for many years afterward. It told of two men who had the task of collecting and burying the dead. The daily death toll was so great that the men had to stack corpses like firewood onto a bull cart. The men drank to numb themselves to the unpleasantness. Exhausted from several days of relentless work and staggering drunk, they drove their loaded bull cart to a mass gravesite outside of town. After emptying the cart, the pair heard a feeble voice from the pit, pleading that it was not dead yet. The intoxicated men looked at each other. "Be quiet!" one of them growled. "The doctor said you're dead, so you're dead!"

The story was meant to discourage drunkenness. It may sound insensitive to non-CHamorus, but rather than an indictment of CHamoru character, it exemplified a realization that the newly arrived Americans were different from the Spanish. The Americans, who put great store in scientific proof and almost none in faith alone, had begun to impose their strange beliefs upon a people to whom the spiritual and supernatural were fundamental realities. The epidemic joke exposed the clashing of two realities.

In time, the alien American beliefs and values gained a foothold in CHamoru society, but they also gave rise to a kind of fatalism and sense of inferiority. While maintaining that equality was the hallmark of Americanism, the Americans did not accept us as equals. They badgered us to strive higher but also told us that equality was beyond our simplicity and political immaturity. The messages were contradictory. In failing to measure up to the Navy government's standards of Americanism, we belittled ourselves and each other in jest, not realizing the damage we were causing to our national psyche. I am as guilty as my fellow CHamorus of causing such damage.

While we could disparage ourselves, all CHamorus take offense at Magellan's branding us as thieves. Islas de los Ladrones, the Islands of Thieves. History books and world maps referred to Guam and the Marianas as the "Ladrones" well into the 20th century. No one was immune to the hurt it caused, but I never allowed myself to grow numb to the insult. I am a lifelong victim of racial insults, so racial slurs against other minority peoples repulse me. I wonder if the authors of such slurs appreciate the effect of their words. The effect on me has been complete rejection and dogged determination to prove them wrong.

Like Dad, I wanted to know all issues of importance and to be involved in as many of the goings-on in town. In my own way, I succeeded. Only one escaped me — I was never a Boy Scout. Established in 1935, the Guam Chapter of the Boy Scouts of America was active. By 1939, there were several troops around the island. After the war, Col. Blaisdale and Dr. Joe Sataloff, who later became a dear friend, reorganized the chapter. I wanted very much to be a Boy Scout. Sometimes, if time and chores permitted, I would go to Bilibek School and peek into the classroom reserved for troop meetings. Wonderful Boy Scout symbols and paraphernalia filled the room. I wanted to be a part of it all, to enjoy Boy Scout adventures, but Dad refused to let me join.

Although I asked him many times, Dad would not yield. No matter what approach I made or what reasons I gave, his answer was the same. He always had a counterargument.

"If it is friends you want, you don't have to join Boy Scouts. You have enough brothers and sisters and cousins for companions," he would say.

I wanted to learn survival skills and life-saving techniques, to go on weekend campouts, to march proudly in formation in a Boy Scout uniform and behind a troop pennant, but Dad never shared my point of view. "Camping? You can go camping at Kotot. You'll learn more about survival there than you would rubbing sticks together in the jungle," he would counter. Sometimes he was heartless.

Denied membership, I would alter my route to avoid the Hagåtña troop whenever the boys came marching down the street. I encountered the troop once. They were resplendent in leather hiking boots and canvas backpacks. Several scouts waved at me. Their gesture was friendly, but I cringed in humiliation. They were marching proudly behind their troop pennant while I stood barefoot beside my delivery wagon. My hurt was so bad I could not bear another encounter.

Mayanghulo', a paradise in paradise

Dad was right. I did have access to many scout-like activities. As the eldest of the Bordallo brothers, Dad inherited Mayanghulo', the choicest parcel of the Hågat estate with the largest, nicest house. Uncle Carlos and Uncle Tom also had summer houses on the estate, but theirs were not as showy as Dad's. Uncle Carlos' house was on a knoll further inland, near the vegetable gardens and chicken coops. Uncle Tom's was on the south bank, near the mouth of the Asñåmu River, which coursed through the estate and emptied into the bay.

Every summer, as soon as the school term ended, we would pack our bags for a three-month stay at Mayanghulo'. Mama would begin packing about a month in advance because it was such a major undertaking. By the summer of 1940, she had 11 children and was ready to have number 12, my brother Michael. Mama's packing signaled the start of a glorious and carefree summer for us. We still had chores to do at Mayanghulo', but the work was exciting and different, and our regular discipline was more relaxed.

Mayanghulo' was a small projection on the coast of Hågat Bay, about a mile south of the Orote Peninsula. It was our paradise in paradise. Our summer house sat high on a rocky bluff on the projection. White sandy beaches stretched from the base of the bluff northward to Tipalao on Orote Peninsula. Sumai lay about 3 miles further, on the Apra side of Orote. To the south, Hågat village stretched along the coast where three small, rocky islets lay just offshore. From our vantage high on the bluff, the islets seemed to sit on the horizon. I used to pretend they were pirate ships returning from adventure on the high seas. Our house was spacious and airy and offered panoramic vistas from every room. The west rooms overlooked the sea; the east rooms faced inland toward the hills. We had running water and electricity from a large generator that simultaneously charged several large batteries.

A long driveway led from the house to the Camino Real, the main road from Sumai to Hågat. At the top of the driveway, a crooked, old coconut tree, bent at a 45-degree angle, stretched out over the beach. The horizontal part was a long, natural bench. We would sit there for hours, watching the sea or the sparse traffic on the Camino Real. A gate at the bottom of the driveway separated it from the road. I once witnessed a gruesome traffic accident there.

The accident, one of the worst prior to the war, haunted me for months. I was only 7 then and was walking from the gate toward the house when I heard a car speeding from Sumai. Sensing something dreadful, I froze. Seconds later, the car appeared and veered suddenly. I watched in horror as it crumpled around a coconut tree across the road, opposite our gate. The sound was loud and terrible. Shards of glass, pieces of metal, smoke, and dust exploded into the air. I ran to the car and peered inside. Blood was splattered everywhere. The bodies of several servicemen lay twisted and tangled. One of the men was moaning. I was terrified and started to run for help. Just then, Dad and others arrived on the scene. Dad spotted me near the gate and yelled, "Stay there, Ricky! Don't come over here." But his warning was too late. The rescuers comforted the victims until military police and Navy ambulances arrived. The gate reminded me of the accident and of the helplessness and fear I felt.

Just north of the gate there was a large pigeon coop. We raised pigeons and chickens for their eggs and for food. We also kept honeybees. The chicken yard and the beehives were south of the house. The pigeons would converge on our roof by the thousands, making it look like a living thing. There were so many they carpeted the roof like a cooing, quivering blanket of gray and white. When they took flight, they darkened the sky.

Dad and his brothers divided the Hågat estate into specific work areas. A cattle pen and a milking house, a small abattoir, and a large pasture were east of Uncle Carlos' house. To the east of Uncle Tom's were the rice paddies, the liquor distillery, and a large hog pen. I would spend hours watching the complex rice-threshing machines or the fruit-pressing machines at the distillery. Behind the hog yard were vast mango and breadfruit orchards. There was also a large vegetable garden with another fruit orchard nearby. We would eat our fill of fresh fruit in season. Mangoes, papayas, bananas, oranges, tangerines, avocados, guavas, *iba'* (*Phyllantus acidus* or Guam gooseberry), *bilembines* (*Averrhoa carambola* or starfruit), picklefruit (*Averrhoa bilimbi*), and *åtes* (*Annona squamosa* or sweetsop) were cultivated in the orchards, but wild guavas, *kamachili* (*Pithecellobium dulce*), *pi'ot* (*Ximenia americana*), *anonas* (*Annona reticulata* or custard apple), and *mansanita* (*Muntingia calabura*) grew wild. Hundreds of stately coconut trees dotted the estate.

At least twice during our summer stay, the entire Pangelinan clan would gather for a huge feast. Scores of relatives would join farmhands, housemaids, their families, and Hågat villagers, who had helped with the harvesting. The gatherings were gigantic. Many people respected Dad and called him the "Duke of Mayanghulo'" in jest.

I loved these times. They gave me a chance to show off to my cousins. I was their tour guide and would introduce them to all the activities available. There was fishing, swimming, and canoeing at the beach. There was hunting for birds, monitor lizards, coconut crabs, land crabs, mangrove crabs, and fruit bats or exploring the various work activities and machinery. I especially liked taking them horseback riding since not many knew how. If they were too timid to try, they could opt for slower, steadier rides on the carabao. Astride my favorite horse, Girl, I would lead my braver and more experienced cousins along the beach from Tipalao to Hågat. Often, I would gallop off at full speed and leave them awed by my equestrian skill. Once, as I was showing off, a bee stung Girl's rump. She bolted and threw me headlong over her head. I flew several yards off to the side of the road and lay unconscious. When I came to, Mama and my aunts scolded me for being foolish. My cousins just laughed. I was uninjured but sorely embarrassed.

My grandaunts, Nanan Lia, and Nanan Acha, lived in Hågat, not far from the estate. Whenever Dad brought in boxers from the Philippines, he would house them at Nanan Lia's, where they set up a training camp. Nanan Lia, a religious woman, stored four or five life-sized statues of the agonized Christ in a special room in her house. The statues, draped in ornate velvet capes and robes, were for Lenten services at church. We children would often dare one another to go into the dark storeroom. The rest of us would wait below the window outside and moan like ghosts whenever someone was fool enough to take the dare. We often got our ears twisted for screaming, laughing, and running in and out of the storeroom.

The clan got together many times throughout the year. There were traditional gatherings like the ones at Mayanghulo', or at Nanan Chong's Santa Cruz novenas in Tutuhan, or the beach picnics at Apotguan, Tomhom or Tangison, which was further north and even wilder than Tomhom. There were also special occasions that brought friends and several extended families together. The wedding of my cousin, Clara Mae Butler, was the most elegant one that comes to mind. Mae was the eldest, the first, and the only one of the Butler daughters to get married. Bea and Dolly became Carmelite nuns after the war.

Mae married Milton Champion in April 1939, after a long-distance love affair. Mae met Milton on Wake Island during a stopover. She was 18 years old then and was on her way home from school in the States. Milton, who was 13 years older than Mae, was Pan American's operations manager on Wake. Despite their age difference, Milton proposed, and Mae accepted. Their wedding ceremony and reception rivaled that of any other wealthy and sophisticated big-city American. Milton wore a smart tuxedo he borrowed from Dad. Mae and her bridesmaids wore the prettiest gowns I had ever seen. Mae allowed me to borrow photos of the wedding to include in this book.

To my delight, Mae asked Patsy Notley to be one of her bridesmaids. Patsy lived on San Ignacio Street, opposite the Gaiety Theater. She went to a finishing school in Manila and had returned to Guam just before Mae's wedding. Patsy was much older than me, but I thought she was the most beautiful woman in the world. I would have courted her if I were older, but since I was not, all I could do was admire her secretly. Throughout the wedding ceremony and reception, I gazed upon Patsy with unabashed ardor. My crush on her was easier to conceal in a busy crowd. I finally confessed to her about my boyhood crush and how beautiful I thought her. "And you still are," I said. Patsy smiled. She was in her 70s and hospitalized when I confessed. She died shortly afterward.

Clara Mae Butler and Milton Champion at their wedding in April 1939.

"Mae and her bridesmaids wore the prettiest gowns I had ever seen."

After Mae's wedding, we celebrated Irene's birthday. She turned 16 in December 1939. Mama and Dad threw a big party for her. It served as her formal coming out and was as grand as a wedding reception. Although scores of pretty girls attended, I was 11 years old at the time and more interested in the huge tubs of ice cream and the free-flowing soda pop.

"You're just a native"

To 11-, 12-, and 13-year-old CHamoru boys, pubescent machismo made proper and comfortable behavior in front of girls difficult to develop and master. This was especially true because we had learned from birth that women were special people. Politeness was not just a sign of good training and upbringing; it was a requirement of all children toward all elders and of all men toward all women. Young men were supposed to accord courtesy and respect to all women in their presence. Even before puberty, little girls ceased to be treated like children. They were young ladies who needed to be shielded from anything vulgar and crude.

While we boys struggled to behave properly with the girls, Roger Perry, the son of the Navy government's chief judge advocate, knew he was exempt from our standards of behavior. He flaunted his freedom to flirt openly and would tease our womenfolk. Drawn like moths to a flame, the girls were fascinated by his boldness and self-assurance. They would giggle at his antics, and with heads bowed shyly, they would hide flirtatious smiles behind their hands. We boys were not jealous of him but offended by his brazenness. Roger epitomized the American double standard for us — CHamoru women were attractive and entertaining, but CHamoru men were nonentities. Roger expected us to treat him like royalty, but he basked like a puppy in the attention girls paid him.

Because his father was a Naval officer and a high-ranking government official, Roger was mean, arrogant, and deserved a bust in the chops. I had never hit anyone in anger before I met him. For me, Roger personified the kind of carpetbaggery that is not content with exploitation; it must also destroy what it exploits. I have encountered it many times since the day I punched him. I call it the Roger Perry Syndrome. Roger did not like competition of any sort. As the son of a prominent and well-to-do CHamoru leader, I represented a threat to his exclusive importance. We disliked each other immensely. He saw me as a rival, and I saw him as a jackass.

Although I never antagonized him, Roger chafed whenever he saw me. His frustration got the better of him one day, and he came at me, intent on putting me in my place. He accosted me on the San Nicolas district bridge, opposite the entrance to the Navy Public Works compound. I was on the bridge and heading toward the Torres copra warehouse when he began yelling at me.

"Hey, you! Bordallo!" he shouted. "Hey, big shot, you think you're something special, don't you? Well, you're not. You're just a native. That's all you'll ever be."

Roger rushed at me and punched me hard in the stomach. At 11, I was no match for him. Roger was older, taller, and heavier. The blow knocked the wind out of me and brought me to my knees. No one had ever hit me like that. My breath returned with ferocious anger and a surge of adrenaline. In one swift motion, I balled my fist and swung at him as hard as I could. I struck his jaw and knocked him backward, head over heels, into the river. The Marine sentry at the Public Works gate saw everything. When Roger hit the water, the Marine came running with rifle in hand. Stunned by my own action, I did not know what to do next. I was afraid that if I ran, the sentry would shoot me. If I stayed, the incident would backfire on my family. When the Marine veered toward the river to rescue Roger, I made my escape.

I ran home and hid in the cellar. Breathless and scared, I listened for footsteps, certain that a regiment of Marines was on its way to drag me off to jail and slam me against the doors again. My heart was pounding in my ears, and pain was pulsing in my gut where Roger hit. My hand throbbed also. I waited in the cellar for a long time, but nothing happened, no marching footsteps, no Marines. After a while, I crawled out and crept into the house, praising my luck. But I knew the offense was going to cost me later.

At supper the following evening, Mama said, "I was talking to Mrs. Perry today." I froze in my seat. *"Here it comes,"* I thought. *"This is it."* Mama continued, "She mentioned something about a fight involving her son and you, Ricky."

I looked up from my plate. Mama was studying me. Dad seemed to be ignoring what she said. His behavior was unusual; he would not have deferred to Mama on such a serious matter.

"What happened, Ricky?" Mama asked. I began telling them what had happened, describing every detail. While Mama listened, Dad remained quiet, but there was a gleam in his eyes. When I finished, Mama seemed satisfied, but Dad's silence worried me.

My trouble with Roger Perry faded amid the busy preparations for Mae's wedding. I thought the episode was over until Dad summoned me to his office a few days after the wedding. He handed me a letter and said, "Deliver this to Commander Perry." I was dumbstruck. "What is it, Daddy? Is this about Roger and me?" I wanted desperately to ask but knew better. I hesitated, hoping he would offer some clue, but he did not. *"Sigi! Laguse',"* he said, waving me out the door. Go! Hurry.

I was nervous and scared when I entered the courthouse. I had no idea where to find Roger's father's office. The Navy men working there looked important and busy. Even the CHamoru employees appeared too busy to bother with an 11-year-old boy off the street. I gathered up my courage and asked for directions. A court employee led me to the chief judge advocate's office. Outside his door, I sucked in a breath, hoping no one could hear my heart pounding, and knocked. From behind the door, a man's commanding voice answered, "Come in."

I wanted to complete my errand quickly, so I opened the door, dashed in, handed Roger Perry's father the letter, and whirled around to leave.

"Just a minute, young man," Commander Perry said as I grabbed the doorknob. "Is your name Ricky?"

I turned slowly to face him. Commander Perry was standing behind a huge desk. He was tall, slender, and stern-faced. His demeanor matched the authority of his high office.

"Yes, sir. My father told me to give this letter to you," I said. Without taking his eyes from me, Commander Perry opened the letter while I waited uncomfortably beneath his gaze.

"So, you're B.J.'s son," he said with half a smile.

"Yes, sir," I said, not hiding my discomfort. Commander Perry then unfolded Dad's note, read it, and chuckled.

"So, you're the one who hit my son," he said as he laid the letter down and leaned forward toward me. "Well, Ricky, it seems Roger got what he deserved. Don't worry about it." He chuckled again at what must have been my visible relief. "You can go now."

Commander Perry surprised me completely. I expected him to be as imperious and haughty as his son. I thought he would demand a piece of my hide. I never expected him to see my side over his own child's. Yet, after weighing the facts and the information in Dad's note, the chief judge advocate ruled in my favor. I left Commander Perry's office wondering how a man so just could have a son who was the opposite.

Unlike Roger, who skillfully sought and hungrily lapped up female attention, I did not master the art of being comfortable with girls until I went to high school. I did not even know how to dance before then. I was a miserable wallflower at my first high school dance, but I studied the couples on the floor and memorized their steps and movements. I also practiced at home with my sisters. At the next school dance, I swallowed my fear and asked a girl to dance. I trampled her feet several times, but she kindly said nothing.

I graduated from the Guam Institute to George Washington High School in 1940. My new schoolmates seemed friendlier and more worldly than my previous ones. As a newcomer to public school, I had much to learn and was eager to participate in every activity. But I attended for only a year. The occupation began in 1941.

Students at George Washington wore uniforms. Boys wore denim trousers and white shirts. Girls wore navy blue skirts, white sailor tops, and red ties. We also had different teachers for different subjects, a new experience for me. Bill Lujan, Dad's stadium manager, taught hygiene; his brother Frank, who later became a judge, also was a teacher, as were James Sablan, Lagrimas Leon Guerrero Untalan, Cynthia Torres, and Carmen Dueñas , who was my mathematics teacher. Many other teachers also later became prominent in Guam history.

Guam history is only a recent mandatory addition to the school curriculum. Many of my generation did not have our history as a school subject to learn, to understand, and to appreciate. Few today know of all the famous people — American presidents, kings, queens, princes, prime ministers, statesmen, international diplomats, entertainers, and celebrities — who have traveled to Guam. I do not think many other small American communities can compare, nor can they say that they played an important but uncelebrated part in geopolitical history.

In 1939, the legendary Filipino statesman and scholar, Carlos Romulo, came to Guam to deliver the official charter of the island's Rotary Club chapter. Dad, Uncle Butler, and several other businessmen organized the Guam Rotary Club in 1938. Romulo was vice president of Rotary International then and was instrumental in the chartering of the Guam chapter. Uncle Butler was the chapter's first president. Dad succeeded him and served until the war.

After reorganizing the chapter in 1945, Dad became its first postwar president.

Romulo, who was already a diplomat of international standing, later became Secretary General of the United Nations General Assembly. He revisited Guam during my first term as governor.

Tun Ramon and the Japanese spy ship

Despite its seeming isolation and insignificance as a distant American military outpost, Guam has played roles in most of America's global political fights. In the Spanish-American War, she was an innocent victim. In World War I, Guam became the first U.S. soil to see "enemy action." Germany's control of the Northern Marianas and Japan's entry into the war on the Allied side brought the war closer to Guam.

In 1914, when the German cruiser *Cormoran* steamed into Apra Harbor, the Navy government found itself in a predicament. The *Cormoran* was out of coal and other provisions, but the Navy refused to resupply her. The United States was maintaining neutrality in the war, leaving the Navy government to take the stranded Germans and their ship into custody as "guests of the United States." The Americans and the Germans enjoyed friendly relations until 1917, when the United States entered the war. The German "guests" then became prisoners of war, and the *Cormoran* was an enemy warship. Navy Governor Captain Roy C. Smith demanded the *Cormoran's* surrender, but the German captain refused and scuttled his ship. The *Cormoran's* dead lay buried in the Naval Cemetery in Hagåtña.

Between 1938 and 1940, the war raging in Europe was a distant event, but we read concern in the faces of Navy officials in Guam. News of Japanese belligerence and their ferocious invasion of Manchuria prompted talk of war and eventual U.S. involvement. Some feared a world war, others welcomed it. Times were worrisome for Navy government officials and CHamorus as well, especially with the fortified Northern Marianas so close.

Despite the Japanese build-up on Saipan, Congress rejected President Roosevelt's request for funds to fortify Guam. According to my friend William Manchester, in his book *Goodbye Darkness*, a congressional aide epitomized Congress' attitude by "merrily" crying, "Guam, Guam with the wind" after the fortification bill's demise. When the issue came up again in 1940, Congress authorized the funding, but it was too late.

Fearing the United States would go to war, Dad and his fellow political leaders began to ponder the fate of CHamorus. Everyone's fears increased when the Navy government began evacuating its dependent wives and children to the States in April 1940. In November, a violent typhoon struck Guam. The damage was immense. The typhoon destroyed hundreds of homes, and many government buildings were either destroyed or damaged. Even the power plant's tall smokestack fell victim to the high winds. The Navy made infrastructure repairs with the federal funds earmarked for fortifications but did nothing to help the farmers, ranchers, and businesspeople who lost everything.

Dad went to see Governor George J. McMillin about civilian relief efforts only to learn that it was a low priority, so low that McMillin turned down the American Red Cross' $10,000 relief grant, saying the Navy government did not need it. McMillin's insensitivity angered Dad. My family did not need financial aid, but many other people needed it desperately. The Red Cross grant could have helped, but CHamorus had no say in the matter.

Not long after the typhoon, Dad received word that a Japanese ship had run aground in Malohloh. The ship was reportedly just a fishing trawler, but the uncertainty of the times and the talk of impending war made Dad and several others dubious. They decided to investigate for themselves. Dad woke me at 3 in the morning to accompany the group. As a 12-year-old, I had spent as much time in the company of older men as I did with my peers. Although Dad charged me with man-sized responsibilities, he did not often include me in his undertakings. That morning was different; going to investigate a suspected Japanese spy ship in the dead of night was a man-sized mission. Without ceremony or fanfare, he treated me like a grown man.

We set out before dawn in one of Dad's new International pickup trucks and arrived at Tun Ramon Baza's ranch house in Yoña at around 4 o'clock. Tun Ramon was a village leader widely admired and respected for his wisdom and philosophy. He had little formal education but had an uncanny knack for knowing the right thing to do. He was a hardworking and successful farmer who excelled in all his undertakings. His harvests always won praises for being the biggest and the best. Even his chickens, which produced eggs the size of duck eggs, had a reputation of excellence. He was one of Dad's dearest friends and a man who has had my deepest admiration for as long as I can remember.

Tun Ramon's house was not far from the main road. Breadfruit and mango trees stood sentinel near the house, and nearby banana stands bore heavy bunches of soon-to-be-cut bananas. Except for the chirrup of insects, the morning was quiet and still, the air damp and cool. It was still dark when we arrived, but smoke from a wood burning stove was already rising from the outside kitchen behind the house.

Dad called out, *"Buenas!"* and from deep inside the house came the reply, *"Fanhålom!"* He was calling us to come in with robust hospitality. I always looked forward to visiting Tun Ramon because of it. Heavy ifit wood furniture handmade by CHamoru craftsmen filled Tum Ramon's living room. We made our way through it and to the outdoor kitchen where Tan Rosa, Tun Ramon's wife, was preparing breakfast. A fire was roaring in her fire stove, which was typical of its kind, a raised pit bordered by concrete blocks or large rocks and topped by a grill of heavy gauge wire mesh. Her outside kitchen was typical also. Built like afterthoughts, outdoor kitchens were an important part of nearly every home before and even after the war. They were practical workshops for food preparation, cooking, and other grimy tasks.

Long strips of beef were hanging to dry above the fire, and a large, old-fashioned coffee pot was burbling with fresh-ground coffee that Tan Rosa would strain into mugs. Big steel pots and pans were hanging from nails in the rafters. Warmth and the aroma of coffee and breakfast filled the kitchen. Tan Rosa made a large pot of rice and thick *titiyas*, which were still hot, and bacon and eggs, both boiled and fried. Famished, I sat down and began to eat while the men talked about the grounded ship. I was listening intently until one of Tun Ramon's farmhands said, "Look, B.J., your son eats eggs like peanuts." Everyone, including Dad, laughed. Red-faced, I looked down and in front of me was an embarrassing pile of eggshells. I had eaten more than a dozen hard-boiled jumbo eggs.

After breakfast, we climbed into the truck and picked our way down the narrow road in the dark. We reached Malohloh but were still a considerable distance from the wreck site. We parked and proceeded on foot for another hour through the jungle to the beach. We met several people carrying away items from the ship. They said the police had removed the Japanese crewmen to Hagåtña for interrogation and were allowing anyone to salvage usable items. We reached the beach and found the ship laying at a crazy angle near the edge of the bay. Debris and hundreds of round glass floats littered the beach. A policeman was standing guard nearby, and several people were picking through the debris in the shallows.

We boarded the ship and began inspecting her from stem to stern. Fish filled the holds, but high-powered equipment filled the radio room. It looked too sophisticated for a fishing boat and seemed suspicious. Other rooms contained fishing nets and more glass floats. We helped ourselves to some of the nets, and I picked up a few floats for Mama.

We later learned that the crewmen told the same story: They were just fishermen who strayed off course and hit the reef. Navy authorities were satisfied with the story and allowed them to leave for Saipan. A year later, we watched the same fishermen return as Imperial Japanese naval officers with the invading force.

Abandoned

Apprehension about impending war increased throughout 1941. The 1940 typhoon was a bad omen. While the war in Europe escalated, and the relationship between the United States and Japan deteriorated, we found ourselves digging out of the rubble of a storm only to brace for a more violent, man-made one.

The evacuation of military dependents continued steadily throughout 1940. By October 1941, only a handful of Navy nurses and a pregnant Navy wife remained. As the military dependent population dwindled, many of us made the innocent assumption that the Navy government would next evacuate CHamoru women and children. But it soon became clear that our assumption was wrong.

When the evacuation began, I welcomed it as the noble thing to do. I accepted that the Navy would see to its own first and was certain that CHamoru dependents would follow soon after. It never occurred to me that the evacuation was exclusive. I was 13 and prepared to meet a man's fate, so long as Mama and the children, and all other CHamoru women and children, were safe. It crushed me to learn that they were not. I sat at supper that night unable to eat. I questioned Dad, who was just as embittered. The Navy, he said, was not concerned about the safety of CHamoru women and children. We were not American citizens and not entitled to the same protection.

We numbered around 20,000 in 1941. Not all of us were able-bodied men and boys. Our women, small children, and old folks could not have filled more than one or two military transports. I could not believe Uncle Sam would abandon such a small handful of his wards to a war not of their making. It still angers me that a government could be so cruel, that it would so forsake a helpless people, that it would willfully subject women and children to unspeakable horrors and hardships — horrors and hardships that destroyed so many, including my beloved Mama. To this day, I cannot reconcile my anger over this failure. I have never heard any acceptable justification. There is none.

That anger resurfaced after my trial and conviction in 1987. While hosting dinner for visiting anthropologist Dr. Laura Thompson and several other guests, I listened with a cold and heavy heart as I learned that the Navy had quietly offered to evacuate American-CHamoru families, but many chose to share the fate of their neighbors. The revelation came as a shock. My trial had ended only days earlier, and I was still trying to come to grips with my anger. Having felt the might of a determined federal effort, I was doubly angered that the same federal government did not expend any measure of that same might to save CHamoru women and children in 1941.

Denied humanitarian aid from the Red Cross after the typhoon, we were expendable pawns in the conflict brewing between powerful giants. The United States abandoned us.

PART TWO

Innocents in a Bloody Arena

THE OCCUPATION OF GUAM

Chapter 9

Ai, Santa Maria

We got up early on December 8, 1941, the Feast of the Immaculate Conception, commemorating the Virgin Mary, Guam's patroness and Hagåtña's fiesta. People would fill the cathedral for the 8 o'clock Mass. Mama wanted to make sure we were not late. As we got ready, the telephone rang. Mama answered it, then handed the telephone to Dad. The call was from the Governor's Palace and sounded urgent. Dad left in a rush around 6 o'clock. Mama seemed upset but hurried us along.

Before Dad returned, we heard the strange drone of airplane engines. We looked outside and saw a formation of planes heading west toward Sumai. I had built many model airplanes and was familiar with American military planes. The ones we saw were not American.

We never made it to church that day. Dad burst through the door, breathless and agitated.

"*Laguse'*, Mimang! Get the children out! *Paketi maseha håfa ya nihi! Lachaddek!*"[13] he blurted, mixing English and CHamoru. We knew something had to be terribly wrong as Dad was not one to get upset. His behavior and the appearance of unfamiliar planes frightened us.

"Do what your father says," Mama said. "Irene, Lorraine, start packing. Ricky, get the car. Bobbie, Paul, get your sisters and brothers, make sure they're together." The urgency in Mama and Dad's voices made us follow orders in alarm. The war everyone feared had arrived.

Governor George McMillin had assembled his ranking officers, staff, and Dad and his colleagues and told them of the Japanese attack on Pearl Harbor,

---

13 "Hurry, Mimang (Dad's nickname for Mama)! Pack whatever you can and let's go! Quickly!"

which was still ablaze. He got the word before dawn. Guam lies west of the International Dateline, 16 hours ahead of Hawai'i. McMillin also told them that Americans had orders to surrender, enemy planes were enroute to Guam, and people should evacuate the city. Word of the impending attack spread quickly. The Japanese base in Saipan was just 120 miles north. There was little time to evacuate.

While we packed, Dad made phone calls, first to Auntie Butler, then to his drivers. He instructed them to make every vehicle — automobiles, taxis, jitneys, trucks, and bicycles — available to anyone who needed transportation. Some drivers were still at home; others were already at work. Several of his other employees gathered on our doorstep to await instructions.

December 8 was a religious, but not a legal, holiday. In 1941, it fell on a Monday. Navy government workers had to report to work after church. That morning, the usual rush took on new urgency. The well-established preparations for emergency situations — typhoons, earthquakes, floods, and other calamities — went into effect, but preparing for war was new and frightening. The emergency siren on the power plant's reconstructed smokestack began blaring. Its warning lamps, which flashed green for normal conditions, switched to red.

Mass at the cathedral was in progress. Someone whispered the news to Bishop Olano at the altar. He turned and instructed the congregation to leave the church, but Mass was not yet over. People were confused — one did not leave in the middle of Mass — then became frightened. They rushed out to join others in the streets. Bishop Olano completed the Mass alone.

Explosions sounded in the distance as the Japanese planes attacked targets in Sumai. Black smoke rose into the sky above Piti and Sumai. In Hagåtña, the people knew the city was next. The smoke, the drone of airplanes, and the wailing siren caused a panic. The rush to escape turned into chaos. People poured out of their houses, searching for members who had been at church. Those fleeing the cathedral ran home through streets filling with vehicles scrambling to get people out of town. People began shouting, trying to make themselves heard above the siren, the hollering of others, and the cries of terrified children. Automobile horns and braying animals added to the din.

Mama worried about keeping us together, calling our names, checking for our whereabouts. We packed the car but could not take much because the 14 of us had to fit also. Once loaded, we swept along in the surging traffic draining from Hagåtña. Bundles and possessions rained into the streets from windows and balconies. Bull carts, trucks, automobiles, bicycles, and jitneys clogged the roads. I watched the rear tire of a packed bicycle fold under the weight of its load. The owner unlashed some of the bundles, slung them on his back, and walked away, leaving the bicycle and the rest of his possessions in the street. At the San Nicolas bridge, a jitney broke down and blocked the path. People climbed over it while others tried to push it aside. By midday, Hagåtña was empty.

We inched our way eastward, uphill to Tun Jose Torres' summer home in Maite, about 2 miles from town. Several other families went there also. While the adults discussed the morning's events, a bunch of us boys sprinted downhill to a spot overlooking Hagåtña.

In the distance, about 3 miles southwest of us, we watched the planes buzzing the Navy radio antenna on Mount Tenho. They dipped and spiraled around the antenna like barnstormers in the newsreels. It was like an air show just for us. The planes dropped little black things that popped and flashed without effect. From our miles-safe distance, we cheered and laughed each time the bombs missed. We thought the Japanese were foolish for defying the United States. None of us believed it was possible. Uncle Sam would return and teach them a lesson. In our innocence, we did not yet know the gravity of our situation.

After a while, the planes gave up on the radio antenna and proceeded toward Hagåtña. Above the city, one of the planes dropped a bomb near the palace. We figured it was meant for the radio shack at the edge of the palace compound. Again, the bomb missed; it landed about three blocks away and hit the house George Tweed rented from the Reyes family. Tweed was a Navy radioman on duty during the attack. He and five other Navy men fled into the jungle. The Japanese searched for them relentlessly and tortured anyone suspected of harboring them. Dad and my brother Paul were among the many beaten. Within weeks of the invasion, the Japanese caught and killed all the Americans except Tweed. They also killed the CHamorus who had aided them. When only Tweed remained, the search for him intensified.

Many CHamorus risked their lives to harbor Tweed, who demanded food, shelter, and even sex while in hiding. A Yoña farmer I know harbored Tweed for a few weeks. He denied his family the eggs from their chickens to feed Tweed. Many people met Tweed's demands because they were loyal to the American ideals Tweed represented, but he was an ugly American. Despite the protection he received, and the torture and death suffered in his name, Tweed repaid CHamorus with insults. In his book, *Robinson Crusoe, USN*, a work despised in Guam, Tweed said CHamorus brought suffering upon themselves for bragging too much about helping him.

The returning American forces hailed Tweed as a hero for surviving alone, as if he had no help, and for supplying valuable information, which he got from those harboring him. Tweed never organized resistance groups or harassment raids or recruited spies to gather intelligence. He worried only about himself. Many CHamorus remember him with bitterness.

Tweed had a violent temper, according to Edward Diego Reyes, whose father was Tweed's landlord. Eddie remembered hearing horrendous fights between Tweed and his wife. He sometimes beat her and their son, Ronnie. The Reyes family lived downstairs below the Tweeds. On the day of the Japanese attack, the Reyes family fled to safety uphill on San Ramon. They watched as a Japanese bomb hit their house. It did not detonate but punched a large hole in the roof.

Eddie attended college in the United States and later joined the Air Force. He was a full colonel, the highest-ranking Guamanian in the Air Force at the time. He was unknown in Guam's political arena, but he agreed to be my running mate in the 1982 gubernatorial election. He served as lieutenant governor of Guam and ran for reelection with me in 1986, despite the federal indictments against me.

The bodies were real people, dead people

After hitting the Reyes house, the planes flew off. At Tun Jose's that evening, Dad and several other village leaders listened to accounts of the bombing from people who came up from Sumai. Some of Dad's employees sought him out to report the condition of his businesses. The planes, they said, went after specific targets — the cable company station, the Pan American Airways station and hotel, the Marine Barracks, the USS *Penguin* and the USS *Barnes* in the harbor, the docks in Piti, and the radio antenna on Mount Tenho. The bombs also damaged several houses in the village.

They also told of the fight put up by the men of the *Penguin* and the *Barnes*. As the *Penguin* attempted an escape, a bomb hit it, killing several sailors, including Ensign Robert White, the *Penguin's* gunnery officer who was engaged to marry Marian Johnston[14] in January 1942. The *Penguin* sank at the mouth of the harbor. Her surviving crew swam for shore. Everyone called the *Barnes*, an old oil tanker, the "USS *Nevermove*" because it never left its moorings. The Navy used the *Barnes* as a training ship for Insular Guardsmen. After the invasion, the Japanese removed it to Saipan.

The men at Tun Jose's house stayed up all night on the front porch, discussing the day's events and pondering our future. Almost everyone was certain that war between the United States and Japan would not last long. The Americans were too powerful. But the Japanese already held most of Micronesia and wanted U.S.-held Guam to cement their supremacy in the region. To us, it seemed insane for them to try. We were too young to understand world politics. America was like Hopalong Cassidy — bad guys were not a threat to him. Like Hopalong, the United States could outgun and outshoot any enemy. As innocent bystanders under U.S. protection, we thought we were safe.

On Tuesday, we listened to the reports coming in for Dad and the other leaders. The Japanese fleet was offshore in Tomhom and Apotguan. Thousands of troops were preparing to land. On Wednesday morning, December 10, around 10,000 Japanese troops landed at various places on the island's western coast. Less than 100 strong, the Guardsmen and the Navy men stood against a special force of about 700 to secure the Governor's Palace. Outnumbered and equipped with only a few obsolete Mausers and three old machine guns, the defenders made their last stand in the plaza and fought until their ammunition ran out. The Japanese rolled over them. In the palace, Governor McMillin and his officers surrendered.

We woke up that morning to the distant sound of gunfire. It still seemed like a dream. Armed with a false sense of security and too curious to be sensible, about a half dozen of us sprinted down the Maite hillside and ventured into town to investigate. Halfway there, we came across the machine-gunned body of a man in a ditch. His bowels lay in a pile beside him. The corpse did not seem real. We did not recognize it as having once been a living person. We were too numb by the reality around us and overpowered by curiosity.

---

14 Marian Johnston, born on April 20, 1917, was one of the four daughters born to William Gautier and Agueda Iglesias Johnston, noted Guam educators and longtime friends of the Bordallos and other prominent Hagåtña families.

Like desperados fueled by adrenaline, we stole into the city, darting for cover behind street corners and buildings the way we had seen cowboys do in the movies. We could hear gunfire coming from the plaza and tried to steer clear of it. As the Guardsmen put up their defense, another young man believed as we did that noncombatants were safe. Roman Camacho was a photographer who had opened a studio and was making a name for himself before the invasion. He sought to record the battle on film. He climbed into the cathedral bell tower for a bird's-eye view but soon realized the fighting was real; the cause was real. Roman could not stand idly by, so he joined the beleaguered Guardsmen and died as he helped one of the machine gunners. We were several blocks away from the plaza but heard about it later.

At the San Antonio bridge we came upon another overturned jitney blocking the road. Machine guns had riddled it with holes, shattered its headlights and windshields, and shredded its canvas top. We made our way around it, peering in as we went. There were bodies inside. We came around to its rear and lifted the canvas flap. Inside we saw the bodies of an entire Japanese family — adults and children, about 20 people in all. Blood was everywhere and dripping onto the road. It was a strange irony; the Japanese family was fleeing to safety, as we had done, and were not a threat to anyone. Yet their own countrymen mowed them down.

Among the bodies, I spotted a girl who attended school with me. I had always thought her pretty and wanted to get to know her. She looked like she was asleep and was still pretty, but there was blood on her face and bullet holes in her body. At that moment, death became real; the bodies were real people, dead people. My knees went weak, and I wanted to vomit.

My companions and I came to the same realization together: if the Japanese would kill an entire Japanese family, they would kill us too. Noncombatants were not exempt. No one was exempt. We fled in panic, fearing the Japanese could come upon us and shoot us down too. I could barely breathe as we ran. My senses tingled at the back of my neck. I suspect we reached Maite around the time the Japanese in the plaza had Governor McMillin and his aides in custody at the Susana Hospital. The Japanese held the American civilians in the cathedral while the surviving Guardsmen and Navy men were kept in Dorn Hall and the jailhouse.

Everyone at Tun Jose's house rushed to meet us, bombarding us with questions about where we had been, what we had seen. Admiration and unspoken approval shone on our elders' faces. They would not have attempted anything as daring and foolhardy as we had done but were grateful that we did. It made us feel like brave young warriors, not panicked boys. We related our experience, including finding the murdered Japanese family on the San Antonio bridge. Our elders listened, knowing that death was possible for all of us. They also lamented the destruction of our way of life and how nothing would ever be the same after this.

After our foray into Hagåtña, a Saipanese interpreter came in a car to Maite. He pulled into Tun Jose's yard and announced that everyone was to report immediately to Hagåtña for processing. After barking his message, he drove off to repeat it elsewhere.

"We must not get caught doing this"

As word of the Japanese order spread, the residents of Hagåtña, accounting for almost half of Guam's population, trickled back into the city. People who lived elsewhere also journeyed to Hagåtña. Some defied the order, but most complied, fearful of the consequences. By that afternoon, at least 1,000 people, including my family, filled the plaza. By evening, there must have been around 8,000. The plaza became a sea of frightened people waiting in lines among machine gun nests and armed soldiers.

Everything in the plaza was strange. The Japanese presence was nightmarish. Hundreds of soldiers in combat gear and clusters of stacked rifles bristled everywhere. Some armed with bayonet-mounted rifles herded groups of people into lines. Many milled about in the plaza, glaring at people. Some were squatting along the streets, chatting among themselves. Their squatting was odd. Except as a last resort or to relieve oneself in the jungle, squatting was not a common CHamoru practice. We found it too uncomfortable and were incredulous to see it among the Japanese. Some soldiers were lazing in the portico of the Governor's Palace, something the Americans would not have tolerated. That the Japanese blatantly did so was an indication that we were now in the hands of a different kind of ruler.

Officials of the *minseisho*, the Japanese Army's civilian affairs section, sat at tables before the long lines of people. They demanded the names, ages, addresses, and number of people in each family. The tedious processing lasted hours. Each person received a small, white piece of cloth with a red Japanese character on it. We had to wear the tags, which we called *lisensian ga'lågu*, or dog licenses, all the time. The Japanese pulled all the American priests and civilians, like Uncle Butler, Mr. Johnston[15], and many others from our ranks and took them into custody along with Bishop Olano. Their removal sent new waves of fear and uncertainty through the crowd. The Americans joined the Navy men interned in the cathedral.

We did not receive our tags until after 9 o'clock, and thousands of people were still waiting in the plaza when we went home through dark streets. None of us had eaten or had anything to drink all day, and we were exhausted. We tumbled into bed, too tired to do anything else. Sometime after midnight, Dad crept into our bedrooms, woke us up, and whispered for us to get ready to leave. Once awake, we heard the noises that worried Dad.

The Japanese had commandeered the Mayhew house next door, and someone was barking orders. Despite the blackout and curfew that officials had imposed, as well as the late hour, the soldiers in the Mayhew house were noisy. They spoke loudly and made no effort to be quiet. We could hear their footsteps thundering up and down the stairs and their heavy feet on the floor. We knew nothing about the Japanese soldiers, except that they were unpredictable. The Japanese people who had long made their homes among us were like us — more CHamoru than Japanese but still Japanese.

Dad and Mama worried the Japanese would also commandeer our house and feared having idle soldiers close to their virginal daughters. Irene had just turned 18; Lorraine was 17. Bobbie would turn 13 on January 6, just weeks away. Norma's 10th birthday was on December 20, nine days away. Despite the curfew, Dad decided we had to flee our house before the soldiers detected our presence. He whispered to us to stay together, move quickly, and be silent.

"Try not to make noise," he said softly. "We must not get caught doing this. Do you understand?"

In the wee hours of December 11, my 14th birthday, we tiptoed out of our house in our nightclothes and scurried across the street. To make sure the soldiers did not spot us, Dad led us between the Palting house and the Schroeder School yard to the next street. We stole down San Ignacio Street to the rear of

---

15 William Gautier Johnston, a Marine who came to Guam early in the 20th century, married Agueda Iglesias in 1911. They had seven children: Cynthia (who married Jose Torres), Margaret, Herbert, Joseph, Marian, Thomas, and Eloise.

Auntie Butler's house. Dad tapped on her back door until someone answered. Auntie Butler, James, and a couple of servants were alone. Mae, Benny, Bea, and Dolly were in the States.

Auntie Butler was distraught over Uncle Butler's detention. He was not a military man or a threat of any kind. His only crime was being an American. The Butlers were not alone. Throughout Hagåtña, many other American-CHamoru families — the Johnstons, the Underwoods, the Notleys, the Nelsons, the Elliotts, the Jacksons, the Manleys, and others — were torn apart and grieving also. The Navy government did not consider the children of mixed marriages to be American and neither did the Japanese. My cousin James was 25 but not taken into custody.

In the darkness of Auntie Butler's living room, we settled down on mats on the floor. Mama, who was six months pregnant, made her customary head-count and came up one short.

"B.J., where's Paul? He's not here," she whispered.

Dad counted again. Paul, who was 11, was not with us. Dad grew angry with himself for not having verified our numbers and with Paul for not following orders. Dad nudged me and directed me to follow. We snuck out the back door and retraced our route back to our house. We stopped at the school and waited to sneak across Hernan Cortez. The soldiers overran the Mayhew house, and several were milling on the corner outside. When no one was looking, we ran across the street and into our house. We groped in the dark until we found Paul still asleep in his bed. He woke with a jolt when Dad cuffed him. Paul sat up and rubbed his eyes.

"Shhh! Do not make a sound. Get up, and let's go," Dad said, not hiding his irritation.

We made our way back to Auntie Butler's house without incident. We stayed with her for several days before returning home. Our house was undisturbed, but the fighting cocks in the backyard had gotten free. Left on their own, many fought to death. Dead roosters littered the backyard.

"Tell your father 'Thank you' from us"

After we went back home, Dad sent me to deliver cigarettes to the Insular Guardsmen interned at Dorn Hall. "Pass them out to whoever wants some," he said, as if it were an ordinary delivery. I stiffened at his willingness to risk my safety and send me into a lion's den.

But Dad never acted without purpose. I realized he was defying the enemy in his own way, using me and the cigarettes as the means. I understood his
motives but was scared, nonetheless. I filled a gunny sack with about a doz-
en cartons of Chesterfield cigarettes, slung it on my back, and took the most
roundabout way to the plaza, to avoid having to bow at all the check points.

The *minseisho* required us to bow Japanese style — low and from the
waist — upon encountering any officer, soldier, or other occupation official.
They posted signs all over town, reminding people of the bowing requirement.
Since very few people could read Japanese kanji, the reminders were easy to
ignore. Bowing was not something we did routinely, and we were careless at
first about adhering to the rule. After getting enough slaps in the face, punches
in the gut, and kicks in the pants, we began bowing automatically.

I hated having to bow. It was humiliating. I refused to bow to the Navy
governor on his horse and was infuriated that, on pain of punishment, I now
had to bow to every foot soldier I met. To me, bowing was not a sign of respect but of submission. In 1986, I received an "invitation" to appear before a
federal grand jury. I accepted but did not take questions. Instead, I delivered a
prepared statement, then on impulse, stood up and bowed to the jury, to the
intimidation it represented.

Even though I took the least check-pointed route to Dorn Hall, I met
roving patrols right away. I was terrified. With the sack of American cigarettes
at my side, I stood erect, pressed my hands to my sides, and bowed. Roving patrols of two or three armed soldiers wandered every street. They questioned
all pedestrians or entered houses at random to conduct inspections. With
their bayonets fixed, their rifles poised and ready, and ammunition belts crisscrossed on their chests, the patrolmen were fearsome. The pistols holstered
at their sides and the half dozen or so grenades dangling from their uniforms
gave them absolute authority.

I crossed Hernan Cortez and cut through the Schroeder schoolyard,
crossed San Ignacio Street, then took a shortcut through the alley behind the
Elks Club and Don Perez's house. I avoided Pazos Street, which led to the Governor's Palace and fronted Dorn Hall. Instead, I crossed Dr. Hessler Street and
took the alley behind Leary School and the post office. I crossed San Juan de
Letran Street and turned onto Pazos Street to enter Dorn Hall from the front.
Despite taking the indirect route and staying off the main streets, I met Jap-

anese soldiers and officials at every turn. My back ached from all the bowing.

Inside Dorn Hall, I bowed once more. Soldiers filled the lobby; several sat at a table, others stood around the room. All turned and glowered at me. There were no smiles among them, no glint of curiosity or interest in their faces, only dark and menacing stares. As extroverts, CHamorus are easy to read; the introverted Japanese were impossible. I did not know how to behave in front of them, what to expect from them, or what pleased or angered them. I set my sack of cigarettes down and smiled, but their demeanor did not change. An interpreter approached and asked me what I wanted.

"Sir, my father told me to bring these cigarettes," I said. "I am to distribute them to the men you are holding."

The interpreter turned and said something in Japanese to the officials while I waited. After a brief exchange, a couple of soldiers rose from the table, grabbed my sack, and emptied it. The other soldiers gathered around and began inspecting each carton. I realized why Dad sent me. A 14-year-old errand boy was nonthreatening. Satisfied the cartons were intact, the soldiers returned them to my sack. One of them led me down the corridor to a back room. The room was large but cramped.

The CHamoru Guardsmen and the Navy enlisted men were inside. Their faces brightened when I entered. They swarmed around me, smiling, and reaching out to touch me. I felt like Santa Claus. I tore open the cartons, one after another, and passed out packs of cigarettes. I cannot forget the joy in their faces and their sincere appreciation.

"Tell your father 'Thank you' from us," many of them called out as I left.

There was great anguish on everyone's face when the Japanese removed the Americans from Guam. On January 10, 1942, a month after the invasion, they forced the American Navy men and civilians, including Uncle Butler, the priests, and Bishop Olano, to march to Piti Harbor. Hundreds of people gathered on street corners or at their windows to watch the procession. Tears streamed from the faces of wives, children, and relatives. I watched a young wife try to reach for her American husband. A soldier shoved her to ground. Her husband could do nothing.

Stoop-shouldered and glum, the Americans shuffled down Hernan Cortez Street. Once proud and confident, they wore expressions I had never seen before on any American; they looked defeated. Few of us had seen them since their confinement and were shocked. Many of the men had lost weight and were gaunt, ragged, and dirty.

The Japanese put the Americans onboard the *Argentina Maru* in Piti and sent them to prison camps in Japan. Some, like William Johnston, Agueda Johnston's husband and Marian's father, died in the camps. Uncle Butler survived and came home after the war, but his ordeal changed him. He suffered from malnutrition and stomach cancer and died in 1951.

No graceful death ballet, no death with dignity

Those of us left in Guam learned we were prisoners as well. After the invasion, the Japanese proclaimed their occupation of Guam and claimed all property. They arrested two men, Francisco B. Won Pat and Alfred Leon Guerrero Flores, for theft of Japanese property. Francisco's brother Antonio was once an accountant for Dad and was his colleague in the Guam Congress. I did not know Mr. Flores. Word of their arrest, torture, and upcoming trial was shocking. The Japanese said nothing about barring the public from the trial, so I attended it out of curiosity.

It was in progress when I entered the courthouse. I had been there only two years earlier when Dad sent me to deliver the letter to Commander Perry. I walked past Perry's office door, awed by the drastic change. There was no considerate judge advocate occupying his office now, only strangers who spoke in angry, foreign words. No one paid attention to me when I entered the courtroom and took a seat at the back. I seemed to be the only CHamoru observer there; I did not see any others. Japanese officials occupied most of the seats.

Mr. Flores was standing before a judicial panel, listening to an officer speaking Japanese. An interpreter translated the charges against him. Mr. Flores stood accused of stealing canned food, clothing, and construction supplies from one of the American contractor's warehouses in Sumai. The list was long, and each item was identified: shoes, denim trousers, undershirts, canvas tarpaulin, canned foods, other canned goods, lumber, nails, and carpentry tools. Nothing listed sounded dangerous or subversive — no firearms, ammunition, or explosives. Read first in Japanese then in CHamoru, all the charges took nearly half an hour to be recited.

Mr. Flores' only defense was that the contractor gave him permission to take any supplies in the warehouse. The Japanese official assigned as defense counsel took just minutes to present an argument that seemed perfunctory.

The panel deliberated briefly then announced the verdict in a long speech. The interpreter translated. Guilty. Sentence: death by firing squad. The interpreter then announced the date, time, and place of execution.

Not waiting to answer for my presence, I left the courtroom and ran home. Without admitting that I had attended the trial, I whispered the news to Lorraine and Paul. I knew Dad would find out soon enough, and I did not want to endanger him with prior knowledge.

A day or two after the trial, town criers roamed the city summoning the few remaining residents to the Pigo' cemetery. The Japanese wanted us to witness the penalty for violating the new law. Women and children were not exempt. We all were to understand the Japanese no-nonsense approach to law and order. By then, Hagåtña was no longer the peaceful, bustling city of happy people and music. It was a ghost town. Most of the population deserted the city after the processing in the plaza. Only a handful of families, including mine, stayed behind. Some residents ventured back for a few hours during the day to check on their homes, gather supplies, bathe, wash clothes, and use the electricity. The Japanese were suspicious of any gathering, so stopping to chat with a friend or neighbor was dangerous. Except for quick greetings and exchanges, it nearly ceased, but people devised a code for transmitting information: "The baby's in the cradle" meant go home, the city was not safe that day.

Criers also took the summons to go to Pigo' into the surrounding areas, but not many people complied. About 100 of us still in town could not escape the order. None of us wanted to witness an execution, but we had no choice. Soldiers rounded us up and herded us like cattle to the Catholic cemetery in Pigo'. The Navy had their own cemetery near the beach in San Antonio. The Baptist cemetery was further inland in the same vicinity. A large limestone outcropping, towering about 40 feet tall, with a large concrete cross on top, once marked Pigo' cemetery. It is not there anymore. The soldiers pushed us to a spot a few yards in front of the outcropping. To our right were two new, open graves.

The air was thick with tension. We knew we were going to watch something horrible. We stood in silence, but some of the women whispered prayers. Two army trucks arrived with Francisco Won Pat, Alfred Flores, and a firing squad. The condemned men's torturers had beaten them so badly they could barely stand. They were blindfolded and had their hands tied at their backs. Two soldiers made them stand before their graves.

The Japanese allowed Påle' Oscar Lujan Calvo to offer some prayers before the execution. With missal and holy water in hand, Påle' "Oskat" read the Last Rites while the squad of riflemen positioned themselves between the condemned men and our trembling group. At an officer's signal, the riflemen fired.

In my innocence, I thought Mr. Won Pat and Mr. Flores would die the way men died in the cowboy movies, that they would clutch at their wounds and lurch from the impact of the bullets. They would suck in a dramatic final breath and slump to the ground. I had watched many such "deaths" on the movie screen. Real death does not happen that way.

The bullets slammed into the men's bodies with violent force. Pieces of their flesh and sprays of their blood exploded in different directions. The impact lifted them off the ground. Their bodies twitched and spurted blood. There was no graceful death ballet, no dramatic last gasp of breath, no death with dignity.

When it was over, the soldiers climbed back into their trucks and drove off. The women and children were sobbing. The rest of us stood in silent shock. We had never seen human beings die by gunfire. We had never seen anything so gruesome and horrifying. We dared not approach the graves. The soldiers herded us away while a crew of conscripted men pushed the bodies into the graves and buried them.

One day history will know about this

For the first three months of the occupation, the ruthless combat troops of the Japanese Imperial Army and its civilian affairs division, the *minseisho*, were in command. Their tenure was cruel and intolerant of noncompliance. The escape of the six Americans who fled into the jungle infuriated them. The *minseisho* badgered everyone for information and tortured anyone suspected of aiding the Americans in any way. Before the Imperial Army forces departed in March 1942, they wanted us to witness their invincibility and determination to win their Pacific war.

A summons again went out for all people to report to an area west of Fort Apugan on the Tutuhan ridge. The Japanese had mounted several large cannons along the cliff, and a crew was manning each gun. The cannons faced northeast, toward Alupat, a coral outcropping at the eastern edge of Hagåtña Bay. The islet was about 2 miles away but clearly visible from where we stood.

At a barked signal, the crews loaded the cannons and fired. The first volley shook the ground. The explosion was louder than anything we had ever heard before. It was so loud it masked the terrified screams of the women and children. Our ears rang, and some people went deaf temporarily. Until then, we had never heard anything louder than thunder and the small cannon the Americans used for salutes. A strange, acrid odor filled the air.

The *minseisho* ordered the cannon demonstration and a parade to mark their departure. The parade was not for public entertainment but a show of force. Every tank, wheeled cannon, and combat vehicle the Japanese had in Guam rumbled through the streets of Hagåtña. Behind the convoy came hundreds of heavily armed troops. At the tail end of the parade, there was a single "float."

The float was a flatbed truck. On it was a Japanese boy we knew from down the street. He was wearing a Japanese combat soldier's camouflage gear and relishing his role as the triumphant invader. He was standing on an American flag spread out on the truck bed and jabbing a mounted bayonet into the belly of another boy we knew. He was wearing an American sailor's uniform, with talcum powder caked on his face and hands, to make him white like an American. His arms were raised in surrender, and he was leaning backwards against the truck cab. He was trembling and had a frightened look on his face.

Irene, Lorraine, Bobbie, Paul, and I watched the parade from the window in the girls' bedroom, which overlooked Hernan Cortez Street. The Japanese boy was enjoying his part. Before the invasion, he was one of us, a neighbor and playmate, but afterward, he and his family changed; they welcomed the Japanese. We could not tell whether the other boy was play acting or if the bayonet jabs really hurt him.

"One day," I whispered to my sisters and brother, "history will know about this." They nodded in agreement. We were disgusted by the Japanese boy's treacherous behavior and his family's new-found arrogance and cruelty. To secure preferential treatment for themselves, they and several other Japanese-CHamorus collaborated with the invaders and brought down hardship and suffering to many. They switched sides again when the Americans returned and counted themselves Guamanian again. In deference to the innocents in that family, I will not name the boy and his family. They know who they are.

There had always been a kind of resentment in our prewar society over class distinctions. Everyone wanted to be *manatkilo'* — to be upper crust, or at least appear to be. The Americans were at the top of the ladder. American-CHamorus occupied the next rung, and wealthy CHamorus, the one below. Those who had no claim to social stature chafed at being among the middle and lower classes. The Japanese boy's family was one of those. The occupation catapulted them up in the new social order.

"We are the masters now," the Japanese father told Marian Johnston. "We are in command, and you must do what we say. You no longer have any choice unless you care nothing for your father."

The collaborator blackmailed the talented Johnston children into performing for the troops at the cathedral. Their father, William Johnston, was among the American prisoners shipped to Japan. Mr. Johnston told his children Marian, Herbert, and married daughter Cynthia Torres not to endanger themselves and to do whatever was necessary to survive. Fearing for his safety and their own, the Johnston children yielded to the collaborator's demands. Mr. Johnston died in prison, but his wife Agueda and his family did not find out until months later.

The greed and selfishness of this collaborating family helped bring about the death of my baby brother. Mama's 13th child was born in March 1942, the same month the Japanese Army left Guam. Mama and Dad named him Franklin Delano, but we could not talk about him. Eager to ingratiate themselves, the collaborators would have reported us to the Japanese authorities as treasonous. During Franklin's brief life, we referred to him only as "the baby."

Chapter 10

The Greater East Asia Co-Prosperity Sphere

The Japanese Navy's police force, the *keibitai*, and its civilian affairs division, the *minseibu*, replaced the Army. The Navy's *minseibu* tried to restore some normalcy, but their tenure was not a peaceful, happy time. Like the Army's *minseisho*, the *minseibu*'s mission was to prepare Guam for its role in the "Greater East Asia Co-Prosperity Sphere" and solidify Japan as the colonial power in the Pacific. The reign of the new empire was to last 1,000 years.

Within weeks of assuming control, the *minseibu* attempted to redirect our loyalties. They required us to pay homage to the emperor for liberating us from American domination and exploitation. As part of the "Japanization" process, they renamed Guam "Omiya Jima" and Hagåtña "Agashi." Other villages had new names too, but we ignored them. Many did not even know of the changes. The *minseibu* established new living and working standards, but the curfew and blackout order remained in effect. We could move about during the day but not at night. We had to increase food production to feed the Japanese, leaving little for ourselves. Leisure time was almost nonexistent.

The Japanese used propaganda to win us over, but like the Americans before them, they did not understand our culture and values, causing many of their attempts to backfire. The *minseibu* campaigned hard against the capitalist, imperialist Americans but succeeded only in strengthening our pro-American resolve. To their frustration, we were too ideologically "American," though not American officially. Our tenacious Americanism prompted them to step up their Japanization process. They gathered a bunch of us and marched us up to the Navy golf course near the officer's club in Tutuhan. We had to listen through an interpreter to a *minseibu* official's lecture on how the Japanese had liberated us from the American yoke and how we worked hard while the Americans were on their golf course, wasting the land and playing idiotic games.

The official rambled for hours. He was almost convincing. He spoke some truth and made some sense, but we could not swallow it. The golf course had indeed been the exclusive domain of the Americans who spent an inordinate amount of time whacking golf balls on the rolling lawns. But the Americans' golf course never intruded in our lives or caused us hunger and suffering. According to the *minseibu* official, part of our new-found freedom would be in the happiness we would derive from transforming the golf course into something productive. He then ordered us to plow it up and plant corn. Most of the harvest went to the troops who were liberating others like us. We found no joy in destroying the lawns and planting corn, but we earned a few yen for our labor.

The *minseibu* reopened the schools in April 1942. They brought in some teachers and recruited several young CHamorus for regimented teacher training. The trainees received preferential treatment and more food ration coupons but had to march from their dormitories to their classrooms and be paraded at Japanese parties for propaganda purposes. The Japanese also started language lessons for children and adults. Most did not attend unless forced. I went only long enough to pick up a few useful phrases.

In addition to the teachers, the Japanese imported their own sex workers. There were three specific categories: one for officers and high-ranking civilians, another for the higher enlisted ranks and midlevel civilians, and a third for the lower ranks. The Kerner house in Hagåtña became the upper-class brothel. Tun Pedro Martinez's summer home in Sasa' became the one for the lower echelon. The brothel for midlevel personnel was in what had been the home of Atkins Kroll's resident manager at Ádilok Point, about 4 miles west from Hagåtña.

The building at Ádilok, once called Missionary Point, had been a schoolhouse built by the Baptist Mission. Atkins Kroll, a California-based import-export company, purchased the building early in the 20th century. The American bombardment destroyed it in 1944. After the war, the government of Guam built an elementary school on the small Ádilok peninsula, first in Quonset huts then later in concrete buildings. By then, the name of the area evolved into "Adelup." In 1985, I converted the old school into the new governor's office and built the Hall of Governors at the top of the point on the foundation of the original school and residence.

Near the end of 1942, the Japanese imported two Catholic priests, Monsignor Fukahori and Father Petro Komatsu, to augment the work of Påle' Jesus Baza Dueñas and Påle' Oscar "Oskat" Lujan Calvo. While the Japanese priests confined their ministries to Hagåtña, Påle' Dueñas , pastor of Inalåhan's St. Joseph's Church, served the southern end of the island, and Påle' Oskat served the northern and central villages. Påle' Oskat hid the Blessed Sacrament, the consecrated Communion hosts, in Nanan Chong's chapel in Tutuhan and traveled from village to village to say Mass. The Rev. Joaquin Sablan, the only CHamoru Baptist minister, served the Baptist community.

The Navy's *minseibu* issued food ration coupons and confiscated anything deemed necessary for the war effort. They expanded the program to include mandatory work details and food production quotas from each village. They appointed *sånchos*, or commissioners, in each district to ensure delivery of their district's food quota. To survive, CHamoru administrators and businessmen entered new career fields. Office workers took to farming and fishing and did anything to guarantee some income for their families. Antonio Won Pat, who was a teacher and Dad's accountant, made and sold wooden slippers. Herbert Johnston, whose family owned the Gaiety Theater, made and sold lye soap.

"Take off your shirt"

The Japanese commandeered Tun Pedro Martinez's cattle herds, his ranch in Dåndan, and his summer house in Sasa'. They also took our herds and agricultural operations in Hågat and Mayanghulo'. They seized Tun Pedro's ice plant, and for some unexplained reason, put Dad in charge of meeting quotas of ice production for the military. Dad also had to reopen his businesses and run them as usual, selling allotments of meat and fish to civilians. I ran the market and cold storage plant in his behalf. The Japanese also confiscated Dad and Tun Pedro's vehicle fleets but allowed each to keep one for business purposes. Dad got back one of his three-quarter-ton International pickups and Tun Pedro one of his Dodge trucks.

The truck was an important necessity for us. Without it, we would be hard-pressed to keep the businesses going, not only for the Japanese but also for the people relying on us and for our large family. Dad handed me the keys with a stern but trusting look and told me I was in charge. I took the responsibility seriously and treated the truck like a baby. I also had expert mechanics to help me. No expensive roadster, not even Dad's red race car, received better care.

To back up my regular maintenance, I enlisted Segundo "Sy" Guerrero, the best mechanic in the Governor's Palace motor pool. The Americans hired only the best local talent to work for the Navy government. I do not think the Japanese were aware of Sy's skills. That made him available to me. If the truck made a funny sound, I would take it to Sy. Like a doctor, he would listen and make adjustments until the engine purred again. I would peer over his shoulder like a nervous hen and bombard him with questions.

When the few parts left in Dad's auto parts store ran out, my only recourse was to have new ones manufactured. For this specialized service, I counted on Arthur Anderson, who lived near our house. Arthur owned a small machine shop and a lathe. He was a master craftsman who took immense pride in his work. He never made a part for me that did not meet his own quality standards. To my long-lasting sorrow, Arthur did not survive the occupation.

Gasoline and motor oil were scarce, but the Japanese allotted us 50 gallons of low-grade gasoline a month. I would collect our allotment and stockpile it even though we had a store of better-quality American gasoline hidden away. The Japanese did not question the inventories reported to them and confiscated only what was visible. Like Dad, many other businessmen hid some of their inventories. The underground storage tank at the garage still contained fuel, and we had several full drums in the warehouse in Aniguak. The Japanese knew nothing about these. To stretch my fuel supply, I mixed the inferior Japanese fuel, which was mostly alcohol, with high-grade American gasoline.

As I drove along Legaspi Street one afternoon, the truck engine purred nicely. Curious about its performance, I decided to put it to a test. Legaspi Street, on the southern edge of the city, ran in a long, straight line from the Governor's Palace to Aniguak. It was a perfect raceway. I also wondered whether the numbers on the speedometer were for show or whether vehicles could really reach such speeds. Since the speed limit in Hagåtña was only 10 mph, no vehicle engine ever strained hard. With no one else around, I could not resist the temptation and jammed on the accelerator. I watched in amazement as the speedometer needle climbed past 20 mph then 30 mph. The engine screamed as I sped to 50 mph, then 60 mph. The speed was incredible.

Houses, stores, trees, and fences whizzed by the windows. I pretended I was driving Dad's race car, which was still on blocks in the garage.

The truck reached 70 mph and the city's western limits in seconds. I slammed on the brakes and slowed to the speed limit. Breathless, I satisfied my curiosity about the speed gauge and about driving a race car, even if only in my imagination. The pickup was not Dad's racer, but its performance was magnificent. Its speedometer was not a dashboard decoration.

I checked my driving skill again a few weeks later when I asked John Blas to let me drive his gigantic dump truck. John and his brothers Jose and Mariano were among Dad's taxi drivers. They and Cristobal Hines were Dad's best. The Japanese conscripted John to drive loads of manganese from the mines at Mount Tenho to the docks in Piti. His vehicle was enormous, with tires taller than a man. It arrived in Guam before the invasion with the equipment and supplies the American contractors ordered for the island's fortification. The Japanese confiscated the shipments and sent most of them to Japan. They kept the heavy equipment and began mining manganese, which they also shipped to Japan. They conscripted only the best drivers to transport the manganese.

The dirt roads to the mines were narrow, rutted, and dangerous, marked by tight curves, steep angles, and unstable shoulders that dropped into ravines 600-to-800-feet below. The dump trucks were so wide that their tires took the entire width of the road. Unskilled drivers could easily kill themselves, but John did not balk when I asked to drive the course. He no longer worked for Dad and was not obligated to me, but he continued to accord me respect as the boss' son. He also trusted my skill and knew that driving such a big rig was too great a temptation for me. He was not surprised by my request but was quick to caution me about the danger.

I was always doing daring things, pushing myself to see how far I could go. Mastering any wheeled vehicle was a challenge I could not resist. I had learned to perform complex acrobatics on my bicycle and could drive an automobile long before I was big enough to see over the steering wheel. Too brash for my own good, I ignored John's warning and climbed into the driver's seat of the giant truck. I drove it without incident or mishap. In recalling the incident now, I shudder. The road from Mount Tenho is paved and much wider now but still dangerous for huge trucks.

Not long after I raced the pickup on Legaspi Street, Uncle Carlos asked to borrow it. He was building a new house a few miles outside Hagåtña and needed it to haul lumber from Litekyan to his construction site. He knew how vital the truck was to us, and he promised Dad not to let anything happen to it. Dad was hesitant but could not deny him. I toyed with the idea of driving for Uncle Carlos but had too many other chores. I told Dad the truck would be ready when Uncle Carlos came for it the following morning.

Late the next afternoon, my brother Fred ran into the market, wide-eyed and frightened.

"Ricky, come quick," he blurted. "Uncle Carlos is back. Something happened to the truck, and Daddy is mad."

"Calm down. What happened?" I asked.

Fred said Uncle Carlos returned to the house on foot. He was exhausted and upset and muttered something about the truck being dead. He told Dad the engine began knocking and smoking. He switched off the ignition and hurried back to town. Fred heard Uncle Carlos tell Dad that he thought the engine had burned out and asked if I had forgotten to check it.

I ran home in a panic. We needed the truck; losing it meant losing our means of keeping the businesses going and the family fed. The threat to my family's security terrified me. I went through my maintenance checklist in my mind, certain I had taken excellent care of it. That I might have neglected the truck and endangered the family made Dad furious also. Uncle Carlos was gone when I reached the house. Dad was waiting for me in the living room. His face was ashen, and he was shaking with anger. I had never seen him so enraged. In his hand was a length of abaka, a new hemp rope, stiff and sharp-edged.

"Take off your shirt," he said coldly.

I unbuttoned my shirt and peeled it off. Dad yanked me into the dining room, knocking over furniture as he whipped me from one room to another. The rope stung across my back. I could feel it splitting my skin. Still shouting that I neglected the truck, Dad lashed at me again and again. I screamed in pain and tried to stagger away from him. Blinded by tears and pain, I stumbled through the inside and outside kitchens and into the yard. Dad followed, still lashing, still hollering. I could feel long, red welts stinging across my back and blood dripping to my waist. Dad did not stop the thrashing.

I submitted to the punishment, convinced that I deserved it. I sank to my knees and began sobbing. The physical pain was excruciating, but the agony in my mind was worse. Each stinging blow drove home my guilt. Each jagged bite of the rope accused me of dereliction. Because of my failure, Mama and my brothers and sisters would suffer worse pain. They could die without the truck, and it would be my fault. I was willing to die at my father's hand in atonement.

Dad's anger fueled his strength and numbed his senses. Over and over, his rope slashed across my torso and back. "I warned you about the truck," he repeated over and over, his voice hoarse and raspy. "You lied to me. You did not take care of it. We're dead now because of you."

Mama had been cowering in her bedroom, listening but not daring to interfere until she realized that Dad was beyond reason. She ran into the yard and cried to him, *"Basta, B.J.! Basta, sa' un puno' i patgon!"* she pleaded in CHamoru. "B.J., don't kill my child."

Mama lunged at Dad and grabbed his arm before he could strike me again. "Stop," she whispered and began to cry. Behind her, my brothers and sisters had watched my punishment and were sobbing. The lashing stopped, but Dad's rage did not.

"I could kill you," he snarled. "Do something about that truck. Do you hear me? You better fix it!" He stormed away, leaving me crumpled, heaving, and crying into the dust.

My back was raw and bloody, but my real pain was inside. My heart was shattered. I had let my family down; I jeopardized their security. No punishment could absolve such a crime. Before Mama could reach me, I tore out of the yard and ran blindly away. *"Find the truck!"* I screamed to myself. Half running, half stumbling, I raced in the direction Uncle Carlos had come. Blood trickled down my back, and tears streamed down my face. I ran shirtless and barefoot over the hot pavement. I ran 15 miles without stopping, oblivious to everything except finding the truck. I had to find it and fix it, somehow, some way. *"You have to fix it."* The message in my head repeated over and over.

I reached Litekyan at dusk but had no idea where Uncle Carlos had abandoned the truck. By instinct, I bolted down an overgrown bull cart trail marked by flattened grass. A vehicle had passed through it. I headed down the trail, brushing aside branches slapping at my face and back. I came upon the truck and approached it cautiously, as if a sudden move could worsen its condition. I climbed into the cab, drew a breath, and held it as I depressed the clutch and shifted the gear stick into low. I turned the ignition. The engine screeched to life with a horrendous gagging racket. I turned the engine off and exhaled, my heart pounding. I sat in confused helplessness in the truck in the middle of nowhere.

I climbed out and lifted the hood expecting to find a jumble of engine parts, but everything was in order. Relief washed over me. I climbed back into the cab, shifted into neutral, and turned the engine over again. To my amazement, the racket disappeared, but when I shifted the truck into gear, the loud knocking and grinding started again. Thinking the problem might not have been mechanical, I jumped out and crawled underneath the truck. Thick wads of sword grass had become tangled around the drive shaft. Laughing and crying at the same time, I began yanking away the tough, green blades, slicing my hands and fingers. I was too relieved and thankful to care about the stinging cuts. I climbed into the cab again and turned the ignition, depressed the clutch, and shifted into reverse. The engine purred and began rolling smoothly backward out of the jungle.

I drove home, wanting to cheer out the window into the night. When I leaned forward, the blood drying on my back glued me to the seat. I peeled myself and reopened the wounds. They started bleeding again. I rounded the corner of our block and blasted the horn. I revved the engine forcefully to announce my return. My brothers and sisters ran out into the yard to meet me. Mama came running too, with towels to dress my wounds. Her eyes were full of pride. I received a hero's welcome. While Mama tended to my wounds, I explained what had happened in the jungle. From his darkened bedroom, Dad listened to my explanation and knew the truck was safe and his son vindicated. We never raised or discussed the incident. The truck and the market remained my responsibilities.

Whiskey in the cellar and radios in the jungle

The Japanese knew that Dad was a prominent political leader and kept eyes on him for signs of suspicious political activity or resistance organizing. Under such intense scrutiny, Dad knew any resistance would be fatal. With a wife and 12 children to protect, he concentrated on other ways to resist, often risking his safety and ours.

The Army's *minseisho* outlawed everything American, especially currency. People had to turn in their American money for yen at the start of the occupation. After the deadline for currency redemption, anyone caught with

American money was severely punished. Many people believed the Americans would soon return and hid their cash, but as time passed and their supplies ran out, they had to convert their savings to yen. Since we ran the markets, Dad redeemed American money for those who had held out. He also offered a fairer exchange rate than the low one the Japanese tendered initially.

Although hoarding was a crime punishable by death, Dad squirreled away about 10 cases of American cigarettes and almost 100 cases of Canadian Club Whisky. He used these and the empty gasoline drums at the stadium as bartering collateral. With so many mouths to feed, he could not depend solely on our meager share of food ration coupons. Twelve children consumed an enormous amount of food, despite smaller portions. Dad used the cows, the garden, the empty gasoline drums, old automobile tires, and anything else he could think of to increase our food supplies, trading whatever we had for anything we needed.

Dad lied to the Japanese about the number of cattle we owned. He turned the herds over but hid a few heads in the jungle. He often sneaked back to the cattle ranches to rustle a few more. Dad also started a garden in Apotguan to augment our food supplies. With a cute, little Indian bull and cart, he and Paul spent most of every day traveling to jungle hiding places to milk and pasture the cows and tend the garden. While they did, I took care of the businesses in town. Most businesses were stocked for Christmas before the invasion, but the Japanese took almost everything, leaving little for people to buy. With so little cash in circulation, only yen to spend, and dwindling merchandise, business got slower and slower.

One of my more pleasurable chores was driving throughout the island and trading our goods for fresh produce and other foodstuffs. I enjoyed the change in my otherwise boring routine and looked forward to driving for Tun Jesus "Tenbat" Rosario, the fisherman. He was a typical fisherman in that he could almost outswim his prey. His skin was deep brown and leathery from years in the sun, and it contrasted with his sun-bleached, yellow hair. Tenbat was gregarious, humorous, hardworking, short but solidly built, and likeable. He was also a good banjo player. He and several others comprised the Tenbat Band, which was not as polished and sophisticated as the Hines Orchestra but was just as popular.

Several times a week I would drive to Tenbat's house on the beach in Apotguan. My task was to take him and several other fishermen down the steep and dangerous road to Tomhom. I would arrive before dawn and enjoy a hearty breakfast of fresh fried fish, *titiyas*, dried beef, coffee, and potu while the fishermen loaded their baskets, nets, and spears into the truck. I liked being with the fishermen and listening to them talk about their plans for the day. I would pick them up and take them home again after their outing. In return for my service, I would get a share of their catch to take home to the family.

Dad managed the hoarded cigarettes and put Paul, Fred, and me in charge of hiding the whiskey. We spent several days hauling the cases from Auntie Butler's house to ours. We hid a few at a time in a bull cart beneath loads of wood, bundles of clothing, or some other disguise. While we hid the whiskey, Auntie Butler buried caches of American cash in various places. Her family never found the largest cache, a box containing $6,000. It remains buried somewhere in Tutuhan, now the village of Agaña Heights.

My brothers and I dug a hole as well — a huge one in the floor of our cellar. The growing stacks of cases and excavated dirt made work in the confined cellar difficult. We dug during the day whenever we had free time and spent about three weeks on the task. Halfway through our project, when we had the whiskey cases stacked against one wall and a dirt pile against another, a patrol chose to spot check our house.

Paul and I stopped digging at the sound of heavy boots on the floorboards above us. The cellar was beneath the dining room, next to the living room and front entry. We held our breath and listened as the soldiers tramped through the house. We froze when they reached the dining room and walked toward the kitchen, which was two steps down from the dining room. The outside kitchen was another two steps down. The cellar door was to the right of the stairs. The soldiers walked around the kitchen then returned to the dining room and living room. Paul and I did not move until we heard them leave the house. We finished the project not long afterwards.

We eventually traded away several cases of whiskey and dug up the rest to restart Dad's business after the war. The American bombardment in 1944 destroyed our house, but the buried whiskey survived. We dug up as many cases as we could find. I am not sure we recovered all of them. A case or two may still be beneath Hagåtña's new, higher ground level, a good 6 to 8 feet above the old.

In addition to rustling his cattle at night, Dad also listened to radio reports from the United States. Bill Lujan, his stadium manager, was one of many who operated secret radios tuned in to news broadcasts from San Francisco. Relevant reports were written on tiny slips of paper, which were easy to hide and destroy. Dad, Tun Pedro Martinez, Auntie Butler, and a few others received the paper slip reports.

Until the Japanese shut down the power plant, the clandestine radio operators could plug their sets into household outlets. Then they took sets into the jungle and hooked them to batteries which needed regular recharging. Since I ran the markets and had authorized use of the pickup truck, I had unrestricted access to our battery charger. When the radio batteries needed charging, the operators would sneak them to me at the market. I would recharge them along with the truck's battery. In exchange, the radio operators allowed me to be among the first to hear the latest news.

Police Chief Shimada and a lesson in bowing

Hagåtña remained sparsely populated after the invasion. It became a quiet, lonely place. CHamorus stayed away from the enemy as much as possible. Most families moved to their ranches, farms, or summer houses outside the city. We were among a few families forced to return to run the businesses. I would walk along deserted streets and abandoned houses to go to work at the market. The imposition of a curfew and mandatory blackouts made Hagåtña even lonelier at night. With little to do but mind a store empty of merchandise and customers, I would while away the day playing solitaire handball against the market wall outside. As head cashier and floor manager, I would go inside when needed.

I paid only cursory attention when Tita Torres came into the market one day. She wandered toward the fabric and notions area at the back of the store and began talking with another woman. I could not tell who was with her, and wondered if it was Lina, Tita's stepsister. I was sweet on Lina and would have relished seeing her but dared not approach uninvited. I left the women to their conversation and went outside to play ball.

With my back to the street, I did not notice that someone had come up behind me. A booming voice startled me. I turned to face the Japanese chief of police, a man named Shimada, who was tall, heavily built, and ugly. My failure to stop playing and bow to him angered him, making him look even uglier and meaner. I tried to make amends and bowed at once, but it was too late. When

I stood up, Shimada slapped my face. He slapped repeatedly until my lip split. Shouting angrily, Shimada then pummeled me with his fists. I did not understand what he was saying, but his booming voice echoed in the empty streets. When he punched me in the belly, I doubled over toward him. He shoved me back and punched me again. My knees buckled under me, but Shimada held me up with one hand and punched again with the other.

Nearly unconscious, I reeled around and looked toward the market, concerned that Tita might have been watching, or worse, that Lina was the other woman with her in the store. The idea that the girl I liked would see me trounced was humiliating. I was in pain, but my pride took the worst of it. Shimada was older and bigger than me, but strong men did not put up with such humiliation, and ladies lost respect for cowardly men who allowed it. I prayed for Shimada to finish and for Lina not to be in the store. I did not care who saw the beating, as long as it was not Lina or Tita, who might tell her about it.

Shimada stopped hitting me but continued to shout. He pointed toward the jailhouse and wagged his wristwatch in my face. With as much decorum as I could muster, I bowed unsteadily and staggered back into the market. Tita and the other female, whoever she was, were gone. I closed the market and washed up as best I could. My face was swollen, my eyes were black, and my ears glowed red with shame.

I went to the jailhouse without stopping at home to tell Dad. I knew he would become angry with me for being foolish and endangering the family. I did not want them to suffer for my misdeed and decided to bear the trouble alone. At the jailhouse, the CHamoru policemen conscripted by the Japanese looked at me with concern. They did not speak. Their eyes spoke for them. They sympathized, but they could do nothing. Chief Shimada appeared in a doorway and began yelling at me again. He slapped me twice before motioning toward the door and barking what I assumed was Japanese for "Get out." For a second time, I was chased from the jailhouse.

The days that followed were uneventful and growing more boring at the market, especially after all the merchandise was gone. After a while, the ice allotments were all that remained. The only break in the monotony was when meat was available. A crowd would come to buy small portions of beef, pork, horse, or carabao meat. Sometimes we would get some fresh fish.

Meat, especially beef, was in short supply but high demand. The Japanese authorized the slaughter of two steers and the sale of the meat once a month. No part of a slaughtered animal went to waste. People bought bones for the marrow and for soup. They also bought the hides. We sold steer heads whole to those who could afford them. Otherwise, we split the heads and sold the brains, tongues, ears, and skulls separately. It broke my heart to give up my horse, Girl. Dad and Paul managed to keep her hidden for several months. Rather than risk her discovery and lose Girl to the Japanese, Dad slaughtered her and kept the meat for us.

Even before the occupation, unemployment was high, wages were low, and American money was scarce. Not many people had cash all the time, so bartering and trading remained important. At the markets, we dealt mainly in coins and $2 bills. We sold butter in quarter-pound sticks because that was all anyone could afford at one time. On Navy government paydays, salaried workers bought groceries with $5 or $10 bills. Only for special family occasions would we see purchases made with a $20 bill. That was big money. By comparison, yen did not seem like real money. We considered it almost worthless.

Dad's secret money exchange netted him a small fortune in American money. He kept it in quiet circulation by spending it. He bought lumber and other construction materials from Tun Pedro Martinez and hired Ben "Titang" Salas, a carpenter, to renovate our house. He added two indoor bathrooms — one for the girls, the other for the boys. He enlarged the boys' bedroom and added a special room just for Mama. She had always wanted such a room, a private, quiet place for herself. She did her sewing, mending, ironing, and folding in it. It was a workroom, but it was her special place.

The American in the gully

Dad was always looking for new and better ways to provide for his large family, always involving us in projects of one sort or another. Sometimes his projects meant drudgery work; other times they meant fun and excitement. Dad broke the boredom for me one day with instructions to drive Irene to Tun Encho Sablan's ranch in Chalan Pago. I leapt at the chance to take to the road and do something different.

Tun Encho was Dad's head butcher. He was also a good farmer. He knew we were a large family and often offered us part of his harvests, even before the occupation. Tun Encho had again offered some fruits and vegetables, which Irene and I were to pick up. We drove to his ranch, about 4 miles southeast of Hagåtña. He greeted us and invited us inside. Several baskets of fruits and vegetables were ready for us. I began loading them onto the truck while Irene visited with Tun Encho. Moments later, I noticed they had ceased talking and were no longer in the house. As I finished loading the baskets, Irene reappeared. She looked troubled but said nothing as she climbed into the truck.

"What's wrong, Irene?" I asked, angry with myself for not having been more watchful. Irene shut her eyes and shook her head, refusing to answer. "Something's bothering you. What is it? What happened back there?" I demanded.

"Tun Encho took me to a ravine behind the ranch," she said. "There was an American hiding in the gully. He said his name is Tyson, and Tun Encho is helping him. Ricky, if the Japanese find him, they'll kill Tun Encho, too."

Tyson was one of the Navy men who, like George Tweed, escaped into the jungle. The others — Yablonski, Krump, Johnson, and Jones — went from one hiding place to another with CHamoru help. The Japanese were relentless in their search for the Americans. They detained, interrogated, and tortured any CHamoru they suspected, killing many in the process. In the end, the Japanese caught and executed all but Tweed.

The information Irene now had made us vulnerable. She feared the terrible secret would show in her face, that it was something she could not hide, something the Japanese would get out of her if they questioned her. Irene was troubled and quiet all the way home.

Before entering the city, we had to clear a check point at the bottom of San Ramon. I stopped the truck, got out, and bowed to the soldier on duty. When I stood up, he was scowling. He started brandishing his rifle and shouting at me. I was sure I had bowed properly. I did not want to anger him further, so I bowed again, the kind of bow reserved for officers and high-ranking officials. But that did not flatter him. Instead, he shouted louder and jabbed his bayonet toward the truck. I turned my head slowly, careful not to turn my body away from him, to look at the truck. Irene was still sitting inside, lost in deep thought.

"For God's sake, Irene, get down and bow," I growled at her.

Jolted from her thoughts, and surprised we were already in Hagåtña, Irene jumped out of the truck and scurried around to stand beside me. I shot her an irritated glance; hers was penitent. Together, we made a deep, important-person's bow to appease the soldier. He smiled and waved us through.

The Japanese captured and executed Tyson, but by then, he was no longer in Tun Encho's care.

Chapter 11

Securing the pleasures of the flesh

Long before the occupation, John Taitano regaled me with stories of his sexual exploits. The occupation and the rigidness of the Japanese codes could not keep him from seeking and securing the pleasures of the flesh. John, one of Dad's San Nicolas market employees, was older than me, but he took me into his confidence when I was 10 and he was 18. I learned much from John about life and women, about how to pursue them, woo them, and, eventually, how to indulge in life's greatest pleasure, sex. As business at the market slowed, he would spend hours entertaining me with stories of his latest escapades.

John was dark-skinned and had perfect, white teeth. His laugh was contagious — the kind that came from deep down in the belly, the kind that made others laugh along, even before they knew what was funny. John bragged that his dark skin helped him skulk around undetected at night. He would climb through his lady love's window and make love to her while her parents went about their business downstairs. He would describe in glowing, graphic terms every scintillating detail of his bedroom performances. A self-proclaimed expert, he would expound on the virtuosity of great sex partners, and with feigned indifference, talk about mediocre ones.

Before the occupation, whenever Dad's drivers gathered, their conversations always turned to women, sex, and Tan Sepan Eka's latest judgments. The jokes, the wild escapades, and the delightful stories enthralled me long before I was old enough to contribute to the storytelling.

Tan 'Sepa was an uninhibited old lady and a colorful, well-known character in Hagåtña. She took advantage of her age to do as she pleased and used her experience to determine the virility of Hagåtña's developing young males. Everyone knew of her penchant for grabbing at adolescent male crotches for quick examination, but no one ever thought ill of her. Tan 'Sepa was a philosopher, wise in the ways of the flesh. She imparted her wisdom about sex and life without reservation. She told young men how to take proper care of themselves so that they would grow up, please their women, enjoy sex, and have children.

"Come here," she would command young boys, knowing they would respectfully obey. "Let me feel if you're growing up right." She would feel about, laugh, then pass judgement: "A little more time, son, a little more growing for you."

If judged by Western standards as I was, Tan 'Sepa could have been charged with carnal knowledge, lewd and lascivious behavior, sexual misconduct, child molestation, contributing to the delinquency of minors, assault, and worse, depending on the prudishness of her prosecutor. Westerners are quick to apply their standards and values upon others. In addition to their social and political contradictions, the Americans were contradictory about sex. It was taboo, something kept secret and hidden. They were uncomfortable with the casual way CHamorus discussed it in ordinary conversation but were eager listeners. American military men nearly worshiped naked women. Enlisted men plastered their barracks walls with nude pinups. Large, rounded breasts and long legs seemed to be their favorite parts of the female anatomy.

As a youngster, I found the American fascination with breasts odd. CHamorus did not consider bare breasts stimulating. Breasts were for feeding babies. Almost every CHamoru mother breastfed her children. Nursing an infant in public was commonplace, not shocking. As the eldest of 10 brothers and sisters, and as my parents' delivery boy, I had seen many, many breasts. I did not blush at the sight of them the way young military men did. I could not understand their preoccupation with them.

In 1978, during my first term as governor, then-Marshall Islands Administrator Amata Kabua invited me to speak at his nation's constitutional convention. The Marshallese people ratified their constitution and elected Kabua their first president in 1979. Kabua took me on a tour of the islands, and at Arno Atoll, he pointed out its fame as one of the last traditional places for teaching adolescent females the art of sex and marriage. Such schools were common among many Pacific Island cultures until Western influences intervened. Kabua and I agreed Arno Atoll's "love university" would have scandalized the prudish Americans. They would condemn such native practices as evil, obscene, and pornographic, and outlaw them. They would apply their own values and standards of morality, then entangle themselves in their own contradictions.

The Catholic religion, as imparted by the Spaniards, had strict rules about sex and marriage. Many of these conflicted with ancient CHamoru customs and beliefs. Despite centuries of enforced religious education, CHamorus never completely abandoned old beliefs for alien, new ones, particularly about sex. Our own value system decided what was a "sin" and what was not. Sinful or not, sex was not a dark secret discovered in adulthood. CHamoru children knew what the consummation of marriage meant.

Sex for me was not a mystery. It was part of life. I had seen the mating and birthing of livestock and pets so often that I knew how one led to the other. The raucous, risqué jokes of Dad's taxi drivers, along with Francisco "Galabook" Delgado and John Taitano's exploits, whetted my appetite for the experience, as did my childhood spying on American sailors groping the girls in the Suzuki bar. The sailors' glassy-eyed pawing and the girls' giggling responses aroused me in ways animal husbandry never could. I knew sex was a powerful driving force and an incredibly delicious activity, but I had yet to experience what my older acquaintances joked and laughed about. That changed during the occupation.

As our store shelves emptied, John had to find other means of work, and I had little to do but wait for closing time. One afternoon, a young street vendor came into the market. She greeted me with a polite smile and set down the cardboard box of homemade sweets she had been selling. She looked worn out and glad for the chance to rest in the cool of the store. She was from a poor family. Her shapeless dress was threadbare and rumpled, but she was pretty. She was around my age and well on her way to womanhood. I could see her panty and her budding chest through her flimsy dress and was getting aroused.

As I watched her, I realized how the occupation had changed our lives. In an earlier, happier time, girls her age would not have had to peddle doughnuts in the streets to support their family. In her developing womanhood, her family would have protected and shielded her from the lascivious looks of young men like me. Although she said nothing, a glimmer of admiration shone in her eyes. I realized I wanted to do more than impress her.

I liked showing off in front of the pretty girls who came into the market. I would shut down the reefer generators. The sudden silence drew their immediate attention to me. Then, with an air of confident authority, I would restart the generators, making a big to-do guaranteed to impress. I would flip certain switches and climb onto a small lift that raised me up to a complicated panel of gauges and buttons. I would check the gauges, turn knobs, and push buttons, making it seem like technical wizardry. No engineer took the task more seriously. Once the generators were humming again, I would descend before admiring eyes.

At 15, fired with desire and a sense of urgency, I wanted more than the vendor's smile. The occupation was too uncertain a time to leave normal developments to chance. I did not know whether I would survive the occupation, or even the next day, and did not want my life to end without experiencing sex. I think she felt the same way. She was not uneasy or anxious when I approached and sat beside her. We exchanged pleasantries again. After a few minutes of small talk, I touched her cheek and let my hand rest on her shoulder. She did not shrink from my touch. She needed me as much as I wanted her. We did not need any words. I got up, closed and barred the market doors, and turned off the lights. I returned to her side and began groping her body the way I had seen sailors do. She guided my hands and explored me with hers. In the darkened market, I discovered for myself what sex was all about.

She returned to the market several times after that. Sometimes she would be waiting for me outside the market in the morning. Sometimes several days would pass before she came to me again. And I would miss her terribly. Our trysts continued during the most horrible period of our people's history, yet she and I discovered the tenderness and beauty two people can share. But just as suddenly as she had appeared, she disappeared. She stopped coming to the market. I never knew whether she stopped caring for me or whether she fell victim to the precarious times. She still commands a special place in my heart.

The Japanese thought nothing of taking an innocent life, especially that of a pretty girl who rejected their affections. To protect themselves from unwanted attention, many of Hagåtña's fair maidens "dressed down" during the occupation. Hagåtña was home to a number of beautiful girls. Many of them, like Patsy Notley, Marian Johnston, Maria Perez Howard, as well as the Villarde, the Torres, the Martinez, and the Underwood sisters, were beautiful, fashion-conscious, and skilled in social graces. To protect their daughters, several families convinced a sympathetic Japanese doctor to say they suffered from tuberculosis, which worked well. Other ploys did not.

With soldiers in the Mayhew house, Mama and Dad worried about my sisters. Irene was 18, fair-skinned, and blue-eyed. Dark-haired Lorraine was 17 and looked like Mama. Both girls were vulnerable. Bobbie, who was born after me, and Norma, who was born between Paul and Fred, were between childhood and adulthood. Bobbie was 13; Norma was 10. Like Lorraine, Bobbie's skin was a warm golden brown. Her hair was dark and curly, like Mama's. Norma was blue-eyed and fair, like Irene. At ages 5 and 4 respectively, Junie and Bobing were little more than babies, but Mama and Daddy feared for all of them.

Like her friends, Irene went out of her way to look unattractive. Despite her best efforts, she caught the fancy of a *keibitai* officer named Captain Awata, who was based next door at the Mayhew house. He had ample opportunity to watch Irene. We often caught him leering at her as she did her chores. We had to put up with his advances or invite untold abuse for insulting him.

Captain Awata was so ugly we nicknamed him "Bulldog." He looked like one. Awata once bragged to us that he nursed at his mother's breast until he was 10 years old. He was proud of it and snickered at our shocked reaction. He led us to think breastfeeding beyond infancy was a common Japanese practice, but we did not believe it. We decided the real reason it took so long to wean him was because he was ugly.

He came to the house one day with the "request" we dreaded. He wanted to take Irene as his guest to a Japanese party at Ádilok. Mama and Dad knew Awata would make a move and had planned for it. Mama told him Irene could go only if chaperoned. Bulldog reluctantly agreed. On the evening of the party, he arrived with a car and Saipanese chauffeur. He thought he could outsmart Mama by providing the chaperone, but Mama was not gullible. She sent Norma with Irene, Awata, and the driver.

As soon as they left for Ádilok, Mama began reciting a rosary and pleading with the Blessed Mother to protect her daughters. Mama kept vigil at her bedroom window until my sisters were home. Less than two hours later, the car returned. Bulldog and his driver dropped the girls then sped off. We met Irene and Norma at the door. Irene threw her arms around Mama with relief. Norma was calm but ashen. Mama demanded to know what happened.

The girls were scared and glad to be home. There was no party at Ádilok. The building was dark and empty. Awata told Norma to go back to the car, but she refused and clung to Irene. Despite Norma's presence, Awata attempted to seduce Irene, but she froze at his touch and hugged Norma tighter. Awata got angry and gave up. He ordered them back into the car and brought them home. He remained stationed next door but never returned to our house, neither were we penalized in any way. We never knew whether he accepted Irene's rejection or was ordered to stay away from B.J. Bordallo's daughter.

Franklin Delano Bordallo

Dad bore up under the pressures of heading a large family, running the businesses, and trying to figure out what the Japanese wanted of us. Mama was perfect as his partner. She stood steadfast at his side, giving him strength, looking after us, and keeping our home as best she could. Luckily, we all remained healthy. Only baby Franklin was having trouble. He was sickly since his birth in March 1942. Mama fretted about him. Her body had produced ample supplies of milk for her babies, but not for Franklin. She had to rely on canned milk. When he was about 9 months old, Franklin developed severe diarrhea and began losing weight and strength. Mama pumped him with fluids and milk, but the diarrhea did not abate. Franklin grew listless and steadily weaker and cried all the time. We all were afraid for him.

At the height of Franklin's illness, we ran out of milk. Mama sent me to the Japanese family of collaborators who lived a few doors down from us. As "friendly civilians," they had supplies of everything. Mama was certain they would still be compassionate enough to trade some beef for a few cans of evaporated milk. For trade, beef was better than gold. Even a small piece was valuable. I worried about Mama. Caring for Franklin, worrying about Dad, and trying to run a large household was exhausting her. Her readiness to trade our share of beef for milk was a sign of her desperation and growing fear.

Since we had just received the market's monthly quota of two slaughtered steer, I cut and dressed a handsome piece weighing about 40 pounds, certain it was worth half a case of milk. Milk for my sick brother and a measure of comfort for my mother was worth a king's ransom in meat. I hoisted the beef on my shoulder and went to the Japanese family's house.

At their door, I waited on the walk and called out a greeting. I dared not invite myself onto their porch as I would have in happier times. Their yard had always been beautiful — a miniature Japanese garden with a carpet of close-cropped Japanese grass, an ornate stone lantern, and a little half-moon bridge spanning a goldfish pond. I always liked watching the goldfish. I marveled as I looked around. Hagåtña was quiet, all but deserted and gloomy, yet this family's life remained comfortable.

"Yes, Ricky? What do you want?" the Japanese man's wife, a CHamoru woman, demanded from behind her screen door. Her suspicious manner reminded me again of how different and sad our lives had become. Her family and mine had been friends and neighbors for years, but after the Japanese invaded, they severed old bonds and friendships and cozied up to the invaders for preferential favor. Her husband and children flaunted their new status. Mine was not the only family to shun them.

"Mama told me to bring you this meat and ask to trade for some cans of milk. The baby is very sick and needs the milk," I said, humiliated at having to speak up to her from the bottom of the steps with a side of raw meat on my shoulder. Under normal conditions, word of a sick baby would have inspired generous offers from neighbors and friends eager to help, without the need to ask, or even to trade. Our cash-poor community was rich in compassion.

"Take it to the kitchen and leave it on the table," she said. She opened the door, motioned me in, then disappeared into the house. I hopped up the steps and into her kitchen, keen to be rid of my load. Without waiting for her to reappear, I went back outside to the bottom of the steps. She came to the door a minute later.

"Tell your mother I'm sorry this is all I can spare," she said and handed me a half empty five-ounce can of evaporated milk. I stared at the open can in disbelief — half a small can for a side of beef. I was cheated and felt angry but could do nothing. Dejected, I walked home and gave Mama the little bit of milk. Franklin died a few days later.

We grieved for a long time. Franklin's death was hardest on Mama; he was her second loss. We buried Franklin and went back to the business of surviving. Those of us old enough to be productive went to work. Mama and the girls took care of the house and the little ones. Dad and Paul tended to our hidden cattle and the garden in Apotguan. I looked after the truck, the market, and trading Dad's empty gasoline drums for food. I also oversaw Dad's garbage collection service, a concession he secured from the Japanese.

The Hagåtña garbage collector

Several of us had the unpleasant task of scooping up cattle and carabao manure on the streets. I did not mind the work, but I did not want my sweetheart Lina Torres to see me with my bull cart shoveling manure in front of her house. I made deals with the other collectors to swap routes and often ended up with the most disgusting one: emptying the waste bins at the Susana Hospital morgue. As ghastly as it was, the morgue route was better than letting Lina see me shoveling dung.

The Susana Hospital was an expansive complex that served both the Navy community and us. It had large wards, private rooms, and modern, American medical equipment, pharmaceuticals, and supplies. By comparison, the Japanese hospital in Saipan was small and not as well equipped. The Susana Hospital was the only large medical facility in the Japanese-held Pacific. It received the wounded and dying from battlefields all around.

The Susana's morgue was the scariest part of the hospital. It was in a small building isolated at the back of the complex. It reeked of death and formaldehyde. The old CHamoru mortician who haunted the place before the occupation was a gaunt character who looked the part. He had dead eyes and leathery skin bleached by years of exposure to embalming fluid. Children fled in terror of him.

The Susana Hospital garbage route was often a good gauge of the course of the war. The Japanese would boast of their victories and made us assemble in the plaza to yell, "*Banzai!*" They commandeered the Gaiety Theater and showed only propaganda films and newsreels which conflicted with U.S. news reports coming over the secret radios. I could tell by the amount and type of morgue refuse which account was more accurate. The Japanese would claim victories and few casualties, but the morgue garbage cans would contain great wads of bloody bandages, amputated body parts, and gory masses of unrecognizable human flesh. If the radio reports told of a freighter sinking or some skirmish in our area of the Pacific, the hospital garbage bins would validate the news. Despite the years I had spent as a butcher, I never grew numb to the sight of discarded human flesh.

After a while, I worried I would start looking like the old mortician. Garbage collecting was distasteful, but I preferred it to boredom and idleness. Accustomed to keeping a full and busy work schedule, I could not bear the inactivity of the market. I looked forward to the bimonthly beef slaughter and to the road trips with Dad's empty oil drums. Once a month, I would drive to Sumai to get fresh fish from the Pan Am Hotel reefers where the conscripted Korean fishermen stored their catches. Most of the fish was for the Japanese, but we also got a small amount.

Because we were authorized to use the truck, roving patrols did not often stop to question me on the road. As Dad's driver, I did not have to justify my itinerary and could go anywhere on the island. As the war dragged on, and an American invasion became imminent, I could keep tabs on how the Japanese were preparing for it. I knew where they built bunkers and pillboxes. That information became important after the Americans landed. The truck gave me the freedom to be on the road, but driving along quiet, empty roads was lonely work. Vehicle traffic was never plentiful before the occupation, but there were always pedestrians, bicycles, and bull carts going about their business, waving greetings, free and unafraid.

The circumstances that forced a peaceful, gentle people into fearful hiding were depressing. We were like sand crabs on a beach, basking in the sun until a threat approached. In the blink of an eye, we would disappear into our little holes. I was a sand crab, too, but I could still move about freely and did not have to disappear at the first sign of danger. It was a lonesome privilege that gave me time to think about what was happening to my people.

I could drive for hours without seeing anyone, but I knew where they were. I would drive into the jungle and come upon small, secret gardens. In happier, peaceful times, the gardens would be large and proudly tended. The occupation made it necessary for growers to make them small and hidden so that the Japanese would not confiscate the harvests. The privilege of knowing the hiding places of families in the jungles was greater than being able to travel with ease. I would come to trade with families who welcomed me like a hero. I would bring gossip and news about other families, about the goings-on in Hagåtña, about the war and the Japanese. I was their link to a way of life that once was. Because of it, I developed a deep and intimate sense of duty and responsibility to my people. That sense did not end with the war.

"If that is God's will, I will accept it"

Trips in the truck did not occur every day. My usual location was at the San Nicolas market, which was more a cold storage and freezer facility than a grocery store. With no produce to sell and limited ice, meat, and fish allotments, the market was also empty of customers. Alone and bored, I would always look forward to Påle' Dueñas ' occasional visits to Hagåtña. He was a restless, charismatic man, full of wisdom. I thought he was brilliant. He shared his philosophies generously and enthusiastically.

Påle' Jesus Baza Dueñas was the pastor of St. Joseph's Church in Inalåhan. He had studied in the Philippines and was the second CHamoru, after Padre Jose Palomo, to be ordained a Roman Catholic priest. Upon his return to Guam in 1938, Påle' Dueñas taught *eskuelan påle'*, catechism classes. I was one of his students. After his assignment to St. Joseph's, Påle' would come to Hagåtña on weekends to visit his parents who lived near the market. Whenever he was in town, and while the market was still open, I would make deliveries to his parents' house then sit with him and talk for hours. When the market closed for good, I would visit with him even longer.

Påle' Dueñas got me in trouble with Dad when I was 10 years old, but because of it, I came to respect and admire him. I was bored with *eskuelan påle'* and often skipped classes to go swimming at the Minondo, the celebrated site of the legend of Sirena the mermaid. She was a child who spent too much time at the Minondo. Her mother prohibited her from going there again, but Sirena defied her. Enraged, her mother cursed her to become a fish. Sirena's godmother intervened. Since she held Sirena's head beneath the holy water at baptism, she could shield Sirena's upper half from the curse. Sirena became half human, half fish in the Minondo. Sentenced to life as a mermaid, she followed the Hagåtña River to the sea and disappeared forever. The moral of the story was that children should obey their parents and not spend so much time at the Minondo. But it did not work; the Minondo remained a popular swimming hole.

I confessed to Dad that I often skipped *eskuelan påle'* to go to the Minondo. I expected a scolding and a licking, but Dad ordered me to apologize to Påle'. That was worse than delivering Dad's letter to Commander Perry. Påle' would know why I had come before him. I would have preferred a spanking, but the penance was not the misery I expected. Påle' Dueñas scolded me then became kind and understanding. I sensed his concern for me, and I liked him at once. We were friends from then on, and I attended *eskuelan påle'* without fail, even after Påle' Dueñas was no longer my teacher.

His assignment to Inalåhan kept us apart, but his occasional trips to Hagåtña brought us together. I enjoyed philosophizing and discussing important matters with him. He influenced my thinking on many issues, particularly about the preservation of human dignity and the courage to defend it. I still adhere to many of his lessons.

Påle' Dueñas' stand against the Japanese was well known. On the day of the invasion, he gathered a bunch of boys to defend the island. Bishop Olano stopped the attempt. Påle' then fought the Japanese with words. He protested the Japanese government and its tyranny over CHamorus from his pulpit. He condemned Japanese brutality, decried the use of forced labor, and demanded respect for CHamoru civil rights and an end to all atrocities. We knew he was endangering himself. Many people pleaded with him to temper his verbal attacks, but Påle' refused to be silent. The Japanese authorities ignored him at first, but later, as he grew more irritating to them, they threatened to banish him to Rota. One of the Japanese priests interceded in Påle''s behalf, and he remained in Guam.

During one of Påle''s last visits to Hagåtña, I expressed concern for his welfare and attempted to persuade him to ease up. "Ricky," he said, unconvinced and unmoved, "hold firm to your convictions. Speak out against what you know to be wrong. Never be afraid because God always stands on the side of Truth. That is what it means to me to be a priest. I am aware my actions may get me into trouble, but if that is God's will, I will accept it." I never forgot the lesson; it fortified my political convictions.

Påle' Dueñas continued his opposition until the Japanese ran out of patience. They arrested and tortured Påle' and his nephew Edward, an attorney, so severely they were unrecognizable. Nine days before the American landing, the Japanese beheaded Påle' and his nephew in Ta'i. If he had survived the war, Påle' Dueñas would have been an implacable advocate for CHamoru rights. He was a political activist who did more than preach. His death was Guam's great loss.

A need to celebrate life

The Japanese were unpredictable, and we never knew what might set them off. The *keibitai* issued hundreds of rules and regulations. Some would disappear, and new ones would come out. We knew about some but not others. The soldiers themselves did not always seem certain. They sometimes ignored obvious violations or struck innocent people for no reason. We avoided them as much as possible. And they left us alone as long as we delivered our food quotas.

The quotas and labor conscriptions were based on village population, and the Japanese appointed *sånchos* to oversee deliveries. Uncle Felix, Mama's brother, was the *såncho* in Sumai. Hagåtña's *såncho* was Manuel Lujan, who later became a respected political leader. The Japanese police beat the *sånchos* who did not deliver their village's quotas on time or produce the required number of conscript laborers. Some *sånchos* invented excuses if villagers could not meet the quotas. Many risked their own safety to protect the people in their villages.

Manuel had an easier time offering believable excuses. The city's population fluctuated after the invasion so much that the Japanese could not get accurate figures. Manuel took advantage of the fluctuations and delivered new numbers every month, forcing revisions of Hagåtña's quota. Sometimes it was as little as 2 tons of dried corn or as much as 50 hogs and 500 chickens. To fill the quotas, Manuel went from family to family, collecting only what each could spare. If the quota was short, he told the Japanese more residents had moved away. He used the same excuse for labor conscriptions, freeing many of us from labor details early in the occupation. Manuel secured many exemptions for Dad, but after the Japanese stepped up construction for fortifications, no one escaped. Dad eventually joined hundreds of others unloading cement sacks by hand in Piti. I did labor at Halåguak, hand-carving an airfield out of cornfields and jungle.

The Japanese production demands and our own survival needs left little time for leisure. Once in a while, on a free weekend or on some Japanese holiday, there was time to mark the end of a novena with a small celebration or for someone to host a party for some happy occasion. Sometimes someone would throw a party merely to bring people together to laugh and sing and dance again. As I look back on them, I realize the parties represented the triumph

of the human spirit over adversity. They provided a temporary reprieve from
fear and sadness to repair broken spirits, to mend our society, and to reassure
ourselves that we could endure the disruption of our lives.

Unlike our celebrations before the occupation, the wartime parties were
meager. If the only refreshments were slightly sweetened, colored water with
ice, the party was a success. Even without refreshments, every gathering was
a happy affair and a sad one at the same time. No matter how hard we tried to
recapture the peace and joy of earlier times, we could not escape the reality
of our enslavement.

The Villardes often hosted parties in their two-story home across from
Tun Vicente Martinez's house in the Hulåli district. For me, approaching the
Villardes' parties was eerie: I would ride my bicycle along dark, empty streets.
Then, out of the darkness, I would see lights and hear music. They contrasted
with the days when warm, welcoming lights and music and laughter were un-
restrained. Where once the homes of peaceful people lit the narrow streets,
there was now only one small spark in the darkness. Where there was once
joyful music, there was now just faint melodies.

Hannah Chance Torres also hosted parties that brought young people
together in wholesome and traditional ways. Hannah had a deep and appreciative understanding of teenagers. She understood our need to celebrate life, especially because we faced uncertainty. She bolstered young hopes and dreams.
Her great strength and optimism assured us that we could indeed reach adulthood. Hannah's parties also nurtured budding romances, like Lina's and mine,
and sustained those that predated the occupation. Her socials brought lovers
together again without fear, to hold hands and whisper and maybe steal kisses
in a secluded corner.

In happier times, the love developing between couples was almost a
community affair. Friends and relatives were part of the process, sharing in
the delight of flowering love and celebrating when it turned into marriage. But
the constant threat of death overshadowed lovers during the occupation. The
war time denied us the freedom to share their happiness. I started courting
Lina after the occupation began, but like many other couples, we could not see
each other often. Ours was only puppy love, but we thought we were in love
and pined to be together. Hannah was Lina's sister-in-law; she was older and
obligated to safeguard Lina, but she would arrange for Lina and me to have
some time alone.

The parties were sentimental affairs. Sometimes even Japanese officers and civilians attended as invited guests. We spent hours boldly dancing the jitterbug, foxtrot, and waltzes to American music. Musicians like Boy Damian; Nick Manibusan, who went by the stage name Duke Navarro; Cristobal Hines and his musicians, who once formed the Hines Orchestra; Tun Enchu Aflague and his son Alex; and so many other music makers could banish our miserable condition for a while. I mastered the art of dancing at these gatherings. Laughing at my clumsy early efforts was part of everyone's enjoyment, including mine. When I was good enough, I approached Mama in my best gentlemanly politeness and asked her onto the dance floor. With proud delight, she took my hand.

There were parties in the jungle as well as in Hagåtña. Without electricity, party hosts scheduled their gatherings according to the phases of the moon. On full moon nights, when the jungle shimmered in soft silver light, we would come together for the camaraderie, to sing songs, and capture some gladness. The songs were like prayers beseeching an end to the nightmare.

After one such moonlight party in Maite, Marian Johnston's companions inadvertently left her behind. Marian faced the unacceptable prospect of walking home alone in the dark. I was about to leave for home also but was riding my bicycle. I offered Marian a lift if she did not mind sitting on the handlebars. Marian agreed but made me promise never to tell anyone the indignity. Eager for the honor and privilege of taking one of the most beautiful girls in Hagåtña home, I made her the promise.

Marian hoisted herself onto my bicycle and planted herself as comfortably as she could on the handlebars. Her fanny was directly in front of my face. As we headed off, Marian wriggled to maintain her balance and squealed almost all the way home. I was torn between keeping my eyes on the road and watching Marian's squirming fanny. I did enough of both to make the ride unsteady. The more unsteady the ride, the more Marian squirmed and squealed. The ride was unforgettable. It was a wonderful end to a wonderful evening, even though I could tell no one about it.

Forty-five years later, Marian released me from my promise not to tell. I told her I wanted to include the memory of that ride in my book. She laughed and recounted the incident. She admitted she had known I was not watching the road but added that she was never concerned or afraid because it was "dependable little Ricky Boy who drove me home that night."

The parties in Hagåtña and under the moonlight in the jungle occurred only occasionally between 1942 and 1943. In January 1944, the Japanese Army and its *kempeitai*, or military police, returned to fortify Guam against the impending American invasion. They brought with them a new group, the *kaikuntai*, an agricultural force, to wrest as much food production as possible from an already exhausted people.

Chapter 12

Mrs. Riye Dejima, one of us

The Japanese Navy tried hard to win CHamoru support for the Greater East Asia Co-Prosperity Sphere. For the 22 months of Japanese Naval rule, a relative peace reigned. Rather than intimidate us with cannon displays, the Navy tried to normalize community life and reprogram us as productive members of the empire. They imported propaganda movies and newsreels and staged cultural shows and exhibitions for our enlightenment and amusement, which were entertaining but unsuccessful. In addition to teachers, priests, sex workers, medical personnel, and some technical experts, Navy officials even brought their dependents to Guam.

The Navy administrators wanted us to adopt their kind of commitment to regimented discipline, absolute obedience, and unswerving loyalty to the emperor. Our stubbornness frustrated them. The Navy was more tolerant than the Army but was just as relentless about capturing the escaped Americans. The searches, interrogations, and beatings never ceased. They had collaborators and Saipanese interpreters at their command, but the Japanese never understood us.

Among Guam's long-time Japanese residents, Mrs. Riye Dejima, the widow of a Japanese merchant, did know CHamorus well. She buffered many of the differences between the Japanese and the CHamorus. She was Japanese and understood them, but she was also Guamanian and understood us. She was part of our community long before the occupation and was one of us. She was a beautiful woman with skin like fine porcelain. She spoke fluent CHamoru, as had many other Japanese nationals and most of Guam's American civilians.

When the occupation began, Mrs. Dejima quietly sided with the

CHamorus and remained pro-American. While other Japanese nationals curried favor by entertaining the occupying forces in their homes, Mrs. Dejima kept to herself. She continued to run her store, opening it in the morning and closing it at night, never altering her routine. The occupying Japanese assumed she was sympathetic to their cause and accorded her several privileges. Rather than reserve them for herself and her daughter, Mrs. Dejima used them and her status to help others. She often gave food and supplies to those who had little or none. Mrs. Dejima also regularly sent food to the American servicemen in hiding. Had Japanese officials known, they would have executed both Mrs. Dejima and her daughter.

Occasionally, during my delivery rounds, I would find her talking with Japanese soldiers in her store. I could not understand their conversations, but I knew enough Japanese to eavesdrop. To promote understanding and win sympathy for us, Mrs. Dejima would tell the men that CHamorus were not a warlike people and that we had welcomed her into our community. After the soldiers left, we would sit and talk. She would tell me of her efforts to make her countrymen learn more about us.

During the American battle to recapture Guam, Mrs. Dejima and her daughter went into hiding with other Japanese civilians in Yigo. They were expected to commit suicide rather than surrender to the Americans. Some did, some did not. Mrs. Dejima and her daughter chose not to commit *hara-kiri*, the ritual act of suicide to avoid the disgrace of being captured by the enemy. The Americans arrested all who did not kill themselves and imprisoned them in Tutuhan along with captured Japanese soldiers. Many CHamorus, including Dad and Auntie Butler, testified in Mrs. Dejima's behalf to convince the Americans that she was not a war criminal. Mrs. Dejima continued to live in Guam after the war. Her little store, which she relocated to Tamuning, is an old and familiar landmark.

Singing and dancing at the altar

To win us over, the Japanese constantly reminded us of the discrimination the Americans practiced against us. The Americans had their faults, but they did not torture or kill us. The Japanese knew we remained pro-American despite their propaganda programs and the efforts made by the collaborators and the Saipanese CHamorus. Pro-Americans, like Mrs. Dejima and a few other Japanese Guamanians, did nothing to further the Japanese cause.

Although the Japanese ordered all traces of Americanism erased, they also held a strange fascination for anything American, particularly among the lower-ranked enlisted personnel. We would watch them puzzling over a gadget common to us but unfamiliar to them, like American toilets. We laughed at their lack of sophistication but never in their presence. We watched several soldiers kneel before toilet bowls and use them to wash their faces. They also smeared butter on themselves, thinking it was soap, and we snickered as they tried to wash it off.

The Japanese banned American songs and music but liked them enough to ignore their own ban. They slapped Nanan Chong's son Frank several times for whistling "Yankee Doodle," yet they forced others in my family, including me, to perform popular American songs and dances for their entertainment.

Eager to please his countrymen, our Japanese neighbor offered to organize American-style musical variety shows to entertain the troops. He knew who in the community were talented performers and used veiled threats to make them cooperate. He enlisted Tun Inocencio Aflague and his sons Wilfred and Alex to direct the shows. He lined up Auntie Rose, who, like Mama, was a gifted vocalist and pianist, and Nick "Duke Navarro" Manibusan, a popular tap dancer. The troupe was a mix of amateurs and professionals. Boy Damian, sisters Rosie and Nancy Underwood, Marian Johnston and Cynthia Torres, and my sisters and I were among many who performed.

The Japanese stripped the Dulce Nombre de Maria Cathedral of religious statues and altar vestments and converted it into an assembly hall where we were to perform. We could not escape the sanctity of the place. The confessionals, the ifit pews inlaid with the names of cathedral benefactors, the beautiful frescos on the walls and ceiling, and the dome above the altar characterized it as a church, our church, where we had worshipped all our lives. But the acoustics were perfect. Center stage was in front of the altar, the holiest and most sacred part of the church. The sacristy became our dressing room.

The Japanese easily ignored the surroundings, but we could not. We were certain God would send down His wrath upon us as we performed. We were glad for the chance to sing, dance, and make music again, even if it were to entertain the enemy, but we were torn with guilt about desecrating a holy place. With prayers asking God's forgiveness, half-naked hula dancers, their midriffs, backs, and shoulders exposed, undulated their hips to Hawai'ian music. Their legs peeking through their hula skirts enthralled the mostly male audiences.

We sang, danced, and performed skits before a packed house, and audiences welcomed our performances with thunderous applause, whistles, and stamping boots. Between numbers, we would steal into the darkness in the cathedral gardens and let passions reign. Several love affairs developed as a result; existing ones grew stronger. Under normal circumstances, none of this could ever occur. Neither would we be singing and dancing in the cathedral. Our parents sensed our misbehavior but dared not risk refusing "requests" for our talent.

I suppose we should have refused to cooperate and accepted death as an alternative, but the will to survive and the desire to be happy were just too powerful. The shows gave us a chance to gather under happier circumstances and some freedom from our stifling rules of proper behavior. Desecrating the cathedral was the most serious infraction, but it was beyond our control.

All my previous singing performances had been at family gatherings and on automobile trips to Sumai and Mayanghulo'. I had never faced a large audience until I sang for the Japanese. The experience forever cured me of stage fright. I knew if I could sing and dance for an audience capable of torturing and killing me, I could face any audience unafraid.

In return for our performances, the Japanese staged cultural shows for the public. Sometimes in the cathedral, in the St. Vincent de Paul Hall located next to the cathedral, or outdoors in the plaza. We enjoyed the novelty of Japanese music, singing, and dancing, and the ritual of sumo wrestling and Japanese fencing. Their penchant for discipline and regimentation was evident in their entertainment. Sumo wrestling was quite different from our style of boxing, and the black-robed fencers with birdcage face shields and long, split-bamboo swords were fascinating, but we were too accustomed to energetic American entertainment to appreciate Japanese classical music or the stilted style of kimono-clad dancers with white-painted faces.

Our variety shows were such successes that, much to our parents' discomfort, the Japanese arranged for us to perform for the troops occupying the U.S. Marine Barracks in Sumai. We rode a charcoal-fueled bus there. Riding a vehicle with a roaring furnace on board was odd. It awakened me to Japanese ingenuity and how their innovations were so creative and unique. Unlike the Americans, the Japanese military was poorly equipped. They compensated for their lack of resources with ingenuity and practicality. Because gasoline was scarce, with most of it kept for the war effort, they converted the bus's gas-driven engine to a wood-burning one.

The road into Sumai skirted the American Navy's golf course where Navy golfers once paid Sumai's children pennies to serve as caddies. After the invasion, the golf course remained under military control, but its new owners preferred cornfields to putting greens. As they did in Hagåtña, the Japanese turned the Sumai golf course into an agricultural project. Instead of rolling fairways, furrowed fields greeted us. The Japanese made the Americans' military base their own, though everything looked much the same. Like their counterparts in Hagåtña, the people of Sumai moved away, preferring the lack of modern amenities to sharing space with the enemy.

I had never paid much attention to the Marine Barracks before the invasion. The buildings and parade fields had always been part of the landscape. I had only been inside the barracks once before when I was 3 years old. My second visit was a revelation. I had no idea the facility was so impressive or that the Marines had lived in such comfort. The barracks was like another world. Under Japanese control, the complex still had an American look and feel — covered walkways connecting the buildings, sidewalks bordering flat expanses of clipped grass, the neatness typical of Navy orderliness. The Japanese did not change anything and seemed reverent about preserving the barracks' generous appointments. The poorly equipped Japanese must have thought the barracks was palatial. It was indeed better than anything we had.

Our "hosts" escorted us into a two-story building that I assumed had been the Marines' recreation center. The interior was neat, comfortable, and well-furnished. The floors were clean and shiny. We went into a spacious area that I assumed had been an officers' lounge. It was large enough to accommodate our floor show and an audience.

The Japanese received our performance with great enthusiasm and expressed their appreciation by serving refreshments. We did not expect such hospitality and stared in disbelief at a table filled with food selections. At home, rations were meager and always limited. Awestruck, we accepted our hosts' invitation to eat our fill.

We performed at the Marine Barracks only once. It was my only opportunity to see it from the inside. The returning Americans obliterated the barracks and most of Sumai and Hagåtña. The postwar Marine Barracks is nondescript, just one among rows of identical buildings. Only its red-painted staircase, the Marine Corps emblem, and the yellow letters "U.S.M.C." set it apart. It offers no testament to the Marines' hundred-year history in Guam, nor does it memorialize the Marines sacrificed to prison camps in 1942 and those who died here on the beaches and in the jungles in 1944.

After our performance in Sumai, we returned to Hagåtña thinking other show trips would follow, but there were none. Even the cathedral shows continued for only a few months longer.

"I never liked the man"

I ran the market even though we had no stock and few customers. The task was unbearably boring. I also continued making pick-ups and deliveries with the truck, but truck errands did not happen every day. I looked for any excuse to take to the road but made deliveries in the city on foot to save fuel. One day as I returned to the market, I ran into Mr. Tomas Santos, one of my teachers at George Washington. The encounter gave me a brilliant idea that would benefit us both.

Mr. Santos was a tall, slender man who reminded me of Abraham Lincoln without the beaver hat and beard. He had a reputation as an exceptional tennis player, the best among a handful of CHamoru players. Mr. Santos was a very dignified, articulate man whose bearing and thinness made him appear even taller. I had not seen him in months, and his appearance shocked me. He looked gaunt.

As we talked, I realized Mr. Santos was not getting enough to eat. He never admitted or even alluded to it, but I sensed it. I respected him a great deal, and his plight moved me. I sincerely wanted to help him, to give him some food, but I knew his pride would never let him accept charity. Then it occurred to me that I could help him without embarrassing or insulting him, and at the same time, I could fill my idle hours with mental stimulation. As a teacher and government worker, Mr. Santos was a font of wisdom and experience. His face brightened when I asked for his tutelage and offered some beef in exchange. We met for lessons a few times. He would lecture on different subjects, and I would pay him with food. His views turned out to be more conservative than mine, but I benefited from his knowledge.

I always felt good about helping Mr. Santos during the occupation and quite clever in the way I had done it. Our lecture sessions were sporadic and continued only while conditions allowed. In time, the market shut down for good. After the war, when I was a wealthy and successful Toyota distributor, Mr. Santos' son Fred asked me for a job. Out of respect for his father, I hired him. Fred proved to be an excellent salesman, one of my best. He was my senior salesman and earned a good salary and hefty commissions.

Mr. Santos and Fred became ardent Republicans. Despite our political differences, I continued to hold Mr. Santos in high regard. I could never bring myself to address him by his first name, even as governor. He was always Mr. Santos. After my trial and conviction in 1987, a news reporter asked Mr. Santos for his reaction. He said something along the lines of, "I never liked the man. He got what he deserved." His comments stung me more than the verdicts.

In the 1970s, Mr. Santos headed a federally funded senior citizen service program. When I assumed office in 1975, I did not exert pressure to have him replaced. He also kept the position during the tenure of my Republican successor, Paul Calvo. Paul appointed Fred Santos manager of the Guam Department of Commerce's public market, which I had completely rebuilt and dedicated in December 1978, the month before Calvo's inauguration. Under Fred's management, the public market burned to the ground in August 1982. When I resumed the governorship in 1983, I replaced Fred as manager. He and his father decried my action as political vindictiveness. They became among my most vocal detractors.

Like me, Tun Pedro Martinez's son To' operated what remained of his family's businesses. In addition to the one truck, the Martinezes had a few warehouses and some construction materials and plumbing supplies. We never understood why the Japanese put Dad in charge of Tun Pedro's ice plant or why they kept some plant workers but not those who were more experienced. One of them was Jesus "Gadi" Laguaña, an amazing ice wizard who worked for Tun Pedro for many years. As children, before the occupation, we would watch him in awe. Dad rehired him to help me with the ice sales and delivery. I had long admired Gadi's strength, grace, and agility. He taught me how to handle ice hooks and blocks, and I learned with almost the same skill.

Gadi was older than me, but I was his supervisor. He became my "Man Friday" and treated me with the same respect and loyalty he had for Dad. I could trust him to do anything for me, including the delicate task of delivering my gifts to Lina. I could trust him with my life. Despite our age difference and our employer-employee relationship, Gadi and I became good friends.

As governor in January 1983, I grappled with the painful decision to re-place Gadi's granddaughter, Pilar Laguaña, as assistant general manager of the Guam Visitors Bureau. Pilar, a Calvo appointee, did not hide her disappoint-ment at my election victory. She made it clear at the start that she would not be a cooperative member of my cabinet. Like other governors, or even the U.S. president himself, I needed cooperative, supportive cabinet officers. I did not want a bunch of "yes" men to rubber-stamp my ideas and policies, but cabinet officials who believed in the goals I set. I was not above selecting apolitical professionals or even dynamic Republicans willing to work with me. Pilar was eminently qualified for the post, but we did not see eye to eye on anything.

Pilar opposed my action and challenged my gubernatorial powers in court. Although she lost the case, the court battle led to an ugly confrontation between the governor and the bureau's board of directors. When I appointed my daughter Debbie as Pilar's replacement in February 1983, the media led a crusade for Pilar and the bureau board.

Three years after the court battle, I ran into Gadi outside the Depart-ment of Public Health and Social Services in Mangilao. He was standing under a tree, waiting for his ride to pick him up after his appointment. I had not seen him since the court fiasco and was uncomfortable about facing him. I did not know if he would treat me as friend or foe, but I had to face him, even if only to suffer his wrath. We greeted each other pleasantly. I asked how he was, and he answered with the straightforward honesty that I had always admired in him.

"Oh, well, you know, I am bothered about what happened to Pilar," he said in CHamoru. "Why did you have to do that?"

I felt guilty about having hurt him and was relieved that he would even speak to me. He had reason to be bitter. Pilar was his *kirida*, his favorite, more his daughter than granddaughter.

"Gadi, my friend," I answered, also in CHamoru, "politics is like a base-ball game. When the innings change, the guys in the field trade places with those at bat. It is our turn in the field. Baseball teams do not swap players just to keep certain ones in the field. Do you see what I'm getting at?"

Gadi nodded stoically. I knew I hurt him, but he hid his feelings. We talked a while, reminiscing about old times and sharing a laugh or two. I left him under the tree, hoping he was still my friend. We had risked our lives together during the war. I owed him my life. Although they have never known it, at least 14,000 CHamorus also owe their lives to him. Had it not been for Gadi, the Japanese would have slaughtered more of us in the waning days of the occupation.

As goods and supplies grew scarce in the market and in the few other businesses, I finally understood why Dad saved so much junk. In addition to the empty gasoline drums, he also kept old tires, used auto parts, and things that seemed useless but turned out to be a goldmine. We traded the empty drums, auto parts, and rubber tires for rice, corn, beans, bananas, vegetables, and fish. The drums filled the need for water catchments and waterproof storage bins for people in their jungle hideaways. Cut to foot size, and needing only rope or leather straps, the rubber tires became cheap, durable, easy-to-make footwear. Skilled craftsmen hammered old auto parts into knives, machetes, coconut graters, and other implements.

With the truck loaded with empty drums, rubber tires, and a box of metal parts, I would drive around, searching for people willing to trade. In doing so, I knew the whereabouts of many families. The trading trips gave me an understanding of public sentiment and made me a popular politician among grassroots voters years later.

One day, Dad's former cattle agent, Francisco "Galabook" Delgado, the man I called Sir Gallahad, asked to tag along. He had heard about a cow for trade in Talo'fo'fo and wanted to negotiate with its owner to buy it. Galabook always had bawdy jokes and stories to tell, so I welcomed his company. By late afternoon, we were pleased with our day's work. Galabook had sealed the deal for the cow and arranged to return for it later. I, too, had bargained well and was eager to show Mama and Dad all I got. Bunches of green and ripe bananas hung from the truck's sides like decorations on a parade float while boxes and baskets of fruits and vegetables and burlap sacks of dried corn and rice filled the truck bed. The truck creaked and squeaked as we bounced back to Hagåtña.

We crossed the Ilek River bridge then started uphill to Yoña. The road was notorious for its two hairpin curves and treacherous narrowness. It was so narrow in some places with sheer drops on both sides. Galabook and I were not thinking of danger as we started uphill and rounded the first curve, which veered to the left and led to the hairpin halfway up. The hairpin angled to the right on the steepest part of the hill. At the middle of the hairpin, the truck ground to a stop. I slammed on the accelerator, but the truck would not budge.

Then the clutch began slipping. The truck would not move forward, but neither did it roll backward. The slipping clutch kept us stationary.

As I continued revving the engine, Galabook looked at me with concern. He opened his door and made ready to jump out, but the road on his side dropped off into a ravine.

"Basta, Ricky, it's not going to make it," he said and carefully climbed out of the truck. "Quit before you get us killed."

I knew he was right. The truck refused to climb any further. There was no sense trying to force it. Galabook searched along the roadside for a large rock to use as a chock.

"I want to back it up," I called to him. "I want to get back down the hill."

"That's crazy, Ricky. For God's sake, don't chance it!" he yelled back.

"I'll go slow. You keep the rock ready and follow me down."

I inched the truck backwards downhill while Galabook complained about my getting both of us killed. Each time he removed the rock, I let the truck roll a few feet. When I stopped, he would chock the tire again. We repeated the process until we reached the bottom.

"Let's leave it here and go for help," Galabook said, his face flushed from his efforts. "Maybe we can get some men and some carabaos to pull it uphill."

That would have been the safest, smartest thing to do, but I rejected the idea. Sundown was upon us, and it would take too long to find help. My load of traded goods was too valuable to leave unguarded. People in the area would know the truck belonged to B.J. Bordallo and would not have molested it, but the Japanese would have confiscated the truck and its load. I was not willing to give up the fruits of my labor or my family's food supply. Even if we found help right away, it would take another couple of hours to hitch the animals and pull the truck uphill in darkness.

I decided the safe way would not work. Galabook grumbled and argued, but I ignored him and tried to figure out something else to try. I remembered something about low gear being stronger when the vehicle was in reverse. I did not know if it was true, but it sounded logical and worth a try. Galabook paled when I told him I was going to drive the truck uphill in reverse. He exploded into a long-winded lecture. I was crazy, he shouted, I was out of my mind; I would kill myself for sure.

"I don't want anything to do with this crazy idea," he ranted while I surveyed the road. "If you die, don't blame me. When they bring back your dead body, I'll tell your father I warned you."

He was still scolding when I climbed into the truck. I turned it around and began the slow, backward ascent. I had to hang out the window and crane my neck to watch the road uphill behind me. The clutch's low gear strength in reverse proved true. The truck rounded the first curve without problem. I kept careful watch of how close I came to the edges of the road and the drop-offs on both sides. My heart raced when I reached the hairpin. If the truck stopped again, I would careen headlong back to the bottom. But the clutch held, and the truck climbed little by little.

My hands were shaking, and I was dripping with sweat when I reached the top. I jumped out and yelled down to Galabook at the bottom of the hill, "I did it, Gallahad! I did it!" I started jumping up and down, waving my arms, and whistling and hooting as Galabook scrambled up the hill. He scolded me all the way back to Hagåtña. Galabook was right. It was idiotic and irresponsible, but I was 16, full of self-confidence and foolish enough to take the risk.

"They crushed my shinbones, Ricky"

By mid-1943, the Japanese had captured and killed five of the fugitive American escapees. George Tweed was the only one left. Without the help of the CHamorus who kept him sheltered, clothed, and fed, Tweed would not have managed. Yet he boasted that his own cunning kept him ahead of the Japanese. He discounted the pain and suffering CHamorus endured in his behalf and criticized them as loose-lipped braggarts who nearly got him captured. He also accused Påle' Oskat of violating the seal of confession. Rather than keep his wits sharpened, Tweed often came out of hiding to attend celebrations in the jungles. There were rumors he even had mistresses whom he often visited.

The search for Tweed was relentless. The Japanese arrested, interrogated, and tortured dozens of innocent people on suspicion alone. A mysterious black automobile that everyone called the Black Hawk roamed the island picking up suspects. Its appearance meant the Japanese had new information, and more people were in danger. Marian's mother, Mrs. Agueda Johnston, the much-respected principal of George Washington High School, pleaded with Tweed in a letter to give himself up and spare anymore CHamorus beatings and executions. In his reply, delivered to her from his hiding place, Tweed warned that the United States would deal harshly with subversives like her.

Mrs. Johnston kept Tweed's letter and hoped someday to confront him with it. She died in December 1977. Marian keeps Tweed's letter as proof that he was an ugly American.

When their efforts failed, the Japanese turned on Hagåtña's prominent leaders, arresting whole families at a time. Mine was among the first. Without warning, well past midnight on August 7, 1943, the Japanese took us into custody. It was one of the most frightening experiences of my life. Mama had given birth to my sister Rosamunde just six days earlier. She sneaked from her bedroom to the one I shared with my brothers and woke me up.

"Ricky, wake up. I think your father's in trouble," she whispered. I sat up and rubbed my eyes. There was a commotion in the living room. "What's wrong, Mama? Where's Daddy?"

"He went out to see what they want."

I hopped out of my bunk and made for the door, but Mama held me back. "Wait, Ricky," she said. "Be careful. There are a lot of men out there. I don't know what they're doing here, but Daddy's been out there for quite a while, and I'm worried."

Silver, a little mongrel dog that someone gave my younger siblings, stood guard at the dining room doorway, snarling and yapping at the soldiers in the living room. They were in combat gear with bayonets fixed to their rifles. I crossed the dining room and came up behind Silver. "Quiet, Silver. Come here, boy," I whispered. Silver ignored me and continued growling.

"Call off your dog, or I'll shoot it," a Saipanese interpreter ordered.

I tried to quiet the dog again, but he continued to growl. I grabbed his collar, dragged him away from the door, and forced him into the kitchen. Silver stopped barking and began whimpering and scratching at the locked door.

Mama clutched at her nightgown and followed behind me. We stood together trembling. The soldiers glared at everything around them, as if they expected an attack. Dad was nowhere in sight. An officer brandishing a sword spoke to the interpreter who then turned to us and said, "Get everyone in the house assembled in here."

Irene, Lorraine, and Bobbie had been listening from their bedroom. They woke Norma, Junie, and Josephine and came out together slowly. I went back to the bedroom and woke Paul, Fred, Rodney, Donald, and Michael. We gathered in the living room as ordered, dressed in our pajamas and nightgowns. Some of us were wearing shoes or slippers, others were barefoot. We assembled according to age and stood single file from tallest to shortest. I stood beside Mama. Irene carried 3-year-old Michael, and Lorraine carried newborn baby Rosamunde. I thought the soldiers were going to beat us and quickly changed places with Mama to be at the head of the line. I did not want her to be the first.

The soldiers flanked us and ordered us to follow. They marched us in the dark to the jailhouse. A full moon lit the way. The dark and silent buildings were eerie. Terrified, we huddled together, holding on to each other in fear. As we approached the plaza, the cathedral bells pealed. Two gongs pierced the silence. I shall never forget their low, almost mournful sound. At 2 o'clock in the morning, we were in the streets in our nightclothes, herded at gunpoint.

We entered the jailhouse where the bright lights inside blinded us. Squinting and shielding our eyes, we stumbled down a long corridor and into a pitch-black jail cell. As soon as the heavy door slammed shut and its bolt locked, Mama calmly began reciting a rosary. Trembling, we prayed along, drawing strength from Mama's courage. We could not see each other in the darkness. The cell was damp and chilly. We huddled together in the small space, but we still shivered with cold and fear.

As we prayed, a woman somewhere in the jailhouse began screaming in pain. We jumped at the sharp sounds of an open hand slapping against flesh. We heard furniture grating against the floor as the slapping continued. The woman cried out prayers, sending them heavenward along with her screams. After a while, the beating stopped, and there was only silence and darkness.

We had not seen Dad, but we knew he was somewhere in the same building. We tried not to think about what was happening to him. Mama continued to lead us in prayer. After what seemed like hours, the door of our cell opened. Bright light flooded in, blinding us. A soldier, his rifle pointed at us, and an interpreter entered.

"Paul. Which one of you is Paul? Step forward, and come with us," the interpreter said.

Mama stifled a cry as Paul rose to his feet. The interpreter shoved him out of the cell and slammed the door shut again. Mama began another rosary. Fear and worry made her voice tremble. I mumbled along, too distracted to pray. I was sure the Japanese were going to torture us one at a time but wondered why they would start with Paul, not me. I was the eldest. I had been free to travel the length and breadth of the island for months. My activities should have been more suspicious than Paul's. He and Dad just tended to the garden and cattle. I held my breath and listened for sounds of Paul's torture, but there was only silence.

About an hour later, the soldiers opened the door of our cell and tossed in Paul's limp body. He hit the floor beside me with a heavy thud and let out a moan. In the darkness, none of us moved for fear of hurting him further. We listened to his labored breathing.

"Paul? Paul, are you all right, son?" Mama asked. She reached in the darkness, trying to feel for him. Paul did not answer. In a dry, raspy voice, he whispered to me instead.

"I think they crushed my shinbones, Ricky," he said.

"What did they do to you?" I asked.

"They wanted me to tell them about Tweed," he said. "I told them I didn't know anything, but they didn't believe me."

Paul was in great pain but never wept. The Japanese had taken him outside the jailhouse, tied him to an inclined ramp, and interrogated him about his activities with Dad in the jungles. To make him confess that he and Dad knew Tweed's whereabouts and had been assisting him, Paul's interrogators struck his legs and shins with a 1-by-2-inch length of lumber. In what I attribute to his great strength and courage, Paul never cried out during his ordeal. He was only 13, but he would not let the Japanese break his spirit. Mama inched closer to comfort him. We huddled close to her and continued to pray.

The cell door did not open again until noon the next day, August 8, 1943, Dad's 43rd birthday. We had had no food or water since our arrest but were free to go. Mama and I helped Paul walk the distance to our house while Irene and Lorraine guided the children. Tan Isabella "Beck" Guzman, our neighbor from across the street, and several other people were waiting in the yard when we arrived.

When Tan Beck awoke to silence that morning, she realized something was wrong at our house. She missed the familiar commotion of a house full of children and became concerned when she heard no noise. She crossed the street to investigate and found our front door wide open. The soldiers had searched our house and scattered our belongings on the front steps. She went into the house and found it ransacked. Her concern then turned to fear.

Tan Beck spread word among the few neighbors left on the block that something dreadful had happened to the Bordallos. Auntie Rose came running from her house on the other side of the Spanish stone bridge when she heard the news. Others gathered as well. Someone went to the authorities and confirmed our arrest. Auntie Rose, Tan Beck, and our neighbors kept watch outside our house. They were reciting a rosary when we staggered home. Auntie Rose ran to Mama in tears. When she realized Dad was not with us, she feared for Mama, who had only recently given birth. Auntie Rose and Tan Beck helped Mama into the house.

Mama withered at the sight inside. The house was in shambles. While we were in custody, the soldiers opened every drawer and cupboard and emptied the contents onto the floor. They overturned the furniture and scattered papers and clothing throughout the house. Mama collapsed in tears and feared for Dad. We did not know if he was still alive or whether the Japanese had already executed him. Paul needed medical attention, and baby Rosamunde needed care. Dad's fate, Paul's wounds, Franklin's death, baby Rosamunde, 12 other children, the Japanese, and finally, the desecration of her home became too much for Mama to bear.

In the way CHamorus share hardships and bolster each other's strength, Auntie Rose and Tan Beck put Mama to bed while our neighbors began picking up debris. They took charge to see to our needs and put our house back in order. Everyone took on specific tasks: some straightened the furniture while others collected trash, some started preparing food while others tended to the younger children. Someone took care of baby Rosamunde while another ministered to Paul's wounds.

Paul's legs were black and swollen. Lacerations scored the skin and flesh of both shins from his knees to his feet. I could see his bones in some spots. Some wounds were bleeding, and dried, black blood covered others. While a neighbor treated his wounds, Paul described his interrogation and beating. As I listened, I realized why the Japanese did not question me. They had kept tabs on me and knew my every movement. They did not know where Dad and Paul went, or what they were doing when they disappeared from town for hours at a time. Dad was secretive about his activities for fear the Japanese would discover the hidden cattle. His suspicious behavior made the Japanese think he and Paul were in contact with George Tweed.

Paul's wounds were slow to heal. Mama remained anxious about Dad. Our arrest made her realize how vulnerable we were and how easily death could come to us. Rosamunde was only a week old and not yet baptized; she could have died and not gone to heaven because she was not free of Original Sin. Mama asked Marian Johnston to be Rosamunde's godmother and arranged a baptism right away.

"Please hurry and christen my baby. She has seen the inside of a jail before the inside of a church," she told Marian.

"Help me get your father home"

Our release on Dad's birthday was difficult. We did not know whether to be happy or to mourn, to celebrate or to grieve. We did not know if he was dead or alive. We commemorated his birthday by beginning a novena for his safe return. Friends, neighbors, and employees also offered daily Masses for him at the Santa Cruz church. Five days passed without word.

On the sixth day, one of my younger brothers who was playing in the street started yelling frantically. We became easily alarmed since our arrest, and at my brother's cries, we ran outside. My brother, I do not recall which one, was pointing down the street to a small, hunched figure coming toward us. It was Dad, crawling on his hands and knees. Pain racked his face each time he threw one arm out, then the other, to drag himself along.

Dad was shirtless and wearing only the tattered shreds of his trousers. His shoes were missing. He was bleeding from gashes all over his body, and flies buzzed around him. His movements were slow and unsteady. Exhausted and nearly spent, he stopped before he reached us. His arms began to quiver. Mama ran into the street and dropped to her knees beside him. We followed at her heels, uncertain and frightened. Dad crumpled and fainted into Mama's arms. She cradled his head in her lap. Tears streamed down her face.

"Help me get your father home," she said.

The Japanese tortured Dad for six days. They stripped him naked and hung him by his thumbs from the rafters of the jailhouse. Two Japanese officers questioned and beat him every day. They took turns whipping him with automobile fan belts. One man was especially brutal. The other was not as harsh. They whipped him to extract information about George Tweed. The Japanese would not accept that a top political leader like Dad would not know anything about the American in hiding. They were certain Tweed's custodians would have kept Dad informed of his movements and condition. Dad could have gotten that information if he wanted, but he chose not to know. He could tell the Japanese nothing.

After the interrogation sessions, the Japanese threw him into a cell already occupied by Jesus "Chada" Cruz. Dad would have died if Tun Sus Chada had not washed his wounds with vinegar and water to fight off infection. Two years after the war, while I was a student at the University of San Francisco, I learned that Tun Sus Chada had passed away in San Francisco. Although I did not know him, I attended his wake on Dad's behalf and to represent my family. I felt an obligation to pay my respects to the man for saving Dad's life.

With the kind of gratitude CHamorus understand, Dad returned to the jailhouse and gave the kinder torturer a bottle of Canadian Club Whisky from our buried cache.

As soon as he was able to get out of bed, Dad began searching through his bureau drawers for something he had hidden. He refused to say what. He knew the Japanese searched our house but not whether they found what he hid. We knew nothing about his secret until he began tearing through the cupboards and drawers. We had spent days putting the house back in order but found nothing missing, unusual, or suspicious. We worried the Japanese might already have found what Dad had hidden.

Dad was relieved when he found it — an old, dog-eared copybook. It did not appear important to us or to the Japanese. It was a journal Dad started keeping after the invasion, his own account of the occupation. He listed as many names and incidences as he knew firsthand. The journal entries were to serve as evidence of war crimes. Dad was confident the Americans would win and return to Guam. The journal was valuable but dangerous. Dad knew that if the Japanese had discovered it, they would have put us all to death.

Our arrest and Paul's beating convinced him that keeping the journal was not worth the risk to his family. Dad told me to burn it and to scatter the ashes. I burned the journal page by page in the backyard. I watched each page blacken into ash and felt bad. I knew I was burning some carefully documented history.

Dad knew but never let on that he was under suspicion. As chairman of the Guam Congress' House of Council, he was the island's highest ranking political official. The Japanese gave him some respect for that, but Dad knew it was only a pretense. The Japanese believed he was the one most likely to organize resistance and would direct the efforts to protect the American escapees. When they could not beat a confession from him, the Japanese released him with an ultimatum to deliver Tweed in 30 days or die.

Dad spent half that time recuperating. During his recovery, a Japanese priest came to visit him. He told Dad to ignore the threat and assured him he would get him relieved of it. We did not know what prompted the priest's intervention or if we could believe him. Dad thought it best not to ignore the order and at least pretend to look for Tweed. He left Paul in charge of the garden and the cattle before setting out on foot every day. He walked as far as Hågat and Dededo so that the Japanese would see him searching. On the 30th day, he presented himself to the authorities without Tweed. An official shouted at him then ordered him out. The priest was true to his word. The Japanese did not kill him.

Chapter 13

"You must find safer quarters"

Most of us learned to be suspicious of all Japanese officials, especially those who by nature were cruel and brutal and who savored their power over helpless captives. Many were mean and harsh, but some among the enlisted men were compassionate and friendly. Whether they were mean or not, many officials defied posted rules about trading or fraternizing with the locals. Japanese high officials banned American goods, but many among the lower ranks would trade items worth hundreds of yen for a pack of American cigarettes. Dad's cases of Chesterfields gave us considerable trading power and made us a few Japanese friends.

One friend, a sailor whose name I can no longer remember, stopped to watch my brothers and sisters playing in the street one afternoon. He spoke only a little English but joined them at play. The children took to him right away. His fondness for the children touched Mama, but Dad was not impressed. Neither were we older ones; we remained distrustful and skeptical. The sailor was still outside when Mama called the children in for supper. The sailor seemed reluctant to leave. He stood in the yard and smiled shyly at Mama. Something about him convinced her he was harmless.

Without consulting Dad, she invited the man to join us. He accepted with great politeness and followed Mama into the house. Dad was dubious but said nothing; he knew Mama was a good judge of character. She would not have invited him if she mistrusted him.

The sailor sat at our table, shared our meal, and marveled at the size of our family. He told us in faltering English that he did not consider himself a military man but was loyal to his emperor and country. He also spoke about how sorely he missed his parents, his sister, and his brother and how much he wanted to go home. He said being with us reminded him of home. He wore a downhearted look for most of the evening. After supper, he asked if he could return. Mama told him he was welcome anytime. The sailor was a decent, personable fellow.

Over the following weeks, he would come to visit whenever he was off duty. He brought little presents for the children and some sundry items for Mama and my sisters. He spent most of his time playing with the children but also conversed with Dad about the war. He did not believe in the Japanese cause or in fighting the war, but he was not a traitor to his homeland.

"My country is too small to pit itself against a giant like the United States," he told Dad. "I do not believe we will win. I fear my country will suffer greatly for trying."

Our Japanese friend expressed his sadness for our situation and apologized for the tyranny his people held over ours. As the weeks and months of 1943 wore on, his disillusionment about the war grew. He began telling us that despite the propaganda, Japanese forces were losing battles in the Pacific. His reports matched those we received over our clandestine radio news reports. At the beginning of 1944, he told us the war was going badly for his side. A showdown with the Americans was coming soon, and the Japanese were planning a strong defense. They were not going to give in easily.

Our sailor friend warned us about staying in the city. He urged us to move away from Hagåtña. The Navy would soon be relinquishing the island to the Army in anticipation of the fight to come. The fighting, he said, would be ferocious. "You will not be safe here. You must find safer quarters," he said with genuine concern. We heeded his warning.

Moving into the jungle seemed the safest thing to do. There was little left in Hagåtña. The power plant was no longer running, and there was no electricity. We closed the market because there was nothing left to sell, and no one came into town anymore. The stepped-up labor demands made wandering the streets dangerous. The Japanese conscripted laborers on the spot, gathering anyone who appeared idle. Without the businesses, we were easy targets for labor details. To avoid that, we moved to a part of the Torres estate in Pado, an area in Mongmong behind Maite, less than a mile east of the Japanese airstrip at Halåguak.

Pado was a deep, untouched jungle area. It was rugged and beautiful, thick with trees, *lemmon di china* brush, thick vines, wild taro, and hundreds

of other wild plants. The undergrowth blanketed a nightmarish terrain of corrugated knolls, limestone outcroppings, narrow gullies, and deep ravines. No
roads or trails led to Pado. We had to hack our way through rough terrain
with machetes to carve a path wide enough for our bull cart. We cannibalized
lumber and roofing sheets from the stadium in Aniguak and our warehouse in
Pigo' and hauled them to Pado to build a suitable home.

We spent weeks covertly hauling the supplies, all our furniture and belongings, our cattle, pigs, and chickens, and Mama's piano. The cart broke
down many times and caused us countless delays. In deference to Mama, we
transported her beloved piano with painstaking care. We were moving into
the wilds, but not without Mama's most prized items of civilization. We also
brought our gramophone, all our phonograph records, Mama's photo albums,
and several books. Because of our numbers and Dad's flamboyance, we built
a large and picturesque bungalow and moved in before we could finish it. We
added walls, doors, and partitions later.

Uncle Tom's family and Mrs. Johnston's family built their jungle shelters near ours. We all selected areas close to protective knolls and a freshwater spring in a ravine nearby. Uncle Tom dug a bomb shelter into the side of
his knoll.

Without electricity or refrigeration, Mama used old-fashioned methods
to preserve food. She made beef jerky and stored it in an empty gasoline drum.
She salted fish and packed them in jars. She discovered that deep frying *titiyas*
prolonged their storage life. They were hard and leathery, not like modern
corn chips. Mama made, fried, and stored hundreds of *titiyas*. She also stockpiled crab biscuits, *pån tosta*, and *rosketi*.

Our sailor friend occasionally visited us in Pado. He arrived one evening in a downcast mood. His bandana, which always held small gifts for the
children, was bulkier than usual. He tried to be cheerful during dinner, but
we sensed he was sad. He untied the bulging bandana and distributed gifts
to everyone after supper. As he made ready to leave, tears filled his eyes. He
was leaving Guam and was bidding us goodbye. He was going off to fight and
feared he would lose his life and never see his family or homeland again. He
thanked us for allowing him to share time with us "even though I am your enemy. I have thought this war was wrong, and you have proven me correct. We
should be friends, not enemies," he said.

Tears dribbled down his cheeks, and he bowed low — the bow reserved only for people of the highest rank. His gesture and his tears moved us all. We cried with him and for him. He was a Japanese military man, but he was not our enemy. He was a friend we had grown to love. My younger brothers and sisters — his favorite playmates — cried bitterly. We followed him to the road and watched until he was out of sight. We never saw him again.

In January 1944, the Japanese Navy returned control of the island to the Army. In preparation for the showdown, the Navy did as the Americans had done in 1941 and evacuated their dependents, and their nonessential civilian personnel. The Army returned with its military police force, the *kempeitai*, and with the *kaikuntai*, a unit of agricultural production experts proud of their reputation as the most brutal and cruel of the Japanese military.

Eerie concerts in the jungle

Until the first American attack in February 1944, life in Pado was pleasant. It was like camping out but not for fun. It was necessary, and we were trying to survive. We had little to do but work on the house and tend the livestock. We lacked the conveniences of city living but were comfortable. With so much free time, we whiled away the hours. Irene and Norma took turns at the piano and practiced regularly. Many evenings after supper, we would gather around the piano and sing while Irene played. Paul, an avid reader, dove into *Don Quixote*. I read *Gone with the Wind* but could not enjoy it. There were too many parallels between Scarlet O'Hara's situation and ours. Like us, war disrupted Scarlet's peaceful, well-ordered life. As I read Scarlet and Rhett Butler's wild ride through the blazing streets of Atlanta, I did not know I would have a similar experience.

I disliked the disruption of routine and the strange inconsistency we were in — the house in the jungle, the extreme change in the way we lived, and the uncertainty of our future. The difference struck me one day as I carried the slop buckets to the pigpens. We hid them in a small clearing downwind from the house. I could not escape the oddity of living in such primitive, makeshift conditions, yet in such pristine beauty. The jungle canopy was so thick I could not see the sky. The pigs squealed and grunted as I fed them. I emptied the buckets and as I followed the path back to the house, someone began playing the piano. Music wafted through the jungle with unusual clarity and volume, echoing as though several pianos were playing. I was not yet near the house, but the piano sounded as if it was near me. It was beautiful.

I turned one of the slop buckets over and sat down to listen. I closed my eyes and pretended to be in a box seat in a grand concert hall. The concert included classical pieces, sentimental old songs, and popular modern tunes. When the music ended, the silence jolted me back to reality. The wild, green jungle closed in on me again. The pigs were grunting behind me. With a heavy heart, I picked up the slop buckets and went home. The eerie concerts and my pig-feeding chore were daily occurrences. Each concert filled me with conflicting emotions, made worse whenever Mama sang. Her sweet soprano voice was haunting.

On February 23, the Americans bombed the Japanese airstrip on Orote Peninsula. The bombing triggered a tragedy in Sumai. We learned of it from Uncle Felix Pangelinan, Mama's brother, the *såncho* for Sumai. A man named Dumanal thought the Americans would land soon after the bombing. He had hidden a .45 pistol, certain the Americans would return. Brandishing the weapon, Dumanal accosted a Japanese officer and a Saipanese interpreter, demanding their surrender. By the time Uncle Felix arrived on the scene, the Japanese police were already there, and tensions were high. Uncle Felix tried to reason with Dumanal, but he remained belligerent. When the interpreter lunged at Dumanal with a dagger, he pulled the trigger of his rusty pistol. It misfired. The enraged interpreter stabbed Dumanal in the chest several times. He died believing the Americans had returned to rescue us and had chosen the day after George Washington's birthday for our liberation.

Dumanal was five months too early. After bombing Orote, American fighter planes appeared in the skies over the island. The first air attacks were the prelude to a storm of nonstop bombing, shelling, and strafing that would intensify and last for days.

American flyers engaged Japanese planes in dogfights almost daily. We went wild with delight, not only at the Americans' return, but also with enthusiasm for the exciting air shows. We would run to the cliff south of Halåguak or find openings in the jungle canopy to watch. Planes often buzzed the treetops and sent us scurrying for cover. Thousands of spent bullet casings clattered down on metal roofs and rained on us, but unlike rain, the casings were hot and heavy, and they stung. After all the bullet casing stings and burns, we lost interest in the dogfights and dove for cover whenever we heard engines in the sky.

From Påle' Oskat's place on the Maite cliff line, we could look out over Hagåtña Bay and watch American battleships steaming into position. There were hundreds of all shapes and sizes, indicating the Americans' serious intention to recapture Guam. We cheered the Americans but hid when roving patrols came near. The patrols shot anyone signaling to the Americans in any way. From our vantage, we also watched Japanese troops prepare to hold the island at all costs. Our sailor friend was right: The battle for Guam was going to be fierce.

In June 1944, the Americans launched their offensive in Saipan. Their initial plan was to attack Saipan and Guam simultaneously, but they met fierce resistance in Saipan. The bloody battle for Saipan was a preview of what the Americans would face in Guam a month later. To minimize hand-to-hand combat on the ground, the Americans "softened" Guam with aerial bombardments before landing their troops. On July 8, they began bombing and shelling the island night and day, believing that nothing could withstand such a pounding.

Without regard for our safety, the Americans tried to pulverize their Japanese enemies. The strategy failed. We and the Japanese survived the intense and continuous bombing.

When the American bombardments began, we would cram ourselves into Uncle Tom's bomb shelter, which was just a large hole dug into the knoll. After the first few cycles, it was clear that both families, especially ours, did not fit inside. We needed a shelter of our own. Paul, Fred, Rodney, Donald, and I began digging one into the knoll near our house. We did not have the correct tools, but we did the best we could to finish a shelter before the next bombing cycle. When we finished, our bomb shelter was large and deep enough to hold all of us. We were proud of it. Auntie Butler did not share our confidence. During one of her rare visits to Pado, the bombing began again. We packed ourselves into the shelter to wait it out. The explosions scared Auntie Butler so badly she dropped to her knees, covered her head with her hands, and started reciting a rosary. We could hear her muffled prayers, but all we could see of her was her rear end. Despite the horrible, frightening din, Auntie Butler made us laugh.

Auntie Butler, her son James, and his new bride Angelina were staying with Nanan Chong's family in Pa'åsan, east of Tutuhan. As conditions worsened, they moved further inland to Eton, east of Sinajana. They could hear and feel the bombing and strafing of the Halåguak airstrip, but distance cushioned them from the terror of it. They did not know how terrible and frightening the action was at close range. Nor did we realize the danger we were in. Once, an 8-inch projectile whizzed through the treetops near Uncle Tom's shelter. It ricocheted off a coconut tree, struck a corner of Uncle Tom's roof, and plowed into the ground without exploding. We crowded around the crater to inspect it. The shell was red hot. We poked at it with sticks and marveled at how it smoked and sizzled.

"A dog more valuable than you"

As the American softening-up bombing intensified, the constant, deafening noise and the quaking jolting became nerve-racking on the Japanese and CHamorus alike. Under pressure, the Japanese vented their frustrations on us and set a breakneck pace for the island's fortification. With Japanese guns at their backs, laborers worked day and night beneath the rain of American bombs and shells. Many died of exhaustion. Exploding shells or gunshots killed others. The combatants on both sides of the war considered us expendable. The Americans tried to blow our island to bits and us with it. The Japanese tried to work us to death.

The intense American bombing and the damage it caused drove the Japanese to force more people to repair the airstrips, gun emplacements, pillboxes, and bunkers or to continue building other fortifications beneath the shower of bullets and shells. The Japanese did not care about CHamoru fatalities. The Americans attacked the Halåguak airstrip many times, and the Japanese forced laborers to repair it after each attack. Laborers were often at work when attacks began again. They would flee the danger from above only to be shot from behind. Several workers once ran screaming past our Pado hiding place. Some were bleeding but did not stop for help.

Manuel Lujan, the *såncho* of Hagåtña, helped Dad, Paul, Fred, and me escape the airstrip labor details earlier in the occupation. But we were not always spared. We also heaved picks and shovels with others to build the airfield. When the Japanese increased the conscriptions, we were among those who returned repeatedly to repair it by hand, the same way we built it.

No longer exempt, I received assignment to a labor detail at the *kempeitai* headquarters in Tå'i. Standard assignments lasted five to six days. My detail consisted of about 75 men — including boys as young as 11 and old men. Having served five days, we looked forward to going home. Most of us had run out of food, which we had to provide for ourselves. If we had to stay, we either had to get word to our families for more food or go hungry. On the sixth day of our assignment, we assembled outside the *kempeitai* headquarters. I stood in the ranks in the third row. A *kempeitai* officer addressed us while a Saipanese interpreter translated. They announced that most of us were going home that day. Others were to remain. They also wanted those who knew how to drive to step forward.

With operational vehicles and gasoline in short supply, and a major campaign impending, the Japanese did not want to train drivers. Instead, they weeded them from the work details, but few CHamorus knew how to drive. Those who did were not eager to volunteer, and that angered the Japanese. Uneasiness spread through our ranks. Many in the detail knew I could drive, and I knew they would not give me away, but I did not know if any among the Japanese knew. I held my breath, my heart racing. All in the ranks stood silent. The *kempeitai* officer went from man to man, examining our faces. Out of the corner of my eye, I saw the Saipanese interpreter glaring at me. He then stepped forward, whispered to the officer, and pointed at me. The officer's face darkened. I was in trouble. My hands became clammy, and I broke into a cold sweat.

The officer ordered me from the ranks. My legs felt like rubber as I went forward, clutching the shoulders of the men in front of me for support. I dared not speak or look at them as I passed. We were all scared. When I reached the front, the officer struck me and began shouting at me. He pummeled me with his fists until I fell to my knees. He pulled his sword and raised it above my head. I shut my eyes and began to pray, waiting for the blow. I felt the horror and fear coming from the men and boys standing powerless behind me.

While the interpreter translated, the officer accused me of lying. He threatened to kill me for not stepping forward voluntarily. He shouted a challenge for everyone to hear. I opened my eyes. He was still holding the saber above me. He was leering at me. There was something sadistic in his eyes.

"Arrogant dog," the interpreter spoke for the officer. "A dog more valuable than you is tied to that tree. Kill it, and prove your worthiness to live. If it escapes, you lose your head."

It never occurred to me that, as a driver, I was valuable to the Japanese.

Their strange behavior and cruel actions often defied logic. They needed drivers but were quick to terrorize or kill anyone who defied them. The ultimatum was my only hope; it was the dog or me.

A scrawny, half-starved mongrel whimpered and looked up at me with pleading eyes. I looked away, trying to numb myself. The only weapon I could find was a strip of dry åkgak (*Pandanus tectorius*). I picked it up and approached the dog. It sensed danger and began yelping and tugging at its tether. I froze. If the dog broke lose, I was dead. I waited until the dog calmed down then aimed at its head, hoping a swift, hard blow would kill it quickly. If I missed, the dog would bolt and break free. As I lashed forward with all my might, the dog reeled around. The whip bit into the dog's rump. It shrieked in pain and yanked hard at the cord around its neck. Gagging, it fell to the ground. I started whipping as hard and as fast as I could. The animal recovered its legs and began running around the tree, winding the cord as it ran. I chased after it, still lashing.

I glanced at the *kempeitai* officer who was still holding up his sword. He was laughing, enjoying the show. Humiliated, I started to cry. The dog was howling. We were both terrified, both fighting to survive. The officer's maniacal laughter, my whooshing whip and labored gasping, and the dog's painful yowling filled the air as the other conscripts watched. I grew lightheaded and dizzy but continued to strike at the animal. Everything seemed to move in slow motion. The dog's hide began to split in places and ooze blood. I tried to hit harder with each blow and begged God to hasten the dog's death and end the nightmare. It felt like hours since it began. The poor beast finally quieted and just whimpered, its tongue dangling. Its eyes were glassy and unseeing. Its legs quivered then buckled. The dog collapsed, convulsed, and died.

I gasped for breath. My chest ached from the effort. My mouth and throat were dry. My arm throbbed. I stood stoop-shouldered over the dog and stared at it. I released my grip on the whip then walked back to the formation. The *kempetai* officer was no longer laughing. His face darkened into an angry frown, his jaw set. He did not think I would succeed and was irritated that I had, but he kept his word. He lowered the sword, grunted, and walked away.

The Saipanese interpreter told me to take the carcass behind headquarters and to skin it. I stared at him in disbelief. My punishment was not over. I walked back to the tree, untied the dead animal, and dragged it to the rear of the *kempeitai* headquarters. There, hanging from pegs, were the skinned and butchered carcasses of several other dogs.

Skinning and butchering the dog was distasteful but not difficult. I was an experienced butcher, and the animal was small. I cut off the paws and peeled the skin away. It was skinny, but its belly bulged. The dog was female, and it was pregnant. As I sliced through its midsection to remove the intestines and internal organs, a litter of fetal pups tumbled out. I looked at the dead puppies but felt nothing. I was too tired and too numb to have any feeling. I gathered the pups with the dog's severed paws and hide and discarded them. I hung the carcass to drain with the others then reported inside the headquarters, certain that my punishment was over at last.

That evening, because my own food supplies were gone, the Japanese fed me a small cup of rice, some watery miso soup, and a small chunk of dog meat. I stared at the meat but was too hungry to care. I ate it and hungered for more.

Hagåtña inferno, the city in flames

The *kempeitai* kept me at their headquarters for another three or four days. My nightly mission was to drive a crew of five to Sinajana to draw water for the *kempeitai*. Several large spigots along the main pipeline to Hagåtña supplied water to rural areas. The nearest spigot was in Sinajana. Our task was to fill several 55-gallon drums and haul them back to Tå'i. During the day, we repaired the camouflage on the truck or did whatever the *kempeitai* ordered.

After returning from the water run one evening, I heard someone's painful screams coming from inside the *kempeitai* headquarters. I did not recognize the voice, but I knew the *kempeitai* were interrogating and torturing one of Tun Pedro Martinez's children. I could see the silhouette of a stooped figure through the window shade. I could hear questions barked at him and hear the loud slap and thud of fist against flesh. I could hear painful moans and jagged crying. I kept vigil outside the window, and with an aching heart, offered a prayer.

After my family's arrest, the *kempeitai* took other prominent families into custody one at a time. The Martinezes, who had moved to the cattle ranch at Dåndan, were the last arrested and brought to Tå'i. Because the family had fled so far from town, the *kempeitai* were suspicious of their activities and kept them longer than other families, certain they knew something of Tweed's whereabouts. The Martinez family had been at Tå'i for several days before my work assignment there. It hurt knowing close friends were suffering, and I was powerless to help.

A few nights later, the *kempeitai* sent me, Manuel Manley, Marian Johnston's brother Tom, and three other men to Hagåtña. The American invasion was imminent, and the Japanese were preparing for it. They transferred men, equipment, and supplies to hold up in Yigo. The bulk of their food stores were in the Japanese family's warehouse on Hernan Cortez Street. Our assignment was to break into the warehouse and get as many supplies as we could. It was a suicide mission. The Japanese knew it, and so did we. We were expendable and not expected to succeed. If we did, they would have their supplies. If we did not, they would do without.

The Americans were pounding Hagåtña and the western coast with around-the-clock bombardments by then. The city was in flames. Tå'i was 6 miles away, but we could hear the explosions and feel the ground quake. We left Tå'i and rumbled in the dark through Chalan Pago, Ordot, and Sinajana. Dim beams of light shone through slits of black electrical tape masking our headlights. I had to lean out the window to see the road. I held the steering wheel in one hand and drove almost blind. As we neared Hagåtña, the explosions grew louder, and the ground shuddered harder. One after another, double, triple, and quadruple blasts jolted our path. The sky ahead of us glowed red above the city. Explosions, whistling missiles, and the roar of the gigantic fire grew deafening as we drew closer.

At the top of San Ramon, we looked down into Hagåtña. It was a seething inferno, but we had no time to mourn the loss of our beautiful capital. We could think only of getting down there, getting out, and staying alive. Manuel and I looked at each other but said nothing. We knew we would either succeed or die in the flames. I turned and hollered to the men in the back to hang on. I threw the truck into gear and slammed on the accelerator. We careened down the hill and into the city on San Ramon Street. Missiles were falling and exploding all around, above, and ahead of us. One of the guys in the back screamed in fright, but the horrendous explosions drowned his cries. I spun the wheel to the right then to the left, trying to avoid exploding parts of the street ahead. Clumps of dirt and pavement flew up and shattered against the truck. Burning pieces of lumber and fragments of building stones rained down on us. The choking dust and smoke were so thick I could not see beyond the hood. The roar of the gargantuan fires was deafening. The heat was unbearable.

I headed for streets lined on either side by thick walls and concrete houses, believing they would better shield and protect us. I turned at the plaza and sped down the street between the palace compound wall and the St. Vincent de Paul building and the cathedral. Telephone poles along the streets were ablaze from top to bottom like pillars of fire. They sizzled, sparked, and emitted a strange popping sound, like small firecrackers. The cathedral was burning. The roof and dome were gone. Long licks of fire reached beyond the roof into the sky. The interior was alight with blinding brightness. White, yellow, orange, and red flames flickered through windows empty of their great stained-glass panels.

I turned onto Hernan Cortez Street and headed for the warehouse. It was intact, but the buildings around it were burning. I glanced down the street to our house. It was still untouched, but I knew it would not be for long. If a shell did not hit it, the fires would soon claim it. I looked away, not wanting to see its destruction. The loud, high-pitched shrill of incoming rounds reminded me of the swishing sounds our fighting kites made on carefree Sunday afternoons. Those peaceful, wonderful days seemed so distant. For a few moments, my fear gave way to heartache. Hagåtña was in her death throes, and my companions and I were helpless witnesses to her agony.

I backed the truck up against the front of the warehouse. We jumped out and began searching among the debris for something strong enough to pry open the doors. Someone found an iron bar. We used it to break the padlock and unchain the warehouse's huge double doors. We worked quickly and silently, aware that a lucky round could reduce us to cinders in an instant. It took all six of us to swing the heavy doors open. The sight inside stunned us. For a moment we were awestruck. American goods and foodstuffs packed the warehouse from the floor to the rafters — cases and cases of goods, great bolts of fabric, crates and boxes of sundries, and huge stacks of canned food. There were mountains of 100-pound sacks of rice, flour, and sugar and barrels of salted salmon and fish. There was more food and supplies than we had ever seen before in one place. I surveyed the scene and wondered how the Japanese military and the Japanese family managed to keep such a huge store so secret.

I looked to the right and saw something that made my heart grow cold with hate. Stacked against one wall were over 100 cases of evaporated milk — more milk than all the babies in Hagåtña could consume, more canned milk than I had ever seen. My heart rose into my throat, choking me. The woman who begrudged my dying brother a half-empty can of milk had hundreds in her possession. Her greed hastened my brother's death. I was in the middle of an inferno, but the bitterness in my heart burned hotter. Franklin's ghostly sobbing rang in my ears, muffling the thundering explosions and the roaring flames.

My mood blackened. I helped the others load the supplies, including the milk. As I drove out of the yard and past the woman's house, I saw that her Japanese garden, with the little half-moon bridge and stone lantern, was still intact. I prayed for a direct hit to obliterate it.

None of us spoke during the ride back to Tả'i. We had driven into the jaws of Hell. We had watched our beloved city die in agony and had seen overwhelming evidence of greed. We were too shocked, too pained, too sad to say anything. The Japanese were surprised when we arrived at headquarters. They did not expect us to succeed. They were pleased to have their supplies but did not congratulate or thank us. They let us go the next day.

Chapter 14

A seething chaos of humans and animals

The American bombardment began on July 8 and continued until July 20, 1944. The bombing lasted for six to eight hours at a time, around the clock. The whistle and whine of incoming shells and the deafening explosions were constant for minutes at a time. The Americans threw everything they had at the island. It rained bombs. The continuous pounding nearly drove us insane.

Although we were safe in our bomb shelter, there was no escaping the noise. Without the lulls between bombardments, we would have gone mad. During a barrage, we could not speak or even think. We could do nothing but wait for a lull and blessed silence. After several hours of such nonstop torment, we would begin to lose all sense of reality. Nothing existed except the horrendous, deafening noise. The lulls were too brief. As soon as our ears stopped ringing, the bombing would begin again. We would dive back into the shelter, muffle our ears as best we could, and cower in fear again.

As Japanese hopes for the Greater East Asia Co-Prosperity Sphere crumbled, their cruelty in Guam increased. There was widespread belief the Japanese would redirect their revenge by executing the stubborn, pro-American CHamoru people. On July 10, 1944, at the height of the American bombardments, the Japanese ordered everyone into staging areas around the island. People from the northern and central areas were to go to Mañenggon, a rugged area inland from Yoña.

Limited to one cart load, we packed only a few items of clothing and some tools. Our main concern was our food supply. We packed as much fried *titiyas*, dried beef, rice, dried corn, canned goods, and salted fish as the cart would hold. Mama had foreseen such an emergency and had stockpiled ample stores. We did not know why we had to move or how long we were to stay. We did not know if we would survive. In the uncertainty, an ample food supply was reassuring.

We deserted Mama's beloved piano and our jungle hacienda to journey inland over rough terrain. As usual, Mama took roll before we set out. There was Daddy, Irene, Lorraine, Bobbie, Paul, Norma, Fred, Rodney, Donald, Junie, Bobing, Michael, baby Rosamunde, me, our little Indian bull, and Paul's loaded bull cart. Sadness filled Mama's eyes. She had always wanted a large family, but forces beyond her control threatened to end the lives she and Daddy had started. There was little she could do but keep us together, like a hen protecting her chicks. She made sure we had food to eat and clothes to wear.

With heavy hearts, we left Pado and joined other refugees on the trail. Our train of people and bull carts grew as the trails to Mañenggon converged. At dusk, a sky of black clouds opened and dumped heavy rain. We stumbled in the darkness and slid in the mud. A huge throng of people was already at Tå'i when we arrived. The larger group had come from Yigo to make way for the Japanese stronghold. They reached Tå'i a day before us. Throughout the night and well into the next day, groups of people from other parts of the island arrived. The Tå'i encampment soon turned into a sea of humanity wallowing in mud. There was no clean water, no shelter from the rain. The Japanese crowded us all together like cattle.

Mrs. Johnston's 8-year-old daughter Eloise was ill at the time and not expected to survive the night. Heartsick, Mrs. Johnston went from hovel to hovel, trying to find someone with a shovel. She was determined to give her daughter a proper burial, even if she had to dig the grave herself. She found one with Kitty Tenorio's family. Upon overhearing Mrs. Johnston's need for a shovel, a compassionate Japanese doctor, working near the Tenorios' camp, offered to take care of Eloise. In desperation, Mrs. Johnston accepted the offer. The following morning, a truck came and took Eloise to the hospital. She survived her illness and the war.

Later that morning, the Japanese routed the encampment and the march to Mañenggon began. I will never forget the terrible scene. Thousands of people rising slowly from their makeshift camps and preparing to move out. They lashed precious belongings — pathetic bundles of every size and description — onto bull carts and travois, or they shouldered or cradled them. Almost everyone carried something. Fear filled everyone's faces. Old people looked sad and confused. There was pain and uncertainty in the faces of the sick. Even the draft animals were frightened. The carabao and bulls were nervous and skittish. Many balked, threatening to overturn carts and crush people in the cramped and crowded encampment. People on foot near the panicky animals rushed to help, grabbing at reins and harnesses. They tried to soothe frightened animals and patted them for assurance. Drivers shouted, whistled, and purred to steady their animals.

At a barked command, a column of soldiers with fixed bayonets began the march. The jumbled mass of people, animals, carts, bundles, and packs slowly assembled in a strange order. The seething chaos of humans and animals compressed and uncoiled like a huge snake. Hundreds of drivers shouted commands to their bulls and carabaos. Families followed on foot, alongside and behind carts and travois. Flanked by armed soldiers, the great human snake inched forward.

Progress over the narrow cart trails and winding country roads was slow. By midmorning, the sun baked the roadway and beat down on us, sapping everyone's strength. We climbed steep inclines or inched down deep ravines countless times. Impatient Japanese soldiers jabbed and prodded our slow-moving procession with their bayonets, driving people like cattle to slaughter. The soldiers had even less patience for the old, the sick, and the weak. They clubbed anyone who slowed progress with a rifle butt or jabbed people with a bayonet to hurry them along. No one could stop. If a bull cart broke down, the owner had to abandon it. Some people tried to salvage their belongings; others had to leave them behind.

Everyone tried to help one another along the way. Whenever anyone stumbled or fell, others would reach out to lend a hand. Though fatigued, many people carried small children and those too weak or unable to walk. I watched people share what strength they could spare with those who had none left. What struck me was the undefeated spirit of people in darkest hardship. Witnessing their strength and courage made me a proud and life-long advocate for my people; I shall never be afraid to sing their praises. If that is nationalism, then I am a nationalist.

As if unsympathetic to our plight, the sky opened and let loose another hard rain. The dry season, which ended in June, had been very dry. Everyone had prayed for rain, but Heaven answered our prayers when we least needed it. The rainy season began with daily downpours that lasted for hours at a time. The rain made our path muddy and slick and slowed our progress even further. All along the column, exhausted people began to slip and fall. Cart-wheels sank in the mud; bull carts bogged down, and draft animals bellowed with fright. The blinding rain turned the march into a nightmare of mud, bray-ing animals, calls for help, angry shouts, the thud of rifle butts on human flesh, and cries of pain.

Hundreds more people joined the march when we reached the Chalan Pago crossroads. From there, we descended the steep road down to the Pago River. We followed the road through the marshy banks of the Pago River and across the bridge. On the other side, the road rose upward again, along the steep flank of the hill to Pago Point and Yoña.

Just before we entered Yoña, a bull cart, about two or three carts ahead of ours, broke down and halted progress. I craned my neck to see what was wrong and grew alarmed. Hannah Chance Torres and her children were pas-sengers in the stalled cart. They were in danger; the Japanese did not tolerate holdups. Though I wanted to, I could not go to their rescue. Like everyone else in the column, I could only watch in fear as a soldier made his way to-ward Hannah's cart. He began shouting at her and jabbing his bayoneted rifle toward her in a threatening manner. Hannah began to scream. The soldier stormed off in disgust, but Hannah continued screaming.

Hannah, the hostess of many of our parties, had always been a pillar of strength. In that moment, I realized her great strength had run out. She began kicking and thrashing in the cart. Several women ran to her side, swooping her infant daughter out of harm's way and trying desperately to calm her. Al-though she was no longer in danger, Hannah screamed for a long, long time. She never recovered from the terror. Exhaustion eventually reduced her to semiconsciousness. She whimpered all the way to Mañenggon and gave up the will to live.

From Yoña, we drove inland, into the rough hill country to Pulantat, where the road ended. We reached the edge of the plateau as night fell. The Japanese would not allow a slow, careful descent into the Mañenggon valley; instead, they drove everyone downward at gunpoint. The descent was horren-dous. The people at the head of the column cut a path through the jungle with machetes. For those of us who followed behind, the rough path was stubbled with hacked-off stumps and cut branches, which stuck out like spears on all sides. The sharp stumps and branches tore at legs and feet, both human and animal. They snagged clothing, flesh, and cart wheels.

As we began our descent, heavy rain fell again. Rainwater and mud streamed down the slopes. In the darkness, people slipped and fell, tumbling helplessly until they slammed into rocks, trees, or other people. Or until cut stumps snagged or impaled them. Men, women, and children dug their feet into the mud, trying to keep their carts from careening downward out of control. When they could not, they shouted warnings to the people further ahead. Terrified beasts howled, and terrified people cried out and prayed for help and mercy.

Halfway down, our little bull let out a mournful wail. Its legs buckled, and the bull collapsed. Its eyes rolled back, and it struggled to breathe. I lashed at it, ordering, and pleading with it to get up, but it refused. I jumped from the cart and yanked at its harness. It would not budge. Then Dad, Paul, and my younger brothers tried but could not get it up. In desperation, I began whipping it again and again, but it seemed numbed to my beatings. Now, when I recall the incident, I realize I had been harsh on the poor animal.

For a few moments, we thought the bull was dead. Without it to pull the cart, we would have to carry whatever we could and make the descent on foot. We coaxed the exhausted animal again and again, taking turns pulling at its harness and pleading with it. Just as we were about to give up, the little bull flinched as if we had startled it from sleep and rose to its feet. Relieved, we continued downward.

The voice in the darkness

Hard rain fell again when we reached the valley floor. We were on level ground again, but it was a swamp. The rain-swollen stream, a tributary of the Ilek River, turned the valley into a sea of mud. In some spots, the mud was knee deep. Exhausted people collapsed on both sides of the stream. Rain splattered down on uncaring bodies, heaving in the mud.

When the downpour ended, the camp began to buzz with the sound of murmuring voices as people searched for space to settle. It was a strange sound. It seemed muffled, distant, and unreal. It reminded me of the honeybees at Mayanghulo'. At that moment, everything seemed distant and unreal — the honeybees, Mayanghulo', even Hagåtña seemed like a dream. The only realities were the mud, the rain, and our miserable condition.

Despite the darkness and the mud, constructing some sort of shelter became everyone's immediate priority, and an encampment began to take shape. People automatically organized themselves to be near family, friends, and neighbors, as if staying close provided a sense of order and security. Like others, Mama insisted we look for space near our Hagåtña neighbors. We found a spot large enough for us close to Uncle Tom's family, the Torreses, and the Johnstons.

While Mama and the girls checked our belongings, Dad, Paul, Fred, and I cut down a lot of saplings and coconut fronds to build a lean-to large enough to fit us all. In the meantime, my younger brothers and sisters huddled together, shivering in the cold, wet night air. When we finished the shelter, we piled in and cuddled for warmth. Outside, the camp settled into a stillness broken only by the buzzing of mosquitoes and an occasional cough.

Despite my exhaustion, I could not sleep. I tossed and turned for hours. In the wee hours of morning, I heard a man's voice calling out in the eerie silence, *"Felis, Felis, mangge hao? Maila', sa' chachaflek si Hannah."* Someone was calling Felix Torres. The doleful, solitary voice pierced the stillness like a sharp knife. More than 40 years have passed since that night, but that voice still haunts me. Sometimes, just before I drop off to sleep, I hear it again in all its clarity and sadness, piercing the night. I had listened to the voice that night but had been too dazed and exhausted to realize its message. "Felix," the voice called. "Come, because Hannah is dying."

At daybreak, Hannah Chance Torres was dead. Felix and his grieving family wrapped her body in a blanket and buried her near the camp. They marked her grave and hoped someday to move Hannah and give her a proper burial. In the following days, other burials took place in and around the camp. After the war, their families returned to Mañenggon, exhumed their loved ones, and buried them where they belonged. Some may still lie in Mañenggon, their markers and burial sites lost.

To keep from starving

The air in Mañenggon was clean and sweet when we first got there. Smoke from thousands of cooking fires would blend with the morning mist and dissipate as the day wore on. But within a few days, the smoke and mist began to accumulate into a thick, steamy layer above the hovels. It never dissipated. The blanket of smoke and steam sealed in all the odors in camp. As human and animal waste piled up each day, the odors and the air grew foul. Soon, the whole camp reeked with a horrible stench.

The smells were my gauge to conditions in camp. As a butcher and meat vendor, I could tell the kind and quality of any meat by its aroma as it cooked. I could sniff the air and know whether someone still had good beef, pork, or chicken for supper. As conditions worsened, so did the cooking odors. The stink of rotting meat replaced the fragrance of good meat. It turned my stomach and sickened me to think people were eating spoiled food to keep from starving. After a while, an odor I could not identify replaced the rotten meat smell. It was a strange odor so repulsive I wondered what people were cooking. The possibilities were frightful.

The small stream that coursed through the valley was our only source of water. With several thousand people using it daily, it quickly turned into a cesspool. There was no clean water, and the ground was always wet and muddy. And we were wallowing in it. Marian Johnston and her friends found a tiny spring trickling from a rock face and thought it was clean. They kept the spring secret, hoping to keep it for themselves. Later they discovered that it came from upstream, where thousands more had encamped and where the water was just as filthy.

The physical misery was terrible; the emotional trauma we were experiencing was worse. As food supplies ran out, people began to suffer tremendous guilt. The ingrained CHamoru tradition of sharing clashed with the need to keep enough for oneself. Denying someone's request for food was as humiliating and difficult as the need to ask. Those who had no food relied on those who still had some. But no one stole food; no one could bring themselves to such degradation.

Gathering food was the main preoccupation in camp. People of all ages were involved. Men sometimes went into the jungle with nothing more than small knives and sharpened sticks to hunt for game. They would often be gone for days, foraging far for anything edible. If they were lucky, they would catch a deer or wild pig, a few small birds, or some fish. They shared their catches, but there was never enough to go around.

As our own food supply dwindled, we would eat only a few pieces of Mama's leathery fried *titiyas* for supper. Like others, Mama made ersatz coffee from toasted corn kernels or *tangantångan* seeds. Although she had many children to feed, she could not be stingy with food. A woman who asked for food told Mama she and her children had not eaten in two days. Mama could not refuse.

If not for the coconut trees around us, thousands would have gone hungry. Without clean drinking water, we drank coconut water or coconut milk squeezed from grated coconut meat. We ate *månha*, the jelly-like meat of green, unripe coconuts; ripe coconut meat; *fåha'*, the spongy substance filling the shell of a sprouting coconut; and *patnitos*, or heart of palm. We used the trunks, fronds branches, spathes, and *gunot* — the netting around the base of the fronds — for everything from building materials and kindling to kitchen utensils and toilet paper.

Except to conscript laborers every morning, the Japanese left us alone. They posted two machine gun squads at the edge of the camp but allowed us freedom to forage in the surrounding area. The only requirement made of us was to assemble at daybreak for labor selection. On one morning, Lorraine was among several women selected and taken from the camp. No one knew what labor the women were to perform and feared the worst. We learned later they were cooks and domestics at Tå'i, not sexual playthings.

Most of our women tried not to attract Japanese male attention but were not always successful. Among Lorraine's group was Maria Perez Howard, a pretty girl who once worked as Dad's secretary. Her husband Edward, a crewman on the *Penguin*, was among the American prisoners taken to Japan. Maria's good looks and her marriage to an American Navy man made her a favorite target for Japanese harassment. She was under arrest at the *kempeitai* headquarters when her family and two children marched to Mañenggon. The Japanese had held her for more than a month. She made her way to Mañenggon and had been in camp only a few days when the Japanese conscripted her with Lorraine and the other women. In Tå'i, Maria attracted the interest of a Japanese officer who had her beaten after she rebuffed him. A few days before the American landing, Maria's captors led her into the jungle at gunpoint. No one ever saw her again.

Edward Howard returned to Guam after the war and searched in vain for Maria's grave. Grieving, he returned to the States with their children, 5-year-old Chris and baby Helen, born just before the invasion. In 1980, Chris Perez Howard returned to Guam to learn about his mother and his CHamoru roots. Through research and countless interviews with his maternal relatives, Chris became reacquainted with Maria and mourned her death a second, more painful time. In 1981, he published *Mariquita*, a book about her life and death. He later became an outspoken proponent for CHamoru indigenous rights, war reparations, and just land claims settlement. In 1985, he signed onto my staff.

The grave in the banana grove

In Mañenggon, we were safe from the fighting, but we could hear it raging in the distance. The Americans were concentrating their bombardments in the north where they knew the Japanese had gathered. An American plane would fly over the camp occasionally and stir up everyone's excitement. On one such occasion, my brothers and sisters and I were splashing about in a deep spot in the river near the camp. As we headed to the spot that day, we came across a freshly dug hole in a banana grove. It was obvious that it was to be a grave. We passed it by without giving it much thought. Graves were common. A few minutes later, as we splashed in the water, a plane appeared overhead. It circled above us and came in closer. Some of the children even claimed they saw the pilot's face.

I realized we were in danger if the pilot mistook us for the enemy. Before I could shout to my companions to smile and wave at the pilot, they were already cheering and jumping up and down. The pilot dipped his wings in acknowledgment, and we got more excited. "Did you see that? He smiled at us. He waved back," someone said. Seconds later, our excitement turned to fear. The pilot suddenly started firing his machine gun. We thought he was going to mow us down. The bullets sliced through the trees beside the swimming hole. A man tore out of the machine-gunned thicket. His hands were bound behind him, and he was barefoot. He galloped past us, screaming in CHamoru, "Move away; they're going to kill me!" As he disappeared into the jungle, a Japanese patrol came out of the thicket.

Years later, I learned from my cousin, Joaquin "Kin" Pangelinan, that the man was Ignacio "Kalandu" San Nicolas. The Japanese were going to execute him that day. The hole in the banana grove was to be his grave. The American's machine gun fire scattered Kalandu's executioners long enough for him to escape. Barefoot and bound, Kalandu ran from Mañenggon to Chúchugo', 10 miles over rough terrain. In Chúchugo', he ran into a Japanese patrol that shot and wounded him then left him for dead. Kalandu crawled under an abandoned house to die but was found near death two days later. He survived.

My cousin Kin sought safety in the same area. His family had hidden in Chúchugo', which is only a few hundred yards north of where we had hidden in Pado. When the concentration order was issued, Kin was among the laborers conscripted to work on the Japanese airfield at Halåguak. His family went to Mañenggon without him. While on the labor detail, Kin stole a nap on the job. A Japanese soldier discovered him, kicked him awake, struck him with his rifle butt, and marched him off to the commandant, who was a cruel man. The commandant ordered Kin to bow repeatedly, recite praises to the emperor, and denounce Uncle Sam. Although Kin complied, the commandant was not satisfied. He beat Kin himself. Kin got even that night. He ambushed a guard and beat him with his own rifle. Kin fled back to Chúchugo', but his family was gone. He did not know that they were in Mañenggon. He hid out in Chúchugo' alone.

A few days after Kin's escape, a Japanese officer on horseback caught him by surprise. Kin thought his luck had run out, but instead of killing him, the officer offered him a job. Kin could not believe the offer but dared not refuse. The officer turned out to be the commandant of an agricultural project and a decent fellow. Kin and the other field workers were treated well. Later, when a soldier from the airstrip recognized and reported him, Kin feared for his life. He did not know how the commandant would react. To Kin's surprise and relief, the commandant slapped the informing soldier and threw him from the camp. When the Japanese position deteriorated, the commandant scribbled a pass for the CHamoru workers and told them to flee for their lives.

"I don't know what he wrote, but it got us to Mañenggon," Kin said in recollection. He and his companions reached the camp as the Americans were liberating it. Lorraine's detail also returned only a day or two before the Americans arrived.

While Lorraine was gone, the Japanese selected Paul for a labor detail in Yigo, where the Japanese were amassing. The plan changed at the last minute, and Paul's group went to Yoña instead. There they unloaded and stacked supplies in St. Francis church, which the Japanese used as a supply depot. A few days later, an American plane strafed the church. The attack panicked the Japanese and gave the laborers a chance to escape. Paul and several others made their way back to Mañenggon.

Like Paul, Adrian "Nito" Cristobal, and Vicente "Ben" Blaz, who I once considered a friend, were also supposed to work in Yigo. Their crew went instead to Lonfet to cut coconut fronds to mask the white gravel of the airstrips from American planes. Nito, who later became a political colleague, was adept at learning languages, and as the eldest in the group, he served as group leader and spokesman. As the men cut fronds, an American plane strafed their work site. The attack killed one man and wounded another who died the following day. Nito prodded his companions to work faster. They stopped only long enough to eat.

During the meal break, a wounded Japanese soldier staggered out of the jungle toward them. He gestured to some green coconuts in a tree then to his mouth; he wanted a drink. Ben, who was about 16 years old, refused to climb a coconut tree for the enemy. The soldier jabbed a finger at Ben and barked, *"Kura!"* which means "quickly." According to Nito, Ben shimmied up the tree faster than a panicked monkey. Ben later became a brigadier general in the Marine Corps. His ego rose accordingly. To Ben's embarrassment, Nito often relates the Lonfet incident with great relish.

The crew that went to Yigo never returned. After completing their assignment, the men, including Gadi's younger brother Ramon, were bound and bayonetted. None survived. After routing the Japanese and reaching Yigo, the Americans discovered the crew's bloated bodies. If plans had not changed for Paul and Nito's groups, they would have also been executed.

As the American offensive intensified, word about similar killings elsewhere on the island filtered into camp. The crew sent to Hagåtña to dig caves into the base of San Ramon and Tutuhan hills also died by execution. That crew included my friend Arthur Anderson. The reports of more executions grew daily. Uneasiness spread in the camp. The Japanese never explained why they drove us into the raw jungle. No one believed it was to shield us from harm. Some thought it was a form of control, a way to keep us from aiding the Americans. Others thought the Japanese had more sinister intentions. There was a rumor that a collaborator bragged about how the Americans would land only to find the island swarming with flies. The rumor and the reports lent credibility to the belief that the Japanese were going to execute us. They had slaughtered thousands in Manchuria; we were an insignificant handful by comparison.

"American, no shoot"

Dad was among the first to receive whispered reports. He was worried. The Americans had landed in Hågat and Asan and were fighting their way inland and northward. CHamorus were at significant risk. If the Japanese were going to execute us, the time was at hand. Since overcrowding in the camp made confidential conversations impossible, Dad took me aside. He did not want anyone to hear. He looked around to make sure no one was nearby.

"The news I've received is not good," he said. The mass killing had started. The Japanese herded two groups of Malesso' villagers into caves at Tinta' and Fåha' and tossed hand grenades in after them. Forty-five people died. Less than a dozen survived. Dad feared Mañenggon was next and that political leaders would be the first to die.

"And you know what that means," he said. "I won't order you to do this; I will just ask because it will be dangerous. Try to make contact with the Americans. They must get here before the killing starts. Once the Japanese weed out and execute the leaders, people will panic. The Japanese will turn on them, and thousands will die. The Americans need to know this and must send help."

Dad looked tired and old. His flamboyance was gone. He had always been self-assured, trim, and handsome, but hunger, worry, and fear had taken a toll. He was gaunt and haggard. Worry etched deep lines in his face. He looked much older than his 43 years.

"I'll go, Daddy," I said, pretending to ignore the risk. I felt as helpless as I did in 1936 when he went to Washington, but I was no longer a 9-year-old child. Dad's request was not meant to teach me responsibility. The mission meant life or death, not only for me or Dad and his colleagues, but for everyone in the camp.

I asked Gadi to go with me. I needed his sharp eyes and his skill for moving stealthily through the jungle. Although it meant risking his life, Gadi did not hesitate. He is an unsung hero who deserves praise. I regret that as a two-term governor, I did not give him that recognition when I had the chance. Without him, I am not sure the mission would have succeeded.

Gadi and I waited until the camp settled for the night before creeping into the darkness. We sneaked across the stream at 3 a.m. and sat on the muddy banks, shivering with cold. The morning dampness and chill kept us cold and wet for hours. We crawled through the jungle on our bellies in the dark. By dawn, we were halfway up the hillside below Yoña. We could hear explosions and gunshots in the distance and knew we were heading in the right direction, but we did not know which camp we would meet first — the Americans or the Japanese. The grassy hills and slopes slowed our advance. In daylight and with little cover, we were easier to spot. As we crawled through the grass, Gadi called out in a loud, hoarse whisper.

"Ricky, look! There's someone over there." He shimmied up beside me and pointed ahead. I saw nothing. "There, Ricky, right there. Look! There's a man right over there."

Still, I saw nothing, but said, "Keep your head down."

A few moments later, Gadi tugged at my shirt. "Ricky, look! Cigarettes! American cigarettes!" He threw me a wide, toothy grin and stuffed the half-filled pack of cigarettes into his pocket. We found more cigarettes and the half-eaten remains of Army rations.

As we crawled further, we found unopened tins and packets of food, including chewing gum and chocolate candy, strewn in the grass. Each packet and can was olive green and had long strings of black numbers and letters, the most heartening were, "U.S.A." Like children on Christmas morning, we scrambled for the rations, both grabbing at the same time, stuffing tins and packets into our pockets and shirts.

"We must be near the Americans," I said. "They're the only ones who could be so extravagant with food."

We found more abandoned rations and gathered them as we advanced. After a while, the treasures made crawling on our bellies uncomfortable and clumsy. We jettisoned some and made mental notes to retrieve them later.

Suddenly, ahead of us, a deep voice called out, "Halt! Who goes there?"

A grim-faced soldier pointed his rifle at us. There was no recognition in his eyes, nothing to suggest he understood we were natives. We had to identify ourselves before the American shot us. I looked at Gadi. We feared he would shoot us anyway.

"Come on, Gadi, get up slowly, and put your hands up," I said as I raised both arms and stood up. Gadi followed.

"American, no shoot! Me, CHamoru. No kill us," I called out. I was scared, relieved, and embarrassed all at once. In my fear and nervousness, I forgot to correct my English. Speaking perfect American English roused Japanese tempers, so those of us who could do so intentionally mangled the language. It was often the only way we could communicate with the Japanese. After almost three years of it, speaking broken English was second nature.

Gadi and I stood side by side with our arms up, waiting for the soldier to recognize us as civilians. Our presence attracted several other soldiers who approached with their weapons ready.

"Turn around," one of them barked. We turned our backsides to them. One of them came forward and began frisking us, searching for concealed weapons or booby traps. The Japanese were known to surrender with grenades, firing pins pulled, tucked at their backs. The Americans quickly learned what to search for first.

"It's okay. They're not Japs," the soldier said. The soldiers lowered their weapons. Gadi and I lowered our arms.

"We're natives of this island," I said. "We must see your commander. Many of our people will die if we don't get help."

The soldiers led us quite a distance until we reached Yoña village. As we neared Tun Ramon Baza's property, I saw a large concentration of soldiers, tents, and weapons. Machine guns shielded by sandbags crouched near a command post, which was a tent beside Tun Ramon's house. A man emerged from it and came toward us. I was not familiar with Army insignia and did not know who or what he was. He carried himself with authority, and soldiers snapped at his orders, so I assumed he was the commanding officer.

"Sir, I am here at the request of my father, who is a political leader of our people. We need your help," I said.

"What's your name, son?"

"My name is Bordallo. My father and the other leaders are down in the concentration camp. The Japanese are going to kill us. Do you know about the camp?"

"Yes, we're aware there's a large concentration of civilians in the valley, but as you can see, we're heavily engaged right here," the officer said.

"There are almost 14,000 people and only two machine guns down there. You can take them easily, but if they open up on the camp, thousands will die," I said.

In the distance, we could hear several machine gun fire and mortar shells exploding. Even as we spoke, we had to crouch or take cover as some shells hit closer to the camp.

"Sir, you must rescue the camp because the Japanese are planning to kill us all, and they're going to start with the leaders. They have already started in Malesso'. They've already massacred people there. Please, you must send help," I said.

The officer looked sympathetic. "Well, son, I don't know if we can do anything. I have to check with higher authorities, but like I said, we're pretty busy here."

"Please, sir, please talk to whoever you need to, but you must come. Our situation is desperate. We need your help, or we will all die down there. Please," I pleaded.

Gadi and I had come a long and dangerous way. We never dreamed the Americans would deny our plea for rescue. If they did not come to the camp, there was no hope for anyone. The officer looked at Gadi and me and read the desperation, disappointment, and fear in our faces.

"All right," he said. "I'll see what I can do."

He walked into another tent a few feet away. Through the open flaps, we watched as he cranked up a field telephone. He spoke into the receiver, but we could not hear his words. A few minutes later, he hung up and returned to us with a dejected look on his face.

"I'm sorry, son. Our command said it's not likely we can offer you any assistance," he said. The decision troubled him. I sensed he would have helped if he could. The Americans were going to abandon us again because they could not spare the effort.

Until that moment, I believed like others that the Americans had come to rescue us. My heart sank at the realization that we were wrong. Our rescue was not their mission. The Americans came only to reclaim stolen property. Four decades later, on the 40th anniversary of "Liberation Day," Jesus Barcinas confirmed what I had long known. Barcinas, a Malesso' leader, was one of the first CHamorus to contact the U.S. Navy in 1944. In a desperate effort to get help and stop the murders in his village, Barcinas and a handful of men jumped their Japanese guards, made their way to the ocean, and sailed out to the American warships. The Americans held Barcinas and his companions at gunpoint until they were sure they were not the enemy. As I had done, Barcinas pleaded with a Navy officer for help. In recounting the incident for an anniversary documentary, Barcinas said, without bitterness, "We were told that they didn't come to rescue the natives of the island ... they were ordered to shell the island down to the level of the ground."

Gadi and I could not hide our despair. We had risked our lives, certain the Americans would charge to the rescue like the cavalry in the movies, flags waving and guns blazing. CHamorus were loyal, patriotic pro-Americans, but we were not Americans and not worth the effort. Gadi and I looked sadly at the officer who seemed to care but could not help.

An instant later, artillery fire erupted a few yards from where we stood. Gunshots rang out. Several men ran about, hollering and shooting. The fighting had moved closer to the camp but had not reached the command post. I suddenly remembered that there was a pillbox hidden behind a large hibiscus bush beside Manuel Lujan's house, which was directly across the street from Tun Ramon's house. I had my back to the street and the pillbox. My spine tingled. I did not know if the Americans knew about the pillbox or if they had already secured it. I looked at the Army officer.

"Sir," I whispered. "There's a pillbox behind me to the left. Have you cleared it?"

"What?" My question shocked him.

"A Japanese pillbox. Over there behind the hibiscus."

Before he could react, machine gun fire erupted from the pillbox. We threw ourselves to the ground. Some soldiers in the line of fire were killed; several others were wounded. Gadi, the officer, and I stayed pinned to the ground; the Japanese did not have a clear shot at us. While the wounded screamed in pain and other men began yelling, several others crawled across the street on their bellies. They inched around to the rear of the pillbox and lobbed hand grenades into an opening. The grenades exploded, and the pillbox erupted in flames. Chunks of metal and lumber and shredded clothing, blood, and pieces of flesh flew out.

"Christ, son, you just saved our lives," the officer said when the uproar ceased, and we stood up. He clapped his hand on my shoulder and added, "If you hadn't warned us, I'd have lost more men. I'm grateful for that."

I wanted his help, not his gratitude. I must have looked sullen, despite his praise. He studied me, then said, "To hell with orders. I'll send a squad to your camp. That's all I can spare. That should be enough to get your leaders out. Go back to your dad with that message."

"Is that the best you can do, sir?" I asked, hopeful but still disappointed. Only one squad?

"Just the leaders for now. A squad will be at your camp at around 1 o'clock," he said.

Before retracing our way back to camp, Gadi and I retrieved some of the rations we had found earlier. We did not take a lot. I took some cigarettes for Dad and some chewing gum and chocolate for Mama and my brothers and sisters. Word of such things in the camp would have stirred jubilation and attracted the guards' attention. The items were proof we had made contact with the Americans and would have gotten us shot, along with anyone celebrating prematurely.

Nine men to rescue thousands

The trip back to camp was quicker but more dangerous. In daylight, we were moving targets more easily seen. It took us hours to get back and sneak into camp. I was eager to share my news and the goodies I had brought, but when I reached our shelter, something was wrong. Dad looked more worried than relieved to see me. And Mama looked scared. My report about the incident at the Army camp and the arrival of a squad did not lift Dad's spirits. Mama, Irene, Lorraine, Bobbie, Paul, and Norma, who had gathered to listen, also did not appear heartened.

"Well, Ricky, I don't know if they'll get here in time," Dad said. "That Saipanese was here earlier. He wanted to know where you were. I made up some story, but I do not think he believed me. The Japanese may already be on their way to arrest us."

Despite our numbers, the Japanese kept tabs on everyone through their Saipanese collaborators. The one who questioned Dad was arrogant and mean. Everyone feared him. He had kept a close eye on us and found hundreds of excuses to harass Dad. He delighted in insulting Dad and reminding him that he was no longer a wealthy businessman or an important political leader. My absence from camp gave him another opportunity to needle Dad. As the interpreter questioned Dad about my whereabouts, he withdrew his dagger and stropped it against his open hand. Dad ignored the veiled threat and told him I was pasturing our bull. Not satisfied, the interpreter also questioned Mama and my sisters.

"When your son returns, we will want him for questioning," he told them and left.

"We must buy more time, son," Dad said. "As long as he doesn't spot you, we're safe. The Japanese must not find you. Look for someplace to hide. Let's hope the Americans get here before they find you."

More frightened than I had ever been, I got ready to flee. My family's lives and mine were in danger. We did not know what was in store for us. We knew we might never see one another again. Saying goodbye was indescribable. Mama hugged me and whispered in CHamoru, "God bless and protect you, my son."

My heart pounded, and my mind raced as I sneaked out of camp again. Running and stumbling, I fled into the hills above camp. Ignoring thorns and branches that tore at my skin, I forced myself into a *lemmon di china* thicket and started to pray. I drew my knees to my chest and started trembling. Alone, hunted, and scared, I gave in to my fear and helplessness and cried.

Except for the buzz of insects, the jungle around me was quiet. After sitting in the thicket for about an hour, I began to hear a strange sound rising from the camp. At first, it was distant and faint, then it grew louder as I strained to listen. It was a sound I had not heard in years, the same sound that came from Bradley Field on Sunday afternoons when someone hit a home run — the roar of a happy crowd. It was coming from the camp, and my spirits soared. "The Americans. It must be the Americans," I thought.

I crouched in the thicket, listening and feeling my fear wash away. I was sure the Americans had arrived, but I stayed in hiding. Dad would send for me if all was safe. Moments later, I heard Paul calling out, "Riiickyyyy, come out. The Americans are here!" He galloped toward me as I came out of the thicket. "Hurry!" he shouted. "The Americans are here! The Americans are here!"

The uproar from the camp and Paul's excitement made me think an entire battalion of Americans had arrived. We ran down the hillside and into the frenzy in the camp. No celebration could have been more wild and joyful. People were laughing and crying, hugging and kissing, shouting and jumping, dancing and singing.

I worked my way into the crowd until I found Dad. Together, we elbowed our way toward nine, dumbfounded American soldiers who were surrounded by hundreds of people. The Americans did not expect such a reception or so large a crowd. One of the soldiers raised his rifle above the crowd and shouted, "We have orders to find Bordallo. Where is Bordallo?" No one listened or paid attention to him. The soldier turned and glanced meekly at his companions.

Dad and I pushed through the crowd to reach them. Dad shouted, "I'm Bordallo! This is my son, the one who went for help."

The soldier strained to hear then nodded and shouted back, "Sir, they told us to get the leaders only." He looked around and realized the task would be impossible. "We were told to get the leaders, but, sir, you will have to let them know and follow us."

"Follow us" was all anyone heard, and the word spread quickly. Everyone wanted to be where the Americans were, to go where they went. They would have followed them anywhere. If it meant follow now, this very minute, then that is what it was. There was no way to control the crowd. No one tried. Like magic, the chaos disappeared, and nearly 14,000 men, women, and children turned into one gigantic entity. Within minutes, the great throng fell in line and followed obediently behind the Americans. Only those who could not leave — the old and the sick and their families — stayed behind.

Like me, the camp guards thought that the entire American Army had arrived when the camp erupted in celebration. They panicked, fled their post, and hid in the underbrush. As we left the camp, one of the guards opened fire. Several people shouted, "Get down! Get down!" Many dropped to the ground and cowered; others ran. As one of the Americans took aim at a fleeing Japanese guard, a man darted into the American's line of fire and got hit in the head. He died on the spot. I watched it happen and felt awful. The man had survived nearly three years of occupation only to die accidentally on the brink of rescue. His family could only wail over his body.

Although I never knew the man's name, he became for me a symbol of tragic irony. The Mañenggon liberation story is not complete without the memory of his unfortunate death. During my second term, while reminiscing with a visitor whose family had also been at Mañenggon, I related the tragedy I had witnessed. To my amazement, my visitor said, "Governor, that man was my father." Forty years after the fact, I expressed my condolences.

Tears among the soldiers

From Mañenggon, many from the camp, including my family, climbed into the hills and headed west toward Hågat and the coast. We followed paths beaten down by the soldiers who had fought their way up from the Hågat beachhead and across the island to the eastern coast. We found evidence along the way of the battle that preceded our passage. Empty ammunition boxes and spent bullet casings, crumpled cigarette packets, and lost helmets and combat gear littered the paths. We reached the grassy hilltops in time to watch a spectacular sunset. It seemed happy to greet us.

At dusk, people gathered into family or neighborhood groups on the plateau. My family, Uncle Tom's, the Torreses, and the Johnstons chose a spot beneath some ironwood trees. The American soldiers camped nearby. As the encampment settled for the night, someone started singing. In what I can only describe as a beautiful and spontaneous release of pent-up fear and a real gladdening of hearts, everyone joined in. The song spread slowly from group to group until several hundred voices were singing at once. As a peaceful people forced to subdue our happy nature, we sang to make ourselves whole again. Each song seemed to nurture our spirits and renew our strength. We sang to confirm that the time of our misery was over. We sang popular songs from happier times. We sang throughout the night. Many of us did not stop until daybreak.

In the morning, we continued westward toward the 77th Army Infantry Division's base camp in Hågat. When we reached the slopes above the coast, an incredible panorama of American military might came into view. Hundreds of ships of different shapes and sizes speckled Hågat Bay. There were so many that they darkened the ocean all the way to the horizon. Several battleships were still firing shells toward the northeast. Their heavy guns were booming with bright orange flashes and great billows of smoke. It was an impressive sight. Hundreds of landing craft, loaded with soldiers and equipment, shuttled among the ships and back and forth between the shore. The beach was alive with activity. Everywhere, men and machines were moving about, too busy to notice our presence above them.

Cheering and waving, we poured down the slopes. Men, women, old people, children, and babies, dressed in rags and smiles, slipped and fell in the mud, but no one cared. No amount of mud could have dampened our joy. Down the hillsides we came, tattered, filthy, muddy, barefoot, homeless, pitiful human beings, who never lost our dignity and who stood steadfast and loyal to the United States. After the Americans spotted us, they sent trucks, jeeps, tanks with bulldozer blades, and amphibious landing craft to intercept us. Bearhugs and grateful jubilant tears marked our first face-to-face meeting with our liberators. We had nothing to offer but our CHamoru gratitude and appreciation, but we offered what we could from our ragged and meager possessions. Tearful "Thank yous" just did not seem to be enough.

There were tears also among the battle-hardened soldiers who transported us to the beach. Until they saw us, the Americans were unaware that the island they were to take included its inhabitants — living, breathing people. Their orders were to wrest a U.S. possession from the enemy, to pulverize him and the island, if necessary. Rescuing the CHamorus was not their mission, yet there we were, innocent, brown-skinned people in their bloody arena. Our appearance gave their purpose a higher meaning. We were their comrades — Americans, at least in spirit and belief. The soldiers would not let anyone walk the last few yards to the beach. They insisted we ride to freedom. When the "ducks" bogged down in the mud, the soldiers did not make us get down; they called for tanks to drag our stranded rides out.

The Americans had no relief supplies for civilians, nor were such supplies following in post invasion shipments. Their ill preparedness confirmed that rescuing the CHamorus was not their aim. Despite this, the soldiers used their ingenuity and generosity to help us, offering anything and everything they thought useful. Field bandages doubled as diapers. Powdered milk became baby formula.

After reaching safety, many people from Mañenggon left the Hågat beachhead to head for home, to search for and rejoin their relatives. We spent one night in Hågat. The following morning, two soldiers arrived in a jeep and asked for Dad. One was a short, red-haired man not surprisingly called "Red," who was the spokesman. The other was his driver. When Red found our tent, he snapped to attention and saluted Dad as though he was a high-ranking officer.

"Mr. Bordallo, sir," he said. "My commanding officer, Col. Chandler of the Quartermaster Corps, extends his invitation to join him at his headquarters."

Dad's face brightened; he knew Col. Chandler. "So, he's a colonel now," Dad said with a smile.

"Sir, we've made arrangements for you and your family if you decide to accept the colonel's invitation," Red said.

"Well, son, you tell Col. Chandler that I do indeed wish to accept," Dad said. "Tell him I look forward to seeing him again. And be sure to tell him that B.J. Bordallo sends his sincerest greetings and thanks."

That afternoon, a weapons carrier and three jeeps, two mounted with machine guns, arrived in camp. We were awestruck. The convoy was our ride to Col. Chandler's headquarters. The unarmed jeep was for Mama and Dad. The weapons carrier was for us. The soldiers hoisted my sisters and the little ones on board. My brothers and I did not need help. The armed jeeps took up positions behind and ahead of us and escorted us to Tipunngan, north of Piti.

Chapter 15

"Someone's baking bread"

The ride was exhilarating. We sped along the coast from Hågat to Piti, veering around bomb craters and smoldering war machines. Swarms of American fighter planes circled the sky above us. They sometimes swooped down to inspect our convoy. We waved at every pilot. Hundreds of Marines and soldiers walked or lounged along the roadsides. We waved at them too. They looked puzzled at first, then recognizing us as rescued islanders, they returned our greetings with whistles, cheers, and big smiles. Complete with an aerial escort, we felt like the prize-winning float in a parade.

Our route took us through the landing areas where fierce battles had taken place. Sequestered in Mañenggon, far from the battles, we were shocked by the aftermath. The once-familiar landscape was ugly and alien, scoured worse than any typhoon. Bomb craters and burned and blackened earth pockmarked the land. Deep holes and mounds of dirt marked the destruction of vegetable gardens and sweet potato fields. An ugly tangle of broken trees and leafless branches replaced the once lush, green jungle along the coast. Broken, topless coconut trees looked like hundreds of deformed telephone poles. And the wreckage of war lay everywhere. Tanks, jeeps, trucks, and landing craft blighted the land. Some vehicles were clumps of burned and twisted metal; bullet holes riddled others.

The devastation surrounded us. To our left, in the shallow reef flats, immobilized landing craft littered the water and the shoreline. Beyond the reefs, the American fleet out at sea was still firing shells northward at the Japanese. To our right were the highlands from where the Japanese fired down upon the American landing forces on July 21, 1944. Hundreds of Americans died in the water, on the beaches, and on the high ground. Despite the difficulties and the carnage, the Americans secured the western coast. The cliffs were silent now, but we could hear the battle still raging in the north and the big guns of the ships at sea. It sounded like distant thunder.

In Tipunngan, the convoy pulled up in front of a house with a gaping hole in the roof. The soldiers had thrown a tarpaulin over the hole for temporary repair and used the house as a command center. A party of smiling officers awaited us in front of it. From our perch on the weapons carrier, we watched as they greeted Mama and Dad with salutes. A couple of officers helped Mama, who carried baby Rosamunde, treating Mama like a lady again after almost three years. An officer, who I assumed was Col. Chandler, embraced Dad, held him by his shoulders and studied him, then embraced him again. The two had become friends before the war. After learning Dad was alive and at the Army camp in Hågat, Chandler sought him out.

The area around the command center bristled with large tents, heavy equipment, and hundreds of men who were moving, unloading, and stacking crates and boxes. As we watched, we became aware of a familiar aroma emanating from the command center. "Bread," one of my sisters whispered. "Someone's baking bread." We breathed deeply and filled our lungs with the wonderful fragrance.

While the officers greeted Mama and Dad, several men helped us down from the weapons carrier. We were the center of camp attention. The soldiers stared at us as curiously as we stared at them. They had spent over a month on board the ships before invading the island. They had known nothing but warfare and had not seen women and children in months. We were out of the ordinary. We might have reminded them of their own families, their brothers and sisters, and home. There was tenderness in their faces. They wanted to help all of us, whether we needed it or not. It was amusing to watch them push and shove each other, trying to act like gentlemen to help my sisters. Irene, Lorraine, and Bobbie blushed and giggled and welcomed the help but worried about their rumpled, muddy appearance. Paul, Fred, Rodney, and I jumped down without help while Junie, Josephine, Michael, and Donald rode the shoulders of some of the men.

Those of us who could walk assembled beside Mama and Dad. The soldiers, with the little ones still riding on their shoulders, stood behind us. Col. Chandler announced that we were to be his guests for dinner that evening. The men then led us across the road to two large military tents on the beach.

"We apologize for the tents, Mrs. Bordallo," one of the men said. "We've tried to make them as comfortable as possible for you and the children. If there is anything you need, please just let us know."

The soldiers seemed to be at our beck and call. A handful played with the children while others helped Mama and the girls. Several of them measured my brothers and me for new clothing. In our excitement, we fired off hundreds of questions. "What is this? What is that? What is this for? How do you do that?" We did not wait for answers; there was much to see and do. The wonders tumbled in faster than we could contemplate. Each was better than the last.

Then they led us to the two large tents. The tents were like mansions compared to what we had in Mañenggon. There were tables, chairs, a gas stove at one end, and new cots for each of us at the other. The cots were narrow and not like regular beds, but after sleeping on the ground, they were wonderful. Clean white sheets, olive green blankets, and real pillows lay on each cot. There were also candles and lanterns for our use. The second tent held several boxes of food; there were cans of corned beef, tins of powdered milk, and even chocolate candy. Mama was beside herself. She thanked the soldiers for everything.

We marveled too, overwhelmed and excited. We ran in circles, trying to explore everything at once. We bounced on the cots, plumped the pillows, unfolded the blankets, sat in the chairs, and tore open boxes. Everything was too good to be true, and we feared it was all a dream, and we would wake up hungry and still be in Mañenggon.

A steady stream of officers and enlisted men came to our tents to welcome us and ask us about the occupation. They congratulated us for surviving and for giving purpose to their fighting. As the recipients of their generosity and hospitality, we felt humbled by the accolades and noble thoughts. We were safe among friendly forces again. We had a clean, new place to stay. We received a windfall of food supplies and brand-new clothes and shoes. I did not know it then, but the best surprise was yet to come.

Mama and my sisters inspected the boxes of food and unpacked the bundles of our best surviving clothes. Mama, a fastidious housekeeper, hated the filth of Mañenggon. Despite the horrible conditions there, she and my sisters managed to keep our clothes relatively clean, even though they were little more than rags. My brothers and I later received clean, adult-sized military undershirts and underwear, khaki shirts and trousers, and new combat boots. My brothers put on their boots, even though they were too big. We also received helmets, canteens, and web belts; we looked like ragtag, miniature soldiers. I had gone without shoes for two years and found the boots uncomfortable. I went to dinner barefoot that night.

A few hours before supper, a man carrying a tray covered with a large, white napkin came to our tent flap and asked to enter. After Mama acknowledged, he entered, set the tray down and said, "Mrs. Bordallo, we thought you and the children might like something to hold you over until supper."

We tried to be polite and wait until he was gone, but the aroma of fresh bread was overpowering. Under the napkin lay several loaves, still hot and sliced thick, along with butter. We stared at the tray for a long time before reaching for a slice. We ate the bread slowly, with reverence and gratitude.

Later, before we headed across the road to supper with Col. Chandler, Mama assembled us and reminded us about our table manners. We almost forgot what those were. For months, we ate with our hands and only had bits of dried meat, fried *titiyas*, and some vegetables if we were lucky. We looked like ragamuffins, but Mama was determined to present a family of proper little ladies and gentlemen. Briefed and ready for action, we went to dinner with Mama and Dad in the lead. Col. Chandler greeted us at his door as though we were Sunday guests, as though there had been no war. We entered the dining room, and the sight took my breath away.

Mañenggon had been the pit of Hell, its misery and stench only a day behind us. Col. Chandler's dining room was the gateway to Heaven. The change was too quick, the contrast too drastic. Gas lanterns hung from the ceiling and flooded the room with bright, warm light. The whitest tablecloth I had ever seen covered a long table in the center of the room. China, glassware, and silverware gleamed at each place setting. More of the fresh bread and butter lay in small dishes in front of each dinner plate. A simple candelabra with lit candles stood in the center of the table. None of our fanciest Christmas dinners before the war was as elaborate. Dazzled, I wondered how warriors in a war zone could dine in such elegance. I could not imagine white, linen tablecloths, china, and silver being standard combat equipment. I decided Chandler and his men might have found the possessions of some well-to-do CHamoru family.

Col. Chandler sat at the head of the table. Dad sat at the other end. Two officers helped Mama into a chair on Chandler's right. With as much decorum as we could remember, we took the other vacant seats. In addition to ourselves, there were about six other dinner guests.

The aromas from the kitchen filled the room and made my stomach growl. They reminded me of our home at Christmastime. As soon as we settled, as many as 15 smiling "waiters" paraded into the dining room with a seemingly endless stream of food.

"Mrs. Bordallo," said Col. Chandler, "this certainly is not the Waldorf Astoria, but my men and I have tried to make it come close. I hope this evening will wash away some of what you've suffered."

Since that unforgettable night, I have had dinner in some of the most prestigious dining rooms and with some of the most important people in the world, but nothing has come close to the grandeur and the ambiance of Col. Chandler's dinner. I have dined in the White House with three different presidents and various governors of the United States, but I have never been as impressed and awed as I was that night in 1944.

"I'd like to note that you are quite the celebrities here in our camp," Col. Chandler said to Mama as he served her from a platter held by one of the waiters. "Our waiters tonight are the best men in the division. We owe them a great deal, and they wanted to serve you as their reward. I can assure you, we had over 100 volunteers for this dinner. We've allowed as many as can fit in the kitchen." We had no reason to doubt him. A new waiter served each new entree, and a different smiling face refilled every empty glass.

With the kind of greed wrought by hunger, hardship, and deprivation, we piled our plates with everything served. There was roast beef and baked turkey, mashed potatoes and gravy, cranberry sauce and applesauce, more hot bread and butter, cut green beans, carrots, and peas. For dessert, there was canned peaches, pears, and fruit cocktail. There was apple pie and peach pie, and most wonderful of all, there was vanilla ice cream. Too hungry to use silverware beyond the first mouthful, we abandoned the silverware and stuffed food into our mouths with our hands.

Mama paled in embarrassment. "Children," she whispered, "please remember your manners."

We ignored the stern look in her eyes and continued gorging. The major sitting beside her sensed her embarrassment and tried to assure her they recognized our unbridled enthusiasm and understood our hunger. We indulged to excess, and for three days afterward, we had diarrhea.

After dinner, we lumbered to our tents and climbed into our new cots, reacquainting ourselves with the feel of real bedding. The cots had a strange odor of military newness, but they also smelled clean and "American." With full bellies, and exhausted from the day's excitement, we fell asleep, secure that we were safe among friends. We thought nothing could harm us anymore.

Hours later, while it was still dark, something sharp jabbed my groin. Half awake, I rubbed the spot, but the pain intensified and knifed deeper into my body. I sat up and called out to Mama. Before she could reach me, the pain spread throughout my body and became unbearable. Howling, I threw myself out of the cot as Mama and Dad rushed to my side.

"It hurts, Mama, it hurts!" I screamed.

"Ricky, what is it? What's the matter?" Mama's voice seemed to fade into the distance.

My right leg and my torso felt like they were on fire. The bones and muscles beneath my skin felt like something was crushing them. Both sensations spread until I lost control of my body. I thrashed wildly and rolled around on the ground, oblivious to everything but the pain. I was conscious but could not think straight; my thoughts became jumbled, and my mind grew fuzzy. Mama told me later that I passed out and began convulsing. Dad held me down for two hours as I struggled against him. Mama was mopping my forehead with a wet cloth when I woke up. Except for a sore spot in my groin, the awful pain was gone. I got up, dropped my trousers, and inspected my leg. There was a large, red welt and tenderness inside my right thigh.

"What was it, Mama? What bit me?" I asked.

Mama suspected a centipede had stung me. While I was unconscious, she and Dad stripped my cot and spotted one scurrying away. The critters lived in coconut trees and once infested the island by the thousands. The Navy government imported giant toads, which fed on them, and their numbers declined. Unfortunately for me, one that survived the toads found its way into my cot. No beating at Japanese hands hurt as badly as that insect bite.

We stayed in Tipunngan for two weeks enjoying the Quartermaster Corps' hospitality. Being among them was an incredible feeling. The might of the great United States was an overwhelming, friendly, and caring presence all around us. The soldiers were eager to comfort and provide for us. They told us to help ourselves to anything we needed. Unaccustomed to such American generosity, we did. I put Paul, Fred, Rodney, and Donald to work. I spared Michael, who was only 4 years old. Like ants, we marched empty-handed from our side of the road, arms loaded when we returned. We looked like the porters in an African safari.

The quartermaster supply tents seemed limitless. We explored them several times a day. We found one tent filled with new combat boots. We each tried on a pair and kept those that would almost fit. Although wearing boots on my calloused feet was uncomfortable, I took several pairs to save for later. They reminded me of the ones I had wished for one Christmas. Within days of our arrival, we filled our second tent with canned fruit, vegetables, meat, powdered milk, dried mashed potatoes, cans of shortening, and sacks of sugar and flour. We took some of everything the quartermaster had available.

The soldiers were good-natured about our shopping sprees. They often met us at tent flaps with news about newly arrived supplies.

"You boys are going to an awful lot of trouble and doing a helluva lot of work," a soldier said after watching us. "You don't have to worry. We're not going anywhere. We're here to stay."

We thanked him and said we were used to hard work. We could not explain the insecurity that drove our diligence or the fear of deprivation that fueled our greed. We had known hunger and never wanted to feel it again. The work of hauling and hoarding was reassuring, and the reassurance was worth the work. Our sense of security grew in proportion to our supplies.

With the second tent filled, Paul and I trotted across the road to the supply tent filled with crated tents. We shouldered a wooden crate marked "Tent, 20'x40'," and like pallbearers, we carried it away. We spent the next few hours erecting it and the next few days filling it. When we filled the third tent, we rigged a tarpaulin lean-to to protect our growing mountain of supplies. In time, the quartermaster ran out of certain items, especially canned fruit. Although the men knew we had hundreds of gallon cans of fruit cocktail, they never repossessed our supplies. They turned down official requisitions and told the troops, "Sorry, ain't none left."

Nestled as we were in the arms of the Americans, we began to believe that the war was over for us, and we were really safe again. But gun fire late one night unnerved us. We were sound asleep when a band of Japanese stragglers infiltrated the camp to steal food. The soldiers caught them red-handed, and a skirmish ensued. The sudden *rat-tat-tat* of machine guns and carbines jolted us awake. We threw ourselves to the ground and cowered in fright until the shooting stopped. Even then, we did not move until someone shouted, "All clear." The following morning, we learned that a dozen or so stragglers desperate for food tried to raid the camp kitchens. The Americans killed several. The rest fled back into the jungle.

The Americans declared Guam secure on August 10, 1944, the day Adm. Chester W. Nimitz, the commander in chief of the Pacific Fleet, arrived to make Guam his Pacific headquarters. But the war was not yet over; the fighting continued in Dededo and Yigo, where the Japanese made a last stand, and sporadic resistance continued elsewhere for several weeks more. The Japanese never surrendered. Those not killed or captured escaped into the jungle and either starved to death or survived as stragglers. Guam's last known straggler, Sgt. Shoichi Yokoi, hid in Talo'fo'fo for 28 years after the war.

For many months after the island's recapture, admirals and generals, along with their aides, came daily to sit outside our tents and brief Dad on the fighting. As chairman of the House of Council, Dad was the island's senior political official, and in the absence of the administering Navy government, the highest-ranking civilian. Officials also sought his recommendations for civilian relief. Dad entertained a steady stream of American journalists, correspondents, and photographers who sought him for interviews.

In an article titled "Escape on Guam," a reporter from the Rotarian magazine described Dad as "an unwashed Ronald Coleman in the last scene of 'Lost Horizon.'" The story appeared in the January 1945 edition with a picture of Dad in front of the ruins of the jailhouse. A reporter for *Leatherneck*, the Marines' magazine, interviewed and photographed Bobbie, and a photographer for another magazine took a picture of all 15 of us in front of our tents in Tipunngan. I then scurried off not knowing that a second photo was taken. That second picture is the one most often published with features about our wartime experience. In 1985, after years of searching, I found a copy of the first photo. In it, I am a scruffy, bare-footed 16-year-old. I had the copy framed and displayed in my chambers as a conversation piece.

In journalist Quinten Reynolds' 1945 article "These Are Americans," he wrote, "There are no more patriotic citizens than the liberated natives of Guam. After thirty-two months of Jap bestiality, they know for sure what it is worth to be Americans." The article appeared in the May 1945 edition of *Collier's Weekly*. Reynolds interviewed Dad, Pale' Oskat, and several others for

B.J. Pangelinan and Josefina Torres Pangelinan Bordallo, and their children, circa 1944.

Front row, L-R: *Fred, Rodney, Donald, Josephine, Michael, and Beverly June*
Second row, L-R: *Norma, Barbara, Irene, Rosamunde (infant), B.J. (in the rear), Josefina, Sylvia*
Lorraine, Paul, and Ricky

the article, which described the CHamorus' patriotism and unwavering loyalty to the United States, despite the Navy government's heavy-handedness. But when CHamorus became American citizens five years later, it was not to reward their loyalty and patriotism but to legalize, after the fact, the military's arbitrary confiscation of vast tracts of CHamoru land.

After its recapture, Guam became a massive staging area for the final assault on Japan. Believing the need was temporary, CHamorus gave up their lands to support the fight. By 1947, two years after Japan's surrender, the American military occupied 75 percent of the island in the name of national defense. It had no intention of returning lands to their owners. Since eminent domain does not apply to noncitizens, Congress made CHamorus U.S. citizens to legalize the military's occupation of private land. The land takings are still a controversy Washington disregards.

In 1972, Congress waived the federal government's right of sovereign immunity and allowed Guamanians, our postwar label, to sue for just compensation. Landowners filed a class action suit, but the judicial process dragged on for another decade. Many original claimants have died. Their heirs, who continue the fight, are not firsthand witnesses to the land takings and cannot fulfill the complex legal and technical definitions involved. The death of each original landowner weakens the case overall. While Washington waits for time and human mortality to resolve it, the issue steeps in bitterness.

Mama's photographs

After about two weeks in camp, Col. Chandler informed Dad that the Quartermaster Corps was relocating to Yoña. He invited us to follow, but Dad declined. He moved us to Apotguan instead. Chandler put a driver and a "six-by-six," a two-and-a-half-ton military transport truck, at our disposal. Our huge accumulation of supplies astounded the driver. By then we had dozens of cases and crates on our side of the road and made many trips to move them.

The first trip to Apotguan was ghastly. We drove from Tipunngan through Asan and Hagåtña. Thousands of bloated corpses littered the roadsides for miles. The Americans were quick to recover their dead, but the Japanese did not. Their dead drew flies by the millions. The sight and stench were sickening. More as a health precaution than a humanitarian act, the Americans bulldozed the Japanese dead into a mass grave near Pigo'. We got our first disheartening look at Hagåtña when we reached the devastated city.

Our driver also helped us move what remained of our belongings from Pado. I led him in the six-by-six to our hacienda in the jungle. I knew we would not find it untouched, but I did not expect to find it in shambles. My heart sank when we arrived. The hacienda had been ransacked. Broken pieces of our furniture and the belongings we left behind lay strewn on the ground and in the surrounding jungle. I surveyed the damage with much sadness. Our ransacked hacienda was a sickening sight, a contrast of nature's beauty and man's destructiveness.

The driver sensed my sadness and stood quietly to one side, leaving me to my thoughts as I picked through the debris. The loss of Mama's photographs was the most painful. She had taken hundreds over the years and had created an extensive pictorial record of the Bordallo family. Mementos of all the birthdays, Christmases, picnics, parties, family gatherings — all the special moments in our lives — were gone. The torn, wet pieces of photographic paper festooned the jungle like confetti. I picked one up but could not identify it. The emulsion on it was just a blob of slime. None of the photos could be saved.

But Mama's piano survived. We moved it to Apotguan and later to all our other postwar homes. Sometime in the 1950s, Dad traded it with some cash to Joaquin Arriola for a baby grand piano, a gift for Auntie Rose, his second wife.

A bedraggled guerilla warrior

We expanded the small lean-to that Dad and Paul had built in Apotguan during the occupation. Because it was to be a temporary home, we improved it only to accommodate all of us. The shack was near the beach, a favorite haunt of Japanese stragglers. We kept firearms ready in case any tried to raid our stores. Thanks to the Quartermaster Corps, we had carbines, Browning automatic rifles, and several cases of ammunition and hand grenades among our supplies. We could fend off intruders, but the need never arose.

We were also located close to the road from the northern frontlines. The traffic was formidable. Tanks, armored vehicles, artillery pieces, and supply trucks rumbled past us daily. As part of their training for the invasions of Iwo Jima, Okinawa, and Japan itself, thousands of infantrymen marched on the road as well. It was the busiest thoroughfare on the island.

We knew the battle in Yigo was going in the Americans' favor and were certain it would end soon. Feeling secure again, we looked forward to a normal, peaceful life. We had everything we needed to rebuild our lives, except a permanent home. Dad spent his time looking for a home and for ways to restart his business. The rest of us had little to do but a few household chores.

Peace was returning, but a regular work schedule for me did not seem forthcoming. Mama and the children were safe. Dad was busy finding a home. I had little to occupy me — no deliveries to make, errands to run, markets to manage, vehicles to maintain, or any of the work that had usually filled my day. The inactivity made me bored and restless. It was then that I realized I was free for the first time in my life to pursue my own interests. Eager for excitement, I decided to test my wings and strike out on my own.

The ongoing battle in Yigo intrigued me. I wondered what it was like to be on the front lines, to battle beside the Americans and strike back at the enemy in revenge. I was missing the most thrilling event on the island. The more I thought about it, the more determined I became to get in on the action. I readied a couple of ammo belts, a canteen, and a carbine so that as a volunteer warrior, I would not show up empty-handed. On the morning I planned to start, Dad called me into the yard and saddled me with chores. Irritated by the delay, I listened as he listed tasks Paul or Fred could have done. My patience wore thin, and for the first time in my life, I answered back.

"But Daddy, I've made my own plans," I said.

Dad ignored the breach of conduct. "Plans? What plans? We have work to do," he said, berating me as though I was a child. His refusal to grant me adult status, his stifling control over me, and my growing desire for freedom steeled my courage. I felt I had earned the right to be a man and stand up to him.

"I told you. I have other plans, Daddy. I won't do it," I said, bravely.

None of us, not even Mama, had ever questioned Dad's authority. My defiance stunned him. His eyes flared in disbelief.

"How dare you talk back to me," he said as he raised his hand.

The sting of his slap across my face unleashed my anger. I had spent my life obeying his every command and had swallowed a lot of hurt along the way. I was no longer his subservient little boy. Whether he accepted it or not, I was a man in my own right. Still haunted by the beating he gave me over the truck, I yielded to my pent-up rage. As impulsively as I had hit Roger Perry, I punched my father but recoiled in horror the instant I touched him. Anger twisted Dad's face into an ugly scowl.

"You think you can beat me? You think you're so big? I'll show you," he growled through clenched teeth. Dad began striking me with both fists.

As I tried to fend off the blows, the shock of what I had done vanished. Anger returned. With strength equal to his, I returned his punches, landing several good ones before realizing how ugly the situation had become. I had to stop; I could not keep hitting my father in anger. I lowered my guard to let him continue. Mama dashed into the yard.

"Stop it!" she demanded. "Stop it right now!" Mama stared at us and began to cry. I did too. Dad and I let go of each other.

I ran to the edge of the yard and grabbed my readied ammo belts, canteen, and carbine from a post and walked away, vowing never to return. I walked about a half mile to the outskirts of Hagåtña. I tried to forget the ugly incident. It was a terrible way to leave, but I was free at last. I was my own man, free to do as I pleased. I crisscrossed the ammo belts on my chest like a bandito and looped the canteen on my belt. I slung the carbine over my shoulder the way soldiers carried theirs. I looked like a bedraggled guerilla warrior — scrawny, barefoot, but armed and ready for action.

The Maite-Hagåtña crossroad was alive with activity. Hundreds of military vehicles, men, equipment, and supplies rumbled back and forth to every part of the island. Hitching rides was easy; nearly every vehicle offered lifts to civilian pedestrians. I got a ride up to Maite where huge 155 mm guns lined the cliff all the way to Barrigada. The guns were going full bore, hurtling missiles at the remnants of the Japanese entrenched in Yigo.

I approached a gun crew and offered to help. The men paused, studied me, then one of them laughed and said, "Sure, kid, grab that shell." I spent a glorious day and a half passing new rounds, stacking spent casings, and following orders. I shared the gun crew's food rations and spent the night in the jungle. It was great fun, but my enthusiasm waned. Firing the big guns was too far away from the action. I wanted to take part in the war in as many ways possible. The following day, I said *adios* to my new buddies and went back down to the crossroads to hitch another ride.

The lumbering amphibious vehicles the Americans called "ducks" fascinated me. They were part truck, part boat. I wanted to get a ride in one so that I could see how they worked. I spotted one and flagged it down. My appearance amused the duck driver.

"Where ya headed, kid?" he asked with a smirky grin.

"Oh, I'm just scouting around, seeing what's happening," I said.

"You enjoying the war?"

"Oh, yes. It's really exciting. Where are you heading?"

"Up to the Third Quartermaster Corps in Yoña."

I did not plan to go to Yoña; I had no specific destination. The Quartermaster Corps seemed as good a place as any. And I had friends there. I climbed aboard the duck and marveled at the "dashboard," which was a maze of dials, gauges, and control levers. To my delight, the driver allowed me to be co-pilot. At his direction, I gave him the dial and gauge readings, flipped switches, and pulled levers as we jounced along the bumpy road to Yoña. In Tå'i, we passed a squad of Marines lounging in the shade beside the road. I changed my mind about going to Yoña and after thanking the driver, I hopped off to join the Marines.

The squad was heading to the battlefields in Yigo and had stopped to rest. Some of the men were eating K-rations, which were individual combat meals. Some were dozing while others were "shooting the breeze." My approach drew their attention. When they also chuckled at my appearance, I realized I must have looked funny. The Marines welcomed me but continued to lounge. Their idleness was disappointing. I was too eager for excitement to sit around and wait for them to get moving. While they relaxed, I started to explore the surrounding area.

Not far away was a damaged house that its occupants abandoned in a rush. The doors and windows were open and household goods littered the yard. I wandered inside for a closer look. Broken furniture and rubbish filled the rooms. Scattered in the debris were piles of trash, papers that looked like official documents, and a photograph half-buried among the papers. I looked at a few and realized some were Navy government documents. The Japanese had used the house as an administrative office. I pulled out the photograph and reeled in surprise. The picture was of the Pan American Clipper's inaugural flight ceremony in 1935. Dad was among the officials in the photo. I ran back to tell the Marines about my find.

"Look, here's my father. The man in the white suit, that's my dad," I said and handed the photo to the squad leader. Several Marines peered over his shoulder to look.

The squad leader examined the photo. "This is your father?" he asked. The men then looked at me. I must have puzzled them. I was a lanky, barefooted teenager who looked more like an abandoned orphan than the son of a man important enough to stand beside high-ranking Navy brass and business-suited American civilians.

"Yes, that's him," I said proudly. "That picture was taken when the Pan Am Clipper first landed." I told the Marine about the papers in the house. "They might be important. I think we should check it out."

Several men returned to the house with me. We rummaged through the debris and collected the papers that appeared official. We later turned them over to an officer.

The Marines did not seem eager to forge into battle. They were either already exhausted or sick of the fighting. Their rest stop lasted longer than my enthusiasm, so I said goodbye and left. I was not sure what to do next or where to go, but I was ready for something different. I hitched a ride with a military truck driver who was heading to the Quartermaster Corps for supplies.

The Quartermaster supply dump was on the Yoña plateau above Ilek Bay. It was a busy place. Mountains of military equipment and supplies in endless rows of green tents covered the land. Hundreds of trucks rumbling in and out of the camp kicked up dust and filled the air with deafening noise. Men were everywhere, moving among the stacks and rows, turning Guam into the largest supply depot in the Pacific. In the bay below, ducks were off-loading huge supply ships. Like ant columns, lines of hundreds of ducks stretched down the slopes, across the water, and around the ships. Empty ducks entered the water and loaded ducks came back to shore.

I watched them in action and realized why they were called ducks. Like their namesakes, the amphibious vehicles were graceful and confident in the water but lumbering and clumsy on land. I offered my service as an experienced duck co-pilot to a driver who agreed to let me. We got in line behind a string of ducks. When we hit the water, the duck's tires continued to spin, but a rear propeller kicked on and pushed us forward. We motored across the bay and pulled alongside a ship. Without formality, a massive crane lowered a heavy net filled with boxes and crates into the duck's hold. To my bewilderment, no one exchanged shipping documents and receipts. When we reached the shore, the driver switched off the propeller, and the duck's wheels took over again. We rumbled up the plateau behind other ducks and dumped the cargo in a staging area.

The lemonade tycoon

I stayed at the supply dump for several days, going with the duck drivers for many more rounds. I also made many friends among the supply personnel who gave me a pup tent. Later, they also gave me the supplies I needed for a business idea I was developing.

In the aftermath of the American invasion, the potential for profit-making became tremendous. The hordes of Seabees, who landed with the invading forces, began their work even before the fighting ceased. From Yoña, I went down to Hågat and watched the Seabees plow through the debris to build new roads and military installations. Working under the hot sun, they had only coffee and water to quench their thirst. I knew they would have gladly paid for something tastier — like lemonade. The demand was obvious. The market was wide open and unexplored. The answer was simple, and I thought it was brilliant. I already had unlimited access to free supplies to make lemonade by the gallons.

With visions of bringing home loads of money for my family, I went back to the supply dump and got several pounds of sugar, some lemon extract, two 5-gallon jerry cans, and some canteen cups. I filled the cans with water, added some sugar and flavoring, and made what I thought was good-tasting lemonade. Then I hitched a ride to the Hågat-Sumai crossroads, which the Seabees were building, and set up shop in a shady spot. I scrounged around for something to use as a counter then lined up the canteen cups. I scrawled "Lemonade 10 Cents a Cup" on a piece of cardboard and propped it in front of my makeshift stand. Then like a carnival barker, I called out, "Lemonade, fresh, sweet lemonade. Ten cents a cup. Come and get it while it lasts!"

The Seabees within earshot stopped working and peered in my direction. As I knew they would, they smiled and headed toward me. "I'll have some," said one man who slapped a dime on the counter. While his companions dug into their pockets, I poured lemonade into the cups then watched as they took mighty gulps. To my horror, they suddenly started sputtering, coughing, and spitting.

"Thanks, kid. Keep your lemonade," my first customer said without malice.

The men walked away laughing, leaving me feeling like an idiot. It never occurred to me that lemon extract made lousy lemonade and serving it warm from a jerry can would not work. Shamed, I dumped the lemonade. My brilliant idea netted me six dimes, a bruised ego, and a first taste of business failure. I had hoped to bring home huge profits, but all I could show for my effort was two empty jerry cans. My failure as a lemonade tycoon was depressing. As days passed, my depression grew. I had been away from home for three weeks and was getting homesick.

PART THREE

The American Re-occupation of Guam

Chapter 16

Return to Mayanghulo'

I had not heard anything from or about my family and hungered for news, though I was not ready to go home. Uncle Carlos and his family were staying in their summer house outside Hågat, so I headed there to visit and hear news about home. Mayanghulo', where our summer house was, had always been my paradise. I was eager to see it again, hoping it would ease my depression and lift my spirits.

From the Seabee worksite at the Hågat-Sumai crossroads, I hitched a ride south. The Seabees were everywhere, working to rid the island of war wreckage and anything else in the way of the American effort to win the war. After landing, American military personnel poured into Guam by the hundreds of thousands. Endless streams of supplies and equipment arrived also. Supply dumps, camps, hospitals, messes, clubs, and prison pens built by the Seabees sprouted up faster than the jungle in the rainy season. The bustling Americans were as inescapable as their intense bombing and shelling had been. I wanted to be rid of them, at least for a while, at Mayanghulo', but to my dismay, they were there, too.

As I neared the estate, my stomach turned. The sight made me sick. The orchards, the rice fields, the gardens and coops, the rice-threshing machines and the liquor distillery, the abattoir and milking sheds, the barns, the stables and storehouses, the cattle pastures and hog pens — everything that made Mayanghulo' a special, wonderful place — lay in twisted, blackened ruins. The coconut grove was a graveyard of mangled, topless trunks, jutting skyward. Bomb craters pockmarked the yards, fields, and pastures. The bees were gone and so were the pigeons. Our house on the point was gone, too. Seabee bulldozers were scraping it into a huge pile of splintered lumber and twisted roofing sheets. The point itself was 20 feet lower than before. Instead of soaring with renewed gladness, I sank deeper into depression.

The military government condemned the entire Bordallo estate through "eminent domain" to carve a new road to Hågat through its heart. Mayanghulo' was to me like a beautiful woman who had rich, long hair. The war had hacked away her locks and marred her looks, but she was still the same beautiful woman. Instead of restoring her beauty, the Americans shaved her bald. Bulldozers and demolition crews swarmed over the landscape, scraping it to bedrock. They leveled hills and knolls, filled in gullies and ravines, and created a flat, ugly expanse of white coral gravel.

Uncle Carlos' house stood directly in the path of the new road. The military government gave him ample time to move, but he refused. When I arrived, he was brandishing a rifle and yelling at a demolition crew. He was standing on the doorstep of his house 20 feet off the ground. The Seabees had leveled the land around his house and left it perched alone on a pillar of limestone. Uncle Carlos was threatening to shoot anyone who came near.

My cousin Carlito had already deserted the house and was living in a pup tent outside. He had landed a military job and tried to convince me to join him. "They need all kinds of people, Ricky," he said. "There's all kinds of work, and you can earn a lot of money." I shook my head. I was not interested in working or in aiding in the further destruction of my homeland. The breakneck momentum of tearing down the old and building up the new swept Carlito up in the excitement of it all. He could not understand why I was not as excited.

Officials removed Uncle Carlos and his family from their home by force. A few days later, a demolition crew blew up their house and the limestone pillar.

Amid this heartbreak, we received word that Uncle Tom's only daughter Betty died of spinal meningitis. She was only 12 years old, and like my other first cousins, she was like a sister. News of her death increased my sorrow. I wanted to go home, to be with my family, to grieve for Betty, and to mourn for Mayanghulo' and for a way of life that would never be the same again.

My route home was along the coast and through busy road-building sites. The bustling work at Mayanghulo' continued in similar projects all the way to Hagåtña. The old, narrow country road in Piti and the old kapok trees that shaded it were gone. In their place was a long, wide stretch of asphalt pavement baking in the sun. The Americans were everywhere, tearing up the landscape, upsetting the balance of nature, molding the environment to fit military needs, not ours. We needed to rebuild our lives but seemed to be in the way of military progress, not active participants in it. I became disgusted with my guerilla warrior gear and dumped them. Military hands were changing my world. It was taking on a new and disturbing shape, and all I could do was watch it happen.

The "rehabilitation" of Guam seemed to me like curing a sore toe by amputating the whole leg. While others seemed oblivious to the massive changes taking place, I could not ignore them. I became a self-appointed auditor of my island's destruction and kept tabs on the projects and changes. Over the succeeding months, I watched the construction of Harmon, Northwest, and Andersen airfields, the dredging of Apra Harbor and obliteration of tiny Fort Santa Cruz islet, the reclamation of swamp lands near Sumai, the construction of the harbor breakwater, and the building of Fena dam deep in the Talo'fo'fo highlands. Guam became a different place when the military finished; it did indeed become a giant military installation. Sacrificed for its construction were hundreds of bird species and wildlife, thousands of acres of farmland and forest, and the simple, peaceful lifestyle of our ancestors.

I reached Apotguan and walked into the house as if I had just returned from doing my chores. There were no recriminations, no questions, no discussions. As though nothing had ever happened, Dad listed several things for me to do. "Yes, Daddy, I'll get right on it," I said, glad that at least that part of my life remained stable.

Hagåtña aftermath

Not long after my return, Dad rented the top floor of Mrs. Kerner's two-story house in the northeast corner of Hagåtña. It was one of the few buildings to survive the American bombardment with only some damage. A plane had strafed the roof and riddled it with holes. We covered the roof with a large tarpaulin. Mrs. Kerner's American husband was among those taken prisoner to Japan. She returned to her home after the American recapture and lived on the ground floor. Her house also had a basement.

The Japanese used the Kerner house as a brothel reserved for the highest-ranking officers and civilian officials. During the calm of the Japanese naval administration, I made deliveries there and marveled at the beauty of the women. They were the finest sex workers the Japanese brought to Guam. The brothel for lower-ranking personnel at Tun Pedro Martinez's summer house at Sasa', which means "to spread apart one's legs," operated under different rules. I had occasion to watch the goings-on there also. It was like an assembly line. Customers lined up at the front door and exited out the back door 15 minutes later, panting, buttoning their trousers, and tucking in their shirts. Unlike the Kerner house clientele, the Sasa' customers could not lounge in the company of cultured females.

After having lived in cramped and primitive conditions for so long, we did not care about the Kerner house's sordid past. We were eager just to live in a real house again. It had a nice living room, dining room and kitchen, a bathroom, and three bedrooms. The ifit wood floors needed only a good scrubbing and polishing to make them shiny again. The bombardment destroyed the power plant and the city's water and sewer lines, so we had no electricity, running water, or wastewater disposal, but these were minor inconveniences. We lit the house with lanterns and candles and filled jerry cans with water for the kitchen and bathroom. We dug a deep hole in the yard, ran drainpipes from the house into it, and covered it for safety.

The bombing and burning of Hagåtña had been devastating. The city was in ruins. All that remained of the power plant was the tall, black smokestack. Broken palms, denuded hardwood trees, skeletal buildings, obliterated homes, and tons of rubble and debris suffocated the once-picturesque little city. Few buildings escaped unscathed, but some were not beyond repair.

I spent hours roaming through the wreckage, trying to locate landmarks. Wandering the empty streets filled me with eerie feelings and made my heart sink. Alone on once-busy Hernan Cortez Street, the mangled remains of places I had known and loved surrounded me. The sounds of our peaceful, happy life — the laughter of children playing in the streets, the cheerful greetings of pedestrians, their jovial conversations, the tinkling of glassware, whistling, singing, and music, even the warnings of "toka hao" — were now just ghostly echoes. The homes of relatives, friends, and neighbors were difficult to find, but I searched and realized that, in some instances, neither the home nor its occupants survived.

Our house sustained a direct hit and had disappeared. Everything except our buried whiskey was gone. Another bomb blew a huge crater in the eastern part of our property. We had buried the Canadian Club in the western part. The whiskey lay deep beneath a small mountain of the crumpled remains of our house. It took us weeks to clear the debris and dig up the cases. I am not sure we recovered every bottle. Some may still remain.

The bombing had cracked and blackened the walls of the cathedral, but the building appeared salvageable. The Governor's Palace was in worse shape; it was a pile of rocks and splinters. Other buildings in the complex seemed repairable. The plaza was no longer a carpet of green lawn. It was brown, pocked with bomb craters and littered with debris. The stately royal palms that once lined the avenues were gone; only broken posts and stumps remained. Bombs destroyed parts of the Susana Hospital. The Navy repaired the salvageable parts and reopened it for civilians.

On the seaside of Hagåtña, the Seabees and their bulldozers were building a new highway. It began at the airfields in the north and skirted the coast to Piti and Sumai. To shorten the distance, the Seabees plowed through all the hills, gullies, and marshes along the way. They shaved down steep hills, filled in valleys, and changed river courses to build a level roadway with few curves. Upon its completion, the new road became Highway One, or Marine Drive, in honor of the Marines.

The Seabees rerouted the Hagåtña River and left the old stone Spanish Bridge near the power plant high and dry. They filled in the Minondo and channeled the runoff into the bay on the eastern edge of the city, a few yards away from the Kerner house. For weeks, I watched crews and heavy machines drive piles and pour tons of concrete to build a bridge over the new river mouth. Not far from the new bridge work, other crews worked on another highway that branched off Marine Drive and led to Camp Dealy in Ipan, about 8 miles away. The Kerner house sat on the corner where Marine Drive, the new concrete bridge, and the highway to Ipan intersected. For the brief time we lived there, frenzied, noisy construction work surrounded us.

The Seabees worked with incredible speed. New roads, bridges, and military installations appeared throughout the island as if by magic. I assumed that construction crews would clear Hagåtña's streets and rebuild the city just as quickly, but I was wrong. The rubble and debris remained in place for more than three years before bulldozers pushed it all into the sea.

With promises to rebuild Hagåtña as the new "Santa Monica of the Pacific," the restored Navy government laid out a new grid of streets and standardized city blocks. The new pattern ignored old property lines and left many landowners with bits and pieces in different blocks. Some lost most of their properties beneath the new, wider streets. When Congress thwarted the Navy's "Santa Monica" plan, work on the new city ceased, leaving Hagåtña's residents with new streets and empty city blocks that did not correspond with original private property lines.

The disparity caused many years of bitter resentment and legal conflict. As a result, Hagåtña's prewar population never returned. Now, the capital city of Hagåtña, once the home of half the island's population, is almost empty at night. It bustles with government and commercial activity by day, but at quitting time, the city grows quiet and empty. The 1980 census listed only 50 families as permanent residents.

As an observer of the postwar reconstruction, I began to sense that Hagåtña's demise was not simply a consequence of war. As the years passed, I became convinced that it was part of a plan to disenfranchise the CHamoru people, to complete the "American duty" to sever our "sentimental attachment" to our city. Hagåtña has been the wellspring of CHamoru culture, identity, and wisdom for untold millennia. Our ancestors believed Guam was the center of the universe, and Hagåtña was the center of that center. It had housed the collective heart and soul of the CHamoru people. The forces who sought the cultural extinction of the CHamorus knew they needed only to deny us our city. With most of its original residents dispersed, an empty Hagåtña could no longer provide a sense of community and belonging or bridge the gap between past and present.

Even before the war, CHamorus were beginning to rankle under the thumb of the patronizing and colonialist Navy government. To this day, the fundamental issues of CHamoru sovereignty and human rights are still unresolved. The denial of human rights, the blatant practice of racial discrimination, and the Navy government's condescending attitudes toward CHamorus had sown discontent. The Japanese occupation and the war plunged CHamorus into physical misery and forced political issues into the background. But before the issues could come to the fore again after the war, American colonialists capitalized on the postwar chaos to prevent CHamoru reintegration and the unified reawakening of political awareness.

To their own detriment, CHamorus remained loyal to the United States throughout the war, despite their grievances against the prewar Navy government's control. In blind gratitude for their liberation and in support of an American military victory, they allowed the transformation of their homeland into a gargantuan military base. The United States has never acknowledged CHamoru loyalty or reciprocated CHamoru gratitude. Instead, it uses these against us, to cloud political issues with conflicting emotions.

Although CHamoru landowners willingly stepped aside to allow the successful prosecution of the war, they began to grow suspicious of military intentions after Japan's surrender. The war was over, but the Navy and Air Force continued to gobble up CHamoru land. The military's appetite for space seemed insatiable. Like many other landowners, Dad and his brothers were skeptical of the military's need for vast acres.

Sometime in 1946 or '47, Uncle Tom went to the newly established Commander Naval Forces Marianas headquarters atop Libugon, which the Navy renamed Nimitz Hill, to find out how long the Navy would hold on to Bordallo property. The Navy had condemned almost all of the family's land in Hågat and Talo'fo'fo. Planners at Naval Forces headquarters showed Uncle Tom their intended land-use maps, which divided the island into thirds. The Navy had planned to take possession of the northern two-thirds. The southern third was to be for civilians — a reservation for natives.

Of the island's 144,000 acres, the Navy planned to occupy 83,600. They would allow CHamorus to keep 60,400 acres. Of those, only about half was tillable. The celebrated "Santa Monica of the Pacific" was to become the new city for American civilian contractors, who came in droves when the massive postwar military construction began.

By the time the Organic Act conferred token citizenship on us, the means for our extinction as a culturally distinct people was well underway. It began with changing — hiding — our identity. We were now to be "Guamanians," the label selected by high school students in an unofficial straw poll. CHamorus in the modern, new unincorporated U.S. Territory of Guam are now Guamanians. For a time, Guamanian was merely the American word for CHamoru. Guamanians did not see themselves as Americans, and "Statesiders" did not see themselves as Guamanians. Now all who live in Guam, no matter their nationality, are Guamanian, at least until they move away.

The Organic Act of Guam extends only certain provisions of the U.S. Constitution to Guam, and that makes us second class U.S. citizens. The federal government removed CHamorus from among "We, the People" to keep control over Guam. Since the war's end, the military has maintained the unspoken policy that Guam's strategic defense importance supersedes the rights and the will of the people of Guam. This is in direct contradiction and violation of the most fundamental principle of the Constitution: The consent of the governed sanctions government.

To distract attention away from the contradiction and eventually rid itself of the dilemma, the federal government launched a campaign to discount the existence and sovereignty of the CHamoru people by eradicating the symbols of our culture and ethnicity and forcing us to fit the mold of white society. The war provided a convenient starting point. The disruption of CHamoru society and economy weakened our resistance to the deceptive euphoria of citizenship and the addictive power of federal subsidy. By maintaining tight grips on the island's economic growth and development, and by having opened the floodgates to immigration, the federal government provided for the eventual dissolution of the CHamoru nation. Washington waits for the last CHamorus to disappear so that it can lay claim to the island they once owned.

In the nearly four decades since the Organic Act's passage, the new Guamanians know little of their history and heritage. They relate more to the glamour and glitter of American big cities than they do to their island capital. They do not share their parents' and grandparents' ties to the land. Someday, they may abandon it as undesirable real estate and let strangers trample the dust of their ancestors.

The wealth of the Nation

In the days following Guam's recapture, more than a quarter of a million military personnel and their war materiel arrived. Hundreds of signs proclaimed their presence and identities. Traditional CHamoru place names gave way to military acronyms and numerical designations. Scores of numbers identified Army, Navy, Marines, and Army-Air Force divisions, battalions, companies, units, facilities, bases, camps, wings, and squadrons. With them came the mind-boggling bounty of American industry.

The second American bombardment consisted of every imaginable American-made commodity in unbelievable proportions — the wealth of the Nation — poured into Guam. The island became a strategic staging area, a major supply center, and a goldmine in the Pacific. It attracted carpetbaggers, profiteers, con men, and racketeers, both military and civilian. With such staggering amounts, military custodians squandered, stole, sold, wasted, dumped, and gave away huge quantities without fear of running out. They also profited themselves at U.S. taxpayers' expense. It was well known that officers, enlisted personnel, and civilian contractors were making illicit fortunes. On an island thousands of miles from Washington, graft and corruption were easy to hide, especially when everyone benefited.

The cargo stacked high on military transport trucks — crates, boxes, and shipping pallets — often fell off, but the drivers rarely stopped to pick them up. I had to swerve many times to avoid hitting supplies abandoned in the middle of the road. Unaccustomed to such waste, CHamorus, including me, gathered any abandoned goods. I would stop, inspect the items, salvage whatever I could use, and leave the rest for the next passerby.

For many months after the war, no one had to buy gasoline. It was free for the taking. Gasoline drums, spaced a few yards apart, lined the new north-south highway for miles. By then, almost everyone owned at least one "surplussed" military vehicle, and driving became a widespread skill. We owned several vehicles, including an amphibious duck. We even considered getting a Sherman tank but gave up the idea because owning a tank seemed too ostentatious. Soon after the arrival of the first nonmilitary vehicles, Dad bought a cab-over-engine Bulldog truck for $200. The new truck became my responsibility. Whenever it needed fuel, I would pull up to the nearest drum and siphon off a tankful. The only requirement was a siphon hose. The military was unconcerned about accounting for the goods entrusted to them.

In a 1946 public hearing, the House Committee on Naval Affairs questioned the Navy Department's chief planning officer, Adm. W. H. Smith, about the alleged abuses, particularly among military officers and men. Smith denied knowledge of the situation and diverted the congressmen's attention. He said, "In view of the recent comments that have been made as to the nature of the Navy's discharge of its responsibilities in connection with the native population, I would like to invite the attention of the committee to the hundred-percent loyalty of the natives to the United States during, before, and after the Japanese occupation." Native loyalty gave carpetbaggers license to operate.

In 1944, winning the war was all that mattered. Whether CHamorus benefited or died in the process was not relevant. After securing the island, the military government established refugee camps for the thousands left homeless by the intense bombardment. Many people could not return to the ruins of their homes and villages because the military had already moved in and erected hundreds of elephant Quonset huts and warehouses. One of the largest resettlement camps was in Sinajana on the plateau behind Hagåtña. A few miles further east, in Chalan Pago, the military built an expansive ammunition depot manned by Black Americans.

The Black soldiers did not often leave the ammunition dump and rarely fraternized with white military personnel or CHamorus. We would see them once in a while driving in town. I thought their somber faces were from the stresses of their dangerous duties as explosives custodians. In time, I realized they were like us, victims of the same white supremacism, racial discrimination, injustice, inequality, and the denial of human rights, but their sufferings had been much greater and for much longer. I felt empathy and a kinship with them.

The ammunition dump exploded one day as I drove uphill toward Sinajana. I was halfway up the hill when a sudden bright flash blinded me. Seconds later, a deafening explosion rocked the ground. Several more followed. It sounded like another enemy attack, and I panicked. I made a U-turn and sped away from the danger. An accident at the dump detonated several large shells and sent thousands of missiles flying for miles in all directions. Hundreds of projectiles rained down on the resettlement camp. A good-sized shell even crashed through Nanan Chong's kitchen in Tutuhan and terrified one of my aunts.

For days after the accident, Navy men drove through a miles-wide area, collecting explosives from people's yards and gardens. They posted public notices as to who to call and the types of and how many explosives needed collection.

"I'm as cool as a cucumber"

Surplussed military vehicles were readily available, but automobiles were a rarity. The heavy bombardment destroyed almost all those in use before the war. High-ranking military officials, even Admiral Chester W. Nimitz himself, the commander-in-chief of the Pacific Fleet and military governor of Guam, rode around in drab-green jeeps. Nimitz had a chauffeur but not a flashy automobile at his disposal. The first new cars to arrive were as ugly as jeeps. They were the same drab green and not impressive. They all had big, black serial numbers painted on their doors and were exclusively for transporting military brass and visiting VIPs.

After hearing rumors about an abandoned car in the jungle in Tå'i, I decided to investigate. I searched for and found a black 1940 Plymouth sedan. To my surprise, it was one of Dad's taxicabs, one confiscated by the Japanese and later abandoned. Dad was not interested in my find and said I could keep it if I could get it running. I wanted to be the first civilian in Guam to own a real car. I knew it needed some parts and engine work but not much else.

With visions of winning female attention, I worked long and hard on fixing, painting, and polishing the car. When I finished, the car looked almost new. I was eager to show it off and to check my workmanship, so I drove it to Hågat for its first long distance run. The Plymouth performed wonderfully. I cruised along the new highway, picturing myself pulling into Nåna's yard and having every pretty girl in Hågat begging for a ride.

Halfway to Hågat, I passed a shore patrol jeep heading north. I only caught a glimpse of the patrolman's face but recognized condescending suspicion and Roger Perry-resentment. I was not speeding, but I watched in my rear-view mirror as the jeep made an abrupt U-turn. With a sinking feeling, I knew trouble was coming toward me. I pulled to the roadside and prepared myself for a Roger Perry punch in the belly. The jeep pulled up behind me, and a tall, heavy-set patrolman climbed out and approached. He stooped to peer into my window.

"Where'd you get this car?" he barked. "Why are you driving it?"

The accusation was unstated but clear: This brown-skinned kid must have stolen this fine car, and how does he get to drive it?

I felt my anger rising. The patrolman was of the Roger Perry ilk — the kind of person who thinks non-whites are incapable of creative intelligence, ingenuity, and sophistication and who attribute evidence to the contrary to trickery. If I had been white, the patrolman would not have bothered with me, but since I was not, it aroused his suspicion. His supremacist attitude infuriated me. I mirrored his arrogance and answered defiantly, "What do you mean? This is my car."

"Your car?" The patrolman's eyes narrowed. He sensed my readiness to question his authority and tried another intimidation approach. "You seem nervous."

"I'm as cool as a cucumber," I said. I heard my relatives use the expression, but I did not know what it meant. It was the most impudent thing I could think of to say.

The patrolman demanded my driver's license and withered when I produced one. He studied it then demanded my registration papers, which I again produced. He made a great show of comparing my license plate against the registration papers, but because everything was in order, he could do nothing. He was annoyed when I drove away.

For many months, my Plymouth was the best looking and most impressive vehicle on the island. It did attract as many admiring glances as envious ones. My ego enjoyed both kinds. I kept the car for a couple of years then sold it in 1947 for $200 to a man who turned it into a taxicab. The money went toward my college expenses.

While we lived in the Kerner house, journalists and photographers continued to seek out Mama and Dad. Dressed in military uniforms, the correspondents and cameramen looked like military personnel, except that their shoulder tags read, "War Correspondent." In November 1945, with her home in good order, Mama agreed to let some writers and photographers share our Thanksgiving supper as a human-interest feature — a liberated CHamoru family celebrates an American holiday. Our meal was not as elaborate as Col. Chandler's, but there was plenty of food, and Mama dressed the table with candles. We ate supper that evening to the blinding flashes of popping flashbulbs, hundreds of questions, and copious notetaking.

To our guests' delight, after supper, we did what we always did at happy family gatherings: We surrounded Mama at the piano and sang. The newsmen and photographers joined in with enthusiasm. Their battle-weary faces softened, and their eyes glistened with wistful, faraway longing. One of the correspondents produced a new-fangled gadget that he said was a new invention, a technological breakthrough in sound recording and reproduction. It recorded sounds on coils of wire. It was the forerunner of magnetic tape recorders. I was fascinated and promised to get one for myself someday. The correspondent asked Mama if he could record one of her songs, and she obliged. He later gave us a copy of the wire recording, but we have since lost it. Mama died in December 1945, less than a month after that Thanksgiving evening.

Dad concentrated on restarting in business, but he met many difficulties. The entire fabric of CHamoru society had been torn to shreds and was being rewoven in a different pattern. The military's appetite for land and sprawling installations drove Dad, his brothers, and many other CHamorus from their farms and ranches, disrupting what had been a self-sustaining agrarian economy. The postwar money economy forced upon us was abrupt and did not allow us time to prepare or adjust. Denied their traditional livelihoods, farmers and ranchers had to look for salaried work. And businessmen had to compete against unfair and unethical practices in a saturated market.

I did my share to add to the family income by making and selling coconut candy. As a child, I had learned how to make coconut candy to satisfy my craving for sweets. I never lost the craving and have suffered with poor teeth because of it. Unlike my ill-fated lemonade business, my coconut candy was a success. With help from Mama and the children, I cooked up buckets in the kitchen. It was easy to make, just sugar and grated coconut meat. We already had plenty of sugar and needed only waxed paper. We gathered, husked, and grated dozens of ripe coconuts. After making several batches, wrapping tablespoon-sized pieces in waxed paper, and filling baskets, I would sell the candy at the public schools. I made enough money to make the effort profitable.

In response to the Red Cross' call for relief for CHamorus, stateside Americans donated tons of used clothing, which arrived in huge barrels and stirred great excitement. Fashion-conscious ladies were eager to discover the "latest styles" in the barrels. The ingenious ones copied popular dress designs or created their own using military parachute silk dyed in assorted colors. It took hundreds of volunteers to sort, select, and deliver clothing for men, women, and children. Mama and my sisters were among many women who volunteered to sort and distribute Red Cross relief supplies. It was like Christmas whenever Mama brought home our share.

Cherry Charote and the bull

We lived in the Kerner house for a couple of months then moved again. Dad rented a house and a commercial building in Toggai at the base of San Ramon. The buildings belonged to Tun Juan Ada. His son John was my classmate at the Guam Institute. I sometimes went to his house for lunch breaks. Tun Pedro Martinez's house was next door. On the other side, an open-air movie theater stood between our house and the "Kuatet," the Navy compound next to the palace. Tun Juan's commercial building was across the street. It once housed the Estaquio Bakery, which was the oldest, largest, and most popular commercial bakery before the war. There was a public washing area — a shed lined with water faucets — beside the building. We moved into the house and opened a coffee shop in the old bakery building. Our new quarters were spacious, but Dad continued to look for a permanent home and good business possibilities.

Our coffee shop had the distinction of being the first civilian spot to offer ice cream. As soon as he was able, Dad ordered a 10-gallon, hand-cranked ice cream freezer and a supply of vanilla ice cream mix from the States. The ice cream was our biggest seller. Paul, Fred, Rodney, and I took turns cranking the freezer and producing as many as three batches a day in the public washing shed. The task was tiring, but it never dampened our enthusiasm for ice cream.

Because the return to normal city living was slow, people flocked to experience any renewed service. They rejoiced at the reopening of restaurants, general merchandise stores, and movie theaters. The restoration of electricity was a glorious event, and the restoration of running water was even grander. We had a thriving business selling ice cream exclusively until Tun Juan "Adot" Lujan opened a soda fountain. After the military began importing ice cream mix by the ton, other businessmen also began making and selling ice cream. Dad benefited from the military imports also. Before then, he had to order his supplies from the States, which was an expensive and time-consuming process.

We were among the first to make bids on the imported military supplies, which were much cheaper and immediately available. I once won a bid on 5,000 cases of ice cream mix at $15 a case. But instead of 5,000 cases, military warehouse workers loaded 15,000 cases onto my truck. When I pointed out the error, a warehouseman shrugged and said, "Just get it out of here, kid. We don't want to have to deal with it." They were expecting new shipments and needed the space, so they were going to throw away the extra 10,000 cases. Supplies of all kinds were so plentiful that any slightly damaged, dented, water-stained, torn, discolored, or imperfect packing case was "surveyed," or discarded. And anything surveyed was fair game. Anyone willing to make the effort could help themselves, free of charge.

The reestablished Rotary Club of Guam held its monthly meetings at the coffee shop, but since it could not hold everyone, Dad put up a tent outside.

Club luncheons drew new members and Rotarian military officers as well. Of those who attended regularly, Dr. Joe Sataloff and Col. Blaisdell stand out in my memory. Active Rotarians, the two men also helped restart the Boy Scouts of America after the war. In 1985, while in Philadelphia for a ceremony on board the USS *Guam*, I got to see Dr. Sataloff again after more than 40 years. I also saw Mrs. Ruth Troy, who had been one of my high school teachers. She attended the ceremony as my personal guest. She was 92 years old.

In 1988, a year after my trial, the Rotary Club of Guam invited me to speak, not as the convicted former governor, but as B.J. Bordallo's son. The Rotarians asked me to represent Dad at a special gathering to honor past presidents. Dad and Uncle Butler were instrumental in founding the Guam chapter, and both had served as presidents. Dad had been gone four years by then, Uncle Butler almost 45. I gazed out at the audience of Rotarians and told them I was uncomfortable.

"I should be out there holding up a tray with one arm and wearing a towel on the other," I said. The comment drew a chuckle. I was the former governor of Guam and a convicted felon awaiting an appeal. The club members, most of whom were repatriates, snickered at what they thought was a public admission of my humiliation. But I explained how I had waited on tables at the coffee shop during Rotary meetings after the war. Only Herbert Johnston, a long-time active Rotarian, knew what I was talking about.

Supplies of fresh meat for the coffee shop came from the cattle, pigs, and chickens that Dad purchased and that I slaughtered and butchered in the backyard. Without the abattoir, I had no choice but to do the work close to home, much to the family's discomfort. After buying a large bull from a farmer in Aspenggao, near Mongmong, Dad sent Venuncio Leon Guerrero and me to pick it up and bring it back to slaughter. Venuncio was one of many dependable jack-of-all-trades Dad hired temporarily. He was a large, jolly man who weighed at least 300 pounds. He had two nicknames: "Cherry," because he was so round and pleasant, and "Charote," his family nickname. Everyone called him by both names. Cherry Charote had a pleasant lilting accent that matched his cheery nature. Before we set out, Dad warned us to be careful — the bull was temperamental.

Cherry Charote and I joked and horsed around all the way to Aspenggao. We were in a silly mood when the farmer led us to the bull tethered by its horns to a tree. It did not have a nose ring; it was a range bull, an unpredictable animal not accustomed to human handling. The bull stamped and pawed the ground as we approached. It did not balk when we untied its bonds and lashed two ropes around its horns. Being the bigger and stronger man, Cherry Charote took the lead line and walked about 10 paces ahead of the bull. I followed in the rear with the second line. We held the lines taut to keep the bull at a safe distance between us. Lashed by its horns, it could do us no harm. The bull seemed docile and remained placid as we led it down the road. I began wondering whether Dad's warning was necessary. The bull did nothing more menacing than snort, twist its head, and try to change directions a few times, but Cherry managed to keep it steady. We were sure the bull would behave and began joking and teasing each other again.

"Hey, Cherry, maybe the bull likes you, and that's why he's being so nice," I called ahead. Cherry laughed and countered, "Ha! You just watch where you step. Remember which end you're facing."

"Maybe he likes your smell. You'd better speed up, or he'll get a good whiff and come after you," I said.

Both of us needed a good bath. Until the return of working waterlines, bathing was a luxury for everyone. Except for an occasional dip in a stream, the sweat of working hard under the sun stuck to us. We often poked fun at our ripening odors.

Laughing at my own wittiness, I realized too late that my rope had slackened. I yanked on the rope, but the bull moved quicker. Before I could shout a warning, the bull lunged forward and gored Cherry's rear end. One horn drove deep between his buttocks. Cherry shrieked in pain as the bull raised its head with Cherry impaled on its horn. I struggled against the line and hollered in fright. The bull flicked its head and sent Cherry flying. He hit the ground with a heavy thud. He lay semiconscious and moaning.

Freed, the bull then turned on me. I had only one escape. I calculated the distance to a coconut tree by the roadside and dashed for it, still clutching my end of the rope. The bull flared its nostrils, lowered its head, and charged just as I reached the tree. I rounded the tree and wrapped the rope around the trunk as quickly as I could. The bull was at my heels, but I managed to tighten the rope and pull its head snug against the trunk. It bucked against its restraints and bellowed angrily.

I ran back to Cherry. He was spreadeagled on the road, glassy-eyed but conscious and in intense pain. Blood covered the whole lower half of his body;

more was pouring from his wound. I dropped to my knees beside him and brushed the dust from his face. I did not know what to do. We were alone on a deserted back road, and Cherry was bleeding to death. Panicked and crushed with guilt, I had to get help, but help was far away.

"Cherry, I'm going for help," I said, my heart pounding. "I won't fail you, my friend. I promise, I'll bring help right away."

I ran as fast as I could toward Fifth Field, a military supply depot, in Mongmong, about half a mile away. I dashed into the compound and babbled to the first man I met.

"Whoa, son. Slow down. Catch your breath first," the man said.

My mouth and throat were dry, and I longed for a drink of water, but there was no time. I explained what had happened.

"...And he's lying there in the road. He is bleeding badly. Please, you must come and help," I pleaded. The man yelled for a medic and an ambulance then jumped into a jeep. "Get in," he said. I climbed in, and we sped off, the ambulance following behind us.

I was afraid Cherry would be dead before we reached him. And it was my fault. Guilt crushed down on me. I wanted to cry but fought back my tears. I kept thinking of Cherry dying in pain, alone, in the dirt because of me.

I led the rescuers to where Cherry lay. He was motionless in a pool of blood. My heart skipped a beat. I jumped from the jeep and dashed to his side, afraid he was already dead. I knelt beside him. Cherry was still alive and conscious but did not speak. He just looked up at me and moaned.

"It's alright, Cherry," I whispered. "I brought help. You'll be alright, my friend. You'll be alright."

Four attendants brought a stretcher from the ambulance. It took all of us to move Cherry onto it. Moving him sent new waves of pain through his body. Guilt and empathy made me feel it with him.

Cherry's wound required 25 stitches. The bull's horn sliced through one buttock and tore his rectum. He spent a month in the hospital. He has never blamed me for the accident, but I have never stopped feeling guilty about it. We have remained friends and can now laugh about it. Many years after the accident, Cherry asked me to be his son's godfather. My godson, Robert, is now a grown man serving in the U.S. Army in Europe.

After taking Cherry to the hospital in Hagåtña, I returned to Aspenggao in a weapons carrier to get the bull. It was still tied to the coconut tree and was docile again. Not taking any chances, I tied the bull to the rear of the weapons carrier, drove home slowly, then led it into the backyard.

"This is for Cherry," I said and drove a spike into the base of its skull. The bull died instantly. We kept a few pounds of round steak for ourselves and the coffeehouse. We divided the rest and gave some to Tun Pedro Martinez, Auntie Butler, Uncle Tom, Nanan Chong, and other friends and neighbors.

The laundry king of Hagåtña

The coffee shop put us back in business, but Dad, always enterprising, won a bid to take over the Susana Hospital's laundry. The industrial facility employed about 20 people who ran the huge boilers, washing and pressing machines, and dryers. Dad kept the workers and put me in charge of marketing and sales. With only the hospital's laundry to do, business for us was slow. The military had their own laundry facilities, and many people did their laundry the old-fashioned way, with washboards and tubs or in the river. As the new salesman, I had to drum up business, or we would have folded.

I decided to check out the merchant ships in the harbor. They were an untapped source that might have needed laundry services, at least for some things. Even if I could only get a few, small loads, our revenues would pick up. It was worth a try. The worse I could get was a "No, thank you." I drove to Sumai and parked on the dock nearest the first merchant marine ship in port. There were at least 20 others tied to the piers. I climbed the gangplank uninvited and asked a seaman for the captain's quarters. He led me to a fat, friendly man puffing a cigar. The captain eyed me curiously and asked my business. I launched into my prepared sales pitch.

"Sir, my name's Ricky Bordallo, and I represent my father's laundry business in Hagåtña. I was wondering if you might need th—"

The captain cut me off. "Son, where the hell have you been?"

I could not tell whether he was pleased or angered.

"This has to be the worst place in the world to get anything washed," he continued. "Why are you just now coming around? We've needed you since day one. Do we need laundry service? Come, follow me."

The captain led me down into a hold in the ship. It was a cavernous room with a mountain of dirty linens piled in the center. "Think you can manage that?" the captain asked. "There's plenty more, too. I'd be mighty grateful for your service."

"Sir, it'll take me a while to count all the pieces and make an inventory for you," I said, awed by the amount of work before me and the profit potential.

"Just get it the hell out of here and bring whatever's clean back," he said.

At the captain's instructions, several seamen helped me load the laundry into the truck. It took several truckloads and many trips to bring the mountain to Hagåtña. Among all the sheets, pillowcases, blankets, bedspreads, tablecloths, towels, and washcloths, we found new linens, still wrapped, and miscellaneous articles of clothing, which the laundry workers kept. We washed and returned about 75 percent of each load and shared the rest among ourselves.

I returned to the merchant ship and handed the captain an invoice for $300. I thought he would balk, but he paid on the spot. He also made me promise to return regularly and to call on the other merchant ships in the harbor.

"If they find out I got laundry done and didn't tell them, they'd kill me," he said. "Make sure you see the captains on all these ships. Tell them I sent you."

For months afterward, our laundry service thrived on the big business from merchant marine ships. Those leaving port sent word about our service to incoming ships whose captains would call us as soon as they docked. They gave us so much business, and we kept so much, we gave away linens to relatives, friends, and whoever wanted them. Our stockpile of blue merchant marine bedspreads, linens, and towels lasted us 30 years. Business was great, and I became the laundry king of Hagåtña until the Navy undercut us.

The Navy built a laundry facility much bigger than ours and turned it over to American civilian newcomers. Similar arrangements were rampant from 1945 until the 1950s. Mercenaries plotted with unethical servicemen and officers for exclusive franchises or special concessions. Although some CHamoru businessmen also benefited from such practices, the widespread carpetbaggery and chicanery stymied the reestablishment of a healthy, wholesome economy. I naively assumed CHamorus would get some preferential advantage since we had been prisoners of war. The military destroyed our homes and towns and took away our lands and our way of life. As a community, we had to start over from scratch. But rather than foster CHamoru economic rehabilitation and the reconstruction of our small, self-sustaining community, many self-aggrandizing military and government officials used their positions and authority to protect their own interests. The military crooks conspired with foreign and American mercenaries who served as fronts.

The military's economic orgies were well known, though not all military men were crooks. The ones who were crooks made for spicy gossip. One of the early commanding officers of the Twentieth Air Force was reportedly on official business in Taiwan when his plane crashed. The Air Force officially listed the men as killed in the line of duty, but gossip from the base was that the men went to Taipei for the brothels, and the pilot was drunk at the controls.

In 1945, the *New York Times* decried the abuses, but federal investigations were rare then. Congress accepted the Navy's word that all was proper and legitimate in Guam.

The massive supply of goods spawned shady deals of all sorts in business as well as personal relationships. Servicemen seeking the company of young CHamoru girls often plied their parents with suspiciously procured gifts — from vehicles and tools to nylons and perfume. American men were of the notion that the right gift could guarantee them all the women they wanted. Disgusted by the idea that local girls would fall so easily, Dad forbade my sisters from associating with servicemen, and he berated any who approached them. But four of his eight daughters married servicemen. Irene married James Little, a sailor. Bobbie, Norma, and Junie married Marines — Peter Siguenza, John Phillips, and Alfred Arroyo, respectively.

Chapter 17

Justice seems capricious

The extensive damage to Hagåtña, and the Navy's plans for the new city, forced many Hagåtña families to relocate to Tutuhan, the rural farmlands above and behind the city, and other surrounding areas. The Tutuhan settlement grew and became the new village of Agaña Heights. Tun Kiko and Nanan Chong owned a large parcel of land and settled there. They parceled lots to each of their children and donated the largest parcel for a church.

Nanan Chong's small Santa Cruz chapel, where we gathered for her annual Santa Cruz novena and celebrated at its end, became where Påle' Oskot offered Mass and stored consecrated communion wafers during the occupation. As more people settled in Tutuhan, a Quonset hut replaced the old chapel. In 1948, Påle' Oskot and the villagers, doing much of the construction themselves, built a permanent church on the land Tun Kiko and Nanan Chong donated. The picturesque successor of Nanan Chong's chapel became Our Lady of the Blessed Sacrament Church. It is the church in which I was married.

The reestablished Navy government also set up headquarters in Agaña Heights and used a portion of Nanan Chong's estate for a prisoner camp for captured Japanese soldiers. The Navy imprisoned Mrs. Dejima, her daughter, and other long-time Japanese Guamanians there until Dad, Auntie Butler, and others testified in their behalf.

When the Navy began prosecuting Japanese war criminals, I often went to watch. After having witnessed Japanese military justice, I was curious about its American counterpart.

American military justice was strange. The military panel showed no mercy toward the Japanese and executed those found guilty right away. Yet, in judging the misdeeds of one of their own, and one of ours, the panel was more than lenient.

Glenn Martinez, the son of Tun Vicente and nephew of Tun Pedro Martinez, was in the Solomons when the Americans recaptured Guam. Glenn, an Army-Air Force pilot, tried to find out how his family had fared but could get no information. He had not heard from them in more than three years. He had heard about Japanese atrocities in Guam and the intense American bombardments and was frantic. Denied any news, Glenn commandeered a B-25 Mitchell bomber and flew to Guam to find out for himself. When he landed at the Orote airstrip, the military police arrested and charged him with theft of government property and going AWOL (absent without leave), among several lesser charges.

Glenn was prepared to accept the consequences and admitted guilt. He said his family was more important to him than his military career. He saw his family again from behind bars. For Glenn's case, the military government applied the principle that laws have a spirit as well as the letter[16] and took into consideration the extenuating circumstances. They exonerated him. What Glenn did was illegal but not done with malicious or criminal intent. I can sympathize with the emotional turmoil that motivated Glenn, and I can appreciate the considerations he received, but I cannot reconcile the legal machinations that can excuse the guilty and convict the innocent. In 1987, the federal government interpreted the law in its strictest sense to judge me guilty of crimes I did not commit. Justice seems capricious.

"Someday, Sweetheart"

In May 1945, Mama gave birth to Anita, her 16th child, but she did not recover quickly. She remained weak for a long time and later complained of pain in her kidneys. Over the following months, Mama's trips to the doctor became more frequent, and she was in and out of the hospital. We worried each time she was hospitalized and rejoiced when she came home, believing she was healthy again. Neither she nor Dad ever discussed her condition with us. We never knew what was wrong or whether her life was in danger. I am not sure that Mama herself knew. If she had, she was confident she would overcome it.

Whenever she was in the hospital, we would take turns visiting her. It

---

16 The letter of the law is what the law states; the spirit of the law is a social and moral consensus of the interpretation of the letter.

struck me as odd that she seemed so close yet so far. The Susana Hospital was near our house, but she was not at home with us where she belonged. Despite her illness, Mama continued to run her household from a distance. She made each of us account for our chores and instructed my older sisters on the care and feeding of the younger ones, especially baby Anita. We always had to keep the standards she set. Her absence was no excuse for relaxing the household rules.

We were at the hospital so often that we became friends with the doctors, nurses, and corpsmen. Irene caught the eye of one of the corpsmen. She found him interesting as well. Amid the concern for Mama's failing health, a love affair between Corpsman James Little and my sister Irene blossomed. Jimmy took extra care of Mama when we were absent, and he was her messenger to get things from home for her. Mama liked Jimmy and approved of his attentions to Irene. From her hospital bed, she helped nurture the match by sending Jimmy to the house often. Jimmy also came up with other reasons to call, much to Dad's displeasure.

To our relief, Mama came home from the hospital for Thanksgiving, but she had to stay in bed. I was concerned by her inability to take charge but reasoned she was recovering and needed the rest. What mattered most was that she was home. I helped her settle in and arranged the pillows under her head. As I adjusted her covers, I saw the bandages around her middle beneath her gown. An ugly, black liquid from her surgical wound had seeped through the bandages and stained her nightgown. The sight frightened me.

"Mama, you're oozing," I said. She read the fear and worry in my face.

"Oh, that's just from the surgery," she said, trying to ease my concern.

Mama valued her privacy and did not share private matters with anyone, but she had always confided in me. I sensed she was not telling me something, and it scared me. Her illness was more serious than she wanted us to believe. I left her room with a troubled mind.

After Thanksgiving, Mama returned to the hospital. Less than a week later, on December 2, 1945, a messenger came to the house. Mama had taken a turn for the worse. I ran to the hospital as fast as I could, but I was too late. Mama was gone. Several members of the family were there, weeping quietly, careful not to interrupt the passage of Mama's soul. I knelt by her bed and stroked her cheek. It was still warm and soft. Mama looked peaceful and serene, as though she was sleeping. I clenched my teeth to hold back my grief and keep my heart from bursting. We stayed with her until hospital personnel removed her to the morgue.

We walked around in numbed shock for days. We were not prepared for Mama's death and could not accept it. We could not believe she would be gone from us, gone from our home forever. Mama had been so strong, so much a powerful and sustaining force in our lives. We never thought she could die. She was always there, always strong, always with us. Her death left a huge, gaping hole in our family. Our relatives, neighbors, and friends came to our aid, offering shoulders to cry on, taking care of details we had overlooked or forgotten, sharing our grief, and lending us their strength. But we still felt alone.

Preparations for her funeral got underway, but I recollect little. More than just the passage of time, the pain of losing Mama shrouds this episode of my life. I remember that her homemade pinewood coffin was fancier than usual. I believe Ben "Titang" Salas, the carpenter and cabinetmaker, built and embellished it with his finest workmanship. He stained and varnished it in tribute to Mama's grace and refinement. Mama's wake lasted the traditional three days before her burial at Pigo' Cemetery.

After Mama's funeral, every reminder of her absence grieved us. The outdoor theater beside the coffeehouse kept playing her favorite songs. Each time we heard "Someday, Sweetheart," new waves of tears and sorrow would sweep over us. The song played again and again for days. The pain was so unbearable that Dad asked the theater manager to stop playing the song and spare us the agony.

At first, I mourned Mama's death with my heart. After her funeral, a different kind of grief overwhelmed me. I struggled with it and grew angry with Dad and with God for allowing her to die. Dad never told us Mama was gravely ill. He did not give us the chance to prepare for her death. He kept the terrible knowledge to himself, and I resented him for it. But Dad was Dad; he could not have managed it any other way.

Mama's death was hardest on him. Mama was his anchor, his *raison d'être*. We would grow up and start our own families, but Dad lost his life's companion, the love of his life. He remained stoic, but the sparkle left his eyes. I could accept Dad's frailty and appreciate the courage and strength he mustered to overcome a major crisis in his life. My anger with God was different. God was all-powerful. He had exacted a tragic toll of human life in the war, but He was not yet satisfied. He took Mama, who had the strength her husband and many children needed. Why, God? Why take Mama, too? It took a long time for me to reconcile my anger and make peace with the Lord.

Kamalin's rescuer

The Feast of the Immaculate Conception, and the fourth anniversary of the Japanese invasion of Guam, came six days after Mama's death. The religious holiday had always been the island's most celebrated. During the occupation, its observance was somber and quiet, but we still commemorated it. In 1944, the ongoing war did not allow for a festive public celebration, but by 1945, despite postwar chaos, CHamorus celebrated the Blessed Mother's feast day with a traditional procession. Thousands gathered in Hagåtña.

The statue of Santa Marian Kamalin, Our Lady of Camarin, Guam's beloved patroness, is the focal point of the procession. Legend says the statue came to Guam during the Spanish days. A Malesso' fisherman spotted it standing on the shell of a large crab in the Cocos Lagoon. The crab held a lit candle in each claw. Each time the fisherman tried to approach, the crab would back away. Wearing only a *såde'*, a traditional loincloth, the fisherman could not retrieve the statue until he covered himself. Villagers kept the statue in a barn and later moved it to the cathedral in Hagåtña and placed it in a niche above the altar. She leaves the niche only for the annual procession.

During the occupation, Tita Torres and her family removed the statue and hid it for protection. In the new Dulce Nombre de Maria Cathedral, the Kamalin statue continues her place in a niche above the altar. On December 8, 1945, parishioners brought the statue down and placed it on a *karosa*, a small trailer decorated with flowers, candles, and fine fabric. Young men in suits and ties draw the *karosa* while little flower girls in fancy gowns walk alongside. The bishop, clergy, altar boys, and children dressed as angels and archangels follow behind. The people follow in lines on both sides. After following a route through the streets, the procession heads back to the cathedral for the brief concluding ceremony. The process has not changed much in over 100 years.

I do not recall where I got the white dinner jacket and black trousers, but I was one of the escorts in the 1945 procession. I was three days from my 18th birthday. On our return to the cathedral, as we pulled the *karosa* in front of the Plaza de España, a plume of smoke rose from the decorations near the statue. A cry of alarm went up just as flames ignited. A faulty connection in one of the battery-operated candles sparked and set fire to the flammable decorations. The flames spread fast and threatened to engulf the statue. I scrambled onto the karosa, wrenched the statue from its attachments, and handed it down to waiting hands.

The fire became part of the Kamalin statue's legendary miraculous ability to survive calamities. Over the centuries, it has escaped unscathed from earthquakes, floods, and typhoons. During my first term as governor, when Super Typhoon Pamela hit Guam in 1976, fierce winds ripped through the cathedral but did not sweep Santa Maria from her niche. Instead, her long human hair was wrapped around her head as if to shield her from seeing the suffering of her people and the destruction of her beloved island. In May 1968 and again in May 1971, thieves stole the statue from its niche. Both thefts left the island in turmoil. People from all villages kept vigils at the cathedral, offered Masses, and said rosaries for her safe return. People made appeals on all media for the statue's safe return — no questions asked. In both instances, Santa Maria came home safe and unharmed.

No accounts of the 1945 *karosa* fire include my role in saving the Kamalin statue. Credit is given to others. Most accounts do not identify the rescuer; others credit an American serviceman. I have never bothered to set the record straight until now. I know Santa Marian Kamalin watches over me. After my indictment in 1986, I committed my fate to her hands. She has not failed me.

Jimmy and Irene

Despite Mama's blessing, Dad was not pleased with Irene's relationship and was hard on Jimmy, speaking to him only in monosyllabic grunts. Whenever Jimmy came to call, Dad would grunt, leave the room, and return 15 minutes later to announce that Jimmy's time was up. Poor Jimmy would comply and leave after only a few minutes with Irene. Dad did everything he could to make Jimmy unwelcome. He was serious about protecting his daughters. As far as he was concerned, American servicemen were the worse suitors of all. Jimmy's only fault was that he was a sailor.

Servicemen were notorious for jilting CHamoru girls. Their beauty and femininity, their charm and grace, and their shyness and naivete attracted many American males. Despite stern warnings from their parents, many girls gave their hearts and bodies to sweet-talking Americans who made grandiose promises. Many were heartbroken and humiliated when their American boy-friends left Guam, never to return. Dad was determined to keep his daughters from such betrayals. He made me promise to look after them and dissuade any American who showed interest.

Jimmy knew what he was up against, but he was in love. And stubborn. With patience and humility, he put up with Dad's coldness. He knew it stemmed from grief, from the overwhelming responsibility of a large family, and from his belief that Jimmy's intentions were less than honorable. Jimmy knew how much emotional damage his military colleagues had wrought, but he was determined to prove himself different. I felt sorry for him whenever Dad was especially gruff. Dad did not dislike Jimmy, but he did not trust him either. Dad knew that only a suitor of true and noble intent could withstand the difficulties and pressures he imposed. He put Jimmy through his harshest tests. Jimmy struggled but passed each one.

Jimmy's difficulties were twofold. In addition to Dad's inhospitable behavior, Jimmy also had to contend with his military superiors. The Navy government no longer prohibited marriage between its personnel and local women but continued to discourage it. Worse than Dad, the military government required Jimmy to undergo psychiatric counseling and an obstacle course of bureaucratic paperwork before getting consent to marry. I suspect other servicemen buckled under the pressure and gave up, leaving their sweethearts brokenhearted.

Jimmy's persistence convinced me that he truly loved my sister. Dad was convinced also. He knew Mama liked Jimmy and had given him her blessing, but Dad made Jimmy earn his. When Jimmy asked for Irene's hand, Dad gave his blessing. Jimmy and Irene were married on March 6, 1946.

Kabayeru

Dad survived Mama's death another 39 years. He died on May 10, 1984, during my second term. By law, the government of Guam accorded Dad a state funeral. As a pioneer statesman and former Guam congressman and legislator, Dad had earned one. As governor, I had to proclaim a state of mourning and order the Guam flag lowered to half-mast. But I balked at the wording of the proclamation my staff prepared. It deviated from the standard. I questioned the legal closing and asked if it were not too self-serving. My staff assured me it was not and encouraged me to sign the proclamation as prepared. It read:

"Now, therefore, I, RICARDO J. BORDALLO, eldest son of Baltazar J. Bordallo and Governor of the Territory of Guam, by virtue of the authority vested in me by the Organic Act of Guam, as amended, do hereby proclaim a State of Mourning in honor of and in tribute to the Late Baltazar J. Bordallo ..."

Dad was a *kabayeru*, a man of principles and unassailable integrity. He was a man of honor who brought honor to his people. I have tried to follow his example and have adhered to his standard of honesty and integrity. Yet the federal government falsely accused, convicted, and sentenced me for violating these very principles. My accusers would have my people believe that I am the dishonorable son of an honorable man. The contradiction leaves me sorely embittered. I shall not give up my fight to clear my name and restore my family's honor, not merely for my sake, but for Dad's.

We buried Dad with full governmental honors at Pigo' Cemetery. We exhumed Mama's remains and reinterred them with his in a burial vault above ground. A green marble tombstone bears both their names.

Chapter 18

Betelnuts and bomber crews

We were still living in Toggai when the new B-29 bombers arrived to set up a home base in Guam. Their arrival flyover was an incredible sight. Hundreds of gigantic planes darkened the sky. The loud drone of their engines was reassuring.

But the Toggai house held too many painful memories of Mama's illness and death. We looked forward to leaving it and settling elsewhere. The profits from the coffeehouse, the laundry, and the sale of our Canadian Club Whisky funded Dad's 99-year lease of a large, former military camp from its owner in Tamuning. The American military had built several facilities then moved and built new ones when time and space allowed. When they vacated the camps, they left behind the infrastructure improvements, buildings, furnishings, and equipment. The wholesale squander was a windfall for the landowners whose properties were returned. Not all landowners were fortunate; most did not get their lands back even after the military abandoned them. The military kept many huge tracts but left them largely unused.

The abandoned camp in Tamuning became our permanent home and business headquarters. Dad dubbed it the Coconut Grove. It covered several acres and contained several large elephant Quonsets, barracks, a galley, and a mess hall. There was a motor pool, several large electric generators, a water storage tank, and a large boiler. A small stream coursed through the camp. A bridge, which was more like an extension of the roadway, connected the camp to the new main highway. A small foot bridge also spanned the stream in front of the mess hall. The foot bridge became our favorite place to gather with cousins, friends, and schoolmates. The mess hall became our new home. A nice, airy, screened-in area facing the footbridge became our living room.

After setting up house, we gradually moved into the other buildings to set up the businesses. A retail store and restaurant came first. The mountain of supplies from Tipunngan became menu entrees in the Coconut Grove Restaurant and merchandise on the store shelves. After the restaurant and store, we started an auto sales outlet for Willis Overland and Nash Lafayette Motors, which later became American Motors, and a popsicle and ice cream plant. I was Dad's general overseer and jack-of-all-trades. Uncle Tom and Dad joined forces and incorporated as Bordallo Consolidated. Business was brisk from the start, and we made a quick financial recovery.

The Coconut Grove was spacious. We could each claim our own special places. I took the commanding officer's quarters beside the restaurant. At 17, I had my own small apartment. It had wide, screened windows, built-in wooden seating, and a canvas-covered roof. The builders stretched the canvas taut and painted it to stiffen and harden it. Cherry Charote lived across the street. I was proud of my apartment. I never thought of it as humble or shabby until six years later when I brought Madeleine to see it. She was my fiancée then and had come back home to Guam for summer vacation. Madeleine shrank at the sight and burst into tears of sympathy for me.

Harmon Field, the expansive new B-29 airfield, was just a few miles northeast of the Coconut Grove. As neighbors, the "Super Fortresses" were noisy. The rumble of their huge engines was a constant distraction but watching them take off was entertaining. They were like huge gooney birds, with great, rubber tires instead of webbed, blue feet, lumbering into the air one after another until hundreds were airborne. They would fly low overhead and not gain altitude until they were far from the island. Their departures and arrivals were like clockwork. Screaming bomber engines at 5 o'clock every morning signaled the day's start. With a deafening roar, the B-29s rose into the sky one by one. They returned at 4 in the afternoon, flying low over us before landing in Harmon.

Everyone held the bomber crews in high esteem. We were not American citizens, but we considered the B-29s and their crews our planes, our boys. The war was not over for the B-29 crews still bombing Japan. We knew that men still died in battle. We would count the number of bombers taking off in the morning and those returning in the afternoon. When the numbers did not tally, we would whisper prayers for the crews who did not come home. Because their jobs were dangerous, and many died in the line of duty, we treated the bomber crews like celebrities. No one complained if off-duty "fly boys" got too boisterous or rowdy at the Coconut Grove Restaurant. They had to let off steam, and we obliged them.

About eight of them came into the store one day while I was at the register. They appeared to be the flight officers of at least two crews. They were young, in their 20s and only a few years older than me, but they were captains, majors, or lieutenant colonels. Their youth and high ranks impressed me. The prewar Navy and Marine officers of like ranks had always been older men. The bomber officers wandered through the store, examining merchandise, and selecting souvenirs and trinkets. They also selected some soft drinks and headed to my counter.

The men were curious about everything, including me. They told me their names and hometowns and asked me about the Japanese, the occupation, and about myself. They were shocked and sympathetic when I told them about the beatings I suffered at Japanese hands. They looked at me with renewed respect, which matched mine for them. We spent a pleasant afternoon learning about one another. They learned that CHamorus were loyal to the United States. I learned that they were not supermen — just brave men who sometimes got very scared.

"What in the world are you eating, Ricky?" one of them asked as we talked. I was chewing *pugua'* (betel nut) with *pupulu* (pepper leaf). We sold betelnuts from a large glass jar on the counter. I helped myself whenever I wanted. A betelnut chewer since childhood, I did not realize until then that they were unfamiliar with the practice.

"Oh, I'm eating betelnut," I said, embarrassed by my unconscious chewing and rude failure to offer them some. I explained that it was an ancient and widespread practice among Western Pacific people, that chewing *pugua'* and *pupulu* together produced a rich, red spittle that one either swallows or spits out, and that it was a mild narcotic. I described how older people chewed *pugua'* and *pupulu* with tobacco and lime, the creamy white calcium oxide of fired limestone, and how that combination packed a power punch.

"I'm only an amateur, so I only chew the nut with the leaf," I said. "Would you care to try it?" Game for anything that numbed the senses, they were eager to try.

I took a betelnut from the jar and peeled it. The officers marveled at my *tiheras pugua'*, a pair of scissors made for peeling and cutting betelnut. The nut was *ugam*, a premium nut that was dark red, bitter, and potent. I cut it in quarters, then into eighths, and distributed pieces to each man. I gave them a *pupulu* leaf and showed them how to nip off tiny bits.

"Just chew slowly and swallow it a little at a time," I said.

I watched for their reactions, expecting them to gag and spit immediately, but they continued to chew.

"It makes my mouth feel twisted," an officer said while the others made funny faces.

"This is not bad. Not bad at all," said another after a few minutes.

To my surprise, the officers liked it. They insisted on buying a couple of dollars' worth. Betelnuts were three for a nickel; a dollar's worth was a lot; two bucks emptied the container. They also wanted some *pupulu* and a *tiheras pugua'*. I could give them the leaves for free but not the tiheras. The special scissors were common before the war but hard to find afterward. I showed them how to use a pocketknife instead.

A few days later, the same officers returned and asked to buy more. I could not believe they had eaten their entire purchase and how quickly they had developed a taste for it. One man said the *pugua'* gave them enough of a buzz to relieve tension. Another said he passed some out to his crew and chewed betelnut all the way to Japan, dumped their bombs, and flew home dizzy and singing from a *pugua'* high.

"I don't know if we hit anything, and I don't really care," he said. "I just like what that stuff does for me and my men. We do not want word of this to get out, so do not tell anyone. It'll be our secret."

I never told anyone. My B-29 friends returned many times to buy *pugua'*, even after Dad transferred me to the popsicle plant. Years later, I hosted veterans of the 20th Air Force who were visiting for the anniversary of Liberation Day. The Air Force vets return to Guam every year. During both administrations, I hosted welcoming receptions in their honor, and I would ask if anyone among them remembered buying betelnut from a teenager or hearing of B-29 crews who chewed betelnut. I never got a positive response, and each year the number of returning vets dwindles.

Always the brunt of American jokes

When Admiral Chester W. Nimitz departed Guam to witness Japan's surrender on board the USS *Missouri*, every B-29 in Guam took to the sky for a flyover in Nimitz's honor. Nimitz, who had moved his headquarters from Hawai'i to Guam in August 1944, was commander of Pacific Forces and governor of the military government of Guam. He relegated his latter responsibilities to Major General Henry L. Larsen, who in turn passed them to Rear Admiral Charles A. Pownall, who became commander Naval Forces Marianas and governor of Guam in May 1946, when the military government ceased, and the Navy government took over again. Admiral Nimitz's sendoff was spectacular. As they had done when they first arrived, the B-29s flew in formation over the ruins of Hagåtña. They filled the sky from horizon to horizon. I watched the flyover from the Coconut Grove with pride and admiration. It restored my faith in the power and might of the United States and cemented my sense of security.

Although Japanese stragglers were still a threat, their numbers were decreasing — either captured and imprisoned or killed. The stockade in Agaña Heights filled rapidly, despite the military government's war trials and executions. Government officials often called Dad, Auntie Butler, and many others as witnesses at the trials and at the stockade to point out who among the Japanese officials had been cruel and who among the civilians were innocent. We had asked Dad to keep an eye out for our Japanese sailor friend, but Dad never found him. The sailor told us he would die for his country. We assumed he did. Like other Japanese combatants, he may have refused to surrender.

At the time, the renegade Japanese were more steadfast than anyone imagined. In 1960, *ayuyu* (coconut crab) hunters Clemente C. Santos and Ben C. Manibusan discovered Masashi Ito and Bunzo Minagawa, who had spent 16 years in hiding. In 1972, fishermen Manuel Tolentino De Gracia and Jesus Mantanona Dueñas were checking their fish traps in the Talo'fo'fo River basin when they caught Sgt. Shoichi Yokoi, who had been hiding for 28 years in the Talo'fo'fo jungle. He lived in an underground cave he dug by hand. Yokoi returned to Japan a hero admired for his obedience to the Japanese army code. He got married later that year and returned to Guam for a visit with his bride. I was a wealthy businessman then and invited the Yokois to a ride on my new jet engine Bell helicopter.

We flew to Talo'fo'fo on a day too dismal and wet for an outing. Rain fell as we toured Yokoi's old underground "home." The chopper would not start when we tried to leave. Its new batteries lacked a full charge. I sent my pilot into the village on foot to call for replacements. Four hours passed before one of my two other helicopters delivered the batteries. The Yokois and I did not get back to Tumon until well past 10 o'clock that night. I had the chopper land in front of their hotel. Despite our misadventure, the Yokois were not put off.

I had always wanted to be a successful businessman like Dad. Although I worked long hours for him, I made time for my own money-making endeavors. For a while, I toyed with the idea of opening my own photo-processing shop. I even set up a darkroom in my apartment. The enlarger, trays, chemicals, and supplies were readily available. All I needed was some experience, so I developed negatives and made some satisfactory prints of photos I had taken. Ben Blaz, who was sweet on my sister Norma and often hung around with me, liked my business idea and marveled at my darkroom. He wanted to be my partner in the venture, but his enthusiasm was short-lived. As the businesses flourished, Dad gave me more responsibilities. I could not spend the time I wanted and gave up the photo business idea.

I came home one day to find everyone excited and starstruck. I had been out on my rounds and had missed the excitement. My sisters were agog. "Oh, Ricky, you missed him. He was here! Right here at Coconut Grove," Irene said.

"Who? Who did I miss?"

"Tyrone Power. He was right here," she said.

I felt badly about missing Tyrone Power, who was a famous actor, but in time I got to see other celebrities, like heiress Barbara Hutton and others. Comedian Bob Hope's USO shows brought many to Guam.

Although the USO shows were meant to entertain American military personnel, Guamanians could also attend. But we chafed at Bob Hope's jokes about Guam. His potshots were insulting. While the service personnel roared with laughter, we sat in humiliated silence. It was not that we could not take jokes or laugh at ourselves. On the contrary, humor, satire, ridicule, and mockery are part of our nature. They are important survival tools. Hope's jokes were not something we could laugh with; they made us the subjects to be laughed at. Rather than promote understanding, Hope expressed sympathy for Americans having to serve in a miserable hellhole like Guam. We took great exception to the spiteful characterization. If Guam was a hellhole, what were we? Demons?

Years later, during my second term as governor, I passed up an opportunity to take Hope to task for his insults. We were both on a flight from Los Angeles to Honolulu and had exchanged pleasantries in the first-class lounge. He was friendly and willing to engage in conversation, but I remained aloof. I knew if I spoke, I would cause an embarrassing scene. As the representative of the people of Guam, I thought it best to maintain the dignity of my office.

Many other celebrities and leading political figures have belittled Guam over the years. Talk show host Johnny Carson's snide remarks on national television have always been unwarranted, stinging blows. President Richard Nixon's celebrated reference to banishing recalcitrant Washington, D.C., bureaucrats to Guam as punishment stabbed us. Astronaut John Glenn and his family were one of the first military families to report to Guam after the war. He knew a lot about the island but never did anything to set the record straight. A few kind words would have sufficed. Even comedian Flip Wilson, who stood sentry duty at Andersen Air Force Base, got his start here. Wilson chauffeured a general who recognized his talent and made important show biz contacts for him. Senators, congressmen, state governors, and high-ranking federal officials have served military tours of duty in Guam, but few have done anything to dispel the misconceptions about Guam and her people.

"Open your eyes and see the world"

When the reestablished Navy government reopened the schools, I was uncomfortable about going back. I had attended George Washington High School only a year before the occupation began. At 17, I would be returning as a sophomore. My only consolation was that I was not alone. Everyone was three years behind. As students who should have long graduated, my classmates and I attended an accelerated curriculum. I graduated in 1947 at age 19.

To prepare us for school, the Navy government ordered physical examinations and inoculations for all students. We took a bus to the Susana Hospital and underwent several tests. One test changed my life forever. I had never had my eyes examined before then.

"All right, son, let us see those eyes. Have a seat in that chair," the Navy doctor said as I entered the ophthalmology office. The chair faced a wall about 10 feet away. The doctor told me to read from a chart on the wall, but the wall to me was blank. The doctor looked at me curiously then opened the door and summoned another doctor. The second doctor conducted a different vision test, but I failed it again. While the doctors conferred, I got scared. The second doctor left the room and returned a few minutes later with a nurse and a tray, which she placed beside me.

"These eye drops will help us see inside your eyes," the doctor said. "I need to dilate them so I can examine them better. This won't hurt."

He lied. The drops burned so fiercely, I nearly jumped out of the chair. Tears started streaming down my cheeks, and my nose ran. My eyes stung for some time. With his nose almost touching mine, the doctor peered into my eyes with a small but intense pencil of light. I had never been so close to another male, especially a Navy officer, and was uncomfortable. I could smell his breath and feel it against my cheek. He studied my eyes for several minutes then switched off the penlight. Blinded, I blinked until the spots disappeared.

"Ricky, have you ever worn eyeglasses?" the doctor asked. I said no, annoyed that he would ask such a question. Only old people wore eyeglasses.

"Have your eyes ever been examined before?"

"No, sir."

"Have you noticed any changes in your vision?"

"Not really, except I had trouble seeing clearly after the Japanese beat me a few times."

"Your vision got worse?"

"Well, I couldn't see as clearly as before, but I thought it would get better in time."

The doctors, the nurse, and two others who joined them huddled again. They took turns glancing at me as they whispered. Their mumblings changed; first puzzled, then surprised, and then concerned.

"Ricky, how did you manage to survive this war?" the first doctor asked.

I shrugged my shoulders. I suspected something was wrong with my vision, but I could see well enough to be a good shot with a slingshot and rifle. Sometimes I could not see what others said they saw, but I always thought they were exaggerating. I never realized my marksmanship was due to my other senses.

The doctor had me sit behind a black contraption that looked like flattened binoculars. He adjusted both sides until I could see the chart on the wall and the letters on it. The machine's ability to improve my sight did not surprise me. I could see just as clearly through binoculars. The machine was just a big, odd-looking pair.

After the tests, the doctor scheduled me for another appointment a few days later. When I returned, the nurse behind the desk greeted me with unusual friendliness.

"Wait right here, I'll call the doctor," she said. Minutes later she reappeared with the two eye doctors and the three nurses who had observed my tests. They were smiling. I sensed they were up to something and grew nervous.

"Sit down, Ricky," the first doctor said. "I want you to close your eyes and don't open them until I tell you to. This is just another test, so be patient."

I sat down and shut my eyes. I could feel him arranging a pair of eyeglasses on my face. When he was satisfied with the fit, he told me to keep my eyes shut and stand up. He and a nurse led me down the corridor. I sensed the second doctor, the nurses, and several others following behind us. We turned a corner and went outside into the yard in front of the hospital.

"Ricky," the doctor said. "Open your eyes and see the world for the first time."

I opened my eyes, blinked, and looked around in awe. The feeling was indescribable. The world was new; it had sharp, clean edges. It had patterns and textures. My head swam with overwhelming details I had never seen before.

"You mean that's how a tree really looks?" I asked. "Look at that coconut tree. Look at the leaves." Until that moment, I never knew that palm fronds spread long, lacy fingers against the sky. I did not know that one could see the corrugations on roofing sheets.

I looked at the sky and saw clouds for the first time. For me, the sky had always been a featureless canopy, either pale blue or flat gray. I stared heavenward for a long time, studying the towering clouds. The clarity and the distinct division between blue sky and white clouds mesmerized me. All around me, colors separated into distinct shapes and hues. I could tell the flowers from the leaves. I could see people's faces at a distance. I could even see the details of their clothing, their every movement.

Behind me, the doctors and nurses were smiling. They gave me a wonderful gift and shared in my amazement.

"Will I always see like this?" I asked, afraid the new sensation was only temporary.

"Yes, Ricky," the doctor answered. "As long as you wear your eyeglasses."

My new-found vision was spellbinding. There were not enough hours in the day to enjoy rediscovering my world. I dreaded taking my glasses off at night, afraid my dreams would be blurry without them. I was happy and disappointed at the same time. Of everything I had "seen" and done, I wondered about what I had missed because I could not really see.

In the yard of the Susana Hospital, I began seeing clearly for the first time in my life. More than 40 years later, near that same spot, I again began to "see" with a deeper, clearer perspective. During my trial in 1987, whenever the prosecutor and my attorney bickered at the bench, I would stand at the window and look down on what had been the hospital yard. I could not escape the sad irony of past and present merging in crazy contradiction.

The Susana Hospital yard now fronts the Nieves Flores Memorial Library, named for the founder of the Guam Institute, which I attended. It also fronts Martyr Street, named in honor of all the CHamorus, like my friend Arthur Anderson, killed by enemy hands at the base of San Ramon. As a young congressman, I authored the bill mandating the street name. The mansanita trees I planted and pruned during my second term have grown tall and beautiful. They line both sides of the street and shade pedestrians and parked cars like giant, green umbrellas. Across Martyr Street, opposite the yard, stands the building that houses the District Court of Guam and the U.S. attorney who accused me of betraying my people.

A fortune in Coca-Cola bottles

I went back to school wearing my new eyeglasses, even though my schoolmates considered it girlish. Wearing eyeglasses was not manly. It was what women wore when they got old. Only old ladies, sissies, and snobs wore them. I took the mocking and taunting in stride. My peers could enjoy the world without eyeglasses; I could not. Nothing, not even the teasing, could force me to give them up.

With schoolwork and my regular chores, I was busy again and had little leisure time, but after the long days of boredom and inactivity during the occupation, I did not complain. I was always looking for ways to add to the family income and earn some money for myself. I wanted to go to college in the States, but I knew that, with so many children to support, Dad could not afford to send me. I had to earn the money myself.

The Navy reestablished the Bank of Guam and restored all prewar savings accounts, including mine, which held about $12. I was proud of my new savings passbook and the $12 entry, paltry as it was. Also, along with Dad and hundreds of other war claimants, I filed for the loss of my 20 head of cattle. I received $350, which went into my bank account. I felt like a rich man, but I had far from enough for college tuition, travel fare, and expenses. My two remaining years in high school did not leave me much time to accumulate an adequate bankroll. I knew that if I wanted to go to college, I had to earn big money fast.

My opportunity came when Auntie and Uncle Butler regained the rights to their Coca-Cola franchise. Uncle Butler survived the three years of Japanese imprisonment and returned to Guam with other American camp survivors after they were freed. He found his family safe but his business empire in ruins. He had to fight to get back his exclusive right to bottle and sell Coca-Cola.

The Coca-Cola Corporation, which had made a sweetheart deal with the Navy government, refused to recognize the Butlers' prewar franchise agreement until Uncle Butler filed suit. Coca-Cola had built a huge, modern bottling plant in Sinajana and was making a fortune in the postwar boom, manufacturing and selling the soda pop to the military. Business was exceptional. The demand for the soft drink was so great that the bottling plant imported Coca-Cola bottles by the millions. The corporation's bottling plant was operating at full tilt while the Butlers' court case proceeded.

Uncle Butler hired Lyle Turner as his attorney. Lyle, who had married Patsy Notley, was a brilliant young lawyer. The Butlers' suit against Coca-Cola was his first major case. And it was a spectacular one because Coca-Cola was already a corporate giant. Coca-Cola was Goliath, and Lyle and the Butlers were David. Lyle managed to embarrass the corporation into settling out of court. Uncle and Auntie Butler received the return of their franchise rights, the bottling plant and all the equipment and supplies in Sinajana, and a $100,000 cash award.

When the bottling plant reverted to the Butlers' control, imports of new bottles ceased, and a shortage ensued. Demand for Coca-Cola was so great, customers lined the road from Sinajana to Ordot, waiting for the soda pop to come off the assembly line. Without the flow of new bottles from the United States, the Butlers had to recycle the empties on island. They offered 2 cents for every bottle. I knew I could make money collecting empty bottles. Although other people were collecting also, I was determined to collect more bottles than anyone else. During my rounds, I scouted for large stockpiles of empties at military clubs and mess halls.

Coca-Cola was delivered to the military in cardboard boxes called V3s, which contained 36 bottles. In the mess halls, a V3 box stood at the start of the chow line next to the food trays. After eating, diners turned in their trays and placed their empty bottles into V3s near the exit. The arrangement was standard at all mess halls. The careful distribution kept the V3s neat and clean. Mess attendants stacked hundreds of V3s behind the mess halls and officers' and enlisted men's clubs. At two cents a bottle, each V3 was worth 72 cents. I did not see them as V3s or empty bottles; I saw them as pennies and dollars.

As I had done with the laundry business, I decided there was no harm in asking outright. No one else seemed brash enough to ask the military for their empties. I sought out the managers of clubs and mess halls and offered to remove their empty bottles free of charge. After receiving the go-ahead, I would spend my free time and Sundays at the task. Because they were like new, loading V3s onto my truck was easy. They made a nice, neat wall of cardboard at our property at Apotguan. My storage area was under some mansanita trees along the base of the cliff. In time, my cardboard wall reached halfway up the cliff.

On my first bottle redemption, I loaded 100 V3s onto my truck and drove to the bottling plant in Sinajana. I felt like a prospector with a bag of gold dust, going to an assay office to get rich. I backed the truck into the loading dock and reveled in the surprised looks on the plant workers' faces. They needed bottles, and I brought them plenty. The first load netted me $72 dollars, paid in five-, 10-, and 20-dollar bills. Although I already had thousands of bottles, I redeemed them only as space ran out. I concentrated on building my stockpile first.

Coca-Cola bottles became my obsession. I kept looking for new sources, wondering where people drank it and in what quantities. With logic and common sense, I found sources and managers happy to accept my removal offer. The hospital turned out to be the mother lode of bottles. Coca-Cola was available to both patients and hospital staff.

The new Navy hospital was in Tamuning, less than a mile from the Coconut Grove. I drove there and found a long row of large, military tents filled with V3s, at least a quarter of a million boxes. The find gave me gold fever. Trembling with excitement, I asked to see the hospital administrator. A lieutenant behind a desk was skeptical. The hospital administrator did not have a scheduled meeting with a scrawny CHamoru teenager. The lieutenant disappeared into another room and returned a few minutes later. "The captain will see you now," he said.

"You wanted to see me?" asked a Navy captain who wore the same quizzical look as the lieutenant.

I introduced myself then launched into my sales pitch. I told him I recognized his growing problem with bottle storage. He nodded. I told him it was a real eyesore. He agreed. I told him I could solve the problem for him. He was interested. I told him I could clear out the tents, get rid of the bottles, and make the hospital grounds presentable again. My initiative and enthusiasm impressed him.

"Okay, son," he said and smiled. "If you're willing to do all that work, the cases are yours. I don't care what you do with them. Just get them out of here."

I was feeling exceptional when I left the captains office. I calculated, tent by tent, all the money I was going to make. V3s filled every tent. There had to be 3,000 or 4,000 cases per tent. And there were at least 50 tents. The thought made me dizzy. I was going to be rich — richer than anyone else in Guam. I spent all my free time emptying the hospital tents. I paid Fred, Rodney, and Donald a nickel for every V3 they loaded. Together, we averaged a tent at a time. Whenever the cardboard wall at Apotguan grew too high, I would redeem 100 or so cases.

We worked quickly and efficiently and had cleared only a few tents, but my sixth sense tingled when a jeep drove up and an officer told me to stop removing the cases. The hospital administrator had revoked my permission. I went to ask why. The administrator said someone from the bottling plant complained that the bottles were government property, and he had no authority to dispose of them. The administrator did not agree, but his superiors did, and he had to comply. I could tell he believed, as I did, that my initiative made someone at the plant envious.

"I'm sorry about this, Ricky," he said. "But let me tell you this: if you can't have those bottles, nobody can. I can ensure that much. Nobody will get them."

I left the hospital disheartened and empty-handed. One of my own relatives betrayed me. I later learned who it was.

The captain kept his word. He did not turn the remaining bottles over to the bottling plant. He had them loaded into trucks, taken to Mongmong, and buried in the Fifth Field trash dump. Word soon spread to other military camps that Coca-Cola bottles were not to be given to civilians. Burdened with so many, the Navy buried huge quantities and dumped thousands more into the ocean. Even now, more than 40 years later, Coca-Cola bottles litter the bottom of Apra Harbor.

Chapter 19

Graduating high school oldsters

When school began again in tents amid the ruins of the old George Washington High School in Hagåtña, uniforms were no longer mandatory. A few months later, the school was moved to a temporary site in Sinajana. Several Quonset huts served as our classrooms. A couple of years after that, the school was moved into the Butler buildings of the old Marine Fifth Field Supply Depot in Mongmong. Construction on a new facility began in the late 1950s, and by the early 1960s, George Washington High School moved into its permanent location in Mangilao.

There were 48 students in my senior class. They elected me class president, but my tenure lasted only six months. I assumed I would serve a full year, like other presidents, but another election took place midway through the school year. I suspect a handful of classmates pressed for it. Ben Perez became the new class president. I was disappointed but did not fight it and stepped down. The class presidency was my first experience with an elected office. I did not know it then, but the unusual circumstances that occurred during my brief tenure set the stage for all my other elections.

I can only guess that I must somehow make running for an elective office highly desirable. I have never run without serious challengers and stiff competition. I have often joked that if I ran for dogcatcher, someone would challenge me. In 1955, I was elected vice president of the Guam Lions Club. By tradition, the vice president rose to become the next president at the end of his term. As an up-and-coming businessman, I looked forward to becoming president, but Gary Fuller, a KUAM disc jockey, broke the tradition and challenged me for the seat. Club elections were an internal proceeding, but in my case, the election became a public battle. With Henry Schnabel as my campaign chairman,

I defeated Fuller and became president in 1956. After my term, the tradition returned; the vice president rose unchallenged to the presidency.

To this day, I do not know what prompted my replacement as senior class president. In the aftermath of the war and our accelerated high school program, our class activities were necessarily different, but I do not think I ever proposed anything unpleasant or difficult. In fact, one of my projects was upbeat. I lobbied among my classmates that, as seniors, we should try to do something lighthearted and entertaining for the underclassmen.

My classmates balked at the idea of staging a musical variety show because we did not have the money for costumes, props, or musical instruments. I solved the problems myself. I enlisted the musicians among the class, borrowed instruments, and put together a funny looking, ragtag group dubbed the "Foofoo Band." Carlos Laguaña and Ben Perez played guitars. Tony Quan played the piano. Another student, whose name I do not recall, played a saxophone. I played drums. The sixth member of the band, Ben Blaz, did not attend George Washington. Ben wanted to become a doctor and was attending special classes at the Naval hospital. He was supposed to graduate with us and thought himself a classmate. Ben wanted a part in the band but did not have a musical instrument or the talent to play one. To accommodate him, I gave him a comb and a piece of tissue paper. With the comb and paper pressed to his lips, Ben squeaked and squawked to our playing.

On the day of the show, when the curtain rose on the Foofoo Band, the student body erupted in laughter. We were a success just standing on stage. When we started to play, the audience roared. The laughter, whistles, and catcalls did not stop until our performance ended. We were a hit, but not because of our talent and repertoire. We had unknowingly provided a release for all the pent-up fears of the occupation. Our schoolmates could at last celebrate peace and the return to normal life. We could laugh again. Life was funny again. We were funny. The band laughed as much as the audience.

I had already decided to pursue a college degree and was thinking about applying to a Jesuit college in the States. A friend of mine, Lt. Smith, tried to talk me out of it. I knew him only as Lt. Smith. He often came to the Coconut Grove, and we became quick friends. Smith took interest in my education and seemed impressed by my ambition. He told me I had good leadership abilities. He invited me to spend a weekend at his barracks to sell me on a career as a military officer. Smith recommended his alma mater, Notre Dame. He wrote to endorse me for acceptance, but I had already applied to the University of San Francisco.

Lt. Smith and I lost track of each other over the years, but I never forgot him. In 1986, at the height of the election campaign and the ruckus over my indictments, my office received a long-distance telephone call from a man who identified himself as Lt. Smith. I was not in the office at the time. Smith told my secretary that we had been friends years ago and that he was traveling to Guam. He said he would try to contact me when he arrived. I was sure he was the Lt. Smith of my high school days and looked forward to his call, but it never came. I do not know whether he decided against calling me or could not reach me. Seeing him and renewing an old friendship would have been pleasant relief from the pressure of my indictment-shadowed reelection bid.

In 1947, as graduation approached, I was no longer class president, but I retained a good deal of influence among my classmates. My successor did not offer our class anything new and exciting, so I stepped up with a novel idea: a picnic at Cocos Island. Most classmates welcomed the plan, but a few, particularly those aligned with the new class president, balked, saying it was far too daring and the school administration would never sanction it. But a boat ride and a day of unchaperoned frolicking was too enticing.

Without the school's permission, we set up a committee that put the plan in motion. The girls enlisted food donations for our picnic, and I arranged for military trucks to take us to Malesso'. Francisco C. Chargualaf, a student from Malesso', secured passage for us on a Coast Guard vessel to Cocos, which lies about 2 miles across the lagoon from Malesso'. I gave Francisco the nickname "Voodoo," which stuck long after we graduated. Voodoo was elected commissioner of Malesso' in 1956 and served until 1976. Before him, another member of our 1947 class, Ignacio M. Reyes, served as commissioner of Malesso' from 1952 to 1956.

Excitement and anticipation mounted as the day of our picnic drew closer. No other graduating class had done anything as imaginative or adventurous. No other class had ever dared such independence or impudence. Jealous of us, the class traitors tried to undermine the plan by ratting us out to our principal, Mrs. Agueda Johnston, Marian's mother, who knew me very well. She did not need spies to tell her the Cocos plan was mine; she already knew I was behind it. On the day before the picnic, Mrs. Johnston summoned me to her office. I stood before her desk and noted her displeasure.

"You've really overstepped your bounds this time, Ricky, and I will not put up with it," she said. "You had better put a stop to this nonsense at once, or I'll be forced to take drastic action. I'm warning you. If you proceed, I'll cancel the graduation ceremony."

Mrs. Johnston was serious. Ours was the second postwar class to graduate. The devastation and unsettled conditions stole the spotlight from the Class of 1946. By the time we were ready, conditions were almost normal, and our graduation ceremony was to have as much pomp and circumstance as Mrs. Johnston could muster. My classmates and I were pleased by the efforts in the works for us and looked forward to the ceremony. But we were not ordinary high school graduates.

"But, Mrs. Johnston, we've grown up. You can't keep treating us like children," I argued. She was adamant. "No ceremony."

Unlike typical high school seniors, we were different; we were three years older than the norm. We were adults completing a process interrupted by the occupation. I could not accept the contradiction that we were adults everywhere except at school. Mrs. Johnston was unreasonable. As word of her ultimatum spread, several students wanted to back out. Others became worried. The class traitors thought they had succeeded and were smug, but I would not accept defeat. I lobbied hard for forging ahead, telling my classmates that exercising our autonomy as adults was more valuable than a ceremonial rite of passage. I managed to convince them that we were old enough and had earned the right to make our own decisions.

Much to Mrs. Johnston's displeasure, the Class of 1947 sailed to Cocos Island. We left Sinajana early that morning and spent a glorious day swimming, exploring, and sharing our picnic lunch. The Coast Guard allowed the girls to use their small galley to prepare our meal. We returned at sunset.

The Coast Guard's Loran station at Cocos was small but well equipped. The station occupied a third of the island. The Rothchild family, who produced and exported copra at the turn of the century, owned the rest. The Guardsmen welcomed our presence, but we stayed out of their way. With two-thirds of the island to ourselves, we had no need to bother the Guardsmen.

Although their romances may have predated the Cocos outing, several serious love affairs resulted. At least three pairs of class sweethearts later got married. John Anderson married Maria Okiyama. My cousin Joaquin Pangelinan married Mariquita Perez. Leonard Paulino married Clotilde Camacho.

Even now, many years later, we tease one another about that day at Cocos. And despite Mrs. Johnston's ultimatum, we graduated with a nice ceremony.

The University of San Francisco accepted my application for enrollment, as well as my classmate and fellow Foofoo bandmember, Tony Quan. I planned to leave Guam right after graduation; Tony would follow later. About a week before my departure, Dad asked me to reconsider going to school. He said college was not promising for me. With Mama gone, Irene married, and Lorraine away at college, he needed me to help with the family and the business. I countered his arguments, saying that Bobbie, who was two years younger than me, was better able to look after the children, and Auntie Rose helped out a lot. Paul, Fred, and Rodney were old enough to take on my work. Dad was unconvinced and unmoved.

"But Dad, if I don't go now, I'll never go," I argued.

Dad frowned and shook his head. I could feel my anger rising until it poured out at him.

"I've spent my whole life working for you, and you've profited very well. It is my turn now. I am going to school. I've earned the right," I said. "I've earned a lot of money for you and the family, but I'm not going to ask you for a penny."

My bankroll surprised him. Despite the 14-hour days I put in for him, I managed to save $2,800 for travel fare and tuition. He demanded to know where and how I got so much money. He had been so busy with business and politics that he paid little attention to me or my independent activities. Our exchange ended on a sour note. He was angry with me for not putting off my college plans, and I was angry with him for asking me. I felt I had earned the right to stand on my own. I resented his wanting to saddle me with his responsibilities.

Dad would not speak to me for days. He knew I was determined to go, but he did not demand my submission to his will. His silence hurt me. I did not want to leave home under such circumstances, but I stuck to my decision. A few days before my departure, Dad surprised me with a farewell party at the Coconut Grove Restaurant. My classmates, teachers, and my entire family were there. Dad even hired a professional band. He told me he still disapproved but wanted to give me a proper sendoff.

"We don't allow Chinese in here"

I would not allow myself the luxury and expense of a new coat. Accustomed only to a tropical climate, I knew I would need one, but cold weather coats were hard to find on an island where no one needed them. Rather than order by mail, I searched the military trash dump and found a heavy Marine trench coat with a bloodstained bullet hole in the chest. I wondered if the original owner died from his wound. The hole was right to the heart. The Marine was about my height and weight; his coat fit me. I managed to wash out the bloodstain, but I left the hole unpatched. At the university, my bullet-holed coat became a conversation piece.

In mid-June 1947, after the State Department approved my application for a security clearance permission to leave Guam, I embarked on the USS *David Shanks*. I paid $150 for passage, a stateroom, and dining privileges in the officers' mess. Auntie Butler's daughter Mae and her husband Milton Champion met me at Pier Seven in San Francisco.

Tony Quan left Guam shortly after I did, but he did not reach San Francisco until two months into the fall semester. Tony's security clearance was in order, but U.S. Immigration officials detained him in Honolulu. They told him the airline should never have sold him a ticket because his father was Chinese. Pan American paid for Tony's stay at Honolulu's Alexander Young Hotel while U.S. Immigration addressed the issue. Tony waited two months before demanding they allow him to proceed to San Francisco or return to Guam. The unsympathetic officials decided to let their California counterparts deal with the problem.

The following year, Bobbie and Paul ran into even worse problems in Honolulu. They were also on their way to college. They were traveling with Uncle Tom's son Rudy, Frank "Junior" Torres, David Flores, and his sister, Nina. Their clearances were in order, but ignorant immigration officials arrested and threw them all in jail like common criminals. The travelers remained jailed and detained until Mrs. Julia Gutierrez Guerrero Pomeroy, a CHamoru longtime resident of Hawai'i, vouched for them.

I had no such problems. My trip from Guam was pleasant. So was my stay with Mae and Milton. I lived with them in Hayward until school opened. Milton was a hard-working, hard-playing man. He made good money buying old houses, which he renovated or repaired and sold at handsome profits. He did much of the construction work himself. I often went with him and spent hours working at his side. At the end of the day, we would unwind by hopping bars and dancing until dawn. I quickly learned to enjoy Milton's brand of relaxation. Whenever he was ready for a night on the town, I was too.

We usually went to a taxi dance hall called the Rose Room in downtown Oakland. With more than 20 10-cent tickets, we would dance with pretty girls. I had never danced with white women, and I savored the occasions. Some of the women were the most beautiful I had ever seen. Milton, who shared my appreciation for pretty faces, was amused by my obvious delight. White people filled the dance hall. I was the only patron with dark skin and was well aware of it but not uncomfortable. I received a few odd looks but perhaps because I was with Milton, the manager never barred me admittance nor did any women reject me as a dance partner.

The same was not true for Ben Blaz. Ben enrolled at Notre Dame and stopped in California on his way to school. With great enthusiasm, I told him about dancing with beautiful women at the Rose Room. Like me, Ben was eager for the experience. Milton agreed to take us out on the town before Ben left for Indiana. We went one evening. A bouncer at the Rose Room door recognized Milton and waved us in, but he stopped Ben.

"We don't allow Chinese in here," he said. Milton tried to reason with him, but the bouncer was adamant.

I could not understand why I was acceptable, but Ben was not. We were familiar with racial discrimination; our people were long-time victims of it but not with its confusing degrees of tolerance. Ben had almond eyes and light skin. People back home considered him handsome. Among CHamorus, children with light complexions were beautiful; those with dark skin were objects of sympathy. Light-skinned boys like Ben and To' Martinez were the ones picked to be pageboys for coronation pageants. I was the kind who never stood a chance. Despite my family's prominence, I was too dark for picture-perfect public ceremonies. Ben knew that. He would not have been surprised if I were the one stopped at the door. As conceited as Ben was about his good looks, he would have expected it. He was always trying to show me up. Milton and I witnessed a blow to his ego, and I was embarrassed for him.

We did not go into the Rose Room that night, but we were determined to have a good time. We put the ugly incident behind us and went elsewhere. Milton was an excellent guide to American nightlife.

A few weeks later, I discovered another confusing aspect of racial discrimination and segregation. Armed with a healthy wallet, I set out alone to
explore San Francisco. I wanted to see and experience everything the city had
to offer. I was eager to taste American life and was willing and able to pay
to do so. After wandering along busy, crowded streets, I walked into a posh
restaurant on Market Street, hungry for an expensive meal in a fancy eatery.

The restaurant was indeed grand, far more sophisticated than any in
Guam and ritzier than the Coconut Grove. Well-dressed diners filled the dining room. Smiling waiters and waitresses escorted incoming patrons to vacant
tables. I should have known something was amiss when no one rushed to welcome me. I was still naive about such things. I decided the staff was too busy
to attend to me, so I made my way to an empty table at the back of the room.
The strange looks people gave me as I passed them went over my head. I figured none of them had ever seen a CHamoru before.

I seated myself and watched the other people while I waited for a waitress. Many were watching me. I was as much a curiosity to them as they were
to me. Still thinking the staff were busy, I waited patiently, but no waitress
came. I watched as several customers came in, sat down, placed their orders,
ate their meals, paid their checks, and left. Entertained by the parade of American life around me, I waited more than an hour, but no waitress came to my
table. No one even gave me a menu. I wondered how such a fancy restaurant
survived with such lousy service. After another half hour, I signaled a waitress.

"I've been waiting quite a while," I said, not hiding my irritation. "Some
people who came in after me have already been served."

The waitress gave me an odd look then walked away without a word. I
waited for another half hour. At tables all around me, patrons ate their meals
and left. New ones replaced them, and they ate and left. Waiters with upturned noses ignored me as they whizzed by my table. It took a while for me
to realize I was not welcome. No one was going to serve me. There was no sign
saying, "Whites Only," but I finally got the message. I would have preferred
someone asking me to leave rather than letting me wait like an idiot. The staff
and the diners knew the rules of the game; I did not. Humiliated, I walked out
like a dog with its tail between its legs. I was too naive and idealistic to think
racial discrimination occurred only in Guam and not in America.

The America of my imagination was perfect. It was the homeland of
freedom, liberty, and equality for all, blind to the differences of race, color,

or creed. I believed my school lessons about America's greatness and her un-yielding adherence to upright justice. I had been eager to experience America's greatness and to be among perfect Americans. But when I came to the fabled Land of the Free, I discovered it shackled by the same intolerance and bigotry as at home.

The gas chamber at San Quentin

I registered for school and took a room at a boarding house at 1908 Golden Gate Avenue, a few blocks from the USF campus. My landlady was Mrs. Catherine Boling, who advertised her boarding house in the university bulletin. She charged $15 a month for a room. Boarders shared the bathroom and kitchen. We each had reserved cupboard space and prepared our own meals. I could afford a more luxurious apartment but was frugal by choice.

When I told Mrs. Boling I was from Guam, she asked if I had driven down. She thought it was somewhere in Alaska. I chuckled and said I came by ship after a two-week voyage. She then asked if Guam was in the Philippines. I explained that it was a small island between the Philippines and Hawai'i. Mrs. Boling was curious about Guam and asked hundreds of questions. I was enthusiastic about answering them, and we became quick friends.

Mrs. Boling was warm and hospitable to all her boarders. There were about a dozen of us. I lived at Mrs. Boling's for eight months and ate ground beef almost every day because it was cheap. She took note of my monotonous menu and asked me about it. She even offered to prepare something different for me. Touched by her concern, I assured her I was satisfied.

Mrs. Boling's son Al and his wife Ruth were as nice and friendly as Mrs. Boling. They lived in the house as well. Al was an avid collector of phonograph records. He boasted that he owned almost every record album ever produced. I had no reason to doubt him. His collection, which numbered in the thousands, was worth a fortune.

A friend of the Bolings, and a frequent visitor at the boarding house, was a guard at San Quentin prison. I do not recall his name. Whenever he came to visit, I peppered him with questions about the famous prison. He said he could secure permission and make arrangements for me to visit. I jumped at the chance. A tour of San Quentin would have been interesting and educational. I was taking a psychology course at the time and had a term paper due before the end of the semester. I had not yet chosen a topic. With the paper due and a prison tour available, I figured I could use one for the other. A few days later, the guard called to say I got a tour, and someone would meet me at the main gate at 9 o'clock.

On the day of my tour, I got up early and took a bus to San Quentin. When I arrived, a small party was waiting for me, including Warden Clinton Duffy, who was well known for his prison reforms and featured in *Reader's Digest* and other magazines. He was well known even in Guam. He was supposed to have been born and raised at San Quentin. No one knew the prison better than he. I was surprised and impressed that he would take personal interest in a college freshman's curiosity. Warden Duffy led the way through the prison gates.

After an introductory briefing, a guide escorted me to the inmate processing center. He introduced me to the processing supervisor who stunned me by saying, "From Guam, eh? One of your people just checked in." My mind raced; who from home would get to San Quentin? I could not imagine any CHamoru committing crimes punishable by federal imprisonment. Such news would have sped through the *tilifon alaihai*, which even spanned the Pacific. I hid my alarm and asked who it was. The supervisor answered with an unfamiliar Anglo name. The new guy was likely someone who came to Guam in the wake of the military. Some were fugitives who thought they could hide out on a remote island. Officials caught many but not all. Relieved, I told my hosts their new inmate was not CHamoru. I was glad to leave the processing center and continue the tour.

We went through the cellblocks, the recreation yard, the guard towers, and the work areas. There were armed guards at every turn. The murmur of voices and the clang of heavy iron doors echoed in long, empty corridors. Everything about the place was cold, stark, and unnerving.

The gas chamber was the last stop on the tour and the most chilling. It stood in the center of a large room. A gallery of tiered stands that looked like stadium bleachers faced it. The chamber itself was a small, oddly shaped cylinder with observation windows all around and a small chair inside in the center. A guard opened the chamber door and invited me to examine the interior. I stepped inside and only half-listened as the guard explained the chamber's features and functions. His voice sounded strange and hallow. It was like being in a tomb. He pointed to a canister attached to the wall near where the condemned man's face would be. It would contain a liquid into which the chemical tablets would drop, start a reaction, and release the gas.

I tried to concentrate on the guard's explanation but could not escape the morbid discomfort of sitting inside a killing machine. I wondered about the men who died there. What were their thoughts? How did they feel? The thoughts made me shiver. As we left the chamber room and headed for the cafeteria, I decided the theme for my psychology paper would be the emotional state of a condemned man. Over lunch, I discussed my theme idea with the warden. He listened and did not balk when I asked to watch an execution.

A few days later, I received word that an execution was to take place in 10 days, and my request to witness it was granted. On the day of the execution, I arrived at San Quentin's gate at 4:30 in the morning. Although I was an unwilling witness to pain and death during the occupation and not keen to see more, this was different. It had an educational purpose. I wanted to be an objective observer, to concentrate on the state of mind of a man facing imminent death. I tried not to think about the condemned man, but my heart was pounding in my chest.

A guard met me at the prison gates and escorted me to the gas chamber room. Half a dozen people were already there, standing on the bleachers. Some were from the press; others were prison officials. Only two were relatives of the condemned man. All were quiet as we waited. A few minutes later, a door opened, but no one emerged. We could hear a minister's murmuring prayers and people whispering beyond the doorway but could not see anyone. Seconds later, the minister's prayers ceased, but the whispering continued. Then the door closed. After several more minutes, guards led all of us from the room. The governor granted a last-minute reprieve and stayed the execution. I was not disappointed.

I returned for another execution, but the governor again granted a stay. I declined a third opportunity. The second stay of execution was a message from Fate; I was not to see another's death, despite my academic interest. I gave up the idea of watching a man die and wrote on another topic. Living was more important than watching life end. From then on, I immersed myself in anything and everything that added to the quality of my life. I wanted to soak it up and make sure I made up for everything the war caused me to miss.

"You are here to learn a way of life"

The University of San Francisco considered me a foreign student, which gave me preference for a dormitory room. When one became available, I moved from Mrs. Boling's boarding house. Foreign student status annoyed me. My education was entirely American. I thought of myself as an American, but everyone else considered me a foreigner. I was a U.S. National, a ward of the United States. Foreign student status made me feel like an alien. But USF's president made me feel better about being a non-white, non-American among upper crust white Americans. In his address at our freshman orientation, he said, "You are not here to learn how to earn a living. You are here to learn a way of life." The philosophy complemented mine.

I looked forward to studying under the Jesuits, the intellectuals of the Roman Catholic Church. I signed up for more than the usual class load and never carried less than 22 credit hours per semester. Since Army ROTC was mandatory for first- and second-year students, I went with my freshmen class to the Presidio to receive Army uniforms. I also signed up for glee club and band, although I could not read music.

Ricky in his ROTC uniform at the University of San Francisco.

I bluffed my way into the USF band, saying I played trap drums, but I never had formal training. I played by ear. The first time the band instructor distributed sheet music, I broke into a cold sweat. I had no idea how to read it or when to strike my drums. I often pretended to be playing. Then I watched and memorized the other drummers' strokes. In time, I played well enough to blend into the band, but my playing was always a little different. The other drummers masked my mistakes and looked at me funny whenever I went off on my own. My playing rarely matched the sheet music.

During the football season and before every game, the band would march from the campus to Kezar Stadium in the Golden Gate Park. Kezar was home ground for the USF Dons, whose colors were green and gold. Our band uniforms were even splashier. We wore green and gold jackets, tight-fitting black trousers, and broad-brimmed Spanish hats edged with dangling ball tassels.

My love of singing was why I signed up for glee club. Fortunately, we did not have to read sheet music to sing. Our instructor, Art McCue, taught at USF during the day, and with his three-piece combo, played the Fairmont Hotel's Cirque Room in the evenings.

Father Willis Egan, whose brother Richard became a famous movie actor, was my speech instructor. I excelled in his class and made straight A's. I could hold my classmates spellbound every time I took the podium. No matter what topic Father Egan assigned, I could relate some personal incident or experience to it. If it was about the war, I talked about the occupation of Guam, our treatment as enslaved people, and the bloody battle to recapture Guam. If it was aviation, I talked about being present when Pan American Airlines landed in Guam during its historic transpacific flights in 1935 and '36. I could speak about Navy Grummands, Marine Corsairs, P38s, and Japanese Mitsubishi Zeroes dogfighting above my head. I could speak from experience about the fabled B-29 "Super Fortresses" and their crews. Whether business, politics, religion, or philosophy, I could speak extemporaneously with ease. Father Egan once told me my life experiences were those of a 60-year-old. I was only 20.

I was the only student at USF who owned a wire recorder. It was like the one a journalist used to record Mama singing. The machine was so captivating that I promised to get one someday. And so, I did, soon after I arrived in the States. Alone in my room, I made recordings of my own voice and pretended to be a radio announcer, just for fun. When other students in the dorm learned that I had one, they gathered in my room for a turn with the microphone. I also bought myself a Rolleiflex camera and took hundreds of photos. It reminded me of Mama and her ever-present camera.

Accounting and business law were my majors, but theology was my favorite subject. I took every opportunity to engage in debates with Father Brolan, one of my theology professors. I once argued with him over the theory of the First Cause. I could not accept his complicated explanation. After I refused to yield to his points, an exasperated Father Brolan told me to rely on faith. He said it was the answer to unanswerable questions.

"Sometimes all we can do is rely on faith," he said.

I also argued with him about equality in heaven. "Father, something is bothering me," I said in class one day.

"Something is always bothering you, Ricky. What is it this time?" Father Brolan asked with a heavy sigh.

"If I make it to heaven, it'll be by the skin of my teeth," I said. The comment sent a chuckle throughout the class. Many shared the notion. But I was serious about exploring the question. Was there equality in heaven? I was not receiving it on earth, why should I expect it in heaven? It seemed unlikely to exist there either.

"Take the saints," I continued. "They won't have any problems. They are bound to get space close to God. Then there are the angels, God's messengers and assistants. They're a notch higher than the saints. The angels and the saints are going to be closest to God, while guys like me must sit at the back. How can you consider that equal?"

Father Brolan's explanation opened my eyes to a perspective that remains one of my deeply held beliefs. He said take two glasses, one small and one large. Fill each to the brim with water. Study the glasses. Note that each is filled to capacity.

"Neither glass can hold any more, correct?" Father Brolan said. "It's the same with men's souls. Some are bigger, and some are smaller. There is no way and no reason for the smaller to envy the larger or vice versa. No soul can be satisfied beyond its capacity. No matter its size, only the soul that is filled with goodness gains heaven."

I took the university president's message about "learning a way of life" to heart. I enjoyed most of my classes for the intellectual stimulation they provided and for the knowledge I acquired. Unlike my schoolmates who only worried about their grades, I wanted to learn, not just pass tests. The issue was the greater value of substance over form, another of my cherished beliefs. The university operated under an honor system that some did not observe. As soon as a professor left the room, students taking a test would start cheating. I could not. Honor was worth more to me than an undeserved good grade. Tests were supposed to measure the knowledge one had acquired. Falsifying the measurement for a high score was opportunity wasted. My grades fluctuated, depending on how well I had studied and how much I had learned.

Braving the unknown: dashing across America

Between classes, and in my free time, I went shopping for products not available at home, like household cleaning supplies and personal sundries, which I bought by the case wholesale. I would ship the merchandise home to my brothers and sisters, who sold it for me at five to 10 times the California retail price. Guam was a wide-open market right after the war, a seller's paradise. Most necessities were available, but luxury items were scarce. I made a $500 profit on bobby pins alone. I bought ironing boards, ladies' slips, saddle shoes, air rifles, and anything else my sellers recommended. I did not worry about earning a living; I was doing it.

I spent almost as much time developing business contacts, nurturing my long-distance business, and satisfying my curiosity and hunger for new experiences as I did in my classes. I also parlayed my original savings into a sizeable bankroll. Along with the profits from my reselling business, I was still earning money from the Coca Cola bottles, which Paul and Fred managed for me. Whenever I needed extra cash, they would redeem a few hundred cases and send me the money.

On one of his business trips, Dad left me a car. I was one of the few students at USF who had one. Dad, who was still the Nash distributor in Guam, bought a new Nash Ambassador from the factory in Wisconsin in 1948. He drove it from Kenosha to San Francisco and left it with me until I could arrange its shipment to Guam. The 1948 Nash Ambassadors had reclining front seats, a new feature promoted in its advertising. People joked about Ambassadors being bedrooms on wheels. Ambassadors were "The Car" to have on a date. I was the envy of the campus for having one but also took a lot of ribbing from my professors and pleading requests from schoolmates to borrow it.

With a car at my disposal, I set out to see as much of the country as I could. I drove all over the state, exploring all the highways and side roads and towns in between. I drove to Reno and Lake Tahoe in Nevada and as far south as Tijuana, Mexico. Over the six-day Easter break in 1948, I embarked with Roy Benito, Tony Quan, and George Michaels on a coast-to-coast trip. We took turns at the wheel and drove around the clock. Like me, Roy and Tony were new to the United States. We had never gone across the country. George, who went on to become a nuclear physicist in Livermore, came with us because he wanted to visit his folks in Buffalo, New York. We hit a blizzard in Wyoming, saw the lights of Chicago, and marveled at Niagara Falls. We went to Philadelphia, toured Independence Hall, and looked at the Liberty Bell. We visited George's family in Buffalo and called on Mrs. Faley in Passaic, New Jersey. Mrs. Faley was a Navy commander's wife who taught American History at George Washington High School. Tony and I had been her students.

We arrived in New York City in time for the Easter parade. I was at the wheel at the time and got us lost. I took a wrong turn onto Fifth Avenue, which was blocked for the parade. A policeman stopped and ordered us to turn around. I apologized and explained that I was from Guam and was unfamiliar with city driving. The policeman was probably a veteran; he recognized Guam and waved us through. With huge crowds on both sides of the street, we drove down Fifth Avenue to the Pan Am building as though we were part of the parade.

On our return, we drove into Washington, D.C., and visited the Lincoln Memorial, the Jefferson Memorial, and Arlington National Cemetery. We climbed to the top of the Washington Monument and saw the Spirit of St. Louis at the Smithsonian Institute. We drove past the Capitol and the White House. It was a whirlwind tour, but I wanted to be able to say I saw all the landmarks. From Washington, we headed south, crossed the Mississippi River, and drove through the deserts of Texas and New Mexico, seeing dozens of small towns along the way. Then we went to Los Angeles and made it back to San Francisco in time for the start of classes.

All my professors in all my classes considered my cross-country marathon a foolhardy and unpleasant undertaking. Many classmates agreed. Their dubious reactions made me realize how differently we perceived things. What to them was a miserable undertaking was to me a grand adventure and a unique experience. I would never have characterized it as miserable. The passing scenery through the windshield and windows was like watching a real-life movie. I saw so many wonderful things, like real Texas badlands, "painted" deserts, saguaro cacti, sagebrush, and tumbleweeds — everything that appeared in cowboy movies — in living color. It was fantastic.

Geography has always fascinated me. No matter where I have traveled, I have left the beaten path for better views. Unfortunately, the generation after mine seems to know little about world geography. In 1985, as one of eight American governors invited to attend a NATO briefing in Brussels, Belgium, I had to convince the young, college-educated staffers with me that a drive to Paris was possible. My chief of staff John Whitt, my legal assistant Lisa Castro, and my tax director Dave Santos were with Madeleine and me. John was one of the first Guamanians to graduate from the Air Force Academy and was a B52 pilot before joining my staff. Dave was a graduate of Regis College in Denver, and Lisa was a Guam Bar attorney with a California law degree. Also with us were Frank "Junior" Torres, who was by then a retired Army colonel. I nominated him, and President Reagan appointed him as adjutant general of the Guam National Guard. Frank's information officer was along to videotape the Brussels trip for the Guam National Guard.

I wanted to take full advantage of the Europe trip and do some good, old-fashioned exploring. Madeleine and I were seasoned travelers and had been to Europe many times, but it was the first for my staff. I wanted them to enjoy it, to taste life as I had, to venture into the unknown, and to learn things along the way. I talked about renting a van and setting out on our own, following the highways until we reached Paris. My staffers tried to dissuade me. Despite their intelligence and education, they did not think it wise to drive from Brussels to Paris and return unscathed. Accustomed to my impulsiveness, Madeleine was ready to go.

"You know, for smart people, you're pretty dumb," I chided them. "You make Paris sound like it's 10 continents away. We can do it, I tell you."

To prove my point, I made the arrangements myself. Much to John's discomfort and disapproval, I hired an air-conditioned minibus and a driver. John, Dave, and Lisa remained skeptical and hesitant. I practically had to order them along. We climbed aboard the minibus, and to the strains of a guitar Dave bought, we sang all the way to Paris. We stopped at a family restaurant in a small town halfway to Paris and enjoyed some of the most delicious, uncommercialized, authentic French provincial cuisine Madeleine and I had ever had.

We whizzed through Paris, climbed the Eiffel Tower, visited the Palace of Versailles, saw the Arc de Triomphe, and dashed back to Brussels in time for my next briefing. The quick side trip left my staffers reeling with delight, as I knew it would. I got as much pleasure from their reactions as I did from the trip. I wondered about their college years and whether they did any of the exciting and foolish things my schoolmates and I did.

Perhaps because I survived the occupation and the war, I needed to catch up on life. I wanted to take part in everything USF had to offer, sometimes with a brashness not tempered with wisdom but luck. With nothing more than school team fighting spirit, I organized and coached a volleyball team for USF to compete in an intercollegiate tournament. The university had formidable basketball and football teams but no volleyball team. After making the suggestion to organize one, I ended up with the task, even though I had no experience or know-how.

With a ragtag team of enthusiasts, we began practicing. We knew we were up against more seasoned, polished teams and had no delusions of winning, but we worked hard to make a decent showing for USF. We played our first game at the College of the Pacific gymnasium in Stockton. We concentrated so much on our game that we forgot about team uniforms. While the other college teams wore handsome athletic uniforms in their school colors, we showed up in a hodgepodge of shirts, shorts, and sneakers, but we survived the season. The USF volleyball Dons finished in second place.

When USF's basketball team won the National Invitational Tournament in New York in 1949, USF students rallied on campus, motored down Market Street, stopped traffic, and marched up the steps of city hall, whooping, chanting, and demanding to see the mayor of San Francisco. It was my first experience with a mass demonstration. The exuberance and excitement were unforgettable. We chanted until the mayor appeared to offer his congratulations. The Jesuits, equally proud of the USF victory, canceled classes that day. The whole city celebrated with us. USF basketball coach, Pete Newell, and basketball favorites Don Loffgran and Rene Hereras were making names for themselves and the school. In football, the Dons coach Joe Kuharich and quarterback Ollie Matson were doing the same. Coach Kuharich went on to coach for the Navy. Matson, an incredibly fast runner who lived in my dorm, went on to the Chicago Bears. He received many athletic scholarships before choosing the University of San Francisco. As minority students, we understood our stations but never discussed them, despite several opportunities. Matson did not have a car. Whenever he needed transportation, he hitched rides with me.

I had been a driver since the age of 8, but I never had an accident until I was a grown man. After shipping the Nash Ambassador home to Dad, I bought myself a black 1932 Ford coupe. I was driving on the Oakland Bay Bridge at rush hour traffic when a bridge tow truck sideswiped my car and clipped in front of me. The damage to our vehicles made the fault appear to be mine, which led the truck driver to think he could escape a traffic citation. He pulled over, inspected the damage, and began shouting at me. I shouted back. We hollered at each other while traffic in both directions came to a stop. I demanded the bridge supervisor settle the dispute. The supervisor decided in my favor.

Chapter 20

"Maybe it was some kind of reminder"

In the summer of 1948, at the end of my first year at the University of San Francisco, I went home for vacation. Doing so meant going to the 12th Naval District to apply for clearance to reenter Guam. President Roosevelt mandated the requirement in 1941, and the Navy continued it for years after the war. The application process was demeaning and seemed unnecessary. Not all applications received approval. We could not understand the need for clearances. The war was over, and the Navy's fleet headquarters was in Hawai'i. The requirement made Guam seem like an ultra-secret installation, dangerous and inhospitable to all, including its natives. I had no trouble getting a clearance, but I resented having to do so.

I made my first airplane trip that summer. I thought I would always remember the name of the Clipper that brought me from San Francisco to Guam, but it escapes me now. Each Pan Am Clipper bore its name on the fuselage just below the pilot's window. Flying was still a new, expensive, and exclusive way to travel. Passengers received first-class service, especially on long, transpacific flights. To pass the time, I played cards with a couple of nieces of China's Chiang Kai-shek[17] who were also on their way home from college. I suppose they were back in school when the Nationalist government fell the following year.

Home looked the way it did before I left. War wreckage was still evident. Some of Hagåtña's streets were clear, but rubble filled entire blocks. Although a few residents had returned, the city remained almost deserted. The sight

---

17 Chiang Kai-shek was a Chinese politician, military leader, and revolutionary of the Republic of China in Taiwan following the Chinese Civil War in 1949.

was disheartening. Having just come from the great, bustling city of San Francisco, I could not help making comparisons. My hometown would never have been as large or as grand, but it could have been as vibrant and alive if it had been rebuilt. Hagåtña was wasting away, and authorities did not seem to care. Without the resources or a say in the matter, CHamorus, especially those who lost parts of their properties, could do nothing.

The Navy government was back in control, but it abandoned the Governor's Palace as the seat of government. The damaged building was razed, and only secondary government offices were housed in scattered Quonset huts in the old compound. The Quonset huts made Hagåtña look like a military base, as seemed intended, and not like a civilian settlement. There was no effort to restore the city's sense of history and tradition. I often wondered why the U.S. military did not "rehabilitate" Tokyo the same way. The Japanese would have gotten Quonset huts in place of their Imperial Palace.

The Navy's new headquarters was in Tutuhan along the cliffs above Hagåtña. Hundreds of Quonset huts set row upon row lined the ridge all the way to Aniguak. An airfield for light planes lay further inland. Years later, the area became the site of the new Naval hospital, and the airstrip became part of Route 7.

Curious about the progress of the new Guam Congress building, I went to the construction site in front of the Cathedral. Dad and Jake Calvo, who kept their seats as chairmen of the House of Council and House of Assembly, respectively, were present for the laying of the cornerstone in 1947. The first postwar elections were held in July 1946, but since the old congress building on the seaside of Aniguak had been destroyed, the first postwar congress convened in Quonset huts on the razed site of the Leary School, which was never reestablished.

The family had settled in nicely at the Coconut Grove in Tamuning. Our quarters looked more like a home and less like a military galley, but it was growing steadily emptier. Lorraine and I were already in college and no longer at home. Irene and Jimmy lived in Hagåtña. Bobbie and Paul graduated from high school that spring and were following me to the States. Bobbie was enrolled at Holy Names College in Oakland and Paul at St. Mary's, Dad's alma mater. By summer's end only nine children were left with Dad and Auntie Rose. Coming home to the business was unnerving. Dad and Uncle Tom had incorporated their respective enterprises as Bordallo Consolidated, and the Coconut Grove was its headquarters.

The compound ceased looking like a military encampment. No longer was everything painted gray or drab green. It had grown into a busy commercial center peopled with many more employees who were strangers to me. Everything seemed businesslike and impersonal. I had hoped to sell my California merchandise out of the Coconut Grove department store so that I could continue financing my own education and travel fare, but I got the impression my independent enterprise was unwelcome. Rather than throw my weight around, I peddled my wares by word of mouth within the compound.

Having just completed a course on the formation of business corporations, I was curious about how Dad and Uncle Tom had executed theirs. I learned to my dismay that Dad had done exactly what our textbook warned against: he tendered his lease on the Coconut Grove and his franchises on Willys Overland, International Harvester, Nash Lafayette, Goodyear Tires, and Willard Batteries to the business. Uncle Tom, who offered his inventories of merchandise, benefited with the lion's share of the stock and controlling interest. Dad got the short end of the stick.

One afternoon, as Fred drove away from the compound in Dad's car, I noticed the license plate. It read "2." I assumed Governor Pownall's vehicle bore the "1" plate. As chairman of the Guam Congress' upper house, Dad was the island's highest-ranking civilian, which entitled him to token acknowledgment as Guam's No. 2 man. Although he and his fellow congress members were popularly elected, they had no power to legislate. They continued to serve merely as advisers to the governor and could do nothing without his approval. Like his office as chairman of the House of Council, Dad's No. 2 license plate was just for show, although he did enjoy a few official courtesies. There was one he wished he had declined. At Pownall's request, Dad witnessed an execution.

"Why, Dad?" I asked. We had seen too much suffering and death. Why would Pownall ask him to see more?

"I don't know," he said. "The governor specifically requested my presence. The reason was never explained, but since it was an official request, I went."

The rape and murder of an American woman in Guam had made news in San Francisco. So had the subsequent arrest of four suspects. I had read about the murder and the arrests while I was at school and had followed the story to its end. The victim, a Mrs. Farnum, had been the owner of a gift shop concession at the Air Force post exchange in Yigo. Her killers were four Black soldiers, who were court-martialed, convicted, and sentenced to death by hanging. I read about the hangings but did not know Dad had witnessed them.

Dad's involvement was puzzling. Although he was the highest-ranking civilian, he was not an American. As far as Guamanians were concerned, the affair was an American problem. Prior to the war, the Americans kept their internal problems to themselves. We were never involved. Dad never knew why his presence was necessary. He was free to draw his own conclusions.

"Maybe it was some kind of reminder," he said. "Maybe they wanted me to see how justice was served, not just among themselves, but for all of us if we step out of line."

The implication was disturbing. It was the same indirect intimidation the Japanese used to control us.

A one-man welcoming committee

Before returning to San Francisco, I called on Nanan Chong in Agaña Heights. Among my grandaunts, she was one of my favorites. As is our custom, I went to say goodbye and to receive her blessing for a safe trip. Nanan Chong was a stern woman, a matriarch and ruler of her household, but she was also a gentle, soft-hearted, and emotional soul, not afraid to show her feelings. She cried when I said goodbye the year before, and she cried as though we would never see each other again. With tears streaming from her eyes, Nanan Chong stuffed a few dollars in my hand — *chenchule'* for my trip — and told me she would pray for my safety on the long journey, for my success in school, for my protection in a strange land, and most of all, for my return. Like a mother, she warned me to look after myself, to study hard, and to stay away from dangerous situations. She also asked me to look up her son, Francisco, who was in the Navy in California.

"Of course, I will, Nanan Chong. What's his address?" I asked.

"Oh, Ricky, when you get to California, just ask around in the neighborhood. They'll know where he is," she said.

I laughed and threw my arms around her. She had no idea of the immensity of the United States or of California. In her mind, every place was like Guam: small, close-knit and friendly, a place without strangers and where no one could get lost. Just knock at any door and ask for help. Someone would help, no matter what the problem. I pictured myself knocking on some stranger's door in Alameda, asking for Francisco Cruz, and having the door slammed in my face. Nanan Chong could not imagine such treatment. She made her first and only trip to the States in the late '60s. "It's too big, too cold," was her reaction. She died in February 1976, during my first term as governor.

I boarded another Pan Am Clipper for the return trip to the States. Enroute to Honolulu, the plane stopped at Wake Island and Midway Atoll, yet despite the stopovers, travel time to Honolulu was a swift 15 hours. I reached Honolulu well before the Navy transport, the USS *Mitchell*, arrived from Guam. I waited for the ship because my sweetheart, Isabel "Belle" Perez, was on board.

As had happened to me, the Navy government recorded Belle's first name as Elizabeth on her birth certificate. She never bothered to get it corrected. Legally, she is "Elizabeth," but everyone calls her Belle. She was very pretty and bright, the salutatorian of her class. I had been courting her since high school. By 1948, our relationship was serious, but I encouraged her to go to college and to put off making commitments to each other until we finished school. Belle was enrolled at Rosemont College in Philadelphia. Concerned for her welfare, and because she was making her first trip from home, I saw Belle off at dockside in Guam and greeted her at dockside in Honolulu.

While on board the *Mitchell*, I met Mr. Christian Zeien, who was on his way to Guam to become the new principal of George Washington High School. Mr. Zeien replaced Norbert Tabery, a stern Naval officer who ran the school like a ship. Students feared him. Mr. Zeien had heard there were Guamanians on the ship and had come to meet some. He seemed enthusiastic about his position and plied me with questions about the people, the language, the culture, and the students of Guam. He talked about his family and how they would join him from Minnesota as soon as he was settled. From his wallet, he took out pictures of his wife, Evelyn, and his children, Madeleine, Diana, and Jimmy. I paid only courteous attention to the pictures, little realizing that one of the girls in them was my future bride.

Belle and I were not destined for each other, but we have remained friends. Belle eventually became a dynamic Democrat senator in the Guam Legislature and one of my staunchest political supporters. We were still sweethearts when we parted company in Hawai'i. We hooked up again in San Francisco a few days later. Belle stayed for a couple of days, and I showed her the sights of the city. With a promise to visit her as often as I could, I put her on a train to Philadelphia. At Christmastime, I joined her in New York where she was visiting her uncle, Manuel Perez, for the holidays.

Belle and I took in the Big Apple and spent a day at Coney Island, which was then an incredible amusement park. For us, it was gigantic and crowded with people. The raucous enthusiasm of the barkers and vendors added special flavor. The color, the sounds, and the excitement swept us up right away. The parachute ride was new then. I talked Belle into riding it with me. We rose at least 250 feet into the sky, and parachutes opened and brought us to the ground. The view, the rush of wind, and the descent were exhilarating. We had a thrilling, wonderful time.

Filled with nostalgia, I took Madeleine to Coney Island in 1985. I wanted to show Madeleine just as wonderful a time, but my heart sank when I saw the place. The conditions of the fairgrounds were appalling. The place was unkempt and filthy. Its color and magic were gone. Even the fairgoers seemed listless and disappointed. The dilapidated parachute ride was a rusty hulk, its tower stark and ugly against the sky. Coney Island, the once proud and majestic wonderland, had degenerated into a neglected, third-rate carnival.

"You know, Madeleine, it wasn't always like this," I said, embarrassed that I had brought her to such a filthy place. I had so wanted her to enjoy the excitement of Coney Island, but it was not there anymore.

As a college student, I crossed the country many times. I enjoyed cruising the highways and byways and learning much about the land and the people. When I could talk family members out of going by plane or train and driving instead, I would promise a more exciting trip. I would do most of the driving, but I did not mind. Whenever family or friends came to San Francisco, I became a one-man welcoming committee, volunteering to drive them around and show them the town. After one such tour, I had one of the most embarrassing experiences of my life. A close family friend, someone I grew up with, stopped in San Francisco. She was on her way to enter a convent and attend school in the East Coast. I picked her up with some of her relatives and gave them a tour of the city. I was to drop them off at the home of another relative afterward.

When we arrived at the relative's home, I opened the car door to let them out and froze in horror. Blood stained the back of my dear friend's skirt. CHamoru women kept such feminine matters secret. Unless married, most men knew little about the monthly "sickness," as it was called then, even if they grew up in a house full of sisters. If revealed to her by a male, an accident could send a woman into humiliated seclusion. Horrified, I did not know whether to tell her and humiliate her or say nothing and pretend not to notice. I chose the latter. I bid her and her relatives a cheerful goodbye and drove away as though nothing was wrong. Many years have passed since then, but I still cringe at the memory.

Most of my one-man welcoming receptions were pleasant. Some were even profitable. I looked forward to Uncle Tom's visits. He and Auntie Chong came to San Francisco once or twice a year for business and vacation. I was their chauffeur. Uncle Tom would give me money for gasoline, plus an extra $20 or $30 for myself. By then, he was a wealthy Guam businessman. On one of his visits, he bought a new Oldsmobile to ship home. I got to drive the new car until the end of his stay.

Like Dad, Uncle Tom was flamboyant. He reveled in luxury and high living. He and Auntie Chong always stayed at the best hotels and ate at the finest restaurants. As his nephew and driver, I enjoyed many extravagant meals at posh places. The first time I ever ate crepes suzette was at an elaborate breakfast with him at the St. Francis Hotel. Uncle Tom would give Auntie Chong as much as $1,000 to go shopping while he conducted business. At the end of the day, we would meet her at a prearranged spot and load up her purchases.

During Christmas vacation in 1949, Uncle Tom decided to drive to New York City. Lorraine, who was attending Holy Names in Oakland, went with us. We took a southerly course across the country to avoid as much cold weather as possible. I did most of the driving.

New York City was in the midst of a blizzard, one of the city's worst. Traffic was at a standstill. Uncle Tom wanted to check into the Waldorf Astoria, but it was fully booked with stranded travelers. He checked us into the Jefferson Hotel near Central Park instead. Since Uncle Tom could do little in the way of business, we went to as many Broadway shows as we could get in to see, discovering in the process how difficult it was to get tickets to the most popular ones. We were amazed to learn that tickets to certain shows sold out years in advance. I saw the Rockettes for the first time at the Rockefeller Music Hall and watched *South Pacific*.

We grew concerned as the days ticked by with no letup in the weather. Our Christmas vacation was running out, and Lorraine and I had to get back to school. Uncle Tom put us on a pullman coach at Grand Central Station and shipped the car as well. He and Auntie Chong stayed in New York to wait out the snowstorm while Lorraine and I chugged back to San Francisco in grand style.

"That's the kind of leader I'd like to be"

When singer Bing Crosby appeared at the Portola Festival in 1948, we in the USF glee club were to be his on-stage musical backup. Dressed in our varsity sweaters, we entered the San Francisco Civic Opera House through the backstage doors like privileged entertainers. On stage, we faced an audience of thousands. I had never performed in front of so large a crowd and felt privileged to stand just left of center in the first row, directly behind The Crooner.

Midway through the show, Bing asked the audience to give us a hand. We beamed with pride at the accolade and the applause. Bing then told the audience that we reminded him of his college days. He reminisced a bit then turned to us and said he wanted to sing the next number in one of our varsity sweaters. To my surprise and awe, Bing came up to me and said, "May I borrow your sweater, son?" I pulled it off and handed it to him. He put it on and continued his performance. He returned my sweater after the show. I never had it cleaned and kept it for years.

I did not mind group activities but was still a loner. The glee club, the band, the volleyball team, and ROTC supplied ample opportunities for the cohesiveness of cooperative effort I enjoyed. ROTC was mandatory for freshmen and sophomores. To go further, juniors had to take tests for admittance into the advance courses, which culminated in an Army commission and a two-year stint. I was not interested in an Army career but figured the advanced training and experience would be worthwhile. I took the tests and passed the written exams but flunked the physical. I knew the vision tests would be a problem, so I tried to memorize the eye chart and bluff my way through, but it did not work.

The doctor examined my eyes and my eyeglasses and concluded that I was as blind as a bat. "You're not combat material," he said. "At most, you'll probably push paper behind the front lines."

His assessment did not offend me. I was willing to serve my country whether it was to be behind a rifle or a desk. An officer's commission would have required two years of my time, which did not seem excessive. My non-citizen status also was a strike against me, but I was granted conditional acceptance. I became a second lieutenant and later, a platoon commander, which was my formal introduction to leadership responsibility.

In June 1948, with the presidential election campaign in full swing, I listened to an American president, in person, for the first time. I was an impressionable, young CHamoru desperately wanting acceptance as an American. The fire and spirit of President Truman's rousing speech from the steps of the Golden Gate Park bandshell enthralled me. I was less than 100 feet from the podium and felt every vibration of his amplified voice. His words moved me. No wonder he was called a fighter.

I remember thinking, "Now that's the kind of leader I'd like to be." I wanted to be strong and decisive, a fighting man like Truman. A few years later, I read comments Truman made about Blacks and racial discrimination. Asked what he thought about American Blacks, Truman was said to have answered, "How would you like your daughter to marry one?" I felt the sting of the insult, and my admiration for him vanished. In his autobiography, *Mr. Citizen*, Truman wrote, "We have never sought to dominate the world, or exploit any people, or force our will or system of government on any nation, firm and dedicated as we are in our democratic institutions." In signing the Organic Act, Truman contradicted himself.

While the Organic Act was making its way through Congress, legislative unrest was brewing in Guam. On March 5, 1949, the Ninth Guam Congress' House of Assembly walked out in protest. The walk-out was Guam's first public demonstration of defiance. It precipitated action on the Organic Act and eventual transfer of jurisdiction over Guam from the Department of the Navy to the Department of Interior.

Two years earlier, in August 1947, the Secretary of the Navy issued a proclamation, an interim organic act, granting the Guam Congress limited legislative powers. So vested, the congress launched investigations into questionable business activities. A special investigating committee summoned a federal civil service employee accused of taking advantage of his office and investing hidden capital in a local enterprise. When the employee refused to submit to questioning, the investigating committee charged him with contempt of congress and issued a warrant for his arrest, but Governor Pownall overruled the order.

Disillusioned and frustrated, 34 assembly members, under speaker Mr.

Antonio Won Pat, adjourned on March 5, vowing not to reconvene until the U.S. Congress acted on Guam's Organic Act, which promised U.S. citizenship and self-government. The bill was stuck in the Senate at the time. On March 12, Pownall called for a special joint session of congress. The House of Council, chaired by Dad, appeared, but the House of Assembly did not.

In what amounted to a "State of the Possession" address, Pownall defended his veto of the arrest warrant by saying, "Although recognizing the inherent power of a legislative body to exercise investigative power and to enforce its authority, the Governor requested the execution of the order to commit be stayed in the absence of governing legislation without which the Governor felt that the government might have been placed in an untenable position. The Governor did not then and does not now hold any brief for the activity of this witness in local business or his conduct before the Committee."

A week later, on March 19, 1949, Pownall issued a proclamation, which concluded, "Now therefore, by virtue of the authority vested in me as Governor of Guam I proclaim: 1. The holders of thirty-four seats in the House of Assembly have by their actions vacated their offices and have no further right to act or be known as Assemblymen during the remainder of the terms of office." Pownall then appointed 34 new assembly members.

The House of Assembly's walk-out made national news, drew national attention to the disenchantment in Guam, and stirred action on the Guam bill. President Truman signed the Organic Act of Guam into law on August 1, 1950. The promised self-government turned out to be illusory.

Since hearing Truman's reelection speech in 1948, I have listened to and spoken with Presidents John F. Kennedy, Lyndon B. Johnson, Gerald Ford, Jimmy Carter, and Ronald Reagan. I am no longer awed.

The Anheuser-Busch-Bordallo mansion in Pasadena

Dad thought about moving the family to the States in 1949. With four of us in college and Norma and Fred also college bound after their high school graduations, Dad saw little point in having the family split in two places. His many business trips were also expensive and exhausting. Dad's close friend and St. Mary's College classmate, Fred Sutherland, did his best to encourage him to make the move. Sutherland, who was then the postmaster of Pasadena, even tried to convince him into settling in Pasadena.

Dad gave in to Sutherland's sales pitches and bought a house in Pasadena. But it was no ordinary tract development house. Dad also gave in to his flamboyance and bought the Anheuser-Busch estate in Pasadena's ritziest neighborhood. The mansion was huge with a formal receiving room, two impressive winding staircases leading to the second-story rooms, and more bedrooms and bathrooms than we ever needed. For the first time in our lives, we owned a house with enough space for all of us. The "backyard" contained a gigantic swimming pool, a pool house, and a bungalow.

Whenever we were free from school or just wanted to be together as a family, we would converge on the mansion and stay a few days. Lorraine at Holy Names, Bobbie at Mills College, and I at the University of San Francisco would drive down for the weekend. Paul, who transferred from St. Mary's to Stanford, would meet us there. For as long as Dad owned the mansion, it served as our getaway.

Although he bought the house, Dad never relocated the family permanently. He instead turned the tables on Sutherland and talked him into moving to Guam. He also lobbied with friends in Washington, D.C., for a promotion for Sutherland, whose position as postmaster was a political appointment. Dad hoped Sutherland would be appointed Guam's next governor after Carlton Skinner. Dad's lobbying efforts paid off, but not in the way he hoped. Sutherland was appointed lieutenant governor of American Samoa. Dad was not disappointed. Sutherland was at least in the Pacific. Late in 1949, Sutherland was packed and ready to head to American Samoa when he suffered a heart attack and died.

Skinner, a Democrat, resigned after Eisenhower's election. In 1953, Eisenhower appointed Republican attorney Ford Q. Elvidge who revealed his colors in a December 1956 *Saturday Evening Post* article entitled, "I Ruled Uncle Sam's Problem Child." Elvidge resigned in 1956. His successor, Richard Barrett Lowe related his stint as governor in his book *Problems in Paradise*.

A new and alien economic structure

In 1950, at the start of my senior year, I quit school and left the sheepskin for Paul to earn. He had always been the studious and intellectual one in the family. By then, he was working toward a bachelor's degree in economics, which he earned in 1952. Two years later, he earned a master's in business administration from Harvard University's School of Business. For me, college seemed like a waste of time. I wanted to learn about business but got frustrated just studying it. I did not think I was learning anything I did not already know. Doing business was far more educational and rewarding.

Financing my college education with money earned from my little part-time, wholesale-retail business taught me more about business than my classes. I knew if I devoted all my time and attention to an enterprise, I would succeed whether I had a college degree or not. President Truman never went to college. I, at least, had three years at the University of San Francisco.

My waning enthusiasm for school was coupled by a growing weariness for fast-paced American life. My status as a non-citizen, American racial intolerance, and big city living made me long for the warmth and familiarity of home. I returned to Guam with great ideas for business and, idealistically, for the betterment of the people of Guam. I believed the time had come for me to buckle down, get to work, and help rebuild my island. I had enjoyed its peace and prosperity as a child; I witnessed its destruction during the war; now, I wanted a part in restoring it. The future for Guam seemed bright and promising then, like a phoenix rising from a fire.

For a while, I thought about turning Alupat Island in Hagåtña Bay into an amusement park like the spectacular ones I had seen in the States, like Coney Island. The Navy government provided for the recreation and entertainment of its personnel and their dependents but did nothing for CHamorus. Like the prewar palace playground, the military facilities were restricted. For years after the war, the reestablished Johnston Theater was the only civilian movie house. The military bases had many. Not until the '60s were two other commercial theaters opened. After having seen the recreational and entertainment facilities available to the public in the States, I wanted the same for my people. If we could not be accepted as equal Americans, we could at least try to enjoy our lives under the military thumb. There was much I wanted to do, but until I could establish myself as a businessman and amass my fortune, I had to find a job.

The radical changes I found upon my return dashed many of my hopes. Five years after the war, Guam's social, political, and economic framework was different. For CHamorus, adapting to the changes was a sink-or-swim proposition. And no one was giving swimming lessons. Rather than restrict economic recovery opportunities to CHamorus and implement training programs to prepare them for the change from an agrarian to a money economy, the Navy government contracted American civilian "experts." Since Guam's small workforce could not fill the labor needs for reconstruction, the Navy government imported thousands of Filipino workers. Fat-salaried government directorships and upper management positions went to the Americans. Blue collar jobs went to Filipino workers who outnumbered the CHamoru workforce.

CHamoru craftsmen and artisans could not compete against the thousands of Filipinos whose immigration status the Navy controlled. Filipinos were willing to work long hours for low wages just so they could stay on U.S. soil. The Navy allowed thousands to remain and become U.S. citizens after the reconstruction. Imported for construction work, many Filipinos worked as houseboys, cooks, and gardeners for ranking officers and federal officials, ingratiating themselves to secure American "sponsors" and preferential treatment.

Under the guise of protecting the fragile Guamanian economy, the Navy government discouraged military personnel from patronizing local businesses, saying local stores should only serve local customers. In doing so, the Navy limited the customer base for local business. Of thousands of military personnel, few shopped outside their self-contained bases. The Navy government also barred its personnel from starting businesses, but clever profiteers weaseled around the ban by partnering with a Guamanian in name only. Many reaped fortunes then left the island. Others returned to Guam after their tours to lucrative, thriving business operations.

Scheming and wheeling-and-dealing were rampant at all levels. Government officials and military officers took advantage of their positions to line their pockets by setting up exclusive business concessions inside the bases and using alien agents as fronts.

Most CHamorus refused to indenture themselves or prostitute their dignity to *"nginge' dågan"* — kiss ass — disreputable military government officials for fair treatment. They paid for their pride by having their businesses undercut or swindled away by cutthroats.

Bordallo Consolidated was not immune. After receiving word that the regional director for National Distilleries, makers of Johnny Walker whiskey and other popular liquors, was coming to Guam, Uncle Tom recommended they host a party to welcome him. Dad rejected the idea; he felt no need to curry favor. Dad had held the National Distilleries franchise for many years and had done well with it.

When Vance Smith, a Naval officer, found out that Bordallo Consolidated was not planning a VIP welcome, he moved to arrange one with his partner Ambrosio Shimizu of Ambros Incorporated. Smith met National Distilleries director at the airport and offered to carry his briefcase. Throughout the director's stay, Smith sold him on how much better Ambros could do with his products. Before leaving, the director announced that Bordallo Consolidated would lose the franchise to Ambros Incorporated. After reaping a fortune at the helm of Ambros Incorporated and taking an unsuccessful stab at a seat in the Guam Legislature in 1952, Smith cashed in his shares and left Guam.

As early as 1945, the *New York Times* questioned the goings-on in Guam and published several investigative stories about unethical practices. The Navy Department denied any wrongdoing on the part of its personnel in Guam and clamped down more tightly on the security clearance requirement. The graft and corruption continued unchecked until 1962, when President Kennedy abolished the security clearance requirement and opened the island to genuine free enterprise. By then, the economic damage was complete, and profiteers were well entrenched. Even now, they continue to profit at Guamanian expense.

Families like mine, the Johnstons, the Torreses, the Martinezes, and others were no strangers to business and the American system of free enterprise. The occupation and the war robbed them of much of their wealth but not of their skills and experience as entrepreneurs. Rather than draw on such expertise, the Navy government destroyed what it viewed as an economic power base and a threat to the new order. Steeped in the American concepts of materialism and money power, the government could not understand the CHamoru concepts of wealth and affluence. The CHamoru profit motive was, at that time, altruistic. Guam's prominent business families used their wealth according to CHamoru traditions.

To undermine Guam's pre-existing economic structure and impose a new and alien one, the Navy government set up and funded the Guam Commercial, a retail venture with a dual purpose. The propaganda touting it was that it was the American way of opening free enterprise to all people, of spreading wealth, and not leaving it to a prominent few. Without business experience or training, the Guamanian operators of Guam Commercial foundered. When the venture collapsed, the Navy government offered it as proof that Guamanians were inept businessmen in need of continued, paternal Navy control.

I was determined to prove the premise false and to succeed in business through my own initiative. I started from the bottom, as an employee at Bordallo Consolidated, and worked my way up. Uncle Tom recognized my business acumen and promoted me to manager of the ice cream and frozen confection plant at the Coconut Grove. The operation was not doing well when I took over. The government health inspector, an Air Force veterinarian, used his standard-setting authority to impose increasingly more difficult regulations to undermine us. When we could not meet them, he would cite us on health violations and shut us down. Our repeated citations barred us from doing business on any military installation.

We soon learned the inspector was in cahoots with the military's ice cream concessionaire. By keeping us off the bases, the concessionaire had no competition. Such undercutting plagued many other local businesses.

Had we retained our sovereignty and better protected ourselves as a people, we would not have lost so much economic ground, but we fell prey to the colonialist attitude toward us. There were many white supremacists who believed little brown natives should be happy and content with American paternalism.

The colonialist mentality was a distortion of Father Brolan's philosophy about small vessels and large vessels. The colonialists saw themselves as large, superior vessels entitled to anything. CHamoru Guamanians were inferior, little vessels too backward to merit wealth and power, too ignorant to be masters of their own household. We allowed ourselves to believe the nonsense and stood passive while paternalism flourished in the supremacists' favor. It has been more than 40 years since the war, but American paternalism has changed little. Food stamps and welfare have replaced the Navy government's iron hand, but the objectives remain the same: destroy incentive, encourage dependency, and maintain control.

When President Truman signed the Organic Act of Guam, Public Law 81-630, 60,000 CHamorus and resident non-CHamorus automatically became U.S. citizens, but not all provisions of the U.S. Constitution applied to us. Only these applied: Article One, section nine, clauses two and three; Article Four, section one and two, clause one; the First through the Ninth Amendments; the 13th; the second sentence of Section One of the 14th Amendment; and the 15th and 19th Amendments.

The Act also established a three-branched civilian government of Guam. The judicial and executive branches remained under federal control. The governor continued to be chosen by presidential appointment and sent to Guam, as were judges of the new Superior Court of Guam. The legislative branch gave us the tiniest measure of self-government. The new, unicameral Guam Legislature, successor of the bicameral advisory Guam Congress, was only a quasi-official lawmaking body. The Guam Legislature could pass laws, but the president retained final veto power, and Congress could declare null and void all laws enacted by the Guam Legislature within a year of passage.

Although I was aware of the limitations on our citizenship, I was as pleased as other CHamoru Guamanians to be an American at last. But my application for a U.S. passport was denied because my birth certificate identified me as Richard Jeronimo, not Ricardo Jerome. The error seemed trivial, but I had to go to court to correct it and keep the name Mama gave me.

Ricky's first passport photo.

Out of curiosity, I traveled to Saipan, which in 1950, was still the headquarters of the Central Intelligence Agency's Pacific operations. The CIA nerve center on Capitol Hill was a restricted area; no one could approach the hilltop compound. Although the CIA work was secret, the Saipanese CHamorus made sport of watching the agency's activities and knew a lot about what was going on. The Saipanese talked of strange planes landing in the dead of night and shuttling people from the airfield in covered trucks and buses with masked windows. According to the Saipanese, the arrivals were Chinese insurgents undergoing CIA training to repel Mao Tse Tung's forces after the collapse of Chiang Kai-shek's government in 1949. Once trained, the insurgents were flown back to China and dropped by parachute behind enemy lines.

Once vacated, the CIA compound became the headquarters of the Trust Territory government, 20 years after the establishment of the Trust Territories, which were the Micronesian island groups that were once colonial possessions of the Japanese. A United Nations mandate entrusted the island nations to the United States to supervise their political development and prepare their people for eventual political self-determination.

The Trust Territory (TT) government's base of operations was in Hawai'i, but after much criticism in the United Nations about the United States' long-distance administration, the headquarters moved to Guam. In the early '60s, after deputy TT high commissioner Pepe Benitez, a Kennedy appointee, exposed the deplorable conditions throughout Micronesia and the federal government's policy of "benign neglect," the headquarters moved to Saipan.

My brother Paul bought the old TT compound in Maite and turned it into a hotel-apartment complex. It became the site of a showdown between Guam police and a trio of murderers during my second administration. In 1983, as the U.N. Trusteeship ended, the old TT headquarters in Saipan became the seat of the new Commonwealth of the Northern Marianas government.

Unlike Guam, Saipan and the other Northern Marianas were not American possessions before the war. They were possessions of Japan. Yet they celebrate their 1944 "liberation" from the Japanese. The postwar American administrators of the Northern Marianas encourage the celebration to erase 26 years of Japanese influence, promote American ideology, and protect U.S. Pacific interests. The interest in currying Northern Marianas favor has puzzled the Guam CHamorus. It was the United States that separated the archipelago in 1898, keeping Guam only, and leaving the rest to Germany, which yielded them to Japan in 1918. Since the United States "liberated" the Northern Marianas from the Japanese and granted the Philippines independence, does not also Guam merit favor? The United States rebuffs the question and ignores the contradictions.

Since the end of the war, it has become clear that the U.S. objective was not the humanitarian liberation of the CHamoru people of the Marianas but the self-serving acquisition of their strategically located home islands.

Chapter 21

The high school principal's eldest daughter

I was growing aware of the federal inconsistency, but like others then, I did not think the federal government would deliberately hurt us. I was young, enthusiastic, and occupied with my own interests and ambitions. I was known as B.J. Bordallo's eldest son but celebrated in my own right, especially by the ladies. I had advantages over other men. Having returned from college in the States, I was more world-wise and sophisticated than average. I was a manager at Bordallo Consolidated, earned a hefty salary, drove my own car, and was not considered bad looking, either. I was the proverbial eligible young bachelor, and I reveled in the glories.

Almost every evening after work, I would get spiffed up to take a pretty date dancing at one of the many military nightclubs. We could choose from among the liveliest clubs or those with the best orchestras, dance music, and professional entertainers imported to entertain the troops. To get into the clubs, one only needed a military sponsor, who was never hard to find. The Talk of the Town was one of a few decent civilian nightspots then. Without military and federal civilian patronage, local clubs were mediocre at best. The only other civilian clubs of any note were Ricky's Suburban Club and, later, The Office. Ricky's Suburban Club belonged to Ricky Perez, who married Kin Arriola's sister Josephine. Kin married my old flame, Belle Perez. Ricky's brother, Frank D. Perez, married Carmen Dueñas , one of my former teachers and the sister of Cristobal Dueñas , the judge who presided over my 1987 trial. Frank, who won a seat in the First Guam Legislature, was chairman of the Territorial Party of Guam, forerunner of the Republican Party. He also became the Republican Party of Guam's first state party chairman.

Earl Kloppenberg owned The Office. I would have a run-in with him in

1974. The Office had the nasty reputation of being the exclusive watering hole of bigwig colonialists and a few sanctioned Guamanians, much like the prewar Elks Club. Despite the changing national policy growing out of the Civil Rights Movement, the colonialists in Guam, accustomed to privilege and the well-entrenched racial discrimination of prewar days, sought other ways to shut us out. The Office was a key club until someone discovered that Guam law prohibited any form of discrimination by commercial establishments and challenged the club's exclusivity.

Kloppenberg was only one of many who profited from Guamanian expense. Others, like John Webster, tried but failed. Webster was a lawyer with impressive credentials, one of the Stateside pioneers of the legal profession in Guam. In the early '50s, he served as assistant legal counsel to the legislature under John Bohn. He also served under two legislative counsels, Andrew Gayle and Kin Arriola. Webster was a heavy drinker; his alcoholism was legendary, but he derived more notoriety after trying to stake a claim to Alupat Island. Instead of looking upon the islet as communal property for all to enjoy, Webster thought Guamanians stupid for not beating him to the punch. After leaving the legislature, Webster went into private practice, but his reputation as a mercenary drunkard doomed him to failure.

Jim Mackey was another questionable agent that federal officials assigned to Guam. Like Webster, Mackey was a lawyer with an alcohol problem. He was the first U.S. attorney for Guam after passage of the Organic Act, a predecessor of the man who would accuse me of being a Judas to my people. His drinking caused his removal from office. Mackey remained in Guam and went into private practice but failed. He withered away and became a derelict.

There were many who became well-known characters in Guam. Most of them started out as successful business and professional men but ended up living off handouts and sleeping in public places, like the Paseo baseball stadium and the Old Spanish Bridge Park or even in bus stops and abandoned vehicles. In addition to Mackey, Bert Pugh, and Ken "Smitty" Smith were among the most notable. Both were former military men who counted on rank and privilege to see them through. Audacious profiteers, they went into business and succeeded for a time. People considered them colorful, prominent businessmen.

Pugh once ran for the legislature and for the Hagåtña commissioner's seat, campaigning with the slogan "A vote for Pugh is a vote for you." He lost his bids. In colonialist arrogance, Pugh commandeered a huge Navy crane. The Navy arrested him, charged him with grand theft, tried and convicted him, and threw him in jail. After his release, he degenerated. He wandered the streets and slept in a packing crate behind Democratic Party headquarters on my Ricky's Auto lot in Aniguak. He died on the beach, alone and forgotten until his body was found.

Smitty also went from riches to ruin. In his heyday, Smitty was a tall, well-built, and good-looking bachelor who owned a flashy, white Chevrolet convertible. He had his pick of pretty girls. When Dad opened the El Patio Club, he imported two Stateside entertainers, Dolores Gaye and Beverly Miller, and a professional emcee named Russ Byrd. Dolores was a beautiful singer, and Beverly was the most outstanding marimba player I have ever heard. Dad, who was a healthy widower who had not yet remarried, and I would have relished romancing the two ladies, but we could not compete with Smitty. During her engagement at the El Patio, Dolores dated only Smitty. Seeing them drive off in his convertible fueled my desire to become a rich and flamboyant businessman.

Smitty married a Guamanian girl and established himself as an up-and-coming tycoon. He built Guam's first modern, up-to-date gas station in Aniguak in the mid-1960s and began expanding right away. Although he had only the gas station and a small auto dealership, he got a hefty loan from the Bank of America to build a mansion in Tumon's prestigious Paseo de Oro. His mansion project created a laugh when workers forgot to remove a forklift from inside the house. An entire wall had to be torn down to get it out. Smitty's business ventures floundered, and the bank foreclosed. In desperation, he drove his convertible to Pago Bay and set it ablaze, hoping to collect insurance. He was caught red-handed. He ended up a hobo and died a pauper.

I was a part-time dishwasher, janitor, and waiter at the El Patio. I could not compete with men like Smitty, but I never lacked dates or places to take them. I always kept my eyes open for pretty and interesting girls to ask out. I did not keep a little black book, but I did have a lengthy list of eligibles. It included some of the most attractive and desirable young women in Guam at the time. One of them was Emily Perez, a beauty with long, black hair and golden skin. She was in a finishing school in Manila when the war broke out. She escaped the occupation and returned to Guam after the war. Her beauty, grace, and charm, as well as her recent return from metropolitan Manila, made her popular.

One evening in 1951, I took Emily to dinner and dancing at the Tutuhan Lodge, the chief petty officers' club in the Island Command compound. Emily wore a bright yellow dress that complemented the warm glow of her skin and the richness of her black hair. We made quite an impression when we walked into the crowded club. The music was great, and the dancing was almost non-stop. When she was not dancing with me, Emily danced with other men. In those days, relationships were casual and wholesome. It was not unusual for couples on dates to dance with other partners.

While Emily was on the dance floor, two young white girls caught my attention. Their behavior was surprising and not typical. They danced with Guamanian partners and socialized comfortably with a group of Guamanians. White females did not socialize with Guamanians. These girls did, and they seemed charming and friendly. I watched them with interest and asked a friend to introduce me.

The girls were sisters, Madeleine and Diana Zeien, the daughters of George Washington High School principal Christian Zeien, the gentleman I had met in Honolulu three years earlier. Madeleine was a senior in high school and a classmate of my brother Fred. Diana was a regular date of Frank "Junior" Torres. I asked each girl for a dance and complimented both on their skill. They were excellent dancers. I made the mistake of paying both the same compliment, telling them they were the most beautiful girls I had ever met. I later learned they had compared notes about me, and they still tease me about handing both the same stale line.

Madeleine was 17, younger than most of the women I dated, but she intrigued me. She was naive about many things, but her mind was keen and quick. I enjoyed her company and conversation, and I wanted to get to know her better. I thought about asking her for a date but did not right away. Not long after I met her, Junior Torres asked me whether I had a date for an upcoming party. I did not. He was taking Diana.

"Well, you know, Ricky, Diana's sister doesn't have a date yet, either. She might consider going with you. I could ask her for you," he said. I sensed he was trying to set me up and was delighted. That Madeleine might be interested in me was a delicious thought.

"I know Madeleine wants to go to the party, and I'm sure the four of us could have fun together," Junior continued. "Why don't I set it up?"

Junior played Cupid, trying to convince me to agree. He said Madeleine was interested in me, and I admitted I was interested in her. He took the news back to Madeleine.

On the evening of the party, I went to the Zeien home in the compound for off-island government contractors in Mangilao. The Zeiens were not uncomfortable when I arrived to pick up Madeleine. I think back, and it reminds me of the Spencer Tracy-Katherine Hepburn movie, *Guess Who's Coming to Dinner*, but in reverse. The Zeiens were warm, welcoming, and friendly. Mr. Zeien remembered me from our first meeting in Honolulu. He introduced me to his wife Evelyn and son Jimmy. I felt comfortable talking with them while I waited for Madeleine.

The Zeiens were unlike other American families in Guam who kept to their enclave. They were outgoing and sociable with everyone and hospitable, like a CHamoru family. Mr. Zeien was of German ancestry; Mrs. Zeien was English and Scottish. They were from Minnesota, and perhaps because of their Midwestern background, racial differences didn't bother them. My experiences with racial discrimination had occurred in the metropolitan and suburban areas of the east and west coasts and the southern states. To me, Midwesterners seemed more open.

The Zeiens were also Roman Catholics, which put us on common ground and enhanced our understanding of one another. Mr. Zeien's four sisters were Notre Dame nuns; his parents wanted him to become a priest. If he had, the Zeien line would have ended without an heir.

Madeleine was gorgeous when she appeared for our first date. That evening, I learned more about her and liked what I learned. Madeleine was born in Graceville, Minnesota. She did not see people in terms of skin color, ethnicity, or economic or social status. She decided what she liked or disliked about people. Madeleine also had many of Mama's attributes. She was gentle, loving, levelheaded, and refined. She had an innocence about her that appealed to my male protectiveness, but like Mama, she also had a quiet inner strength and courage. Madeleine could be formal and reserved, but she could also be free spirited and fun loving. Like Mama, Madeleine loved music and was a studied musician.

After our first date, I continued to date other girls, often double-booking dates with Madeleine and my other girlfriends. Although she was still in high school, I would whisk her away from campus for lunch at the Bamboo Restaurant in Hagåtña. I picked her up after school every day, took her to her part-time job at Dr. Ramon Sablan's dress shop, picked her up after work, then took her home. But there were times when I would be on a date with someone else and forget to pick her up. Madeleine would wait for hours before calling her father to take her home. Once, after I left Madeleine waiting, Mrs. Sablan warned her against losing her heart to a lady's man like me. To my eternal gratitude, Madeleine did not heed the warning. In time, I wanted to be with Madeleine only. I could relate to her in ways different from other girls. I could be frank and honest about myself, and she was as straight with me.

As my feelings for Madeleine deepened, I would go with the Zeiens to watch Madeleine and Diana's performances at military nightclubs. Madeleine and Diana were skilled entertainers whose talents did not escape Dixie Dot, a colorful lady who lined up acts for the military nightclub circuit. Madeleine sang and danced; Diana performed acrobatics. Dixie had the girls booked to perform almost every night of the week, and Mr. and Mrs. Zeien went to every show. They were watchful and protective of their daughters.

Madeleine's regular partner was a Filipino named Johnny Belmas, a professional ballroom dancer. They dazzled audiences with their style and grace. Watching Johnny hold Madeleine in his arms made me jealous. I felt threatened and decided to prove myself equal, if not better. I was a good dancer but not good enough to challenge Belmas, so I started studying their steps and memorizing their movements. When I was ready, I mustered my confidence and made my challenge. When the music for their performance began, I nudged Belmas aside and took his place. My action caught Madeleine by surprise, but I took her in my arms and led her onto the dance floor before she could react. She smiled, and we floated away, oblivious to the audience and lost in each other's gaze. The audience was pleased; Belmas was not. I did not replace him as Madeleine's dance partner, but since then, she and I have stolen the show whenever we dance.

Madeleine was an accomplished singer, dancer, and actress. She landed starring roles in many theatrical productions and musicals at the Soldiers' Show Theater at Harmon Army Base. She performed with Hollywood professionals in *HMS Pinafore*, *The Mikado*, and many other shows. She once performed with American actor Jimmy Stewart. As a high school senior, she played a leading role in the school's production of *Boarding House Reach*. Years later, our daughter Debbie, in her senior year, played Helen Keller in her school's production of *The Miracle Worker*.

Madeleine was George Washington High School's lead majorette. She wore a high hat and a cute little outfit with brass buttons and braids. With a whistle in her mouth and a baton twirling in her hand, she marched ahead of the band. I marveled at her great twirling skill. She made it look easy. One of my most cherished photographs is of her leading the band. I kept it on my desk during my days as a businessman, senator, and governor. It sits beside me now on my desk at home. Madeleine is an extraordinary person. I feel fortunate to have won her heart. I daresay she has impressed everyone who has ever met her, and she has turned heads since she was a teenager.

Young Madeleine Zeien as George Washington High School's lead majorette.

Madeleine's ability to command attention has always delighted me but has sometimes irritated me as well. During my terms as governor, when we hobnobbed with Washington's social and political elite, heads turned whenever we entered a room. Madeleine would get admiring glances. I would get curious looks. No one ever said anything, but I sensed the puzzlement some people had about how such a beautiful white woman could be married to so dark-skinned a man like me. I have seen the question on their faces and even recognized jealousy and condescension, especially among bigots who did not hide their revulsion over interracial marriages. They would look at me as though I had trespassed their domain and duped Madeleine into marrying me. Other men might have reveled in stirring such envy, but I resented the implication that I should not have access to anything above my non-white station.

Once, in a department store in the States, a cashier at a register studied us as we made our purchase. I could read the questions in her face. She finally said to me, "My, what a beautiful, dark tan you have." Before I could respond, Madeleine smiled and said, "That's not a tan, dear, that's natural. He was born with it."

By the time Madeleine graduated from high school in June 1951, I was an accepted member of the Zeien household, but I would never visit empty-handed. I supplied the family with popsicles and creamsicles from the plant. I even lent Mother Zeien my Nash Rambler convertible. Mother Zeien worked as head buyer for the Navy exchanges and needed the transportation.

Madeleine's graduation gift from her parents was a trip to Manila and Hong Kong with Mother Zeien, who was to buy merchandise for the base exchanges. I could afford the airfare and hotel and did not want to be away from Madeleine, so I volunteered to tag along. Mother Zeien welcomed the idea. Since it was a buying trip for her, she could not entertain Madeleine and agreed that she would enjoy the trip more with me as her sightseeing companion. The trip was my first to Asia, Madeleine's as well. Since then, we have travelled the world together.

We flew to the Philippines and checked into the Manila Hotel, the nation's finest. Mother and Madeleine shared a suite while I took a room on a different floor. Sometimes, when we felt lazy, the three of us would have a leisure breakfast in the suite. While Mother attended to her business, Madeleine and I took in the city, sightseeing and shopping, hand in hand. Sometimes we would just splash about in the hotel swimming pool. Madeleine wore a flashy, tiger-print swimsuit that attracted quite a bit of attention. A beautiful, fair-skinned blonde, she was a rarity in the city. The skimpy, body-hugging, tiger-print suit was also uncommon. It pleased me that she attracted so much admiring male attention, but I was possessive at the same time. I rankled with jealousy whenever anyone approached her.

Soon after our arrival in Manila, I contacted Raul Mendoza, a nephew of then-Philippines President Elpidio Quirino. Dad had become acquainted with Raul and his family when he paid a state visit to the president years earlier. Raul went out of his way to entertain Mother, Madeleine, and me. Almost every night of our 10-day stay, we were treated to dinner parties and socials with the cream of Manila society. Each time Madeleine and I took to the dance floor, we became the focus of everyone's attention. Our dancing always cleared the floor of other couples, and we would find ourselves bowing to appreciative applause when the music stopped.

In 1985, during the Manila leg of Pan Am's 50th anniversary transpacific clipper flight, Madeleine and I again cleared the dance floor at an exclusive party hosted by First Lady Imelda Marcos at the same Manila Hotel. What our audience took to be an entertaining dance performance was to Madeleine and me a nostalgic recreation of our romantic trip in 1951.

After seeing Manila, Mother Zeien, Madeleine, and I spent a few days in Baguio then flew to Hong Kong and checked into the Peninsula Hotel. We toured the island, including the Tiger Balm Gardens, Victoria Peak, and the famous floating restaurants at Aberdeen. Hong Kong was still a shopper's paradise then, and we took advantage of the bargains. I bought my first Rolex watch, an 18-karat gold 21-jewel Oyster Perpetual for $500. I now wear a more expensive Rolex, but I keep my first one for sentimental reasons. I bought my graduation present for Madeleine at Mrs. Ada Lum's jewelry shop. It was a heavy, antique gold neck chain with a large, gold butterfly pendant decorated with multicolored pieces of jade and quartz. Madeleine considers it too gaudy and heavy to wear but keeps it for its historic value.

When wealthy Chinese capitalists fled to Chiang Kai-shek's democratic stronghold in Formosa, which is now Taiwan, they sold rare and priceless heirloom jewelry to Mrs. Lum to help set up the new government in exile. Madeleine's neck chain and the rings I bought for Mother Zeien and Auntie Rose came from Mrs. Lum's collection.

By trip's end, Madeleine and I knew everything about each other — the good and the bad. It brought us closer and made our relationship stronger, more honest, and real. Madeleine understood me better than anyone else I knew. She knew of my reputation as a lady's man but was certain about the depth of my affection. I did not often tell her I loved her. Like Dad, I was not openly affectionate. It was not our nature. Dad was never affectionate toward

Mama, but he loved her. What I did not say with words I expressed in actions. I showered Madeleine with gifts and attention.

My ideas and opinions about love and marriage were not common for the time. Romance did not blind me, nor did the complexity of joining the lives of two different people escape me. I knew the kind of person I was, and I was not willing to hide my faults to create an impressive but phony image. I did not want anyone to put me on a pedestal as if I were perfect then discover later that I was not. I was determined to succeed in business and to champion the rights of my people in the political arena. I did not want anyone who could not accept the real me to end up being miserable. I never outgrew my curiosity about life and my thirst for adventure, nor could I give these up. Madeleine knew this. I knew she would be the kind of person who could keep up with me. By the end of our first year of courtship, I knew I had found my life's companion. Now, after more than 35 years of marriage, I still love her deeply.

Madeleine and I accepted marriage as the next step in our relationship, but we never discussed it. We assumed she would go to college, earn a degree, and come home to me. She had spent all her teen years in Guam, in a small close-knit community where no one was a stranger. Before I could ask her to share that community with me forever, she had to know more about the world she would leave behind. She needed more exposure to that world and to other men, other relationships. She had to make a free and well-informed decision about returning and about us. I did not want her to end up hating me if she made the wrong choice.

One of the greatest risks of our separation was Madeleine's talent for music and acting. She had been concert mistress of the Guam Symphony Orchestra, which was then under the direction of violinist Redentor "Red" Romero, who went on to become a renowned philharmonic conductor. Madeleine enriched her violin skills under Red's tutelage. I had no doubt Madeleine could have achieved stardom if she wanted it. She had the talent and the savvy. I knew if she decided on a serious musical or acting career, I would lose her.

Madeleine was accepted at St. Mary's College in South Bend, Indiana. The thought of losing her tore at me, but I encouraged her to go. It was the right thing to do. My heart cried out for her to stay, but my practical mind insisted she go. She was set to leave when the Zeiens learned they would have to leave also. I knew that if her family returned to the States, Madeleine would not come back, except to marry me if we were so destined.

Father Zeien was well liked as principal of George Washington High School. He enjoyed his position and wanted to remain in it, but his contract was not renewed. Many of us knew it was because the Zeiens were too friendly with the natives. Neither the Zeiens nor the students and their parents had a say in the matter. The family's popularity among the locals won them the disapproval of the colonialists — the influential American civilian appointees and contracted professionals in the government of Guam who, like their pre-war counterparts, wanted their community kept separate from ours. Those, like Father Zeien, who did not adhere to the unspoken segregation policy, did not stay in their positions long. Those who disliked their jobs or the island and its people seemed cemented in place and took out their frustrations on Guamanians.

The circumstances for the Zeiens' departure from Guam were depressing. Madeleine and I had yet to discuss marriage, but I also considered her family mine. I wanted to do something exceptional for them, to make their farewell something wonderful and memorable. I decided on a special picnic. They accepted my invitation without knowing what I had in mind. I lined up Dad's longtime employees, Felix "Kundu" Lizama and Juan Muña. Kundu was Dad's head chef and Juan was his butcher at the San Nicolas Market before the war. They took pride in their work, and I took advantage of their expertise.

After church on the Sunday before the Zeiens' departure, we drove to a point overlooking the ocean just north of Umatac. Kundu and Juan had set up the picnic on a hillside with a breathtaking view. We could see the rugged southern coast on the right, Cocos Island in the distance on the left, and the Philippine Sea straight ahead. Cool breezes swept in from the sea, and the sky was sunny and clear. Lunch was hot and ready when we arrived. Kundu and Juan outdid themselves. They had spread a large, white tablecloth on the ground for an American-style picnic, but it was set with china, silverware, and glassware. Nearby was a small bar with ice and soft drinks. A cookfire was keeping our lunch warm. Everything was perfect. The Zeiens were beside themselves. Even I was impressed. The picnic was pleasant but tinged with sadness. The Zeiens believed it was to be their last memory of Guam, and I thought it would be the last I saw of them.

The day the Zeiens departed, a crowd of people — their Guamanian friends and students — came to see them off. Junior Torres and I stood together and waved to Diana and Madeleine, who returned our waves from the rail of the USS *David Shanks*, the same ship that first carried me from Guam. We kept waving as the ship left the harbor. We then dashed up to the Builders Club on Libugon, where we could see to the horizon, and continued waving even though we knew no one on the ship could see us. We watched the *Shanks* grow smaller and smaller.

I was heartsick when the *Shanks* took Madeleine away from me. I hid my feelings from Junior, whose relationship with Diana was only casual. He was sad at Diana's leaving, but he knew he would see her again in a few months when he left for school in the mainland. I was not as fortunate. Madeleine was the center of my universe. Without her, I felt hollow and empty. When the *Shanks* disappeared over the horizon, I felt very alone.

Mamaisen saina

I made Madeleine promise to write every day, and she did without fail for two years. When her letters were late, I would fear she found someone new, but they eventually arrived after being misrouted to Guatemala, Ghana, or some other place. To make sure she never missed a day, Madeleine told me she predated her stationery and placed them alongside stamped envelopes addressed to me. Her letters were a journal of her activities and the events around her. I kept all her letters; I still have them. My letters to her were sporadic but lengthy. Madeleine never asked me to be faithful. She never asked for promises she knew I could not keep. She never broached the subject of marriage and left it to me to bring up in my own time. It came that summer.

Madeleine returned to Guam for summer vacation in 1952. I had missed her so much and decided never to let her go again, whether she finished college or not. My family took Madeleine in long before we were married, and they treated her like a sister. She stayed with my sister Lorraine and her husband Eloterio "Elo'" Calvo, Påle' Oskot's brother, in Agaña Heights. As the brother of a priest, Elo' had a distinct advantage over the other men who wanted to marry my sisters. He had a much easier time than Jimmy did when he was courting Irene. Elo' and Lorraine were married in February and were still newlyweds when Madeleine came home.

Madeleine landed a temporary job at the Radio Corporation of America (RCA) to earn money for her return trip and her vacation expenses. We spent our days at work and our evenings together dancing and partying almost every night. On our way home one evening, I pulled into the lookout on Nimitz Hill, downhill from a wartime Japanese command post. The secluded spot overlooking Hagåtña and beyond was popular among lovers. Madeleine had no idea of my intention. With the city lights twinkling before us, I turned to her and blurted, "I want you to be the mother of my children. Will you marry me?" Madeleine stared at me blankly. I did not know whether she was going to laugh or cry.

I then told her my innermost feelings. I spoke to her as I had never spoken to anyone else. Inspired by the love Mama and Dad had for each other, and how Mama's eyes sparkled whenever she spoke about Dad, I poured my heart out. Marriage to Mama had never dampened Dad's admiration or appetite for other women, but without a doubt, Mama was more special than all the rest. Mama was the one true love of his life. Without her, Dad was lost and empty. I felt the same way about Madeleine. She was the woman I wanted to share my life with and to bear my children. The sentiments may seem corny now, but to me, they have always been genuine and profound. Madeleine remained silent while I spoke. She knew I was serious. After a few minutes, she said, "Yes, Ricky."

Over the next few days, I realized I had forced her into an answer. I did not want to lose her, but I was not sure Madeleine understood what marrying me meant. She was a white girl from Minnesota asked to live out her life on a faraway island with a brown-skinned man. I wondered if she could do so without regret. Assured by her answer, I again encouraged her to return to college, telling her the time apart would test our relationship. I teased her about meeting some rich, handsome man or maybe a husky Notre Dame football star who would make her forget her little island boy. I laughed at my own jokes knowing in my heart it could happen.

To remind her of her promise to me, I gave her a 1-carat diamond solitaire, the largest and finest engagement ring I could afford. Tom Connolly, then Guam's most reputable jeweler, sold it to me for a staggering $1,800. Madeleine returned to Minnesota and announced our engagement to her family. Dad followed with a letter to the Zeiens, asking for Madeleine's hand in my behalf. A CHamoru marriage custom, the formal exchange between parents serves as the endorsement of the match and the agreement of wedding costs.

Unlike the American custom, in which the bride's family pays the bulk of wedding costs, CHamoru custom requires the groom's family to shoulder them. It comes from our matrilineal past when marriages were by mutual agreement to link together families and clans. In ancient CHamoru society, children belonged to their mothers, their clans, and their clans' resources. Men married into their brides' clans and earned rights to use their resources. The Spanish, followed by the Americans, forced changes in CHamoru society, but some aspects remain, especially in marriage customs. CHamorus never gave up their belief in the fundamental value of women. Faced with the expectations of two cultural traditions, Dad and the Zeiens negotiated special arrangements to accommodate us. Dad's letter of *mamaisen saina,* the formal request to the bride's parents, was traditional and eloquent, and is among our treasured wedding keepsakes.

Because our upcoming marriage meant Madeleine would move to Guam, Mother and Father Zeien convinced her to transfer from St. Mary's in Indiana to St. Catherine's in Minneapolis-St. Paul, to be closer to home until then. While at St. Catherine's, Madeleine landed a soprano position with the prestigious and highly selective Minneapolis-St. Paul Opera. I greeted the news with enthusiasm but worried that a promising opera career would threaten our engagement.

The voting public didn't know what to make of me

Rather than dwell on the possibilities, I turned my attention elsewhere. The prospect of getting married and starting my own family prompted me to think seriously about my future. My manager's position at Bordallo Consolidated kept me busy, but I did not give up hope of starting my own business. Perhaps because of Dad's long involvement, the political arena beckoned also.

In its day, the old Guam Congress was like a magnet; it drew me there whenever it was in session. I would stand outside, beneath a session hall window, and listen to arguments, discussions, and floor debates. Although I did not always agree with his positions, I felt proud when Dad had the floor. I would marvel at the reasoning powers of the congressmen with whom I agreed and fidget when the opposition countered them. It frustrated me when my "roosters" got tongue tied; I knew I could argue their points more effectively. After spending countless evenings beneath the window, I realized that unless

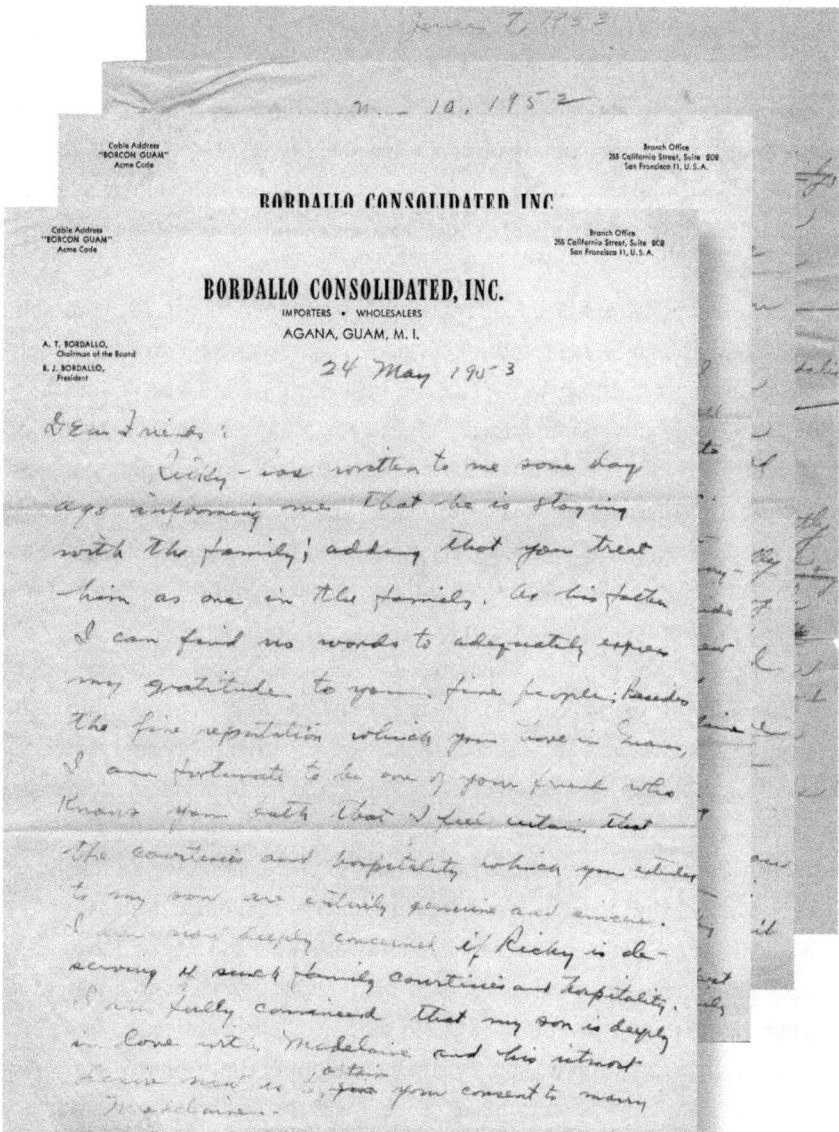

Cable Address
"BORCON GUAM"
Acme Code

Branch Office
255 California Street, Suite 909
San Francisco 11, U.S.A.

BORDALLO CONSOLIDATED, INC.

IMPORTERS • WHOLESALERS

AGANA, GUAM, M. I.

A. T. BORDALLO,
Chairman of the Board

B. J. BORDALLO,
President

24 May 1953

Dear Friends:

Ricky has written to me some day
ago informing me that he is staying
with the family; adding that you treat
him as one in the family. As his father
I can find no words to adequately express
my gratitude to you fine people; besides
the fine reputation which you have in Guam,
I am fortunate to be one of your friend who
knows you such that I feel certain that
the courtesies and hospitality which you extend
to my son are entirely genuine and sincere.
I am now deeply concerned if Ricky is deserving of such family courtesies and hospitality.
I am fully convinced that my son is deeply
in love with Madelaine and his utmost
desire now is to obtain your consent to marry
Madelaine.

"Dad's letter of *mamaisen saina*, the formal request to
the bride's parents, was traditional and eloquent, and
is among our treasured wedding keepsakes."

I was inside as an actual congressman, my ideas and opinions were worthless.

I wanted to try to stop and undo the injustices perpetrated on our people. I wanted to lead the fight against racial discrimination and the economic exploitation long rampant in Guam. I wanted political equality for Guamanians and the economic opportunities I had seen in the States. I wanted to be among those who shaped the postwar destiny of Guamanians and that meant making a bid for public office. In 1952, at age 24, I ran for a seat in the Second Guam Legislature.

As a candidate, I faced several formidable impediments. My youth and lack of experience were stumbling blocks, but getting people to take me seriously was my biggest obstacle. The congress in those days was serious business, and legislators commanded high esteem. Many people thought me impudent for thinking myself worthy and disrespectful for competing against my father. Dad had long enjoyed the respect and confidence of the voting public. I had his name and a growing reputation but not his experience, wisdom, or maturity. My public image was not that of a viable political candidate. I was merely B.J. Bordallo's upstart son.

Despite the obstacles, I filed my candidacy and stirred controversy right away. I was not yet 25 years old, the age set by law to hold public office. The election commission went into a quandary over whether they could certify my candidacy. Old-line congressmen who considered me impertinent demanded my disqualification. But I argued that, while I could not legally hold office at 24, the law did not prevent me from running. The election would take place in November, the inauguration in January, and my 25th birthday in December would make me eligible if I were successful. After long and heated debates, the commission ruled in my favor. This controversy, one of many in my life, was a portend of other conventions I would shatter in local politics and business.

My first campaign was brash, showy, and out of the ordinary. The voting public did not know what to make of me. I was the upstart whose candidacy ruffled the election commission, the youngest of 43 candidates, and an independent running in direct competition with my father, a Popular Party incumbent. Worse, I bandied my picture and personal background for everyone to see. Conservative voters were not accustomed to such bravado. Although it is a standard campaign practice now, I was the first legislative candidate to produce brochures listing my platform and resumé, as well as posters with big pictures of my face. I recruited youngsters to distribute the brochures to who-

ELECT

Ricardo J. Bordallo
(INDEPENDENT)
For Congressman
GENERAL ELECTION   NOVEMBER 4, 1952

WILL INITIATE OR FURTHER PROMOTE LEGISLATION FOR:

1. Curtailment of Government waste.
2. Village street improvements.
3. Equal pay for equal work.
4. New and better roads for the southern districts.
5. Additional facilities for crowded schools.
6. Repeal of the 20% amusement tax on movie theatres.
7. Financial aid towards a more effective promotion of fishing industry.
8. Farm crop insurance and increase in funds for farm loans.
9. Expedition of island power facilities for all villages.
10. A more just and fair pro-rating of the island's water and electric bills.
11. Workmen's accident insurance.
12. A more effective and constructive handling of the juvenile delinquency problem.
13. Old age pension.
14. Monthly allotment for the blind and invalid.
15. A bonus for every Guamanian veteran with sixty or more days of combat duty in Korea.

SAFEGUARD YOUR FREEDOM —— VOTE ON ELECTION DAY

"Although it is a standard campaign practice now, I was the first legislative candidate to produce brochures listing my platform and resumé, as well as posters with big pictures of my face."

ever would take them and to tack the posters onto power poles all around the island. Prior to then, old guard incumbents and experienced candidates relied only on their name and reputation to secure victory. Many raised disapproving eyebrows at my methods, condemning them as a carnival approach to the serious business of running for office. But by the next election they, too, were printing campaign posters and brochures.

Despite my enthusiastic campaign, I only garnered enough votes to rank high among the losers in the November 1952 general election. Incumbent E.T. "Jake" Calvo was the top vote-getter. Mr. A.B. Won Pat, the incumbent speaker of the First Legislature, came in at number nine. He also kept his seat as speaker for the Second Legislature. Dad came in 12th. Mr. F.B. Leon Guerrero, Dad's 1936 Washington companion, ran as an independent and missed the cut, landing the 22nd slot. At number 18, my cousin James Butler, an independent, became one of six new congressmen. The others were Felix T. Carbullido, Paul D. Palting, Adrian "Nito" Cristobal, Pedro C. Lujan, and Greg D. Perez.

I had no delusion of winning and had resigned myself to defeat even before the election. Losing was disappointing, nonetheless. To salve my ego, I convinced myself that my bid had been experimental, a trial run for 1954, and that the campaign experience and public exposure had been valuable. Indeed, my natural gift for oratory, which, thanks to Father Egan, my brilliant USF speech professor, had been honed and ready, was challenged and polished. I had always admired Father Egan. After the 1952 election, I was even more grateful for his tutelage. I think he would have been proud of me.

A notice from the draft

After the election, I received a notice from the draft. It puzzled me; I thought I was too old. My 25th birthday was just weeks away. There were hundreds of younger men eager to join the military and enlisting voluntarily in impressive numbers. I wondered why the armed forces hungered for more, especially older ones like me.

The Korean War was winding down by then. The continued conscription of fighting men from a tiny island of less than 60,000 people did not make sense. The speed with which we were called to military duty made me even more suspicious of our limited American citizenship, granted just two years earlier. We were not accorded all the rights and privileges of citizenship, but the duties and obligations, especially to defend the country, were impressed immediately. The scores of volunteers easily exceeded Guam's draft quota, but Guam's draft board went to great lengths to conscript those who did not. I later learned that Col. Juan Muña was one reason why. A Guam militiaman, he was a member of the draft board and an ardent militarist who advocated mandatory military service for all able-bodied Guamanian men. A flag-waver long before it became fashionable, Col. Muña genuinely believed it was the moral obligation of every citizen.

No other Guamanian was as faithful to the American military cause as he, despite the racial and social discrimination that made his rank little more than tokenism. I did not agree with his philosophy, but I could never fault his loyalty and commitment. Despite the role he played in my conscription, I named the Guam National Guard Headquarters in his honor in 1984. He deserved the recognition, and I said so publicly at the dedication of Fort Juan Muña in Harmon.

I do not believe Col. Muña was entirely responsible for my conscription. I suspect some old guard politicians resented my impudence for challenging their ranks and pushed to get me drafted. It was their perfect solution — teach me a lesson and remove me from their arena and from Guam. In those days, ranking politicians could influence the board and often secured draft exemptions for their relatives and friends. Many of my peers escaped the draft that way.

Dad had more than enough clout to secure an exemption for me or to counter the effort to draft me, but I did not ask for help. It was not necessary. My poor eyesight kept me from qualifying for USF's advanced ROTC program. I assumed it would do so again, and I would be weeded out during the physicals. Near the end of November, I boarded a bus with about 50 other draftees to be processed at Naval Station. I was discharged five months later.

My brief stint in the Army is shrouded in mystery. My detractors and political opponents have generated outlandish tales and rumors over the years to try to damage my candidacies. Their stories are full of incredible details, distorted half-truths, and outright lies. Every election gives rise to improved versions, embellished with scintillating new "discoveries," whispered as if true. I have been accused of fraud, treachery, dishonesty, and insanity. The rumors grow more malicious in gubernatorial campaigns. According to the most popular versions, I am supposed to have dodged the draft, raped the general's daughter, seduced his wife, made homosexual advances, and sat naked atop a flagpole. I have never publicly responded to the myths or defended myself against them. At my sentencing in April 1987, the federal judge asked why my Army record was not included in my court file. He, too, was curious about what really happened. The omission was inadvertent. News reporters jumped on the possibility that my Army record might become public at last. To their dismay, Judge Dueñas sealed the report. Although my critics may scoff, I now recount what happened.

There was only one white face among us on the bus to Naval Station. He was about 19 and did not hide his annoyance at having been drafted. I was not pleased either, but I knew my conscription was a mistake, and I would be rejected. All the other draftees were enthusiastic and excited. For many of them, military service promised training, steady pay, and the opportunity to travel. For them, the advantages outweighed the disadvantages. That was not true for me; I did not need military advantages and privileges. I already had more than the military could offer.

At the processing center, we were stripped down, lined up, and herded through an ordeal of paperwork and medical tests. The process was demeaning, but I had been through it before for ROTC at USF and knew what to expect. As I stood in line, I caught the Marine sergeant herding us along, staring at me. He was a short, burly man who scowled at everyone, but his scowl was worse for me. The look on his face made me uneasy. He seemed to know who I was and was pleased to have me in his grasp. I assumed he recognized me as the privileged son of a prominent congressman or as the legislative candidate who rocked the election commission.

As we moved along, he kept searching for me among the crowd, keeping track of where I was. I sensed he did not like me. The look in his eyes told me I was in trouble. He was like a predator getting ready to pounce. And I was his prey. He reminded me of the Marine policeman who dragged me off to jail by the scruff of the neck and kicked my butt. Both Marines had the same arrogant swagger, the same air of power and authority. He was another Roger Perry, offended by my being more than just a lowly native and needing to be put in my place. Although I did nothing to antagonize him, I knew the Marine would pounce on me somehow, but there was nothing I could do. When my turn for examination came, I was relieved. My poor vision would get me released, and the Marine sergeant would be out of luck.

The examining doctor asked for my eyeglasses, and I handed them over without hesitation. I could read the eye charts with them on, but without them, I was blind. The doctor peered through the eyeglasses and shook his head. As I expected, he handed them back, saying, "Son, you have no business being in the service." He spoke sternly, as if he had caught me trying to sneak into the Army. He wrote, "Disqualified" in large, red letters across my enlistment form and said, "That's it, move along. You can get back on the bus."

I have never liked being deemed unworthy for anything and was not numb to the rejection. I knew it was coming, but it still did not feel good. I got dressed without triumph and started outside for the bus. Before I could reach it, the Marine sergeant stepped into my path.

"Where the hell do you think you're going?" he growled as if I had been trying to escape.

"I've been disqualified. I was told to get on the bus and wait for the others," I answered.

"No, you don't. Come with me," he said.

The feeling of impending danger returned. The Marine knew he had the upper hand. I dared not stand up to him or question his authority on federal ground. I was like other Guamanians conditioned by years of intimidation to cower before the naval government's power. My fear turned into anger, but I resisted the urge to challenge him. The odds were too much in his favor. Instead, I followed him back into the processing center like a little schoolboy. I sensed something sinister was in store for me.

Inside, the Marine ordered me to a corner while he whispered to the doctor who had disqualified me. They glanced in my direction as they spoke. When the doctor shrugged his shoulders and walked off, I knew my fate had been sealed. The sergeant retrieved a file folder and motioned me toward him.

"Sit down here, and read the first line of that chart," he said. There was only one letter on the first line: a gigantic "E" which I could see even without glasses. After I read it, the Marine said, "You're fine. Get back in line."

Too shocked to do anything, I rejoined the men in ranks. They had seen what had occurred and stared at me wide-eyed, fearful, and confused. Stunned, my head swam. I could not believe what was happening. How could a Marine enlisted man overrule a doctor, a Navy officer? It took a few minutes to recover, and then I became infuriated. Why would a doctor yield to a sergeant? I wanted to shout out in protest and demand answers, but to my everlasting regret, I held my tongue and gave in to intimidation again.

I was angry but also confused. I did not know what to do or what I could do. My companions in line were just as dumbfounded. We were all still just draftees, still being processed. We did not belong to the Army yet and had not sworn oaths to obey "superior" officers. We were still civilians, still American civilians. With rights. But citizenship had come to us like a thief in the night. We were Americans without preparation, without indoctrination, without an understanding of what it meant. And all the years of subjugation and discrimination were not easily erased. We had all grown up under the Navy government's autocratic thumb. For half a century, it was all-powerful and had remained so in our subservient minds. None of us were confident enough, or brave enough, to test our freedoms. I truly did not know whether I was within my rights to protest.

Like sheep, we stood together silently and watched as the Marine again whispered to the doctor. We had seen such collaborations among whites before and knew something was afoot. The young white fellow was next in line. In a voice meant for all of us to hear, the doctor ordered him onto a gurney. He then tapped the boy's knee with a rubber-tipped hammer and announced, "You've got knock knees. You're disqualified. You can go."

The boy was taller than the rest of us and built like an athlete. He was in obvious good physical health. He strode past us with a smug, triumphant grin on his face. I have often wondered who he was and whatever became of him. I am sure his name is listed among the draftees processed that day.

The reason for my retention suddenly became clear to me. With a helpless, sinking feeling, I realized I was being shanghaied. A deal had been made to let the Statesider go free, but for the quota of inductees to be preserved, someone had to take his place. Despite my eyesight, I was the replacement. My suspicion was confirmed when we got back on the bus. The Statesider was nowhere in sight. He was so sure of his rejection that someone had already picked him up.

Ma fa'ga'ga' — to be made an animal

"*Ma fa'ga'ga'*" is a profound CHamoru term. It means to be stripped of human dignity and treated like an animal. To a CHamoru, to be *ma fa'ga'ga'* is the ultimate humiliation. Similarly, "*mås ki hao gå'ga'*," which means, "you are like an animal," can be a put down or an insult, depending on how it is said. I had been *ma faʻgaʻgaʻ* by that Marine sergeant. He wanted to prove his superiority, his supremacy, his power over me. He was worse than Roger Perry. He was not satisfied with humiliating me; he had to degrade me, to treat me like an animal. On the bus back to Hagåtña, while the other men celebrated their new status as soon-to-be Army soldiers, the full weight of what had happened hit me, and my stomach churned. I had been dehumanized.

In the days that followed, I looked for some redeeming aspect about my situation, but nothing ever came to mind. I tried to cling to the ideals and principles that were supposed to be the guarantees of all Americans, but too many examples to the contrary haunted me: *...All men are created equal... "You're just a native. That's all you'll ever be."* *...That they are endowed by their Creator with certain inalienable rights... "We are different, Ricky. We are not citizens." Ours is a nation of laws, not of men. "Get back in line."* Why were there such disparities? Why did ugly Americans outnumber noble ones? Tormented, I began to think that partial American citizenship was nothing more than an obligation to die in battle. We were the "wretched refuse," valued only as cannon fodder. We were expendable citizens. I was a loyal American, and if called to serve my country, I would do so with honor. I did not have to be forced to do so or to be treated like an animal to underscore someone else's sense of superiority. I kept returning to the same conclusion: a Marine underling decided my fate, and I let him.

My bitterness toward the Marine sergeant turned into resentment then into intense anger and hatred. I never told Dad what happened to me at Naval Station or that I was harboring such terrible emotions. I did not want him to think I was looking for pity or salvation, or worse, that I was a coward. My pride was at stake, and I tried to deal with my problems. I denied the feelings and turned them inward, not realizing that like poison, they would eat me up. Sick at heart, I boarded a ship for Hawaiʻi with the other recruits in December and started infantry training at Schofield Barracks.

Bootcamp was appalling. I was unprepared for the coarseness of the experience. I could deal with the strenuous physical demands but not the shock to my psyche. The deliberate degradation of human beings in the name of duty and discipline was alien to all my morals and values. To me, picking up cigarette butts on a parade field with one's mouth was tantamount to being *ma faʻgaʻgaʻ*. And being *ma faʻgaʻgaʻ* once was enough. I swore never to commit any infraction that carried the penalty.

I also was not prepared for the foul language and the profanities spewing constantly from the mouths of drill sergeants, recruits, and officers alike. I was 25 years old but not accustomed to hearing obscenities so publicly and so often. Every utterance made me flinch at first. Mama had been tyrannical about cussing and swearing. It was not a sign of good breeding. Just saying "Darn it" would earn us a twisted ear and a mouth full of soap. I could not go back on Mama's teaching. To this day, most cuss words stick in my throat, but I can say them. My sensibilities have been calloused by the constant repetition in bootcamp and in the way vulgarity has become commonplace.

I had the misfortune to be billeted on the second floor in one of the two-story, concrete barracks arranged in rows around a large quadrangle. A second-floor billet meant losing precious time negotiating a flight of stairs.

Time was of the essence at 4 in the morning when the reveille bell rang. We had only minutes to get up and assemble in the quadrangle with all our equipment and gear. That was the rule. Breaking it meant we would suffer. Even if only one recruit was at fault, the whole company suffered. If the formation was not perfect, if we took too long, or did not meet our drill sergeant's standards, he would make us repeat the assembly process as many times as necessary to get it right. For those of us on the second floor, it meant running up and down the stairs. Sometimes, instead of running back and forth, we were made to stand at attention for hours at a time. On hot, sunny mornings, recruits who collapsed in the ranks left the field on stretchers. Leaving the parade field unconscious in an ambulance was a humiliation no one wanted.

The consequences of tardiness or imperfection made every morning harrowing. The ear-piercing sound of the reveille bell, coupled with the sudden switching on of the overhead lights, ignited a frenzy among blinded, groggy men groping for their clothes and equipment and complaining loudly as they did so. Minutes afterward, there would be a deafening clatter as hundreds of men stampeded from the barracks and onto the parade field.

The first weeks of basic training were the roughest. It was a time for lesser men to wash out. Physically exhausted, many men could only rely on male pride to prevent failure. I survived the weeding-out period and was determined to continue. I was not working to become a soldier but a killer. I wanted to return to Guam and kill the Marine sergeant. I pushed myself for that goal. But I started to get headaches. At first, they were mild, and I could ignore them. Later, they grew more frequent and intense. I soon became oblivious to everything but the pain in my head and the desire to kill the Marine.

Even the making of *From Here to Eternity* did not pique my interest. I should have realized then that something was wrong. It was not my nature to be indifferent to something as extraordinary as the filming of a major Hollywood motion picture. The movies had fascinated me since childhood and watching one in the making was the opportunity of a lifetime. Under normal circumstances, I would have performed extra duty for the chance to watch. The presence of big-name movie stars and film crews had the camp in an uproar.

By February 1953, my headaches had become so severe that no amount of medication relieved the pain. When my vision and balance became affected, my condition became noticeable. My eyes were always bloodshot and watery. During pain spells, I could not see straight and would get dizzy. I often stumbled and fell, especially on long hikes and forced marches. Sometimes I had to be held up and helped along. My buddies urged me to see a doctor. Those who knew what had happened to me in Guam wanted me to speak to the commanding officer. I refused their advice, thinking I would be an embarrassment to the other Guamanians in camp. I assured them I was okay, but I was not. I grew weaker by the day and tried to keep up, but it soon became impossible.

After one of my more spectacular falls, my drill instructor, a tall, well-built Hawai'ian, said to me, "I know you're trying, so just hang on." He had been tough on all of us but after making the comment, I sensed he was not pushing me as hard as he could have. He never singled me out for push-ups or policing the field for cigarette butts.

"Would you kill to defend?"

I did hang on, but not for the reason my drill instructor thought. By then, near the end of basic training, I was hanging on for life. More than the physical rigors of the training, the mental anguish I was going through took its toll. Unable to take out my anger and hatred directly on the Marine sergeant, I did not realize how damaging it was to me. The tension and uncertainty I lived with during the occupation was returning. The feeling of insecurity and threat flooded back. I was again at the mercy of an all-powerful military force. The Army was the Army; it did not matter whether it was Japanese or American.

The time and place, the uniforms, and the people were different, but the overpowering presence was the same. I was a captive once again, and like a captive, I was on guard for danger. Although racked with pain, I knew where I was and what I was doing.

Then, after an especially grueling day in February or March, I do not recall when, my head hurt so badly that I could not sleep. At 4 o'clock, when the reveille bell rang and the lights came on, I thought my head had exploded. The sound drilled into my ears like a jackhammer, and the light seared my eyes like fire. Blinded, disoriented, and in severe pain, I jumped up from my cot. I was back in the nightmare, in the terror of driving through the burning city, back beneath the laughing *kempeitai* officer's sword, forced to choose between killing or dying. I did not hate the poor dog that died at my hands. I did hate the Marine who condemned me to misery. I hated myself for not killing him when I had the chance, for not having the guts, for not demanding my rights, for submitting to tyranny with only myself to blame.

As the barracks came alive with men pushing and shoving to get ready, I groped for my eyeglasses but could not find them. I started to panic. Vomit rose from my stomach, but I fought it back. I tried blindly to find my gear — my clothes, my helmet, my shoes, my rifle — and ready myself for the stampede down the stairs. I managed to pull my trousers on, then fearing I would be the cause for the company's punishment, I grabbed the thing closest to me, hoping it was my rifle, and ran for the door. I swept down the stairs with the surge of rushing men. At the bottom, I realized I was half dressed and instead of my rifle, I was carrying a broom.

The humiliation was more than I could take, the degradation more than I could bare. I threw down the broom, grabbed a rifle from the man nearest me, and erupted in total rage. I wanted to kill whatever it was that had robbed me of dignity. I wanted to inflict as much pain as I was suffering. What followed is a blur. I later learned that I shouted profanities and threatened everyone around me with the rifle. Several men pounced on me and pinned me down until an ambulance arrived. My outburst was like a purgative. It lasted until my pent-up anger and bitterness had been discharged. When it was over, I felt unburdened and cleansed. I never lost consciousness. During the ambulance ride to the camp hospital, the pain in my head disappeared.

I was remanded to the care of the camp psychiatrist, who spent a great deal of time talking with me. With my anger gone, I could discuss everything that had burdened me. I spared no details: the draft, the Marine, the doctor, my disqualification, the arbitrary reversal of my disqualification, the reprieved young American. And all the other ugly Americans who had ever tyrannized me. The war. The occupation. The Japanese. Racial discrimination. Subjugation. The American promise. The American failure. American citizenship. Equality. Rights. My immense disillusionment and disappointment. Everything came pouring out.

The doctor listened without comment or judgement. He seemed genuinely sympathetic and understanding. He never gave me cause to doubt his sincerity. He did not believe what I told him about the Marine in Guam until he verified my story. His reaction was, "What the hell is happening on your island?" I explained how officials in authority commonly took liberties at the expense of Guamanians. One of the questions he asked during my two sessions with him was, "If you, or your country, were threatened by an enemy, would you kill to defend?" My immediate response was a vigorous "Yes!" Why he asked it, I do not know. He never explained. It still puzzles me.

Five months after receiving a draft notice, I received an honorable discharge from the Army. My political opponents and detractors have often claimed I cleverly manipulated a "Section 8" discharge[18]. My discharge certificate, which I have not shared with them, reads in part:

Honorable Discharge
Ricardo J. Bordallo, US50005352, PVT2, AUS
16 April 1953
awarded as testimonial of honest and faithful service.

I admit I harbor resentment toward the military, not because of my Army experience, but because the military, like the Marine sergeant, relishes its dominance over civilians in Guam. It is a formidable omnipresence in our lives. It does not blend into our community like a good neighbor; it squats like a warlord, ready to pounce on anything that dares to disturb it. Military installations in the United States are different. There, in communities that must tolerate the military presence, civilians are not the enemy. In Guam,

---

18 Section 8 was the category of discharge for military personnel deemed unfit for service physically or mentally or for sexual orientation.

the lines of separation — the barbed-wire-topped cyclone fences — are like fortress walls warning enemies to keep out. The military has always treated Guamanians like suspicious foreigners, not like loyal fellow citizens. I long for the day when my homeland can be a normal community, where civilian authority prevails.

A Note About Orthography

This book follows the updated Utugrafihan CHamoru, Guåhan (Guam CHamoru Orthography) except in the cases of villages names that have not been changed by law. Village names that have been legally changed at the time of this book's publication and the names of places not considered political jurisdictions adhere to the Utugrafihan CHamoru.

In acknowledging the historical and linguistic importance of the CHamoru language's evolving orthography, the following is a list of village and place names mentioned in this book that have been spelled differently over time. The list reflects both an older spelling (in most cases, how the words were spelled when this book project began in the late 1980s) and the current Utugrafihan CHamoru spelling.

Older Spelling	Utugrafihan CHamoru Spelling
Agaña	Hagåtña
Agat	Hågat
Inarajan	Inalåhan
Malesso	Malesso'
Sumay	Sumai
Talofofo	Talo'fo'fo'
Adelup/Adilok	Ádilok
Annai Island	Anae Island
Anigua	Aniguak
Asgadao Bay	Asgådao Bay
Asñamo River	Asñåmu River
Aspengo	Aspenggao
Atkija	Atkiya
Bilibic	Bilibek

Cetti Bay	Sette Bay
Chochogo	Chúchugo'
Cutot	Kotot
Dandan	Dåndan
Dungca Beach	Dungca' Beach
Etun	Eton
Facpi Point	Fåkpe Point
Faha	Fåha'
Fouha Bay	Fuha Bay
Jalaguak	Halåguak
Julale	Hulåli
Lalo	Lålo'
Litekjan	Litekyan
Lonfit	Lonfet
Malojloj	Malohloh
Mt. Tenjo	Mt. Tenho
Neye Island	Neyi Island
Pa'asan	Pa'åsan
Pågo	Pågu
Pigo	Pigo'
Sagua Mañago	Sagua' Mañågu
Sasa	Sasa'
Satpon Point	Såtpon Point
Sella Bay	Seya Bay
Ta'i	Tå'i
Tanguisson	Tangison
Tinta	Tinta'
Tipungan	Tipunngan
Togae	Toggai
Ylig	Ilek

Special thanks to the members of the Kumisión i Fino' CHamoru yan i Fina'nå'guen i Historia yan i Lina'la' i Taotao Tåno' for their guidance in providing the orthography edits for this book.

Map of Guam Villages

MAYANGHULO'

TOMHOM

YIGO

TUTUHAN

HAGÅTÑA

PITI

TAMUNING

MONGMONG

SUMAI

MAÑENGGON

YOÑA

AGAT

TIPUNNGAN

UMATAC

INALÅHAN

MALESSO'

Ricardo Jerome "Ricky" Bordallo was born to Baltazar Jeronimo "B.J." Pangelinan Bordallo and Josefina Torres Pangelinan on December 11, 1927, in Hagåtña, Guam. His parents were both members of the Pangelinan "Kotla" clan.

Like his father B.J., a pioneering political leader and businessman, Ricky went into business and politics. He landed the first distributorship of Toyota vehicles outside the U.S. and eventually built Ricky's Enterprises, featuring real estate, finance, and other ventures in addition to his new and used automotive sales business. In politics, Ricky was instrumental in the establishment of the Democratic Party of Guam and served as its first chairman. He served seven terms as a senator in the Fourth through Tenth Guam Legislatures (1956-70). He was Guam's second (1975-79) and fourth (1983-87) popularly elected governor.

Ricky's wife Madeleine Zeien Bordallo was Guam's first lady and served as a senator in the Guam Legislature, the lieutenant governor of Guam, and a Guam delegate to the U.S. House of Representatives. Ricky and Madeleine have a daughter, Deborah, a granddaughter, Nicole, and a great-grandson, Ricardo James.

Ricky died on January 31, 1990, at the age of 62.

Catherine Sablan Gault was born in Guam to Navy Chief Vicente "Benny" Leon Guerrero Sablan and Antonia Pangelinan Cruz.

Gault worked as a reporter and feature writer for the *Pacific Daily News* under the byline C. Sablan Gault. In 1983, she became Governor Ricardo J. Bordallo's press secretary. Between 1987 and 2008, she also served as Senator Madeleine Bordallo's press officer; a writer and editor for the Political Status Education Coordinating Commission; communications director for Guam Congressional Delegate Robert Underwood; and deputy press secretary to Delegate Madeleine Bordallo.

Gault authored and self-published two romance fiction novels, *A Mansion on the Moon* and *The Quonset in Tutujan*.

Gault and her husband David, a Vietnam Veteran and Army retiree, live in Agaña Heights. They have three children and six grandchildren.

www.ingramcontent.com/pod-product-compliance
Lightning Source LLC
Chambersburg PA
CBHW022042020426
42335CB00012B/509